In this important study, Dr Brent Neely delves into comparative theology, comparing Christian atonement doctrine with Islamic perspectives, informed by critiques from contemporary Muslim scholars. Assessing three redemption frameworks in response to Islamic critiques centered on divine justice, honor, and sin, the study seeks to deepen Christian comprehension of Islamic thought, inform Gospel communication in Islamic settings, and, primarily, refine Christian perspectives on atonement by integrating incarnational and trinitarian emphases. Bridging scholarly inquiry with practical implications, it provides essential insights for Christians interacting with Muslims.

*Peter G Riddell, PhD, Professor Emeritus, London School of Theology*

In *Atonement Theology in Conversation with Islamic Thought*, Brent Neely provides a model of respectful interreligious dialogue on a central concern of Christian theology. Rather than seeking a lowest-common denominator solution that leaves no one happy, he listens carefully to his Islamic interlocutors and gives a reasoned response affirming the integrity of Christian perspectives on the atonement. Drawing on major Christian thinkers, he articulates the significance of Christ's death on the cross with clarity, sensitivity and appropriate nuance. This book will enrich a wide range of readers, from beginning theological students to seasoned theologians. Highly recommended.

*Sean McDonough, Professor of New Testament,*
*Gordon Conwell Theological Seminary*

It is a noticeable pattern of church history that growth in theological wisdom is often catalyzed by sustained engagement with non-Christian religious traditions. In this book, Brent Neely undertakes the somewhat daunting yet exceedingly fruitful task of placing contemporary Christian theologies of atonement into conversation with Islamic soteriology. The result of the encounter is a learned and insightful study which generates new avenues of reflection for theologians, pastors, missionaries, and students of comparative religion.

*David Luy, Associate Professor of Systematic Theology,*
*North American Lutheran Seminary*

I0895776

In this timely study, Brent Neely provides a path-breaking account of Christian salvation in conversation with Islamic thought. The world's second largest and fastest-growing religion, Islam has been an interlocutor of Christian thought for 14 centuries, but rarely have Christian thinkers seriously grappled with the ways Christian understandings of soteriology might be refined or more carefully communicated in light of Islamic soteriologies. A model of thorough research which draws on an impressive range of Christian and Muslim thinkers, Neely's work succeeds wonderfully in doing just that. Attentive to internal diversity within both traditions and their history of mutual critique, the work points the way toward a faithful and creative restatement of Christian salvation in dialogue with Islam.

*Matthew J. Kuiper, Hope College, author of* Da'wa: A Global History of Islamic Missionary Thought and Practice *(Edinburgh University Press)*

Due to their very different theological commitments on sin and salvation, the death of Jesus Christ on the cross has long been a point of contention between Muslims and Christians. In this meticulously researched and thoughtful work, Dr Neely brings the critiques of atonement theory by some leading Muslim thinkers into serious conversation with the views of influential Christian theologians, resulting in a creative exploration of a central Christian doctrine. Dr Neely is among the few theologians with the requisite skills to unpack both Muslim and Christian perspectives on soteriology. This groundbreaking study is essential reading for anyone interested in the comparative theology of Islam and Christianity.

*Harold Netland, Professor of Philosophy of Religion and Intercultural Studies, Trinity Evangelical Divinity School*

REGNUM STUDIES IN MISSION

# Atonement Theology in Conversation with Islamic Thought

## Series Preface

Regnum Studies in Mission are born from the lived experience of Christians and Christian communities in mission, especially but not solely in the fast growing churches among the people of the developing world. These churches have more to tell than stories of growth. They are making significant impacts on their cultures in the cause of Christ They are producing 'cultural products' which express the reality of Christian faith, hope and love in their societies.

Regnum Studies in Mission are the fruit often of rigorous research to the highest international standards and always of authentic Christian engagement in the transformation of people and societies. These are for the world. The formation of Christian theology, missiology and practice in the twenty-first century will depend to a great extent on the active participation of growing churches contributing biblical and culturally appropriate expressions of Christian practice to inform World Christianity.

# Atonement Theology in Conversation with Islamic Thought

Brent Neely

First published 2024 by Regnum Books International

Regnum is an imprint of the Oxford Centre for Mission Studies
St. Philip and St. James Church
Woodstock Road
Oxford OX2 6HR, UK
www.regnumbooks.net



British Library Cataloguing in Publication Data
A catalogue record for this book is available from the British Library

ISBN: 979-8-8898-3883-8
eBook ISBN: 979-8-8898-3884-5

Cover design by Words by Design

Typeset by Words by Design

Distributed by Fortress Press in the US, Canada, India, and Brazil

## Contents

## Acknowledgements

This book is a revised and streamlined version of my dissertation completed in 2022 at Trinity Evangelical Divinity School (Deerfield, IL). The list of those whose support has been vital to both the dissertation and book projects is too long for specification. It includes family, friends, instructors, exemplary mentors, and more. I suffice with thanking and naming a few out of the many. I am grateful for my dissertation committee headed by Dr. Harold Netland, and including Dr. David Luy and Dr. Matthew Kuiper. Dr. Lisa Neely was supportive and indispensable in helping me think through the revision of the dissertation. I thank my parents, James and Eloise Neely, for the years of love and support, particularly expressed in my mother's faithful proofreading of a draft of the book and my father's modeling of intellectual integrity. Caleb Fischer kindly read a draft and offered theological comment. None of this would have happened without the support of my wife, Loretta. I thank Regnum Books for the opportunity to publish this work. All of the above are aspects of God's generosity to me.

# Abbreviations

| | |
|---|---|
| *Cat. Or.* | *Catechetical Oration* |
| *CDH* | *Cur Deus Homo* |
| *CV* | *Christus Victor* |
| *MHR* | *Meditation on Human Redemption* |
| n | note |
| NT | New Testament |
| OT | Old Testament |
| *OVC* | *On the Virgin Conception and Original Sin* |
| PSA | Penal Substitutionary Atonement |
| Q | Qur'an (often used in noting *sura* and *aya*/chapter and verse) |

# 1. Introduction

> Soteriology anchored in the Trinity is an account of divine sonship that begins in the being of God by nature and is extended to creatures by grace. If soteriology is reduced from a relation of sonship to a relation of lordship and obedience, with forgiveness or sacraments as a way of patching up that relationship when it has been transgressed, then all the richness of the biblical language is flattened out or dumbed down … A depth is missing here, and it is against this kind of reduction that so many modern Trinitarians are reacting, under the slogan of Karl Rahner that many believers are "almost mere monotheists". This minimal soteriology could be underwritten by a unipersonal God; almost by a deistic God; certainly by Allah. Trinitarian theology summons Christian soteriology to go deeper. (F. Sanders, *Fountain of Salvation*, 52)

## The Context of This Study

To suggest that Christianity is a "salvation religion" or a faith centered on the cross is hardly innovative. And thus, to say that I have long grappled with the meaning of atonement hardly sets me apart. However, there is perhaps a little more that might be said about the locatedness of my own theologizing. For many years I lived in Israel working amongst the Palestinian minority. That is to say, the confession of Christ and him crucified was one among three major confessions indigenous to this area, the "heartland" of monotheism. It could even be argued that Christianity was the "odd one out" among the three, whether in terms of population demographics, political contest, or relating Jesus to redemption. Redemption at the cross has long remained a stumbling block, not least for Muslims and Jews – whether the problems are centered on the historicity of the event; a history of scapegoating tied to the event; the scandal of the event; or the alleged ethical deficit of basing divine–human reconciliation on the event. And yet, in the face of the surrounding antipathy to traditional Christian atonement theology, I remained convinced that Christ crucified and risen uniquely answers to the truth about "us," our brokenness and our hopes. For me, the misery, shame, and loss; the love and sacrifice; the power, life, and light of the incarnate Son's living, dying, rising, and reigning – all these precisely intersect with the desperation and aspiration of the human condition in a way that uniquely effects redemption, transformation, and hope. In a region so fractured by pain, violence, and enmity, the broken and victorious Emmanuel himself embodies reconciliation, Shalom. Thus, while this study is in no way "about" the Middle East, much of the motivation for this work arises from life in that setting.

This book brings together two major arenas of study: the Muslim–Christian theological interface and atonement theology. These two domains are constituted by a complexity, contestation, and historical depth that persists. My interrogation of these disparate religious zones constitutes a Christian theological project attentive to contrastive voices from outside the Christian faith.

This book catalyzes a discussion between Islamic soteriology, particularly its evaluation of Christian atonement theory, on the one hand, and the robust intramural Christian debate about atonement, on the other. Atonement is an important conceptual field to bring into conversation with Islamic theology, for at least two reasons:

i) The cross and atonement have long been a critical nexus of Muslim–Christian interaction and divergence.[1] According to Todd Lawson, the crucifixion is "probably the greatest single obstacle in Muslim–Christian relations".[2] That which is essential to the one faith is anathema to the other (cf. 1 Cor. 1:20–2:2; Gal. 2:20-21; 6:14; Q 4:157-158).

ii) The cross and atonement are definitive, a *sine qua non*, for Christianity yet, paradoxically, there is no agreed theological center or creedal consensus as to atonement's contours, content, and mechanisms.[3] The soil remains ever receptive to further plowing. Searching questions from the vector of Islamic theology will help forward this process.

## A Work of Theology and Comparative Theology

At its most basic level, this book is a work of Christian theology. Theology is, of course, socially located and emerges in conversation with voices, ideas, or influences from some cultural or intellectual matrix or another. Schools of thought continue to emerge foregrounding the concerns of particular communities or contexts (e.g. womanist or liberationist). Historically, philosophy has provided the most prominent external interlocutor for Western theology. The current project turns in a somewhat different direction for a conversation partner: to Islamic theology.

There can be little debate that we live in a world that is intensively diverse religiously, culturally, and ideologically, both as a whole and in our North American context.[4] This fact impinges on the lived experience of all of us, however well or poorly our theology takes these contextual realities into account. Daniel Madigan's words help to set the stage:

> It is still the case today, sadly, that even the good-faith questions posed by Muslims, to say nothing of the polemical challenges that are often aired, tend to meet with the same unconvincing answers because our theologizing and our catechesis so often take place, if not in a closed circuit, at least in a world in which the major interlocutor is still too often the skepticism of modernity rather than the world of diverse living faiths.[5]

And so, this theological research may also fairly be seen as "comparative theology". This is not in the sense that my interests are divided evenly between Islamic and Christian resources; they are not. Rather, this work is comparative in the sense that the interlocutor with which we initiate discussion – Islamic thought – stands outside the Christian ambit. In this study, critiques of atonement theory from the world's second largest religious community furnish the opening volleys for consideration.

I am interested in Muslim reflections primarily on the nature of sin, salvation, and redemption, especially when in conscious engagement with Christian atonement thought. This research is, in part, an effort to better understand Muslims' *theological* understanding of and response to the Christian doctrine of the cross and atonement. That is, my interest is more theological than apologetic, polemical, or historical.

## The Purpose and Ethos of This Conversation

The key contrivance of this project is to generate an interface across a religious/theological boundary between unlikely conversation partners. Distilling my endeavor to a single question: *if we appropriate Muslim thinkers' concerns about Christian atonement doctrine and introduce their voice(s) into intra-Christian theological debates, how might this enrich Christian expressions of atonement theology?*

One can anticipate that the results of this interface between Muslim intellection and divergent Christian theological "packages" will manifest a varied texture. This nuance and texture will be manifest in at least the following ways:

i) A process of careful listening, attending, and responding to an outside voice may highlight areas of notable convergence, overlap, or theological traction between Islamic ideas and this or that particular atonement model. Examining how some of these disparate Christian theologies engage fruitfully with (or founder upon) Islamic critiques may indicate more hopeful starting points for dialogue across the Christian–Muslim boundary. Points of marked convergence or overlap with Islam (in one stream of atonement thought versus another) might indicate areas of traction, "on-ramps", in cross-cultural presentations of the Gospel.[6]

ii) However, the mere fact of a given atonement model's relative congeniality towards aspects of Islamic discourse does not in itself necessarily commend the truth, biblical fidelity, or superiority of that model. Indeed, at various points, this exploration may simply confirm certain classic Christian–Muslim divides as irreducibly intractable. Theological, soteriological, or anthropological zones of mutual contradiction, incompatibility, or even incomprehension, may simply be confirmed. But even such conclusions have their place in lucid and faithful interfaith communication.

iii) This study aims at discipline and transparency, not neutrality. A process of Christian discernment remains necessary. So, even as I endeavor to hear disparate voices from within and without Christian tradition, this study will require some assessment of the varied claims forwarded by the interlocutors, Muslim *and* Christian. In some arenas, the pressures of Islamic critique may refine or chasten the articulation of Christian atonement thought. *All this, hopefully, eventuates finally in a better Christian soteriological synthesis.*

This book is a theological venture informed by a concern for the mission of the church. I hope that listening to a major voice from outside the Christian tradition may ultimately serve as a sort of "leavening agent" to elevate *our own* Christian construals of God's reconciling work. In the wake of the inter- and intra-confessional thrust-and-parry, I primarily hope to offer a useful framing of atonement theology. But a further follow-on consequence might be an improved communication of the Christian salvation message back into a Muslim context.

## The Shape of the Discussion

The coming chapters unfold according to the following logical sequence: I begin by exploring a select group of modern (20th- and 21st-century) Muslim thinkers' discourse on Islamic "salvation" and the deficiencies of Christian atonement, as they understand it. With this collective, distilled "atonement protest" echoing in the background, I turn then to the bulk of the study: an examination of three distinct atonement constructs, classic and contemporary – those of St. Anselm, Karl Barth, and Kathryn Tanner. Having brought a discreet range of concerns and complaints about atonement theory into conversation with this grouping of three soteriological proposals, I attempt in my concluding chapter to synthesize the results and to offer constructive suggestions.

### *Three Motifs*

Throughout the study, three topoi inductively distilled from the Islamic writings are used to interrogate theologies of atonement. The three motifs are sin, justice, and honor. One might say that these three are load-bearing themes as they either speak directly to the question of the divine character (justice and honor) or highlight theological anthropology and the human condition (sin). And, of course, tropes like "sin" (evoking anthropology, hamartiology, and soteriology) ultimately entail assumptions about God himself. For example, many Muslim critics take the doctrine of original sin to be unjust, ethically enervating, and arbitrary, and thus to impeach the Christian conception of God himself. So, it is hoped that this assessment of Christian atonement paradigms, in terms of the threefold typology, will produce an enhanced map of soteriology for the sake of a better conception and worship of God, and for the church and her mission.

I want to elaborate further on the taxonomy of the three themes (justice, honor, sin) through which I inflect atonement thought. Let's begin here with the category of "sin", which at times I telescope as "sin and human nature". Although our central interest is atonement rather than sin or anthropology as such, all are obviously interlocking aspects of a larger reality. One might ask, for example, "What is the nature of the human problem to which the cross is supposed to be the solution, and how embedded a problem is it?" In response, Christianity and Islam have generally forwarded divergent conceptions of sin and the human condition.

As for the category of divine honor, it has enjoyed considerable traction in both classic Christian and Islamic theology – even as its air of traditionalism has rendered it quaint, regressive, or superfluous in some quarters of modernist Christianity. In any case, "honor" is intended to invoke traditional affirmations of the surpassing greatness of God, or, perhaps, his aseity. Thus, at times, I pair "honor" with divine "transcendence." In Holmes' words, "God is both transcendent over, and immanent in, his world. These … words express the thought that on the one hand God is distinct from his world and does not need it; while on the other hand he permeates the world in sustaining creative power."[7] God's transcendence or honor, then, indicates something of his unbounded power, infinity, purity, and invulnerability to denigration, corruption, evil, or change. Dishonor speaks to anything that would tend to degrade these perfections.

Some overlap amongst our three themes is hardly surprising, as may be seen, for example, when it comes to justice and honor. After all, a deficit of justice on God's part would hardly redound to his honor; there is no unjust honor nor dishonorable justice. Nonetheless, there are two conceptually separable kernels here. This is why questions of ethics emerge in our discussion of justice in atonement, while questions of transcendence, of God's power or limits, gravitate towards the honor category. One might say that justice references God's dignity in terms of virtue or ethical purity, while honor references his dignity in terms of unparalleled capacity – thus transcendence. But, again, there is no yawning chasm between the two.

Justice itself can be assessed along very different trajectories. For example, theologies of penal substitutionary atonement (PSA) often center on retributive justice. Meanwhile, a fulsome soteriology will attend not only to a) retribution averted or redirected, but also to b) the ends of salvation and reconciliation. A more eschatological or positive framing of atonement, then, would concern itself with restorative justice.

Finally, I sometimes deploy a bifocal approach to God's justice in atonement: "justice from above" and "justice from below". These distinctions are not in fact hermetically separated realities, but there is utility here. Justice from above relates to the effort to discern God's justice with reference to himself. I have in mind issues such as the accusation that the cross is a locus of a war within God as the Father tortures the innocent Son. Justice from below connects more closely to matters of sanctification or community ethics. Think here of protests against an atonement in which God seems to justify those who are clearly not just or, allegedly, punishes the innocent, while granting the guilty *carte blanche*. Justice from below presses questions of the persisting "un-redeemed-ness" of a community that purportedly has been "saved".

And a final comment on our triple typology of themes: the three tropes are a consistent through line of the book. However, throughout the later chapters on Christian theology I only occasionally engage the prior chapters' Muslim authors, sometimes in the notes. It is *the themes* that are the sustaining chord.

### *Three Schools of Atonement Thought*

As we bring the three governing tropes into conversation with three configurations of atonement, I hope that this engagement will result in synergies useful for thinking on salvation. The three Christian-focused chapters do notionally represent different approaches. But in fact, the first two form something of a set, with the starkest boundary falling between them and the third.

The iconic exemplars Anselm and Barth constitute a set in that they foreground substitutionary suffering centered on the cross – an atonement profile sometimes termed "objective". Anselm, with his emphasis on honor–debt satisfaction, is commonly taken to be the fountainhead of Western crucicentric substitutionary theories. Meanwhile, later penal substitutionary atonement (PSA) theories constitute one key branch of the Anselmian genealogy.

On that score, Barth is a major modern theologian at least loosely representative of this penal trajectory. This family of traditional atonement configurations is arguably historically dominant in the West, but has also been subject to withering attacks, generally on grounds of its alleged violence, injustice, legalism, individualism, dearth of love, irrationality, and so on.

In strong contrast to the preceding exemplars of "objective" atonement, I turn in chapter seven to Kathryn Tanner's incarnational, participatory framework. Tanner's theology promises to be generative in terms of its marked contrast to substitutionary paradigms. In opting for a holistic emphasis on the incarnation itself as the driver of salvation and redemption, Tanner dramatically decenters cross theology – without wholly excising the theological significance of the cross and while maintaining a relatively classical God construct.

A reader alert to the Islamic queries will note potential (if unintended) overtures to Islamic agendas in Tanner's soteriological matrix. Consider, for example, her diminished focus on the cross; her "milder" approach to original sin; her lack of patience for juridical and penal categories in redemption; her salvific holism focused on the entire life of the Messiah, rather than on its end; and her vigorous adherence to divine transcendence. However, obvious disjunctions with the Islamic impulse are also evident. For example, her atonement theology is not intensively associated with the justice (or law) motif, and she is, of course, robustly invested in the absolute significance of incarnation (itself a major bone of contention).

To recap, then, I give attention to two contrasting atonement streams: one a broad historical tendency headlined by two key figures, Anselm and Barth, and the other an alternative orientation featuring the feted modern scholar Tanner. The two chapters devoted to Anselm and "his friends" stand in for various atonements of substitutionary, representative suffering. Alternatively, Tanner's incisive theology offers a bracing, but contained, contrast to these more traditional trends in Protestant thought.

To simplify, Tanner provides a fruitful and challenging (while not wholly hostile) counterpoint to Anselm and Barth. And I have chosen Anselm and Barth (beyond their unquestionable importance to historical theology, generally) for two reasons:

i) They may serve as ancient and modern poles in the theological stream eventuating in substitutionary, suffering atonement theology – the stream that has mostly informed my own ecclesial context.

ii) Models of substitutionary atonement at the cross represent in general the "brand" of atonement theology upon which Muslims have most energetically, and negatively, focused. Hopefully the tensions, diversity, and critiques inscribed in all my sources will converge to suggest a deeper, textured, and compelling profile of salvation in Christ.

## Where Do We Land?

At the risk of deflating the tension of discovery, let me reflect briefly on the findings to which my argument builds and on the journey to that destination. This book tries to bring issues raised by Islamic thinkers into a creative interface, challenge, or confluence with "traditional" atonement models (Anselm), including modern iterations thereof (Barth), and to further galvanize the discussion by way of the participatory paradigm represented by Tanner. Writing from within the general matrix of the Protestant tradition, this study assumes the viability of a soteriology centered on a substitutionary atonement at the cross. The point is not so much that this is the only biblically possible emphasis with respect to redemption; but I aim to plausibly unpack an approach to atonement initiated from this traditional starting point.

And so, at journey's end, I hope that the disparate challenges and pressures can point us towards a hopeful, faithful, and capacious soteriological construct. That is, my agenda is more synthesis and integration than critique and deconstruction. For example, even though I would differ with Tanner at many points, critique is not my leading purpose here. Instead, my engagement with Tanner prods us not towards her abandonment of substitutionary dynamics, but towards a broader, more holistic framework of salvation – a creational and incarnational framework *in which to situate* the contributions of something like PSA.

In terms of broadening the scope of atonement theologizing, David Moffitt's critical rethinking (especially of Hebrews) is helpful:

> Jesus's death, resurrection, and ascension are all essential (in distinct ways) for the salvation of his people. In the broadest sense of the word "atonement," these are all important for salvation because all of them do important, saving work … The resurrection and ascension are not just important addenda to the main event of the crucifixion … Rather, Jesus's resurrection and ascension are themselves fully and robustly salvific.[8]

In light of the questions posed by the research – questions centered on sin and anthropology; divine honor; and divine justice – *how* a substitutionary atonement is framed and *where* it is situated both matter. So, for example, in light of unworthy representations of redemption in which God appears grossly unjust towards Jesus and/or alternatively violent or permissive in his ethical response to his creatures, it is important that God's work on the cross is seen to be a unified act of Father, Son, and Spirit to bear the weight of humanity's demise; to overthrow evil; and to renew those who turn to the God of mercy. The cross and resurrection are not to be seen as a hapless effort to satisfy contradictory impulses of love and justice, but rather the mysterious, congruent expression of both flowing from God's own character, and from the power of the ineffable, honored, transcendent Trinity. So, too, the effect of atonement must not be mere justification in its most restrictive sense – some sort of legal papering over, a forensic fig leaf applied to essentially unchanged rebels against God and the Good. No, justification must be intrinsically linked to sanctification, to renewal, to an overthrow of the old, dying order of sin.

So much, then, for *how* cruciform atonement is articulated. But, equally, *where* the cross story is located within the larger conceptuality of redemption is vital. That is, one may well wish to insist that the cross is central, or perhaps that the complex of the cross and resurrection is the white-hot core of salvation. That is fine but, even if one positions the cross as the climax of salvation's story, one must not lose sight of that very story of which it is the climax. The supporting structure is hardly optional, negotiable, or of lesser import. Another way of putting this is simply to say that it is Jesus himself (not only one key move he makes) that saves us. It is the entire life, death, rising, and reigning of the Lord that reconciles humanity to the Father. It is indeed in the incarnation that the very life of God is applied to a sin-sick world so that we are healed. That is, even our talk of "substitutionary atonement at the cross" must be framed in terms of the entire story of Jesus, in terms that are incarnational, holistic, participatory. The death and rising of Jesus are the climax – not the end – of a process by which sinners are "made right", evil is defeated, and the renewal of the cosmos begins. In this way atonement is not simply an act accomplished (which it is), but it is also the launch of a new-old project of human life lived in this world, lived in constructive relationship with our Father and Source.

As I conclude these introductory thoughts, allow me to pivot once again to the interconfessional nature of our theologizing. It is worth noticing the productive but also complex nature of communication across religious boundaries in this endeavor. In view of the trifold typology, how do the Muslim contributions inform, sharpen, or clarify Christian thinking on salvation? The impact ranges from correction to accomodation, from refinement to reaffirmed divergence – once again, the results are textured, nuanced, and hybrid.

Even where Islamic thought encourages a constructive rearticulation, my project remains a *Christian* endeavor. The point is to listen attentively, but in response I am driven back to the resources of Scripture, tradition, and the Spirit-breathed community of faith. Good questions may arise from within the house of Islam, but my answers remain Christian – not necessarily calculated to please or persuade the Muslim interlocutors. So, for example, with respect to concerns forwarded by Muslims – concerns for justice and a this-worldly relevance to salvation – I have tried to listen. However, as a result, my thinking about redemption at the cross (a clear flashpoint for Muslims) has been directed ever more deeply into the mysteries of Trinity and incarnation (no less flashpoints in their own right!). I hope to proceed with gratitude, humility, and conviction, and then to let the chips fall where they may.

## A Word on Comparative Theology

One way to characterize this book is under the rubric "comparative theology". Comparative theology is a burgeoning field whose methods, commitments, and boundaries are quite undefined. No single work was the originating model for this project, but there are many exemplary works touching on Muslim and Christian thought that have influenced me. In an appendix, I offer an overview of some of these. Whatever else may be true of my methods, sources, and approach, it bears repeating that I expound my comparative theology from within a broadly Protestant, evangelical perspective. How might this impinge on the texture of my comparative inquiry? Let me briefly elaborate:

Most of the authors noted in the comparative theology appendix aim to allow voices of the religious "other" to speak on their own terms. *As a starting point*, this is both an ethical and methodological gain. However, I sense that tacit assumptions for *some* of these scholars are that i) "ultimate truth" is an enveloping reality so exceeding our finitude that ii) no religious message will prove to have been uniquely authoritative or true in the final accounting – if there even is such a thing. For my part, I appreciate the epistemological humility of the former (i), without conceding the logical necessity of the latter (ii). That said, I do hope that this project is presented with sufficient humility, integrity, and rigor so as to merit a hearing by competent interlocutors from any intellectual or religious tradition. This foray in comparative theology is a "confessional exercise" that aspires to humble honesty, to listening as well as asserting.[9] In turning to the task at hand, then, let us conclude with an admonishment from Joshua Ralston:

> Witness is an act of humble particularity, which is marked by a non-anxious confidence in the One in whom we place our trust, faith, and submission. The central task, then, for both Christians and Muslims, is not to defend religion or protect one's own religious power or position, but to offer a creative and living witness to God and God's coming just rule. Such a posture of engagement is a sign of faith and trust in the security of God.[10]

# 2. Christian Atonement Thought

## Mapping Atonement

This introductory chapter offers an overflight of the terrain of atonement theology, beginning with a discussion of basic terms, concepts, and the domain of metaphor and model. Once again, while the New Testament (NT) and Christian tradition repeatedly invoke salvation from sin in Christ, there is no comprehensive, detailed creedal definition of atonement. The locus of "redemption" or "atonement" or "soteriology" is a complex, contested, and seemingly endless conversation.[1]

In terms of doctrinal development, I cover certain typologies that categorize atonement thought conceptually (e.g. objective and subjective models) and/or in terms of historical process (e.g. Aulén's tripartite typology). My review will necessarily be incomplete in some respects. I touch on a few common taxonomies of atonement while neglecting others – not because these approaches are comprehensive, more accurate, or clearly superior. I feature them because they generally *have been* important; are commonly deployed in atonement theology; and are heuristically useful. Moreover, they intersect in notable ways with the theologies I most engage in this study (those of Anselm, Barth, and Tanner).

Towards the end of the chapter, I shift attention to atonement perspectives that have a broad scope, that integrate the concerns and effects of several traditional theories. (Oliver Crisp proves a helpful guide at this juncture.) I particularly have in mind "incarnational" and "participatory" frameworks, which typically draw on the patristic heritage. Such integrative theologizing extends atonement beyond a narrow focus on the cross and the individual believer.

I conclude this chapter by anticipating the study's endpoint, suggesting that an incarnational atonement framework is a good matrix in which to situate the traditional Protestant construct: substitutionary suffering at the cross. I argue that we need not abandon these traditional theologies as such, but they must be embedded within a wider redemptive canvas.

In traditional Protestant thought, the term "atonement" has commonly centered on the event of Christ's passion and resurrection, especially the effect of his *sacrificial* death on a cross as applied to the believer. According to Veli-Matti Kärkkäinen, "The most common biblical terms that are translated either as 'to atone' or the closely related verb 'to redeem'…, *kipper* and *hilaskomai*, have their origin in a cultic environment and have therefore close connections with sacrificial rites."[2] Unpacking a Levitical perspective, M. Bennett says, "Atonement is the process given to cleanse and forgive the people such that the people's camp might be made a suitable habitation for YHWH."[3] David Moffitt notes that "the verb [*kipper*] refers to a mechanism (a cleaning, purification, or removal of some hinderance) that contributes to the resulting restoration in the relationship."[4] Thus, he warns, the act of purification by blood sprinkling (כִּפֶּר) *leads to*, but is not synonymous with, reconciliation, being made "at one".

In any case, discussion of atonement may well begin within the notional matrix of sacrifice, with the ways in which sacrifice clears defilement, both ritual and moral. But connotations, concerns, and contestations around atonement very quickly spread beyond those boundaries embroiling many aspects of life, worship, theology, and ideology.[5] As a theological category, the word "atonement" itself is a relatively late arrival and is not native, for instance, to the lexicon of the Church Fathers.[6] The wide referential range for the word "atonement" is a source both of its utility and imprecision. I will commonly employ atonement in a broad spectrum fashion, well beyond the tight lexical confines of any single Hebrew or Greek term. In this book, atonement is broadly conceived as God's work to reconcile humanity to himself and to set creation right from a fallen state, climactically at the cross of Christ, but ultimately through *all* his action in the cosmos.[7]

## Model, Metaphor, Mystery

### *From Images to Theories*

Atonement is not readily separable from other domains of theology; "the atonement is a uniquely synthetic doctrine, for it is the point at which all Christian theology comes together."[8] A balanced atonement theology is concerned with both the retributive or remedial and the constructive; that is, it involves "that which Christ came to save us from and that which he came to save us for".[9] Such scope necessarily extends to the entire life of Christ, to the cross, and to the Lord's resurrected life.[10] Kathryn Tanner makes the following point:

> The cross is the final expression of God's wrathful condemnation of sin, the place where sin, and the suffering and death it entails, are borne by Christ and put to death, destroyed. The cross is the ultimate expression of God's loving choice to be with sinners, in all the sufferings of a spiritual and physical sort that burden human life in its sinful condition. The cross is the final act of divine humiliation, or the intra-Trinitarian act whereby the second person of the trinity is abandoned by the first, in a divine self-emptying that makes room for a world of pain, sin, and death within the very life of God. It is the cultic sacrifice to end all sacrifices. It is the agonizing birth of the new creation to be revealed in the resurrection of the dead and in the new life of those dedicated as Christ was to God's cause. On the cross we find the final form of perfect obedience to God's will, or a man laying down his life for his friends. We see our own sin: the culminating rejection of Christ's mission of love as that takes shape in the execution of a religious and political subversive at the hands of imperial power.[11]

The restorative action of God in the world has been expressed by a range of terms (atonement, salvation, redemption, reconciliation) and a range of formats and constructs (images, models, paradigms, theories). This research does not depend on a tightly defined taxonomy of "models", "theories", and so on, but some further reflection is warranted.

A common designation for an "explanation" of atonement is the word "theory". For some, the use of the term implies the exclusive validity of that one approach against all others.[12] That is not my stance. Ross Hastings can be read to align the descriptive tools for atonement thought along a spectrum: image → model → theory.[13] On this gradient, the "image" end claims little explanatory power; the "theory" end claims much more.[14] Hastings, understandably, mistrusts theory terminology to the extent that it implies modern, rationalistic positivism.[15] He does accept that the term is unavoidable, but pleads for it to be understood as an encompassing "framework", able, in some measure, to embrace the other images, metaphors and models.[16]

Structuring a taxonomy of approaches to atonement can be difficult. For example, St. Anselm's explanation of the incarnation and death of Jesus in *Cur Deus Homo* (*CDH*) attempts to explain the workings of atonement ("theory") in greater precision than, say, the *Christus Victor* (*CV*) patterns ("model").[17] However, in this case, a theory may be highly precise and explanatory on one hand, but also rather narrow on the other, not readily accounting for other important aspects of atonement beyond "satisfaction". Thus, taking *CDH* as a "theory" (which it is) seems to fall afoul of the spectrum scheme presented above. Though all of these terms (and more) appear in the discussion to come, I will not rigorously differentiate between these lexical options, except to say that an "image" generally does represent a smaller unit than either a "theory" or a "model", terms that I often use interchangeably.

### *Diverse Images and Models of Atonement*

The NT manifests a brilliant array of atonement imagery and salvific trajectories. The streams of atonement thought converge at the cross but, even so, they are not exclusively *reduced* to the death and rising of Jesus. As Kärkkäinen notes, such "diversity gives theology unprecedented resources in speaking of salvation in Christ in ways sensitive to cultural and religious contexts".[18] And soteriological truths are generally not expressed in bare propositions or arid syllogisms, but rather by way of image, metaphor, and story, whether one's focus is a specific image (e.g. a sacrificial lamb) or model (e.g. Exodus-liberation). A profusion of pictures or approaches are often implicit even within a single pericope (e.g. 2 Cor. 5-6).[19] It is worth highlighting here that there has long been vigorous scholarly discussion on the nature and effect of metaphor for both epistemology and communication. I cannot pursue the specifics of this debate, but will simply assert that metaphor is often necessary to best express the "literal" truth of things.[20]

### *Mystery and Paradox*

In atonement theology, the ubiquity of imagery and metaphor – with their innate hermeneutical fluidity and refractivity – calls to mind another contested arena in theology, the dimension of "mystery". Theological speech strains after the ineffable and transcendent and, thus, often operates in domains of antinomy, tension, and paradox. The margin granted to mystery or paradox, and the loci in which these are found, varies from theologian to theologian. Unarticulated assumptions often fuel discrepancies in understanding, not least in Muslim–

Christian dialogue. For example, for some Muslim theorists, a simple, linear ethic of judgment and reward with its clarity and austerity is much to be preferred to the complexities and paradoxes of salvation by incarnation, Passion, and resurrection.[21] For these critics, the term "mystery" is but a fig leaf for the irrational.[22]

The range of relevant biblical metaphors and tropes can offer tremendous insight into God's work for us in Christ: we may be healed, liberated, forgiven, sanctified, adopted, vivified, and so on. But a limited grasp of exactly *how* all this has come about is an embedded feature of human existence. According to Hastings, "there is an 'irreducible complexity' to the atonement [… sourced in] 'the diversity proper to the life of the triune God in the fullness of the divine attributes'."[23]

In view of all this, Oliver Crisp's endorsement of the epistemological humility implied in the term "model" is commendable.[24] A model is a rough-and-ready simplification that does not claim to explain comprehensively or exhaustively. "Explanations" should be resonant and coherent, but successful ones are unlikely to be mathematical or mechanistic; they should not overreach. Mystery is irreducible within the story of salvation.[25]

Questions of metaphor often entail further questions as to the nature of analogy between the Creator and creaturely experience. There is potential for meaningful theology, for "God-talk", because analogy obtains between God and his image bearers (and because God has taken the initiative to reveal). But this is a likeness embedded within an even more marked unlikeness; analogy is not univocity.[26] This God–human relationship is grounds for hope, and grounds ultimately for salvation, precisely because *he who will always exceed our cognitive capacities* has at last spoken to us in the Word.

## The Development of Atonement Doctrine

A common depiction of the development of ideas of atonement stems from Gustaf Aulén's *Christus Victor* (*CV*).[27] Aulén's account provides an efficient point of entry to the story of atonement doctrine's fortunes over time, even if there has been ample critique of Aulén's historiography. By his telling, the predominant view of the Fathers was the *Christus Victor*, "classical", or "dramatic" idea of the atonement.[28] Here we have atonement as liberation: at the cross Christ defeats humanity's primary enemy, the Devil, freeing us from corruption into a new creation. For Aulén this "original" perspective's fundamental claim was that "a God of totally self-surrendering *agape* … through pure grace brings about and enacts human liberation from enslavement by evil powers."[29]

For Aulén, this classic position held sway roughly until Anselm of Canterbury (d. 1109) promulgated his satisfaction theory; out of that wellspring his theological heirs have propounded notions of atonement centered on vicarious sacrifice – the so-called "Latin" view, dominant from Medieval Christianity and through the Reformation. However, Anselm's younger contemporary, Peter Abelard (d. 1142), examined the sacrifice of Christ through the lens of self-emptying divine love, *an example* that propels God's people towards beatitude, absent any need for "atoning satisfaction".[30] Retroactively, these two (competing) views have been described as "objective" (the Latin) and "subjective", with the latter often known as a moral influence or moral exemplar view. The terminology is inadequate, but the sense is that in the Latin or "objective" theory, Christ's sacrifice accomplishes an objective change benefitting the repentant sinner – often (unfortunately) assumed to be a change *in God's own essence or disposition.* In the moral or "subjective" theory, Christ's intervention leads *us subjects* – atonement's recipients – to a changed outlook and, thus, salvation.

Penal substitution theory came into its own in the wake of the Reformation. (Emergent from the Anselmian fountainhead, we remain here within the domain of objective atonement.) A. McGowan defines penal substitution as "an explanation of the atonement which says that Jesus Christ, the Son of God, standing in the place of sinful human beings, took upon himself the wrath of God due to those sinners". And, continuing, "The sinners for whom Jesus died are therefore pardoned and accepted by God. This pardon and acceptance is appropriated through faith in Jesus Christ."[31]

Approaches correlating penal substitution and sacrifice became central to conventional Protestant conceptions of atonement, a trajectory traceable from Calvin to Barth.[32] However, in the current of Enlightenment developments, Abelard's "subjective exemplarism" became the point of reference for liberal critiques of tradition. So much for Aulén's line of thought.[33] Intended as a "historical" study, *Christus Victor* does come across as an attempt to validate "classic" atonement over the later Anselmian "objective" and exemplarist "subjective" models.[34]

Such broad-stroke configurations of historical theology are heuristically helpful in imagining the terrain of atonement theology. But rigorous interrogation may also inflict the death of a thousand qualifications on Aulén's mapping. In fact, aspects of all three of Aulén's archetypes, and more, are discernable in the patristic sources. Thus, the historical sketch above is at best an impressionistic profile of actual developments.

### *Ransom Theory and Polyvalence in Patristic Salvation*

If the NT is assumed to be the fundamental point of reference, then the soteriological patrimony of the church's first centuries is an important resource from which to further enrich one's thinking on atonement. We are once again dealing here in general terms with the patristic era from which Aulén claimed to derive his "classic" or "dramatic" theory. One common trope in the soteriological reflection of these Fathers is that of the divine "ransom". Adam Kotsko expounds this salvific imagery in a creative, if contestable, way. On Kotsko's terms, Gregory of Nyssa's depiction of the incarnation as a trap for Satan is the iconic expression of God's shrewd, non-violent deliverance of humanity from Satan's grasp – a "buy-back" representing a redemption more worthy of God's peaceful character and much to be preferred to the allegedly moralistic, individualized, and potentially oppressive "objective" models.[35] In Kotsko's presentation of the ransom stencil, human sin, accountability, and justification are radically de-emphasized, for the Devil alone bears the critical mass of responsibility for cosmic ills.[36]

The ransom template is prominent in early Christian soteriology and, at least as a minimal concept, present in the NT witness (cf. Mk 10:45; Acts 20:28; 1 Cor. 6:19-20; 1 Tim. 2:6; Heb. 9:12; 1 Pet. 1:18-19). But that ransom invariably constitutes a free-standing and comprehensive patristic model of atonement or that there *is* a delimited patristic model must very much be doubted. Theologians generalizing a Ransom theory are sometimes in danger of overweighting Satan's role and underplaying the notion of human guilt (certainly as compared to the NT). Contrary to caricatured portrayals, human guilt is *not* excluded in patristic thought, and Death as the enemy to be overcome is often of greater import than the Devil.[37] But, yes, we certainly see in all this that Christ is victor.

In terms of the Fathers' ideas of salvation generally, McGuckin contextualizes their redemption constructs as multivalent and diffused throughout larger theologies of creation and restoration. Broadly speaking, for the Eastern Fathers, humanity's fall into sin highlights the *deception* in which superior evil beings prey on an ignorant, innocent humanity.[38] In the *paideia* of the incarnate Logos, humanity – fallen in Adam – experiences an ontological uplift.[39] McGuckin styles patristic soteriology as "transfigurative incarnational thought" derived mainly from scriptural exegesis.[40] Patristic ideas of humanity's restoration are diverse and range widely, even enveloping at times notions such as debt, substitution, and penalty – notions typically dubbed "objective", and sometimes assumed to be blessedly absent in the "superior" conceptualities of the Fathers.[41] Nonetheless, an underlying coherence to the Fathers' soteriology may fairly be generalized as accenting the incarnation and humanity's ontological transformation as the enemy is overthrown.[42] *These tropes will be important in the ensuing chapters.*

## The Breadth of Atonement Concepts in Scripture and Tradition

In Johnson's words, "Jesus' death and resurrection accomplished all three of these things: he defeated Satan, satisfied the goodness, honor and justice of God, and taught us to love God and neighbor by means of his absolutely unique and unprecedented example."[43] Now, having briefly considered a vague historical sequencing of the emergence of atonement thought, it is time to turn to more modern and systematic taxonomies and categorizations of the field of salvation, that is atonement in its broadest sense.[44] William Placher (2009) offers a concise typology of atonements. He moves the reader through the objective or penal substitutionary template; its conceptual rival, subjective exemplarism; the *Christus Victor* paradigm; and a "non-violent" atonement *à la* René Girard. He concludes by way of appeal to a broadly integrative posture and a call for renewed attention to a "physical", "mystical", or "recapitulationist" orientation – something like what I have called "incarnational" or "participatory" patterns.[45] (See the appendix on liberationist and "non-violent" atonements.)

Johnson puts it that "The doctrine of the atonement is a conceptually unified account of how the life, death and resurrection of Jesus Christ are effective for the reconciliation of all things to God (Col. 1:20)."[46] In that "salvation" essentially lies at the intersection of everything to do with God and his creation, the dizzying range of what atonement theories may signify is hardly surprising. But, for all that, atonement need not lack for form or direction; there can be a productive norming pressure when the claims of tradition are accounted for.[47]

### *Objective, Subjective, and Other Atonements*

In Kevin Vanhoozer's words:

> The Reformers and post-Reformation theologians worked a penal variation on Anselm … These views tended to stress the saving significance of Jesus's death as a past event (redemption *accomplished*) to which a subjective moment – repentance – was an appendix (redemption *applied*). In modernity the pendulum has swung to … the human response to God in the present.[48]

In modernity one of the most active fault lines in atonement debates has run along the polarity of the so-called objective/subjective models. In Lowe's terms, "it is often unclear in modern theology whether salvation is an event that one knows [objective] or the event of one's knowing [subjective/exemplar]."[49] In accordance with traditional Protestant instincts, I would appeal that our starting point should be the "objective" significance of atonement at the cross – significant to persons, society, the cosmos. Indeed, this book's pair of iconic theologians (Anslem and Barth) can be fairly classed under the rubric "objective" – though to leave matters there risks great reductionism. Even as I condone "objective" models, I hasten to qualify my approach: i) I would eschew any excluding dichotomy between the objective and subjective aspects of salvation; ii) I would gladly foreground the cross in an atonement construct, without ignoring the broader sweep of the Jesus story, the incarnation, his session with the Father even now, and so on; and iii) finally, I would emphasize that the objective aspect of atonement entails a genuine "change in the cosmos", but it need not imply that it is God's being or disposition that shifts.

Jesus died for us, the "callous observers" at the cross, we the violators of the great commands to love God and our neighbor.[50] The unrepeatable victory of unfallen incarnate Man – in whose passion and life is the "reconciliation of all things" – is not reducible to the purely subjective. The death and rising of Jesus is the crucial "pivot" of redemption, prior to any particular human reception, but yet with "subjective" implications on an outsized scale.[51]

Objective models, perhaps especially the flagship PSA, have attracted a large cohort of detractors in our day. (On PSA, see below.) I would agree with some of the protests in so far as they protest objective theories configured as a sort of "cosmic accounting maneuver"[52] or a "Gospel of sin management"[53] – thin and inadequate constructs indeed. In contrast, I prefer to argue for a salvific vision that extends beyond the standard benefits of stereotypical Protestant models, but without dispensing with the constructive resources of objective atonement altogether.

### *Exemplarism*

Peter Abelard is commonly taken as the father of exemplarist or subjective atonement, though it would be a mistake to take him therefore as a unidimensional thinker.[54] Moral example models generally deny that the cross "changes anything about God" – the cross was not a requirement for the satisfaction of justice.[55] The cross and the entire advent of Messiah are rather about God's self-emptying love for us in the face of a violent world. Christ's example changes *us* and our understanding, and sets the stage for *our* renewed action in the world.

The exclusive dichotomies assumed in the objective–subjective binary are sometimes nuanced in actual practice, with certain subjective thinkers insisting that Christ's example is effective as more than mere exemplary data.[56] But strictly subjective models do entail difficulties. In general, this family of perspectives weights sin somewhat lightly; they beg the question of how an example heals the cosmos; and they struggle to answer for the uniqueness of Christ in a pantheon of martyrs and saints.[57] The cross as ultimate *example* of divine love is propositionally true but an insufficient summary of salvation. There something cosmic, something metaphysical, must be achieved aside from human response, otherwise the Lord's death is drained of value *even as demonstration*.[58]

### *Objective and Subjective Views: The Necessity of the Cross*

Why should it be that such a shameful Roman execution was required to reveal the nature of divine love to humanity? An instinctive response on the subjective end of the spectrum is to deny divine design, "necessity", in the Passion.[59] On these lines, "Jesus' death is *contingent*, not necessary – a tragic martyrdom that is the outworking of a moral and revolutionary life."[60] Such subjective intuitions may be positioned as a repair to the (perceived) moral high ground in the face of a supposed objective Anselmian legacy of oppression, injustice, and violence.

But, as Gunton puts the counterpoint, sin's "slavery [cannot be] abolished by appeals to follow a good example".[61]

> We cannot write out of the story the justice – judgment – of God which Jesus voluntarily undergoes: the cross is the baptism – death by water – and the cup of God's wrath (Mk 10:38; cf. Ps. 75:7f.; Isa. 51:17). In view of what, as a matter of objective fact, has happened, there must be a correspondingly objective demonstration of justice, or the world is a morally indifferent place.[62]

Indeed, the dominance of the cross narrative in NT witness seems to demand more than a subjective interpretation (e.g. Ac. 3:14-18, 10:39-43, 17:2-3; 1 Cor. 1:23–2.2, 15:1-4; Eph. 2:13-19; Col. 2:11-15; 1 Pet. 3:18). How many more ways could the NT writers communicate that by God's providence, Golgotha "had to be" (cf. Mt. 16:21-24; Mk 8:31-34)?[63] None of this indicates, however, a diminishment of the *subjective* aspects of the Gospel nor a claim that in atonement God's own nature is changed (cf. Mt. 10:16:24, 24-25; Jn. 15:18-22; Eph. 4:32–5:2; Phil. 2:5-11, 3:10-11; Col. 1:24; Rev. 14:4). The atonement hinges on a strangely particular, once-for-all act with cosmic reverberations. As Katherine Sonderegger says, it is "the forgettable execution of a Jew from the provinces … that remakes the world".[64]

### *Vicarious Suffering: Sacrifice and Wrath*

Again, Anselm of Canterbury is often taken to be the wellspring of "objective" atonements of substitutionary sacrifice, one trajectory of which culminates with PSA.[65] I have already positioned Barth as a later developmental milestone in this line of thought, though, as we shall see below, theologians dispute whether or not to apply the label PSA to his doctrine of reconciliation. The death of Jesus (perhaps also his life) as "sacrifice" is a common construct in the NT, whether one thinks of, for example, the Passover in John's Gospel or the Day of Atonement in Hebrews. Fairly or not, such sacrificial models are frequently also linked to atonement paradigms majoring in penalty.[66] Here, for many critics, complaints about the juridical, forensic, or legalistic sensibility of penal theories merge with worries over their alleged intrinsic violence, arbitrariness, and injustice. Even if Anselm's conceptuality itself does not major in "punishment", vicarious suffering and the "cost" of death are integral to the system.[67]

For further discussion of other important modern atonement frameworks, their criticism of various "objective theories" majoring in sacrifice, blood, death, and/or punishment, and a partial response to some of the criticism, see the appendix on "liberationist" and "non-violent" atonement. Some of these modern trends such as liberationist streams, feminist soteriology, and non-violent atonement are important voices in today's landscape which have developed, in part, from the "subjective" or "exemplarist" impulse. These schools of thought are not featured here for reasons of space and because they are less central to the argument of this book, which largely seeks its constructive provocations elsewhere. However, this broad modern impulse tends to reject Anselm's "objectivism", which is cast as violent, oppressive, and so on. Anselm can hardly be addressed without acknowledging this – so, to a limited degree, I also engage these critical voices in chapter five.

#### Penal Substitution

Hovering over most discussions of vicarious sacrifice is the doctrine of penal substitutionary atonement (PSA). PSA is a frequent lightning rod for atonement polemic, the archetypal theory (it is said) of wrath, violence, oppression, abstraction, hyper-individualization and spiritualization, and so on. Intrinsic to PSA is a legal exchange of status before God, an exchange between Christ and believing, repentant sinners based upon the fact of Christ's bearing our punishment on the cross.[68]

Crisp exposes PSA's logical dynamics and potential vulnerability:

> [So,] in suffering our punishment on the cross Christ "becomes sin" for us [2 Cor. 5:21]. That is, he has imputed or ascribed to him our sin as well as our guilt … so that "the punishment that brought us peace was on him" (Isaiah 53:5) … But having someone other than the felon suffer qualitatively similar penal consequences for the crime committed by the felon, ascribing to the substitute the sin and guilt of the felon, would hardly constitute an example of human justice.[69]

Baker and Green are likewise critical of the PSA construct of Hodge, who "has one member of the Trinity punishing another member of the Trinity".[70] Arguably, when such a theory is promulgated, God becomes a bureaucrat under constraint, and one of dubious justice at that. Such atonement is said to be decoupled from resurrection, ethics, transformation, community, the life of the Messiah, and, worse, may conceptually fund authoritarianism, violence, and the valorization of suffering.[71] Even robust defenses of PSA (that of J. I. Packer, for instance) may evince certain weaknesses, for example affirming the resurrection without successfully demonstrating its integral necessity to the theory.[72]

There may be, however, a constructive counterpoint.[73] Language of divine "wrath" need not indicate an erratic urge to vengeance, but rather an "anthropomorphic [way] of getting at the expression of [God's] justice".[74] Furthermore, the key ideas of PSA can be expressed without entailing a war internal to the Trinity, even if in *some* iterations of the theory, smoke probably is indicative of at least some fire.[75]

Typically, PSA is emphatic on "negative" salvation – that which we are saved from. Well and good. The consequences of death and sin demand to be addressed. PSA's "emphasis on the cost of God's love, on the pain of forgiveness, is not only true to human experience ... but a powerful proclamation of something true and important about the atonement."[76] But, it also matters that the theologian not leave the new creation – "salvation for" – on the cutting room floor.[77]

In one way or another, the cross has classically been the throughline of atonement thought. Suffering and shame, if not punishment, are inextricable from the story. Rather than eliding or deflecting the word of the cross, much better then – with humility, grace, and struggle – is to face its painful offense as in a mirror, and to do so without whitewashing or valorizing the sin, the suffering, the darkness that Christ crucified and risen came to eradicate. Gunton is right: "Justification is not a legal fiction but a new relationship"; the various "juristic connotations" of Paul's thought need not be occluded, but rather interpreted in service of justice.[78]

## The Cross, Ethics, and Time in Divine and Human Perspective

Before proceeding further in sketching out typologies of atonement, and how the various approaches may (or may not) be constructively oriented to one another, allow me a moment to address contentious ethical, logical, and philosophical issues that commonly attend debates on atonement and the cross of Christ. These questions, related to God's freedom to act and his acting justly in salvation, have long swirled around models of suffering "objective" atonement in particular (even without reference to Muslim disapproval). These issues are largely tied to conceptions of God's radical otherness and his independence (or not) from the creaturely experience of time.

Any capacious atonement discourse will have to deal with apparent incongruities between divine mercy and the terrible realities of the cross and to acknowledge concerns about abuse and violence in our world.[79] At stake in all this is a constellation of divine attributes – God's justice, mercy, and love, for example. The revolt against any sort of linkage between God and the cross's violence, while not entirely new, is intensified by shifts in modern cultural values as well as emergent philosophical perspectives involving time, eternity, and freedom.

Of course, already in the NT we are confronted with the tension of human evil and divine design coinciding at the cross. Non-violent critiques of vicarious paradigms commonly operate on assumptions in which God himself is subject to a linear space-time continuum. Divine and human autonomy amount to essentially the same sort of thing, distinguished in terms of quantity more than quality. For some, a classical theological imaginary of a God transcending even time – one in which reality subsists at two radically distinct ontological levels – is unacceptable. Operating within such Enlightenment parameters, theologians have reacted on grounds of conscience, freedom, and human dignity against an arbitrarily powerful God jostling humanity about in the competition for metaphysical space. At worst, Colin Gunton says, "God [comes] to be conceived as a competitor of, or threat to, human freedom rather than its source."[80]

Defining human freedom in terms of sheer autonomy, many moderns recoil at traditional ideas of "ultimate" and "secondary" causes, at construals in which freedom is "God's orienting the [human] will to its proper end".[81] If unconditioned autonomy is all there is to freedom (divine or human), then it becomes difficult for any theologian to explain the logic of cruciform redemption. If in fact God operates on the same and only metaphysical plane that we do, it becomes more difficult to distinguish the intentions and design of God in the cross from the intentions and design of Jesus' violent opponents.

With respect to these recondite issues, my modest aspiration is to express my theological intuitions with reasonable coherence, without remotely claiming to have "proven" my case. In traditional fashion, I affirm the analogical relations between Creator and creature – with all the ambiguities and epistemological "gray areas" that necessarily implies. We must reckon always with a "likeness enclosed in Greater Unlikeness".[82] "The God–world relation is unique."[83]

From these foundations, I assume that God is not bounded by the metaphysical frame that constrains us, even as he is free to participate in it. So, in this book I generally assume divine timelessness and can merely acknowledge, rather than engage, the vigorous dispute it occasions. Both levels of existence (God's and ours) enjoy their own proper integrity, but in asymmetry. For the apostles, the cross was the ultimate shame and travesty at the human level, and *also* the sovereign, subversive, gracious design of God for reconciliation at the divine level (e.g. Ac. 2:23-24, 3:17-18, 13:27-33; cf. Gen. 45:8; 50:20). David Burrell's exposition on these metaphysical tensions is particularly helpful: in "the detailed structure of biblical stories … the omnipresence of the divine actor in no way suppresses but rather enhances the poignancy of human initiatives and failures."[84]

The possibility that volition, action, and freedom – human and divine – occur symbiotically, while distinctly, on more than one level, is pregnant with potential. The paradox extends beyond our ken, but divine and human freedom need not be mutually negating.[85] In this productive mystery, the wrong of human agents is truly wrong – a wrong not imputable to God – even as God's creative act upholds all that is. This traditional Christian lens on reality strongly counters pervasive epistemological scientism.[86] The counterpoint here endorsed is the "notion of created freedom, or the freedom proper to creatures".[87] As divine and human freedom do not subsist in a "zero-sum" relation, human freedom is real, but is never synonymous with sheer autonomy – definitionally not an option for a creature.[88]

And so I contend that in both the creation of the world and at the cross God acts in justice and timeless freedom, not under any alien requirement, not subject to human chronological constraint.[89] But, thankfully, the radicality of God's freedom is congruent with the radicality of his virtue: "the freedom of the act of creation stems from the inner life of a God of love."[90] Thus I invoke the following paradox: the cross is genuinely a travesty of human rebellion; it is also the locus of God's liberating love for those selfsame rebels, a revelation of his own being.

## Incarnational or Participatory Atonement

Increased attention has been given of late to a family of salvation frameworks, variously termed physical, incarnational, recapitulationist, participatory, and so on – typically centered on human participation in the divine nature or *theosis*.[91] These perspectives draw on patristic sources to emphasize holism, the redemptive impact of the incarnation *in se*, and integration of redemption with creation. Jesus, the "prototypical human being," acts on our behalf to heal the world.[92] So-called incarnational atonement tends towards a preoccupation with ontology, construing salvation in terms of transformative union with God, participation in the divine nature (2 Pet. 1:4). "[Christ] became Man that we might be made God … He underwent insult at the hands of men that we might inherit immortality" (Athanasius, *On the Incarnation* 54). This is the "deification" of a worshipping dependent linked into the life of the Trinity who alone remains non-contingent. The line between Creator and all else remains.

A weakness of some Protestant theology has been the demotion of the incarnation, life, and ministry of Jesus to a perfunctory precondition to the crucifixion – a failure to bridge the meaning of Jesus' life to the meaning of his death. Ideally, the subversive life and ministry of Jesus must coinhere with his death – together ushering in the Kingdom.[93]

Unfortunately, in some reactions, the pendulum swings entirely away from the cross. Incarnation and *theosis*, accented by a focus on creation, resurrection, and death's overthrow, are played off against sin, guilt, death, and vicarious suffering – an alleged "Eastern" vs "Western" theological polarity. The opposition is unhelpful. Matthew Baker rightly says, "What the language of atonement [at the cross] indicates is not an alternative 'model' to *theosis*, but rather a crucial dimension of that multi-faceted plan of the Creator to save his fallen creatures from death and destruction and to raise them up into union with him."[94] Incarnational redemption and ontological transformation also entail exchange, substitution, and representation that are effected at cross *and* resurrection (cf. 1 Tim. 3:16; Athanasius, *On the Incarnation* 13; Augustine, *Confessions* 10:68; Irenaeus, *Demonstration of the Apostolic Preaching* 69).[95]

Incarnational redemption is framed in light of the ongoing purposes of original creation; salvation is not a "spiritual", disembodied, stopgap measure instituted retroactively to a failed creation agenda. Salvation "cannot be presented as a remedial act on the part of a disappointed or puzzled creator: it brings about a state of affairs which this creator has in his loving freedom intended from the first."[96] Thus, at their best, incarnational streams hold together that which is too easily divided; they maintain a holism in which atonement is relevant to who God has always been and what he has always been doing. This concerns spirit and body, creation and redemption, Beginning and End, individual and community. As a constructive foil to the Anselm–Barth axis of "objective" atonement, in chapter seven I engage Kathryn Tanner as emblematic of this modern incarnational or participatory disposition.

## Composite Approaches: Commending Integration

With the increased appreciation for the spread of atonement thought, contemporary proposals frequently draw on a multiplicity of sources and models. For the most part, this is a gain promoting holism, balance, and a better account of reconciliation and restoration. A danger though is that salvation is articulated in an amorphous manner without a sense of proportion or direction of travel.

Crisp envisions two categories of incorporative holism:[97]

i) The first is associated with Joel Green (along with Mark Baker), who is known for expositing the diverse mosaic of atonement imagery in scripture without reference to a controlling outline or hierarchy – the "kaleidoscopic" take.[98] For Green, atonement at the cross is central, but there is little impetus towards centering any one of the many "contextual" accounts of this salvation.[99] Green is agnostic about any fixed atonement structure, but rather calls for pastoral sensitivity and contextual awareness in applying the varying models and images.[100] Crisp points out that this amounts more to a theory about atonement theories, rather than a model of atonement.[101]

ii) Crisp promotes an alternative approach to composite models under the moniker of "mashup". Here there is generally a controlling paradigm with aspects of other models subsumed within the structure. Such hybridity is not inherently problematic; the proof is in the pudding. With respect to a proposed configuration, one must ask: Are the parts appended to one another logically? Is the whole coherent and proportional? Is the model ultimately convincing, cogent, and biblically faithful?[102]

Crisp's own "mashup" filters atonement through a quasi-Athanasian matrix of participation in a rhetorical register calibrated to modern auditors. But importantly, the resultant frame also encompasses "forensic" dynamics of substitution and penalty (cf. Heb. 2:14-16; 2 Pet. 1:4; 1 Jn. 3:5-10).[103] Alongside other generative resources (e.g. Hastings 2019; Anatolios 2020), I would also commend Adam Johnson's work for its healthy integrative instinct. Johnson's theologizing values "fittingness" and "demonstration" while honoring the coinhering "dimensions of the mystery" of salvation.[104]

The best frameworks will be wide enough to incorporate the virtues of "salvation from" and "salvation for". And yet their expansiveness will not drain momentum or specificity from the atonement doctrine. "Everything" from creation to the life of the Nazarene matters, but, consonant with the gospels' own harmonics, the Passion and resurrection comprise the *pièce de resistance* of redemption's panorama.[105]

## The Task at Hand

Clearly, the complex and contested arena of atonement doctrine can be a raucous public square. My intention is a soteriology with an open – not relativistic – stance. For example, the subjective and objective profiles are, arguably, edifying inverses of one another, the subjective lacking the necessary "negative" and the objective the necessary "positive" components of redemption. Similarly, one could distribute restorative (subjective) and retributive (objective) justice across this polarity; both are vital.[106]

Underlying the stories we tell about the human condition and its remedy are convictions about God's own self. To ask how severe the human predicament is is to ask with reference to our Maker. How like us, how unlike us, is God?[107] In his likeness (immanent nearness), we encounter solidarity; in his unlikeness (transcendent distance), we encounter saving capacity. In dialogue across difference at such junctures, incommensurable claims will pierce the surface, whether the interlocutors are Muslims and Christians or Christians and Christians. These sorts of concerns will accompany us as I order the discussion around the triple tropes of humanity in sin, God's justice, and God's honor.

Let me once more trace the contours of the study's final proposals with respect to atonement doctrine: I grant ample space to traditional templates of suffering substitution or so-called objective theories. At the same time, I aim to be integrative. This entails, first, nesting substitutionary atonement within a much wider participatory framework – one that manifests a holism about the saving impact of the incarnation as such and is relevant to human life in both old and new creation; and second, articulating traditional theories themselves (even PSA) in a way that gives attention to the power of the transcendent Trinity, attends to questions of justice, and insists on a change in both the legal status and actual person of the believer.

The argument aims to ensconce salvation within the meta-story of the Trinity, creation, and the incarnation. Equally, it maintains the cross and rising of Jesus as the climax of the incarnational miracle. There we find a just, vicarious offering for sin; an overwhelming upending of demonic evil; a model, path, and worshipping life for the people of God; and much more. And so, I now cede the floor to Muslim thought and critique hoping this will be a propellent to our process.

# 3. Islamic Theologizing of Salvation

The plan of this chapter is as follows: first, I offer a very brief summation of Islamic attitudes to Christian atonement theory. (This is merely a thumbnail sketch, which seeks to orient the reader towards the central concerns looming in chapter four.) Next, I comment on the key Muslim scholars whose work propels this book's discussion – most importantly, again, in the key following chapter. Finally, I devote the bulk of this chapter to a summary outline of "Islamic soteriology". These are the "positive" Islamic commitments that underwrite the "negative" protests to come. (Though I do make use here of my collection of critical Muslim interlocutors, this chapter is not about their thoughts as such. Rather, in an introductory mode, I survey Islamic claims about "salvation" in a loose and general way that at best skims the surface.) This current chapter, then, aims to lay the groundwork for chapter four's substantial Islamic criticisms of "Christian salvation".

## Islamic Response to Atonement Theory

So, I begin with a passing reflection on Islamic reaction to Christian theologies of the cross. In Kenneth Cragg's terms, there is "an Islamic consensus" that the crucifixion "did not, historically, it need not redemptively, and it should not morally, happen to Jesus".[1] The second element, "redemption", along with the third, "morality", is central to my interests in this project.

Generally, Islamic theology has stalwartly rejected a salvation theology centered on the crucifixion and resurrection of Jesus. The historical, philological, theological, and ethical critique of the cross as central to Christian faith; the exegesis of relevant qur'anic passages; the scholarly or apologetic debate on this topic (pro and contra); and so on – this literature is voluminous.[2] Most of it cannot detain us here.

The impetus for this negative Muslim reaction may be parsed into several categories. i) Most obviously, the Qur'an seems to deny the facticity of the crucifixion. ii) A claim for the historical verity of the crucifying of Jesus would be taken as a denigration of the dignity and perfections of God and his prophet. iii) Qur'anic theology, anthropology, and Christology generally disavow incarnation, a precondition of cruciform salvation. iv) Finally, Islamic theology and soteriology tend to disallow an atonement rooted in representative mediation – let alone vicarious suffering and death – on grounds of its injustice, ineffectiveness, and soteriological redundancy. We shall soon become familiar with such remonstrances.

## A Collection of Modern Muslim Writers

The work of a selection of modern Muslim intellectuals (writing in the 20th and 21st centuries) provides the theoretical springboard for this book; the critical questions I wish to pose to atonement theology arise in their writings. In this research, I engage the Islamic discourses as a bloc. My goal is not a granular or thick reading of each theorist, but rather a sort of composite distillation of key themes, tropes, and critiques. For the most part, these authors are situated as academics, theologians, "clerics", or intellectuals rather than popular-level apologists and polemicists. The general confessional leaning of this conglomeration is Sunni, but not without exception.[3] It is also worth noting that Sufi thought as such is not a focus of this study.

As a group, the trend in terms of theological perspective is towards "Islamic modernism" rather than "traditionalism". This, however, does not indicate homogeneity of outlook. Nor does "modernist" in this sense necessarily indicate a "liberal" or "pro-Western" inclination – frequently this is not the case. Rather, for example, an author's "modernism" might be indicated by an emphasis on the Qur'an that sits fairly loose compared to the hadith Tradition.[4] Similarly "modern" is many of the authors' recourse to sources outside the Islamic religious canon or their deployment of direct commentary on the contemporary scene within the text of their *tafsir* (Qur'an commentary).[5]

The intention behind my collection of these works is not to speak for Islamic thought comprehensively. This group is not necessarily "representative" of any demographic majority in the heartlands of the Islamic world. In any case, the group covers too great a chronological and geographic spread to justify drawing demographic conclusions. Nonetheless, many of these thinkers were and are enormously popular in Islamic countries and beyond (e.g. Rida, Qutb). The central point is that the cadre represents an important, influential, and modestly diverse body of Islamic thought. The collection is deep enough – with authors of substantial notoriety and influence – to offer legitimate soundings in Islamic intellection on atonement and to provide a constructive provocation for this theological endeavor. For brief biographical notes on many of these authors, see Appendix C.

## Islamic Soteriology

We will soon be engrossed in Islamic assessment of Christian soteriology, most of it decidedly negative. Indeed, such criticism is the catalyst for this study. However, if Christian atonement theory is taken to be problematic, then at least implicitly underlying this judgment is a presumably superior Islamic salvation construct, a path to beatitude before the Maker. Let us then give some attention to a generalized portrayal of "salvation" in Islam.

While one of the relevant qur'anic terms, *naja*, can be rendered as "rescue, escape, or salvation", one may question its equivalency to "salvation" in routine English-Christian usage.[6] Any hesitation about speaking of Islamic "soteriology" or "salvation" stems from the possibility that such a "Christianly" loaded term might come freighted with theological connotations inappropriate to

Islam. Nonetheless, Gordon Nickel is right to challenge the idea that "salvation is not something Islam is concerned with."[7] "Salvation" may be taken as a locution covering a person's ultimate destiny and beatitude before God; one might likewise speak here of "individual eschatology" (although the point certainly would not be the absence of a communal accent in Islamic thought). Thus, while Islamic conviction may arguably negate atonement or redemption as commonly conceived, it *is* intensively concerned with "salvation", warning us from the Qur'an onward to live life in this world (*dunya*) with acute attention to the looming Hour of Judgment and the life to come (*akhira*) (cf. Q 19:72; 39:61; 40:41; 61:10-14; 70:14; 81:1-14).[8]

> Every soul shall taste death, and you will indeed be paid your full rewards on the Day of Resurrection. Whoever is delivered from the Fire and admitted to paradise has certainly succeeded (فَقَدْ فَازَ). The life of this world is nothing but the wares of delusion. (Q 3:185 Qarai; cf. 2:286; 29:64)

My interest, then, is salvation or individual eschatology in Islam, with the added proviso that I aim not so much at a depiction of Judgment Day, or the Fire and Paradise (punishment or reward) – as significant as these are – but at the conditions that make for one's ultimate disposition in blessedness or damnation. Again, the primary contribution of Islamic scholarship to the agenda of this book lies in its collective and (mostly) critical assessment of Christian ideas of salvation. However, underlying such criticisms are implicit assumptions about positive Islamic claims about salvation, the "right" way of framing judgment and reward, and "setting humanity right before God." I offer an outline of such matters in the remainder of this chapter.

### *Just Judgment by Works*

Advocates of Islamic "salvation" often construe their soteriological model as rational, just, and knowledge-based, correlating with Islam's self-image as the "natural religion". The irreducible core of Islamic proclamation is the radical oneness and unicity of God (*tawhid*) which overthrows all idolatry, polytheism, or infidelity (*shirk, kufr*). Were one to generalize the basis of salvation in Islam, a reasonable starting point would be God's straightforward and just judgment of one's deeds at the eschatological Day of Reckoning – beginning with the question of one's submission (*islam*) to the One God, or one's idolatrous infidelity. Of course, intervening factors can complicate such apparently simple paradigms.

However that may be, Hamza Yusuf cites classical authority in describing "God as *Master* (or Sovereign) *of the Day of Judgment* … The Day of *din* can thus be understood as the day when debts fall due."[9] A standard template places the individual's fate in the balance – between the Garden of Paradise and the Fire, as "winner" (*muflih*) or "loser" (*khasir*) – contingent on the preponderance of works, good or ill (cf. Q 3:85; 7:8; 28:67). In the Qur'an, and Islamic thought generally, there is typically a strong sense of the linkage between one's works, one's piety or dereliction, and the consequent outcomes – now but also, especially, "then" (cf. Q 2:25; 3:180-82; 8:50-51; 13:35; 80:33-37; 99:6-8).[10]

## Fitra *and Original Sin*

In the standard Islamic conception, humans are born with a relatively unproblematic orientation towards God, that is, as "true monotheists" or Muslims; it is environmental distortions that lead to the straying of persons and societies. This native innocence is signaled by the Arabic term *fitra.* A famous prophetic saying holds that every child is born into the *fitra*, and then his parents turn the child into errant paths (Jewish, Christian, Zoroastrian).[11]

Reading Isma'il al-Faruqi, for example, one would infer that saving knowledge of God is innate to humans as a sort of steady state of creation, diverted or distorted at times by historical contingency, but always accessible "in a state of nature". Islam in reality is simply "*din al-fitra* (*religio naturalis*)" and the true human is "*homo Islamicus.*"[12] The *fitra* has even been dubbed an "original righteousness".[13]

There is an Adamic Fall narrative in the Qur'an, but its trajectory does not imply the emergence of "original sin" or a redemption narrative.[14] As Emmanuelle Stefanidis puts it:

> In Christian understanding, Adam's fall is only redeemed by the sending of Jesus and his death on the cross. The Qur'an follows a similar narrative pattern where Adam's fall brings about a divine rescue, but the means to salvation is different: to follow God's guidance whenever it reaches humanity, as is the case through this Qur'an.[15]

## Sin Awareness in Islam

The robust Islamic critique of original sin will occupy us in the next chapter. Suffice it here to note that in an Islamic ethos, sin is commonly taken to be a matter of "weakness", "forgetfulness", or simply "erring" rather than a devastating marring of the divine image or an indelible guilt (cf. Q 4:28). In any case, Islam's construal of humanity in sin is conventionally, and understandably, depicted as less rigorous than the Christian preoccupation with human depravity. But this oppositional polarity should not be exaggerated. It would be a mistake to cavalierly screen out Muslim attempts to come to grips with sin.[16]

One must beware of underplaying the lament over human sin, weakness, and forgetfulness which *is* present in Muslim anthropology.[17] Sin must be taken seriously for, according to Rahman, it is a pervasive instinct to "gravitate downwards" in resistance to God. This *kufr* (unbelief, paganism, infidelity, ingratitude – definitions are contested) must be resisted (cf. Q 7:175-76).[18] Fazlur Rahman eloquently invokes the minutely calibrated terror, justice, promise, and threat of the Qur'an's eschatology with an awareness of the deep darkness, deception, and desolation that can characterize the human soul:

> Man's conscience itself becomes so perverted that, through long habituation with particularized interests and persistent worship of false gods, the holy seems unholy, and vice versa. This is what the Qur'an terms *ghurur*, multi-layered self-deception.[19]

Nonetheless, in summation, the Islamic anthropology of *fitra* and instinct against original sin is coordinate with the rejection of substitution as redemption: none rightly can or should redeem another, and given the inborn human capacity for meritorious obedience, there would be no need (cf. Q 53:38). Some Muslim authorities eloquently express sin's seriousness, but, to my mind, their general tendency is still to overestimate the innate human capacity to resist its seductions.

### *Salvation in* Gnosis

For most Muslim theologians, human attainment of a blessed eschatological outcome hinges on the gift of divine revelation, but revelation *specifically as knowledge*. The Qur'an comes as God's highest revelation – but not as personal apocalypse – it is instruction, guidance (*hidaya,huda*). In al-Faruqi's terms:

> Islam regards God primarily as the Just Being whose absolute justice – with all the reward and doom for man that it enjoins – is not only sufficient mercy, but the only mercy coherent with divine nature. Whereas the God of Christianity *acts* in man's salvation, the God of Islam *commands* him to do that which brings that salvation about.[20]

Essentially, we have to do with salvation through *gnosis*. (As I use the term here, *gnosis* refers to divinely given *knowledge*, the path to salvation; I do not intend the usual connotations of *esoteric* or *secret* knowledge.) The need is not "vicarious intervention", but guidance leading to a harmonization of the human will with the divine, leading on to peace.[21] Revelation of divine requirements, acceptable worship, the unseen, judgment, and so on should produce, in responsive persons and societies, social uplift and the possibility of individual purification and salvation.[22]

In Seyyed Hossein Nasr's words, "Islam addresses the human being not primarily as will, but as intelligence. If the great sin in Christianity is disobedience, which has warped the will, the great sin in Islam is forgetfulness and the resulting inability of the intelligence to function in the way that God created it as the means to know the One."[23] Salvation, al-Faruqi intones, comes by way of epistemological intervention because sin's "locus and genesis [… is] in perception. Its effect is in intent and doing. Accordingly, it can be counteracted only in the faculties of perception and its solution must therefore be in education."[24]

### *Law and Obedience, Not Atonement*

Thus, the facts of the matter call for both divine intervention and human effort. Rahman, again:

> Therefore, God's role, his succor, and his support … are very crucial: no man can say, "I am going to be a good person" and automatically become one. He has to struggle, and in this struggle God is his willing partner. Yet, God may not be taken for granted as though his partnership were automatic … [I]t can be described almost literally as God's mercy.[25]

On the dominant Islamic typologies of sin and anthropology, the soteriological mode is enlightenment, not redemption. Law, not atonement. Information, not incarnation. Of course, *guidance* must be *received*. Salvation requires the twin inputs of revelation *and* moral exertion.[26] Shabbir Akhtar contends that,

> [S]in is primarily *zulm al-nafs* (self-wronging; Q 18:35) but it also injures our relationship to God though not irreparably. According to the Hebrew Bible, this relationship is restored typically through sacrifice – an external form of atonement (Lev. 5-7). An internal or spiritual purification is also required (see Isa. 1:11-17). Muhammad's Islam requires only the internal process. Muslims, like modern Jews, hold that they can repair and maintain their relationship with God through daily canonical prayers, accompanied by supplication and repentance, fasting and voluntary charity.[27]

Judgment – punishment or Paradise – hurtles towards us; God has given revelation and intellectual and moral faculties. So, "at this point … man's crucial test comes: will he use his knowledge and power for good or for evil, for 'success or loss', or for 'reforming the earth or corrupting it' (as the Qur'an constantly puts it)?"[28]

At one level, eschatological beatitude seems a straightforward ethic of accountability and requite. A classic text is Q 2:286: "Allah does not task any soul beyond its capacity. Whatever [good] it earns is to its benefit, and whatever [evil] it incurs is to its harm" (Qarai; cf. Q 2:233). "The decisive factor is man's choice either to adhere to and obey God's commands, or to hanker after Satan's deceptive allurements."[29] Human capacity for gratitude, submission, and piety (*taqwa*) are a sort of presupposition to the searing eschatological warnings threaded throughout Islamic scripture (cf. Q 6:94; 81:1-14).[30]

Rahman is adamant that God does not play games with the economy of salvation – last-minute repentance does not avail.[31] But admonitions to law, threat, and punishment are not the sum total of Islamic soteriology and individual eschatology: appealing to God's compassion, his inclining to mercy in judgment, and so on, all indicate a conceptuality of grace as well. The prominence of the "grace" theme in Christianity can generate a stilted dichotomization in which Christianity becomes the religion of grace, a virtue (supposedly) vacated in Islam. Akhtar responds that Christian soteriology posits an over-robust role for grace (χάρις). Meanwhile, grace (فضل), while distinctively calibrated in the Qur'an, is hardly an alien category.[32]

> Deliverance from the life of the flesh is part of salvation. This stress on deliverance, not merely on forgiveness of sins, distinguishes Christianity from Islam. Paul moved decisively from his inherited Judaism to a new view of faith as essentially salvific, not merely legal and didactic. Islam is not a mystical faith of salvation wholly by external grace through a holy savior, human or divine, but rather a practical law-centered faith requiring human effort albeit aided by grace. While the divine initiative of grace is the *decisive* basis of human moral effort, it cannot be its *sole* basis since we have free will, which supplies the grounds for human accountability to divine judgement.[33]

Instead of a Christian-style "grace extremism", Akhtar would have us understand, Islam's legal orientation with its more "realistic" standards – fine-tuned to human capacity *and* moral weakness – is itself an extension of grace.[34] Rahman posits a sort of divine tolerance or "generous realism"; God is "realistic" in that he accepts repentance and weighs the overarching trends of one's life.

Rahman's modernist reading of the Qur'an allows for neither intercession nor "saviorship" in the divine economy.[35] Interestingly, he does grant the *appeal* –

not the validity – of "the psychological factor involved in the ideas of intercession and redemption".[36] But, again, retribution and reward are typically seen as relatively straightforward. Hear al-Faruqi:

> Ethical salvation ... is a progressive achievement open to all men by birth; and it is judged and measured on the scale of an absolute justice that knows no alternative or attenuation of the principle, "Better among you is the more righteous", for "whose doeth good an atom's weight will see it then, and whose doeth ill an atom's weight will see it then." (cf. Q 99:7-8)[37]

Where does one find the instruction to be followed for success in this life and at the Hour of Judgment? Quintessentially in the Qur'an, but, drawn from a wider base of tradition, divine command is distilled, ordered, and applied across the spectrum of human behavior through divine law, the *Shari'a.* As Nasr says:

> In the Islamic perspective God has revealed the *Shari'a* to man so that through it he can reform himself and his society ... The presence of *Shari'a* in the world is due to the compassion of God for his creatures so that he has sent an all-encompassing Law for them to follow and thereby to gain felicity in both this world and the next.[38]

Salvation can in great measure be reduced to the lone individual's moral exertion before the Judge, particularly in terms of the Judge's will refracted through revealed law.[39]

### *Forgiveness: Repentance and Realism, not "Saviorism"*

Differing Islamic configurations of salvation or individual eschatology straddle tensions between a God of justice and exacting judgment and his receptivity to repentance and "best efforts" by sinful humans. On aggregate, contemporary reflection attempts to situate God's perfection alongside his tolerance of human imperfection, a divine realism that honors the sincere repentance – a turn to submission (*islam*) – of morally wavering subjects. According to Sayyid Qutb:

> It is with absolute justice that God deals with all His servants. He requires them to try their best to implement the same rule in their dealings and transactions. They should endeavor as hard as they can to adopt these standards of perfect justice: "He who does evil or wrongs his own soul, and then prays to God to forgive him, shall find God Much-Forgiving, Merciful. For he who commits a sin, does so to his own hurt. God is indeed All-Knowing, Wise." (Q 4:110-12)[40]

Sin is not inconsequential, but its remedy lies ready to hand: sinners must simply repent and obey. For Rahman, Islam instills "a healthy moral sense rather than the attitude of self-torment and moral frenzy represented, for example, by the teachings of Paul and many Sufis, which require some sort of *savior ex machina*".[41] After all, God's justice inclines to mercy.[42]

For Rashid Rida, genuine "atonement" (تكفير الذنب) or reform issues from purity of heart, moral effort, restitution, and repentance. Sheer sinlessness is an unnecessary standard.[43]

> God endowed every person with the innate capacity (بقواه الفطرية) to do corrupt and evil deeds and pious and good deeds. [The individual] is the one who either purifies himself with the latter or implicates his soul with the former. The one who guards his doctrine and sets aright his deeds, his soul is restored and purified and qualified

> for bliss in that upper realm. As for him with mythical and vain doctrine, and evil deeds, he has corrupted his morals and degraded his soul. And he is accountable for its plunging and tumbling into hell (تدسيتها ودهورتها إلى هاوية الجحيم).[44]

The grace that guides the believer towards submission correlates with God's willingness to foreswear penalty. Repentance is efficacious for error-prone humans because God forgives. "*Mercy wards off punishment.*"[45] Conventionally, forgiveness is always possible except in the case of unrepentant polytheists, those guilty of "associating" (*shirk*) anything with God, setting any other entity at his transcendent level.[46]

Now, the apparently easy linearity of Islamic soteriology conceals complexifying factors beneath the surface (some of which are discussed below). Still, on a typical narration, divine guidance, a just-but-realistic reckoning, God's mercy, and human capacity for faith, repentance, and obedience – these together constitute sufficient access to final benediction with no recourse to a savior. Once again, then, we encounter the undergirding instinct that the revelation required for salvation is "knowledge" rather than a "savior".

### *Intercession*

One of the factors that might disturb the seemingly tranquil surface of Islamic soteriology is the trope of intercession (*shafa'a*) for sinners at the Judgment. On strictly qur'anic terms, the concept is not quite vacant, but, generally, there is precious little hope of a third-party intervention for otherwise doomed souls (cf. Q 2:254). Again, it is the "associators" whose ill fate seems the most certainly sealed (Q 2:123, 254-55; 4:17, 31, 116, 123-24; 91:7-10).[47]

Nonetheless, varieties of last-minute intercession for mercy at the Judgment do leave their mark in time-honored tradition and popular imagination.[48] In the Hadith, the quintessential intercessor at the Hour is, of course, the prophet Muhammad, but in the books of prophetic reports, he is not alone in this role. In general, the more traditional the scholar, the larger the scope allotted to intercession; the more modernist and "qur'anist" the scholar, the smaller. So, forms of "mediated salvation" cannot be entirely excluded from the Islamic ethos. Nonetheless, it is very much the rare minority reading that ties intercession in any way to sacrificial redemption.[49]

### *Faith and Works*

An interesting soteriological dyad may be injected into the discussion here – a crux of dispute within Islam, as in Christianity, namely, "faith and works". Read off the surface, salvation may be distilled down to "right belief and right action".[50] "As for those who have faith (*amanu*) and do (*'amilu*) righteous deeds – we task no soul except according to its capacity – they shall be the inhabitants of paradise, and they shall remain in it [forever]" (Q 7:42 [Qarai]).[51] But, the definitions and metrics for faith and works provoke debate: does faith itself entail works, and, if so, in what manner?

The famous "hadith of Gabriel" contains a precis of six essential components of Islamic faith (see *Sahih Muslim* 1.1).[52] This prophetic tradition draws distinctions between faith (realia to be believed), Islam (submission – necessary acts), and virtue or righteousness (*ihsan*).[53] Seemingly, cognitive assent, work, and internal motivation are all invoked. In any case, the dialectic between faith and works remains taut. On one hand hadith seems to support the salvific sufficiency of faith understood in terms of minimal commitments: "I heard the Messenger of Allah say: He who testifies that there is no god but Allah and that Muhammad is the messenger of Allah, Allah would prohibit the fire of Hell for him" (*Sahih Muslim* 1:10:49).[54] On the other hand, we have already encountered a heavy accent (in scripture, tradition, and theology) placed upon the soteriological gravity of works, on pious action.

### *The Mystery of Predestination: Qadar*

Even if salvation appears to be reducible to a calculus of merit and mercy, certainty as to one's own destiny remains elusive. Enter here one of the most significant complexifying factors of personal eschatology: the arena of divine sovereignty and human agency. Enter here the doctrine of God's predetermination, *qada' wa qadar* (or simply *qadar*).[55] All the preceding discussion notwithstanding, at times in Islamic discourse God's volitional power seems to overwhelm any other consideration, including that of his own attributes (e.g. justice or mercy). A radical accent on untrammeled divine power and inscrutable will seems to obviate the need to even entertain theodicy: the redoubtable Ibn 'Abbas (d. 687) is quoted as saying, "God forgives heavy sins to whomever he pleases and punishes for minor sins whomever he pleases" (cf. Q 3:129).[56]

God is the all-sovereign Compeller (العزيز الجبّار), his operations impervious to any restraint, perhaps unconditioned even by his own virtues (cf. cf. Q 59:23).[57] Where divine voluntarism is radicalized, justice may be entirely lost to view and human morality indexed to Law as a formal matter without reference to any intrinsic "rightness".[58] Akhtar says:

> Orthodox [Muslim] theologians angrily insisted that God was under no (moral) obligation even to reward a virtuous monotheist, let alone a virtuous pagan. Both could be justifiably sent to Hell. God does whatever he wills. Paul affirms a similar understanding of God's will when he ponders the mysteries of God's inscrutable sovereign choices (Rom. 9:13-21) which must appear arbitrary to the creature's limited reason.[59]

To my reckoning, Daniel Brown rightly avers that a balanced comparative theology "allows us to see in particular that the theological dogma that sets Islam apart most clearly, and that comes to be the foundation of Ash'arite theology, is the overwhelming and all-encompassing power of God."[60] The doctrine of *Qadar* sits front and center.[61] And so, many have with reason discerned a tilt towards determinism in Islam. Nonetheless, the judgment is not unanimous.[62] And, certainly, we must be quick to acknowledge the intensive claims made for divine justice and human accountability by Muslim theologians. Resolving the countervailing pressures between this and a radical divine voluntarism may be an intellectual quest without end.[63]

### *The Path to Paradise*

I would suggest this as an approximate Islamic salvific sequence: *huda* (guidance) → *tawba* (repentance) → *ghufran* (forgiveness) → *islam* (submission) → *falah* (success or prosperity).[64] Simply (or simplistically), salvation depends on judgment and reward grounded in a strict weighing of good and evil. But, as we have seen, this soteriological template represents only the beginning of a winding discursive pathway.[65]

Nonetheless, as the next chapter demonstrates, a commonplace among many Muslim scholars is that Islamic salvation is rational, reasonable, and ethical – against Christianity's mystic irrationalism. Rida intones that:

> Muhammad … explained that Islam was the religion of nature, of reason and thought, of knowledge and wisdom, of evidence and proof, of the inner being, and of freedom and independence … Thus, Allah had sent prophets to instruct and guide people, and to give them good tidings and to warn them at the same time.[66]

Elsewhere he insists that no vicarious intervention is needed for the morally industrious if they will only follow "the path of the *fitra* and the order of creation (لسنن الفطرة ونظام الخلقة)".[67] Personal and social reform in response to the call to *tawhid* is all that humanity requires – good deeds performed in good faith will produce a good outcome.[68]

# 4. Muslim Theologians on Atonement

> [T]he crucifixion and atonement [are] the foundation of [the Christian] religion. It is the Alpha and Omega of their call and mission – in the same manner as the Qur'an has made tawhid the foundation of the Islamic mission. (Tabatabai, *Tafsir al-Mizan*, "Discourse on Jesus and Christianity", 151, translation altered)

Recall Kenneth Cragg's words that there is "an Islamic consensus" that the crucifixion "did not, historically, it need not redemptively, and it should not morally, happen to Jesus".[1] Put in bald terms, redemption is not an Islamic construct. It is true that a few Muslim scholars take the Qur'an to affirm "Christ's ultimate triumph over death rather than [... to flatly deny] the historicity of his death on the cross".[2] But this remains a far cry from endorsing a theology of cruciform atonement. Understandings of the cross remain a closely policed frontier between the faiths. We may take Tabatabai in the above heading as emblematic of the incompatibility between "genuine monotheism" (*tawhid*) and a "redemption religion"; indeed, for him Jesus is "not a redeemer".[3]

## Mapping the Chapter

In the last chapter, I sketched an Islamic construction of the path to judgment, beatitude, punishment and/or reward. Now we attend to modern Muslim thinkers in their assessments of Christian atonement thought. This swivel towards Islamic critique is intended as a productive catalyst to our theologizing of atonement.

Again, the collection of Islamic scholars deployed here is a sort of "core sample" of learned opinion in the modern era, by no means an exhaustive sounding, but one adequate to the task. (In the preceding chapter I characterized this collection of intellectuals as a whole. Appendix C offers brief biographical detail on many of them.) This composite of voices manifests a spectrum of theological visions, but there is greater congruity than divergence in terms of the concerns of this book. Most of the Muslim reaction to Christian theologizing that I survey is negative. However, a slightly more positive "minority report" is discussed briefly in Appendix D.

The chapter unfolds in this way: after an aside on the aesthetic texture of theological reflection, I trace the arguments of these Muslim scholars as they expound salvation, the human condition, and, mainly, problems with Christian atonement. Special attention is directed at our (by now familiar) three themes: i) sin and the human condition, ii) the justice of God, including the ethics implicit to a given soteriology, and iii) divine transcendence or honor. While the themes are "native" to the Muslim writers' discourse, their writings are not necessarily ordered according to this typology.[4] These are my selected analytic categories. Finally, I conclude the chapter with a synthetic summary of the cumulative effect of the Islamic critique. The contents and impulses of this chapter “lay the table” for the rest of the argument in which I tackle the “Anselmian legacy” in two chapters, then “participatory atonement”, and finally offer an overarching synthesis in chapter eight.

*An Aside on Aesthetics*

A tangential glance may be useful here; I pause to comment on a term that occasionally surfaces in my negotiation of the boundaries between Islamic and Christian soteriology, namely “aesthetics”. It seems fair to say that a spiritual aesthetic is at least implicit in most theological constructs; that is, in some form or another, we expect God’s truth to be coherent and, arguably, also “beautiful”. That which is ultimately right, moral, and “so” is expected to be intellectually cogent and morally elegant – aesthetically virtuous. The problem is, of course, that judgments as to aesthetics vary as greatly as other theological judgments. Divides over aesthetic sensibilities are none too rare in Christian–Muslim interface. This felt tension is hard to describe with precision and emerges at different junctures in the debate. One example we sporadically confront is the Muslim distaste for Christians’ allegedly gratuitous appeal to mystery and paradox, purportedly an appeal to the irrational and indefensible.

Hazarding an etic characterization of an Islamic aesthetic, I would suggest that the preference is for the linear, the simple, the evident, and the austere in terms of an economy of salvation – coupled with a vision of divine transcendence that is aggressively abstract and anti-anthropomorphic. First, anything perceived to constrain God’s transcendence, to demand his limitation, or to entail his immanent condescension will appear to be a threat to divine honor, and thus a degradation of the moral aesthetic. We see this sort of intuition played out in the frequent complaints about incarnation, the Passion, the subjection of a prophet to humiliation at the cross, or, worse still, of God himself to bodily indignity. Second, in addition to the “bodily indignity” intrinsic to the death of the Son, some Muslims detect an aesthetic defect in the complex, developmental, “roughly-textured” aspects of Christian salvation history as such; for some critics, it is simply logically, morally, and aesthetically unworthy that redemption should require so lengthy, messy, and contingent a process, worked out in the history of one people. Thirdly, the mystery of (what Muslims construe as) a “third-party” saving intervention (Jesus as God and man) is seen not as wondrous paradox, but as unworkable unreason. These types of theological instincts must be borne in mind as we explore Islamic concerns about atonement thought. Their impress is felt throughout, but particularly in discussion below on theological boundaries around God’s honor and transcendence.

## Original Sin

Recalling conceptions of both “salvation from” and “salvation for”, let us turn to the nature of the sin predicament the cross is said to resolve (salvation from), and to a specific storm center of debate, namely original sin.[5] I have already touched on the ways in which Islamic theology commonly construes sin, whether as weakness, error, forgetfulness, or even willful pride. For all the significance of sin in their accounts, Muslim scholars have persistently rejected the weight and ontological depth accorded to sin in many Christian anthropologies.

Islamic critique of the Christian framing of sin, and especially original sin, is profuse in its rejection of the purported exaggeration, irrationality, and injustice of Christian theology's "sin obsession". Rida styles the problematic of original sin this way:

> Adam, when he transgressed against God by eating from the tree from which God had forbidden eating, Adam and all his descendants became sinners deserving punishment of eternal destruction in the hereafter. So all his descendants became guilty sinners. They became deserving of punishment for their own guilts/faults just as they were deserving of it for the guilt/fault (ذنب) of their father which is the source of their guilts/faults.[6]

Islamic disapprobation of Christian theorization of sin runs along several trajectories. A dominant assessment is that sin on Christian terms is articulated in a mode that is overly heavy, too ontological, and unrealistically ultimate. In contrast, the faith of law and justice (Islam) presumes an allegedly more realistic, less overwrought understanding of sin and a milder assessment of innate human depravity.

al-Faruqi is among the sharpest critics of original sin (as he understands it). The doctrine is execrable in its irrationality and ethical derogation; it is, for him, fundamentally dehumanizing, denying that anything basically good remains in humans as created. Christian thought on humanity in sin is practically nihilist.[7] For al-Faruqi, the humanity-in-sin dogma is "extreme" and "absurd". Worse still, the error is viciously, intentionally obdurate: from Augustine to the Reformers, saving grace is commended (!) as "mysterious, inscrutable, irrational".[8]

Here we encounter the recurrent disjunction between the two faiths over the location and nature of theological mystery; note the marked impatience with apparent paradoxes or conundrums in Christian soteriology however many tensions and inscrutabilities persist in other domains of Islamic theology itself.

Muslim interlocutors generally take original sin to be a concept that fails the tests of both logic and justice, and is symptomatic of a morality that twists a properly sober evaluation of sin into sin obsession.[9] Not only does original sin hold culpable those who are not, but the severity of sin (starting with Adam) is overblown. For Tabatabai, in the case of Adam, the entire scenario of "forbidden fruit" does not rise to the level of universal human guilt or corruption, nor even to deserving sovereign punishment (عقاب مولوي). Adam's mistake simply earned an appropriate, moderate consequence – removal from the Garden.[10] Tabatabai harangues Christian theology's failure to account for nuance and varying legal severity in sin; he holds that Christian soteriology, contrary to reason, pronounces all infractions (including the most trivial) to be catastrophic iniquity meriting perdition.[11] For his part, al-Faruqi insists that sin is "a moral category; it is not ontological".[12] And, as such, Christian anthropology overreacts in its dour pessimism, for "there is ... in the world ... far more virtue than sin."[13]

A distinct, but not unrelated, complaint is directed towards sin's overall role in the Christian redemption narrative. In a sense, the problem lies with the kind of religion Christianity is understood to be – the problem with Christianity is that it is a "redemption faith". If we take the radical doctrine of the cross as central to Christianity, if this offensive redemption mechanism is the emblematic *solution*, then a *problem* of equally garish contours – original sin – had to be contrived to match.[14] The whole structure is seen to be a farce, with original sin playing a starring role. al-Faruqi ultimately traces this "unworthy and illogical" theology to Paul the apostle.[15] For all intents and purposes, Paul – with his conflicted posture towards the law – conjured the concept of original universal depravity, retroactively supplying the missing datum required by a faith that takes redemption as key not only to salvation but to the very essence of God himself.[16]

In concluding this segment's ruminations, allow me once again to highlight that Muslim theologians frequently observe the mutually reinforcing interplay between a Christian framing of sin as a lurking, inveterate, almost self-propelling force and a soteriology of radical divine intervention and redemption. This is typically set in contrast to an Islamic insistence on humanity's original innocence, basic freedom, and adequate capacities before God's "reasonable" and "realistic" enforcement of the law.[17] The following citations, from Rashid Rida and Shabbir Akhtar respectively, manifest a more and a less polemical tone, but they both follow familiar lines in contrasting Islamic and Christian salvation constructs:

> Does not this Islamic doctrine raise the ability of humanity and elevate his importance, and motivate him to seek perfection by his faith, fidelity, and good works? Isn't this better and more beneficial than relying on this cross story the likes of which was influenced by pagan myth, stories which the independent mind won't believe, nor the sound heart entrust itself to. Isn't this the violation of the path of the *fitra* and of the order of creation (المخالفة لسنن الفطرة ونظام الخلقة), which [violation] corrupted mind and morals in the Christian lands [time immemorial]?[18]

> For Paul, the cross was a necessary event. For the Quran, it is an avoidable tragedy, though not anathema ... Muslims dismiss the cross as suffering that is pointless or, in the nomenclature of theodicy, "dysteleological". The Quran would not see it as the necessary precursor of the salvific victory of the resurrection. Does sin possess us? Does sin possess such ontological integrity that only the death of God's only son on the cross could redeem us from its power? Is not God's fiat sufficient? For Muslims, God forgives whomsoever he wills. It is not in vain that he is God! Or does this Muslim attitude betray too casual a view of sin?[19]

## Justice Critique of Substitutionary Atonement

### *Objections to Cultic Mediation*

Akhtar describes atonement theory as typically fixated on the death of Jesus, thereby universalizing an otherwise local ministry:

> How does the life, healing ministry, death, resurrection, and ascension of Jesus accomplish (for others) forgiveness and reconciliation with God? Christ's death, as opposed to his life and ministry, secures atonement for all humanity as opposed to the few who knew and accepted him in first-century Palestine. It universalizes what would otherwise have remained a local and parochial transaction. His death was an expiation – redress or compensation – for universal sin.[20]

As with Akhtar, in most modern Islamic theorizing of salvation there is marked opposition to a mediated salvation. There is no vicarious bearing of sin, no bloody expiation, indeed no mediator in God's "saving" – this "saving" is a *direct*, just, and merciful dispensing of consequences, promises, and threats. The cross as ultimate cultic sacrifice simply has no place in the theological framework. Sacrifice ritual as a socio-historical reality of monotheism may be admitted, for "the prophets ... offered sacrifice as an expression of worship. It was accepted as righteousness, but the Quran rejects the dogma that blood cleanses us of sin, a Jewish view inherited by New Testament writers."[21] Indeed, for Akhtar:

> The Quran would see this obsession with eliminating sin through sacrifice, animal or human, as corrupt *pagan superstition* ... According to Muslims, whatever may have been ordained by God in the past, the revelation of the Quran terminated the need for animal sacrifice as expiation for sin and instead demanded that human beings surrender and sacrifice only their will and purpose to God – the very meaning of Islam.[22]

It is then abundantly clear that Jesus cannot be a redeemer or mediator of reconciliation between God and humans. The Shi'i scholar Tabatabai proffers an interesting explication of Q 5:116-18 in which Jesus is seen to disavow deity, to assert that all judgment or forgiveness is God's alone, and to limit his role amongst humanity to that of "witness" (شهيد) – and that only so long as he remained on earth. In these verses, Jesus is emphatic about the limits of his knowledge and authority. According to Tabatabai, were Jesus' role truly atoning, he would not have disavowed responsibility for his people after God took him away.[23]

Christ crucified is not simply the terrain of historical dispute between the faiths; rather, for most Muslims, the cross does not even belong in a discussion of salvation, righteousness, or eternal life with God. Muslim apologists may even attempt to "turn the tables" on Christian claims about God's intimate interface with humanity achieved in Christ crucified: the claim is that Islam's lack of mediation reveals a God *more* present to the believer than in Christian theology. Allegedly, counterintuitively, Islam's radically transcendent God is the "nearest of all", and *directly,* for no mediation is permissible in Islam (cf. Q 2:186; 11:61).[24]

There is no third-party expiation, propitiation, or mediation. There is no redemption by death (and rising). There is no question of a personal reconciliation somehow "costly" to God, still less of a blood-based redemption narrative.[25] The modernist theologian, Fazlur Rahman, amplifies the Qur'an's own stress on individual accountability, on the temptations of "this life" (*al-dunya*), on eternal outcomes hinging on personal response to the claims of monotheism, and so on (cf. Q 7:179; 8:53; 13:11; 23:115).[26] For him, this is "the qur'anic rejection of redemption".[27] While God's decision to forgive or condemn must remain *somewhat* inscrutable, his capacity to do so is entirely unconstrained and without mediation (see Q 3:129).[28]

### *"Justice from Above": Atonement's Failures in Reason and Justice*

In Islamic analysis, a common concern about atonement thought is that a vicarious bearing of sin and its consequences – a transfer of responsibility – results in an illogical and unjust salvation architecture. This can only reflect poorly on the Architect.[29] For a range of Muslim critics, the God of atonement appears to be an arbitrary and capricious being, one riven with internal contradictions as he attempts to effect justice. On inscrutable whims this God transfers guilt and innocence, even to the extent of visiting horrors on his own innocent prophet Jesus – who may even be in some absurd manner "God himself".

For critics, this more-or-less straight-line impugning of God's character and essence underlies atonement theory; such issues fall under my category "justice from above". But Islamic critics also perceive a problem when guilty sinners enjoy a blanket justification from God based on mere cognitive assent towards Christ. I turn to this "justice from below" issue – the resultant deleterious social ethic – in the following section.

Rida is one of the more vociferous opponents of atonement theory's twin ills of irrationalism and injustice. On Rida's construal of the atonement dynamic, God's effort to reconcile justice and mercy at the cross finally produces neither:

> [The Christian redemption story amounts to] the total abolition of justice and mercy in the crucifixion of the Messiah, for God punished the Messiah in the flesh when he did not deserve punishment because he was in no way guilty. So his torment in crucifixion and piercing by the spear (according to Christian claims) results in neither justice nor mercy whatsoever (لا يصدر من عادل ولا من رحيم بالأحرى). How can it be reasonable that the Creator is neither just nor merciful? Or being just and merciful, he creates something that places himself in the dilemma of abolishing one of the two characteristics, and, trying to unite the two, loses them both together?[30]

For Rida, to claim that it required the cross to resolve the tension between mercy and justice is fallacious from all angles. A sovereign can forgive without compunction and without elaborately contrived intervention.

For his part, Akhtar picks up on the ancient dispute over the recipient of "ransom" at the cross to highlight the ethical and justice tensions attending atonement theology. For Akhtar,

> There is a lacuna in Christian soteriology: to whom is the price of redemption paid? If paid by God to God himself in a different personal form or incarnation of himself, it makes him a narcissistic and avenging deity rather than the allegedly loving and generous God of Christian faith. It could not have been paid to the Devil since that would make him God's morally equal opponent.[31]

The straightforward, individualized accountability between creature and Creator is warped and delegitimated by the insertion of any "third party"; Jesus Christ at the center of atonement is precisely such a destabilizing insertion (cf. Q 6:164; 17:15; 39:7; 53:38).[32] Further, any "payment" involved in redemption invariably leads, says Akhtar, to God-constructs which violate reason, aesthetics and ethics; they are altogether unworthy. Adding a "third party" only exacerbates the ills.

al-Faruqi's portrayal of substitutionary atonement is stark, blunt, and unconcerned with nuance: "The act of Jesus is sacrifice; the act of God the Father ... is mercy; and the act of God who demanded that the Father do something in expiation, is justice ... God demanded it as retribution and ... Jesus carried it out as expiation."[33] For al-Faruqi, such a construct is hopelessly problematic; being unjust and irrational, it is also unworkable, operating with unworthy moral archetypes.

First, al-Faruqi thinks, this theory of redemption takes pain as "adequate retribution," when in fact infliction of pain is itself retrograde, unjust, and reflexively destructive. "It is hard to see ... how the pain of crucifixion" would work to requite or undo sin.[34] This complaint is reminiscent of Tabatabai's indictment of disproportionate retribution in Christian soteriology, albeit with a more modern sensibility – invoking pain and violence in redemption is *ipso facto* a debased proposition.

Further, al-Faruqi objects to the injustice and inevitable failure of any attempt to transfer guilt or consequence. Moral evil cannot be transferred or atoned for in any reasonable way by the intervention of an external actor. Vicariousness elides individual agency as "the ineffably personal character of repentance and of moral transformation" are lost.[35] The truth is, rather, that salvation comes when humans "fulfill their own vocations", and thus salvation "is [their] own doing or it is worthless".[36]

Essentially, it is wrong and ineffectual for God to "go over our heads" in trying to save us. Comparably, Sayyid Qutb insists that the Islamic alternative to original sin and atonement is the "right balance" of each one accountable only for their own works before God: no guilt transferred and no atonement needed except the making right of one's own transgressing.[37]

### *"Justice from Below": Irrationalism Correlates with Moral Dereliction*

We are now familiar with the Islamic commonplace that vicarious intervention at the cross is irrational and, equally, unjust.[38] Hear Ibn al-'Uthamin:

> And so the Christians in their foolishness, delusion, and paucity of reason, adopted the cross on which their prophet was crucified as a god, or at least as holy, whereas if they were actually rational, upon seeing the cross they would break and burn it. But they are deluded fools, unable to distinguish between truth and falsehood (سفهاء ضلال لا يميزون بين الحق والباطل).[39]

There is copious commentary on the destructive fruits of this "unreasonable" doctrine in the realm of human morality. Rida is especially loquacious about atonement's theological, spiritual, and ethical deficiencies, particularly in comparison with Islam's morally robust proclamation of *tawhid* in view of a looming Judgment.[40] According to many critics, atonement is a morally counterproductive dogma, for that which does not make sense, *in the nature of the case*, won't work. Irrationality correlates with ethical derogation. The nonsensical transfer of guilt (onto the innocent One) is tantamount to an inducement to antinomian license – morality collapses when reward or punishment are no longer at stake.[41]

Rida sees the Passion as the climax of a pitiable narrative involving God on the horns of a dilemma (Adam's sin), a story that culminates in the unworkable doctrine of vicarious redemption. According to Rida, the upshot of this doctrine is that those ready to "extinguish the light of [their] mind" are saved by faith in this teaching; this is so even if they "kill, commit adultery, drink alcohol … and [are] the bane of civilization … [Meanwhile, on these grounds, Muslims'] faith in God and his angels, books, and messengers [… and] disciplining of moral character and reform of actions" are taken by Christians to be of no benefit.[42] For Rida, the basic proclamation of the cross lacks all moral suasion and rather appeals to base appetites, proffering a sort of moral indemnity.[43] Tabatabai voices similar objections: an atonement already "accomplished" is tantamount to a law-free system in which both excellent and execrable people are absolved. Moral incentive has well and truly disappeared.[44]

Islamic critics discern unjust irrationalism not only in the moral calculus of atonement's transfer of guilt and innocence, but also in the status of the death and resurrection of Jesus as a "finished work". al-Faruqi censures "salvation" as a problematic concept laden with assumptions of fallenness and humanity's being "pulled out of the sinful predicament … from which [they] can never extricate [themselves] by [their] own effort, no matter how great or moral [they] be".[45] When atonement is predicated on an external action of God, received as a punctiliar experience of grace, this is tantamount to arbitrary justification "by divine fiat".[46] Instead of this "*fait accompli* redemption", al-Faruqi avers that "salvation" is in reality an ever-present, contingent process.[47] "There is no time at which the Muslim may carry his title to paradise, as it were, in his pocket. Instead of 'salvation', the Muslim is to achieve felicity through unceasing effort."[48] Indeed, "[s]alvation must flow out of morality, not *vice versa.*"[49]

For al-Faruqi, Christian theology inculcates "habits [… such as] irrationalism and paradox, an obsessive clinging to the paired doctrines – the necessary fallenness of man and nature, redemption as an event already accomplished by outside agency – with their inevitable consequences: a deep distrust of the processes of human effort and history, and a bleak individualism".[50] So, "the committed Christian is by nature complacent, a passivist, a proclaimer of an event past, whereas the committed Muslim is a moral activist, seeking and determining a future."[51] Tragically, it seems, atonement theology leads to ethics and worship that negate the virtues of life in this world.[52]

### Atonement Theology Generates a Deficient Social Ethic

Atonement as a finished work of grace, then, is frequently paired with Christianity's supposed hyper-individualism and abstracted spiritualization. As a result, the attending ethical vulnerabilities of atonement theology manifest not only in personal lifestyle morality, but also in sociopolitical ethics. This debilitating impact can be extended even to the burden of the colonial legacy. On al-Faruqi's terms:

> [I]t is no wonder that the Christian who acts consistently with the logic of [redemption] doctrine … is vulnerable to spiritually fatal attacks of ethical complacency. It ought not to be denied, for example, that what Christendom has allowed itself to do to the non-Christian world during the last five centuries … is

> one effect of that self-righteousness which belief in a savior engenders and cultivates. From this dark shadow that accompanies the doctrine of necessary sin and mysterious salvation, there is no escape except in paradox. The shadow, in individual and collective life, cripples the moral imagination so that with all the power in the world to do good, that power creates only more intractable problems for itself.[53]

We cannot afford the motif the space it deserves here, but the Islamic charge that Christian soteriology is morally effete precisely due to its gaping legal lacuna also echoes in the literature.[54] There is a marked disparity between the faiths when it comes to confidence in human ethical capacity and the salvific worth of the moral sanction of revealed law (Torah/*nomos*/*Shari'a*). Some Muslim critics allege that the Pauline reticence about the law results in a deficient Christian social ethic in terms of both constructive vision and also deterrence of malfeasance.

At its worst, atonement theology's bypassing of the law leads Christians into the dead end of a paganized, bereft mysticism. Note Akhtar:

> Thus, for Muslims ... Christianity must finally emerge, after one has taken account of nuances and shades of scriptural meaning, as essentially a primitive faith, closer to a primordial paganism, a mystical pantheism infused with a vague notion of a human–divine interface whereby nature and the supernatural meet. The problem is that such a view offers no guidance on how to live well. Thus, for Muslims, the law is not a curse but a blessing, a reminder and a commandment from God, sent down for our collective benefit rather than to oppress us (see Q 20:2–3). A robust moral virtue is not beyond the law but rather through the law.[55]

Muslim critics suggest that if one's hopes are suspended on a vicarious redeemer, the restorative energies of the law, God's *way*, have been passed over. On this reckoning, atonement theory exacts a punishing cost on individual virtue, eschatological salvation, and contemporary social uplift.[56] For Akhtar, if indeed the law was divinely given, then reason demands it can and must be salvifically effective for those willing to submit. The alternative is to construe God as toying with his helpless subjects, deceptively calling them to the impossible.[57]

And so, Akhtar bemoans the "fact" that a cross gospel is devoid of Islam's ethical activism buttressed by legal sanction:

> The gospel of the cross, like persecuted Meccan Islam, would appeal to powerless victims, often struggling at the lowest levels of Roman society. Such were probably the majority of Paul's hearers (see 1 Cor. 1:26-28). The Gospel, like the Quran, was to be an alternate source of power, sacred power. But the Quran attempted to absorb politics into religion so that utopian politics would appeal not only to the marginalized but rather confront all the solidarities that oppress peoples and societies everywhere at all times. Faith was not merely a school of social criticism but rather the effective weapon of revolutionary change in every structure that resisted universal justice. Muhammad moved from the soothing catharsis of merely moral outrage into the tougher arena of effectively activist agency.[58]

al-Faruqi's claims serve well to conclude this section. By his lights, atonement doctrine, majoring in forgiveness, vicarious intervention, and justification delivered "once for all", is a heady elixir, but the patient's malady has been misdiagnosed.[59] al-Faruqi may be taken as broadly representative when he says that for ultimate benediction, humans need a divine "education" far more than they need a blanket "justification".[60] For many a Muslim thinker, a soteriology of human capacity (Islam) or incapacity (Christianity) is a critical watershed in which the latter is found wanting in terms of reason, justice, and morality.

## God's Honor: Atonement as Violation of Divine Transcendence

Upholding the honor of God against all pretenders is a near-ubiquitous pressure in the religious rhetoric of Islam (cf. Q 9:33). And in terms of a standard Islamic theological and moral aesthetic, there is little surprise that atonement theory falls afoul of its sensibilities. Zeal for God's honor can be expressed with visceral flourish against Christian doctrines taken to be debased or unworthy. In other cases, the critique may be expressed in a more philosophic register. The clashes often emerge along boundaries where atonement theology is perceived to threaten divine transcendence. At these junctures, contestation over atonement also implicates incarnation.

In the Chambésy consultation, al-Faruqi engaged in an eloquent and sharp interchange with Christian theologians on the nature of the Creator–creation divide. Islam, for al-Faruqi, strongly resists any implication of divine entailment in or obligation to creation, or that God's relationship to humanity exposes the divine essence or character to view. Indeed, a major preoccupation of Islamic theologians is the robust policing of the frontiers between the Creator and his world, a border that Christian thought (allegedly) has left all too porous and vulnerable to infiltration.

According to al-Faruqi, both Islam and Christianity begin their projects with this vital metaphysical duality in place. But, he thinks, Christianity strays all too quickly, contriving the doctrine of incarnation *en route* to salvation. Doctrines such as incarnation hang on the "impossible paradox" of the coincidence of transcendence and immanence. For al-Faruqi, it is vital that God's nature and essence stands across an unbridgeable chasm from creation and humanity.[61] Regrettably, the "immanentism" of the Trinity and incarnation, defaces *tawhid* by "apotheosizing nature" and "objectifying the transcendent God".[62]

Tabatabai likewise expresses offense at the "anthropomorphic" instincts of incarnational theology. The physicality and development inherent to human existence negate the notion *a priori* as rationally incoherent and philosophically absurd.[63] Citing 1 Cor. 1:19-23, Tabatabai takes Paul as emblematic of the Christian disdain for philosophical insight and rational judgment (الفلسفة و... الاحكام العقلية)[64]:

> In the end you will have to admit that there is no relationship between a thing that has a physical body with all its accidents and concomitants (اوصاف الجسمية وآثارها) and a Being that has neither a body nor any of its concomitants or accidents (like time, space, movement, etc.). How can one even think of unity between the two in any way?[65]

The incongruities of incarnation, for Tabatabai, throw the stability of God's being, difference, and essence into question in such a way that contrary attributes (justice/injustice, knowledge/ignorance) may be found to inhere in him.[66] Christ as God incarnate constitutes a veritable parade of unbearable contradictions.[67]

Hamid Algar's elucidation of these problematics for atonement theology is typical and convergent with Tabatabai's misgivings:

> If one takes as true, for the sake of argument, the Christian belief that Jesus ... was indeed crucified, then the theological problem is acute. Because if he is of entirely human nature, then the whole claim for special status for him falls away. If on the other hand there was a divine nature in him, then the death of a divinity is a self-negating concept. And if the two natures were first joined but then separated at the time of crucifixion, again the distinctive nature of Jesus, according to Christian belief, is negated.[68]

Incarnation's cavalcade of slights to the divine honor builds to the ultimate "impossibility" of the Passion. For Rida, irrationality matches ignominy – that God should indwell a womb, should have a digestive tract, and so on.[69] And then, for this innocent One to suffer unjust torment – on God, by God. "Heaven forbid!"[70] The teaching that Christ bore the divine "curse" is seen by Tabatabai as utterly fantastical (التعليم العجيب بتمام معنى الكلمة).[71] He quotes Q 35:15: "O mankind! You are the ones who stand in need of Allah, and Allah – He is the All-sufficient" (Qarai). A curse of whatever sort can hardly be applied to God – let alone "by himself, to himself" – as God is *in se* above, beyond, impervious, invulnerable to any defect.[72]

There is profound resistance to connecting Jesus to the eviscerating shame of crucifixion. For most Muslim scholars, the concept remains impermissible whether or not a theology of incarnation is factored in. Such dishonor applied to Jesus – even presumed to be only a great prophet – would redound to dishonor. God cannot be seen to be so weak, unreliable, so feckless as to have "abandoned" the Messiah. Hear Ali Merad:

> God does not abandon His own: how then could He have abandoned Jesus, a being whom he produced miraculously, by His *Kalima*, a being whom He assisted by His Spirit, whom He had singularly favored? ... Islam refused to accept this tragic image of the Passion [i.e. the suffering and death of Jesus]. Not simply because it has no place for the dogma of the Redemption, but because the Passion would imply in its eyes that God had failed.[73]

### *Vicarious Mediation: Pagan Immanentizing*

In Islamic discourse, an intertwined nexus of Christian doctrines (Trinity, incarnation, crucifixion and atonement) are sometimes seen as vectors injecting malign pagan influences into early Christian monotheism.[74] For example, vicarious mediation "by blood" is decried as a pagan distortion of monotheist purity.[75] For many Islamic intellectuals, redemptive intervention of this sort is a thoroughly immanentizing, pagan paradigm.[76]

Naturally, questions of mediation being pagan may provoke counterchallenges around the template of "intercession", a trope, as noted, embedded within some sectors of Islamic thought. Thus, Tabatabai labors to sharpen the contrast between Islamic intercession (الشفاعة) and the errant Christian teaching of atonement (الفداء).[77] For Tabatabai, the Qur'an excludes intercession as any sort of mediating moral transfer; it is simply the humble request of a pious worthy before God (cf. Q 2:48, 254).[78]

Purportedly, the polytheistic impulse of paganism pushed Christian theologizing and worship in detrimental directions pre-eminently with respect to Christ, but also including the over-exalting of apostles, leaders, and saints.[79] The pagan undercurrent in Christianity portents a fatal parting of the ways between the faiths: Sayyid Qutb holds that Jesus came offering only a strict monotheism (in no way inserting himself into divinity), but too quickly the Christians strayed in their creeds and dogmas, admixing paganism, contriving notions of Christ's deity, Trinity, cross, atonement, and so on.[80] Indeed, having taken on "lords beside God", Christians have lost their *bona fides* as monotheists, for "those who claim that all sins are forgiven through a holy communion with Jesus Christ, which is the only way to achieve forgiveness [... cannot] be described as believers in God or in the Last Day."[81]

### *Muzzling Divine Power?*

Islamic antipathy to the gospels' portrayal of the crucifixion extends beyond a denial of the event's historicity. Whatever one makes of the original context of Q 4:157-58, Islamic theology counters the crucifixion on grounds of theology proper, soteriology, prophetology, and so on. We have already seen the tendency to disallow the shame of the Passion because it would attribute an indignity to both a prophet of Jesus' stature and to God.[82] This instinct may be developed along various arcs, for example, a pious rejection of the cross because it, by definition, represents defeat – which is impossible for God. According to an al-Azhar commentary:

> God elevated [Jesus] to a place, undertaking for his protection and safety, preserving him from his enemies' designs. "God is Almighty, All-wise." God is and remains unceasingly victorious, not overcome by anything. He is wise in all he does and so he saved Jesus from his enemies. It was not possible for [Jesus'] honored body to be overcome by the opponents of the truth (لم يمكن من جسده الشريف خصومَ الحق).[83]

al-Sha'rawi insists that the death of Jesus on a cross would not make sense because God never commissions a messenger and then allows people to kill and overcome him prior to his fulfilling his mission.[84] There can be no diminution of God's power nor attribution of limits to the One who is limitless.

Cruciform atonement is seen to be inimical to Islam's relentless insistence on God's limitless sovereignty and untrammeled rule. This objection obtains at the more pedestrian level of history: the mission of the prophet cannot be seen to fail. It also obtains at the level of soteriological grammar: no elaborate interventions or devices are required to mediate, validate, or instantiate God's forgiveness. His capacity to save, forgive, and judge must remain utterly unqualified (al-Azhar commentary):

> The amazing thing is that even the Christian gospels have Jesus telling the disciples they will doubt him, so how would they know the real events of the crucifixion. As it is they made obligatory vapid interpretations of the event based on their divinization of him and presumption about his crucifixion, to the point that they make him a redeemer for all the world's sinners! ... This is quite contrary to reason.

> If he was God or God's son as they claim, he could readily forgive whomever he chooses (يستطيع أن يغفر لمن شاء) or overcome in his body the weapons of his enemies. As it is, on their telling, he becomes the cause of their sinning further – contrary to intentions (عكس المقصود)![85]

Tabatabai concurs with judgments noted above to the effect of agreeing that redemptive exchange (البدل فدية وفداء) is problematic because it is a category mistake; one that runs afoul of divine transcendence at that.[86] As such it insupportably transposes restrictions onto the divine essence. Redemption is an operation in which charges, penalties, and claims are transferred away from the one liable, who thereby benefits. In intrahuman relations this sort of thing may be allowed, but not with God. His rights are absolute and inalienable, and not to be toyed with.[87] What we owe God can't be shunted elsewhere and, equally, no one may say who he may or may not judge or forgive. His sovereignty gives no account and none may expect a "ransom" from the Fire (cf. Q 57:15).[88]

Tabatabai insists that God is not subject to external constraint (غلبة المانع الخارجي) of any sort.[89] God has "outright ownership" (ملكه المطلق) of all; there is before God no "partner, ransom, associate, or intercession" with influence over him (شريك أو فدية أو خلة أو شفاعة).[90] The Sovereign has full rights (شؤون المولوية) of punishment and reward, and has no need of any external justification for forgiving and withholding punishment. For Tabatabai, this pattern is simply a consistent fact of human experience and divine revelation (الوحي الالهي), even including, for the most part, *the Bible*. That sin without vicarious intervention should remain indelible, impervious to "repentance, change, return, and regret, is unacceptable to sound reason and righteous nature (عقل سليم و... طبع مستقيم)."[91] We may not foist the "need" for an atonement mechanism onto God.

Indeed, this open door for repentance is one evidence of "grace" in Islam. Akhtar is eager to pre-empt any notion that atonement doctrine positions Christianity as a religion of "grace" as opposed to Islam. For him, the fact that Islamic thought rejects vicarious suffering in no way intimates an absence of "grace". Rightly related, grace and works are synergistic, with no need for a vicarious Savior.[92]

Rida, too, is strident in his objections, claiming that atonement at Calvary is a farce featuring a God of limited sovereignty, constrained by boundaries, supposedly caught between justice and mercy.[93] Rather than extracting God from a bind, for Rida, atoning crucifixion actually puts God *into* one wherein neither justice nor mercy are achieved. The implied "need" of the cross is a denigration of divine authority and an offensive limitation on God's unfettered capacity to punish and forgive.[94] Similarly, Mohammad Hassan Khalil insists, on the basis of the Qur'an and Hadith, "that God may choose to pardon the sincere, whatever their sins".[95]

Naturally, few Muslim thinkers would deny the justice of God, but the impulse to assert the unfettered freedom of God appears at times to trump any expectations of what God "must" do to satisfy justice. Akhtar tells us, "Islamic doctrine is entirely innocent of the temptations of theodicy since Muslims recognize no puzzle here."[96] On Islamic terms, there is no "problem" requiring a cruciform solution, nothing to "justify" – not least God himself.

### *God's Honor and Metaphysical Intuition*

Islamic and Christian interface on atonement thought tends to underscore discrepant preunderstandings. Definitive for Christian soteriology is the insistence that God is uniquely, personally revealed to us in Christ. But for many of our Muslim thinkers, exploration of divine ontology is theologically inappropriate *in se*, a hubristic feint towards the boundaries that sanctify a God unknowable in his own essence. Thus, the harder the Christian presses the economy of salvation as the lens by which to know God as he is, the more the chasm with the Islamic interlocutor widens.

Christian discourse on atonement is intellectually challenging, running up against the limits of the knowable and commonly thematizing concepts such as paradox, intuition, reversal of expectations, and so on. (Thus, it is well in keeping with classic orthodoxy, for example, to insist that in Christ God is truly known, "savingly" known, without indicating that one therefore has epistemic command of God's "essence".) Meanwhile, for many Muslim critics such ruminations are rank irrationality. According to Akhtar, Muslims "regard any deep inquiry into such matters [of ontotheology] as presumptuous since the Qur'an is silent only on matters that are ultimately humanly unknowable but also *irrelevant to the attainment of success in the life of faith.* Theology, as the study of God's nature as opposed to his will, is anathema."[97]

Indeed, Islamic affirmation of the divine transcendence can be prosecuted so vigorously that a notable gap seems to open up between the Revealer and the Book he reveals. So, Akhtar holds that:

> The Qur'an, by contrast [with Paul's notion of revelation *through* Christ], is revelation from (*min*) God, not through God. *Distance is preserved between the revealer and the reality revealed.* The mother of the book (*umm al-kitab*; Q3:7), meaning its essence, is with (*'inda*) God. This preposition, frequent in the Qur'an (e.g. 9:19), literally means "at God", that is, in his sight – implying intimate connection albeit at a fixed location rather than, so to speak, during an agent's continuous movement or transfer.[98]

Both Christian and Muslim scholars generally intend to acknowledge God's grandeur, greatness, and exceeding of creaturely reality – that is to say, "his honor". However, the guiding presuppositions and intuitions here can radically diverge, not least when salvation or human rectification are being exposited. Perhaps some overstatement for the sake of clarity may be permitted, as follows.

Within the Islamic parameters, the category of "mystery" does apply to theology proper. But the mystery of God's person or character must remain inveterately opaque; investigation and speculation are discouraged in that God's essence is by definition inaccessible. Right human engagement with God is, for the most part, deflected away from relational knowledge towards knowledge of and submission to his revealed will or law.

It is this *forensic* dimension that is soteriologically relevant. In a religious ethos centering law, instruction, and divine guidance, it is little wonder that reason, linear rationality, legal predictability, and so on inflect its soteriological grammar. By way of contrast, categories of mystery, paradox, or productive tension appear to be more at home within a Trinitarian framework of salvation.[99] For their part, Muslim scholars tend to receive these themes of Christian soteriology with considerable perplexity and discomfiture, frequently assessing them to be fatal aporias.

Thus, we do well to remember that an Islamic advocacy of a "simple" and "rational" soteriology (or doctrine of human beatitude) is often the inverse side of a defense of divine dignity, even when the conversation is not focused on the nature of God but rather on the destiny of humans. Protecting the "reasonableness" of salvation is bound up with avoiding an intrusion on divine transcendence.

al-Faruqi's analysis of Christianity is emblematic here in that he aims above all at an allegedly dispassionate realism. In his *Christian Ethics* he proposes a principled "logical" critique of Christian concepts as opposed to even a "Muslim" perspective.[100] It becomes clear, however, that he sees little daylight between the "rational" or "natural" and "Islam," for the *fitra* is tantamount to Islam, which is the innate, reasonable religion.[101]

al-Faruqi claims, purportedly in contrast to Christian thought, that God's ways in salvation operate along rational, patent, and sequential channels of accountability. We have already seen him decry the nihilism and pessimism inherent to the determinism of the doctrine of universal original sin – the "inevitability" of sin as a looming power is defeatist and enervating.[102] And again, he construes original sin as an after-the-fact construct engineered to match the equally malformed doctrine of vicarious atonement. He warns that such ideas derogate the linear dignity of Islamic salvation via command and free obedience. For al-Faruqi, sins and temptation, alongside individual self-mastery aided by revelation, adequately account for the malady and grandeur of the human condition.

Islam's offer of salvation on evidently rational grounds is often contrasted with the intellectually suspect Christian penchant for paradox, subversive reversal, and inverted values. In this regard, Cragg captures al-Faruqi's stance well:

> For al-Faruqi, paradox was evasion, the sign of an untidy mind or a perverse will. It offended against the sure principle of rationality which Islam, as he saw it, possessed and enshrined … There was, he thought, something he called metareligion which "approved" faith as based on certainty of evidence assured on the ground that "whatever is repugnant to reason is repugnant to Allah." Such conformity of the true faith (Islam) to internal coherence as constituting the validity of "revelation" was not to be seen as an imposition on God, but was a necessity for man.[103]

Akhtar's angle of approach is distinct from al-Faruqi's, but remains similarly suspicious of Christian appeals to the mysteriously inverse dynamics of God's economy – for example, the cross as strength manifest through weakness:

> Paul is variously an apostle and servant of higher beings – and his strength derives from that liaison. To serve a voluntarily powerless Lord is, however, still to serve in weakness. Where is the strength in this arrangement? Christians need to know that such claims, whose charm and truth seem self-evident to Christians, are dismissed particularly by Muslim and also by Marxist critics. They see it as special pleading, self-deluded reasoning and, in any case, ineffective in our kind of world which resists goodness, not evil, and does so with determined force and tenacity.[104]

And so, firmly operating within a specific tradition of "rational" theologizing – with particular assumptions about what might be possible for God, and with presuppositions as to the ontological "givens" of reality – Islamic scholars often appeal for a universal convergence around "rationally discernable religious truth". For al-Faruqi, this reduces to a challenge that Christians abandon their "figurization of God in Jesus as normative".[105] Rahman, too, pursues a similar gambit.[106] Thus, while Christian and Islamic monotheism assiduously intend fidelity to the transcendent Creator and his unimpeached honor, the compatibility of their intuitions about "rationally discernable religious truth" will undoubtedly remain contested.

### *The Contradictions of Biblical Salvation-History*

In the Muslim–Christian engagement over soteriology, a fascinating divide emerges around salvation-historical schemes. We have seen Muslim scholars assess cross atonement in terms of injustice, irrationality, and deleterious human consequences. Interestingly, at times the criticisms of Christian redemption are projected from a slightly different angle: the scholarly deconstruction can be aimed at the illogicality of salvation history's structure or simply at the scandal of its historical particularity. In all this, recall our point above that the subtext of much Islamic demurral is intended to bolster God's honor and transcendence.

Akhtar poses the issue:

> In the Christian scheme of history, the era of promise (Abraham) and the era of law (Moses) culminate in the era of fulfillment of the age of promise (Christ). The fourth era is the eternal life of faithful fellowship with Christ ... Islam has no corresponding scheme of sacred history. Instead, this world in present history will, for each person, end and lead to death, resurrection and the enduring next life (Q 7:24-25; 20:55). For Muslims, the law is not probationary but permanent. The Muslim critic of Christianity can see the motives for eliminating the law – the desire to include Gentiles and the impossibility of obeying the whole law without the aid of grace. But what are the revealed grounds, the dominical sayings, for that stance? The Islamic alternative states that every human being received divine guidance and that we are all individually accountable for our actions. God expects us to do our best, no more. He never burdens any person with more than he or she can bear (Q 2:286).[107]

We have here an Islamic salvation framework – individuals are pre-programmed for the "innate religion" and have been from the beginning bombarded with calls to return to this truth by a prodigious succession of prophets. What is required is knowledge and a conscience attuned.[108] On these grounds, the Christian narrative – a slow historical development leading to the cross – is seen to be unhelpful, unworkable, and unnecessary. God's summons to "saving" monotheism – in effect, to Islam – must in principle be on offer in (virtually) complete form, always and ubiquitously.

Tabatabai links the NT's "malformed" profile of salvation history to the legal lacuna in Christian theology. His perplexity is palpable. He wonders that if revealed knowledge or law is not the constituent component of human salvation, then why the promulgation of the Torah in the first place? If Adam's sin results in guilt and damnation for all – a dilemma only resolved at the cross – then what virtue is there in the legal promulgation of religion (تشريع الدين) whether before or after Jesus' coming?[109] If eternal punishment for sin was not to be resolved by "religion" or deeds, then why did God go through the charade of sending a sequence of prophets, books, and laws? He charges that, if the atonement construct holds, the missions of Moses and Jesus, not to mention the very purposes of God, come to rather meager fruition at best; the atonement narrative represents a corruption of reason (فساده عند العقل) that vitiates the majesty and capacity of God to create and then guide creation (Q 20:50).[110] For Tabatabai, Christian soteriology is beset by an internal contradiction for, by revealing an ineffectual law, God deceived humanity and himself.[111]

The Sunni intellectual al-Faruqi is likewise pointed and probing as he argues that atonement theology places the cart before the horse. al-Faruqi takes to task redemption, the Christ event, and the economic Trinity (my terms) for distorting Christianity's basic God construct. The centrality of redemption for Christianity leads to insuperable absurdities, making redemption definitive of God.[112] "Strict monotheism" has been compromised when "the Christ revelation is [taken as] the supreme moment *in the Godhead itself*".[113]

As al-Faruqi sees it, atonement theory necessitates and valorizes the "blessed Fall"; this inverse valuation hopelessly distorts the entire picture.[114] He suggests that sin is so vital to the Christian paradigm of redemption that God might have needed to compel sin if Adam hadn't fallen (a sort of *felix culpa*). We are left with an untenable antinomy: for Christians, sin is exaggeratedly dark and yet strangely vital to the true revelation of God. And yet, ultimately, bereft of a divine law, Christians are ill-equipped to counter it.[115]

Yes, we have previously explored al-Faruqi's argumentation on original sin, but with a *primary* concern for its deleterious effects on ethics and anthropology. The focus here is his contention that the intertwined structure of sin and redemption besmirches the honor of God, injecting instability into his very being.[116]

> Unless the necessity … of human sinfulness is presupposed, the mission of Jesus Christ … loses its point. Now, since the mission of Jesus Christ as universal redeemer is a necessary part of what defines God as God[, …] the necessity of human sinfulness has also to be a presupposition of God being God.[117]

Rashid Rida expresses similar concerns about atonement as historically realized in a narrative running from Adam to the Passion, albeit with a rhetorical pungency all his own:

> And so, from the time of Adam's transgression, a problem occurred for God (heaven forbid!) who is characterized by justice and mercy. The problem was this: If God punished Adam and his descendants, this would contradict his mercy and he would not be merciful! But if he did not punish him, that would contradict his justice and he would not be just. It's as if since the transgression of Adam, God was thinking of a way to bring together justice and mercy. God was not led to this way (solution) until 1922 years ago, according to current reckoning (heaven forbid!). And this was for his Son, who is God himself, to indwell the belly of a woman of Adam's line and to unite with an embryo in her womb and to be born from her. So her son was fully human as her son and fully divine as Son of God – and the Son of God is God. And he was sinless, free of all human transgressions. Then after

> living a time with people, eating what they ate and drinking what they drank, and enjoying as they enjoyed and suffering as they suffered, his enemies contrived to kill him with the most awful killing, and that is the crucifixion, the victim of which is cursed in the divine book. So he bore the curse and the cross for the sake of the redemption of humanity and to save them from their sins. As John says in his first letter: "He is the atoning sacrifice for our sins, and not our sins alone, but for the sins of the whole world too."[118]

In a following segment Rida further ridicules the image of a limited and befuddled God trying to work out a solution to his internal conundrum over justice and mercy. Oh, the folly of this metanarrative, which "implicates the Creator in ignorance and having an origin", but only "those who stipulate that their religion need not cohere with reason have accepted this story (ولكن قد يقبلها من يشترط في الدين عندهم أن لا يتفق مع العقل)!"[119]

Christianity's concocted salvation scheme running along a storyline from Genesis to the gospels is, to Rida's mind, riven with insupportable incongruities. For example:

i) To begin with, it is problematic that salvation is historically developmental rather than a "steady state". As the unitary message of *Islam* ought in principle to be available in virtually complete form in all times and locales, particularity – attributing cosmic import to the death of the Man from Nazareth, ca. 30 CE – is a scandal.[120]

ii) The Syro-Egyptian scholar decries the opposition of justice to mercy. None of God's attributes are in tension, and his capacity to forgive and punish remains without constraint. There is no "need", no logical bind requiring the cross as a sort of resolution between competing goods.

iii) Christianity's sort of "historical" salvation scheme unacceptably humanizes the sovereign God. This Entity, caught up in space-time, haplessly struggling to work out a cosmic solution, is risibly anthropomorphic even before the offenses of incarnation are addressed. Contrary to these *paganized* depictions, God in truth is ultimate Reality characterized by aseity, simplicity, infinity, and authoritative power.[121]

Many Christians see in the biblical narrative the mystery of God in time, the wonder of incarnation, and the realistic but hopeful (if rough-and-tumble) texture of the Bible's progressive revelation. But all of these offend Rida's theological imaginary. Indeed, most Muslim assessments conclude that Christian preoccupation with a doctrine of reconciliation through the death and rising of the incarnate Lord runs aground on the shoals of truth, reason, and justice. A crucial aspect of this collective rejection is the implicit indignity, the injured honor, that Christianity's governing metanarrative is seen to foist upon the immutable, invulnerable Sovereign of creation.

## Conclusion

In closing the chapter, I synthesize the preceding Islamic assessments with an eye on the categories of sin, justice, and honor.[122] A pervasive tendency is to establish an unflattering contrast: Christian intellection of salvation swims in waters of unreason, floundering in unjustifiable mystery and paradox, generating an ethereal theology with invidious individual and collective consequences. Islam's framing of the God–human relationship is markedly different; the religion of *tawhid* grounds salvation in a rational monotheism with a law-backed channel to blessing in this world and the next. The content, vision, and processes of salvation in the two faiths diverge sharply. Undergirding this disjunction are contrasting intuitions about God and incommensurable epistemological expectations – moral aesthetics, metaphysical imaginaries, and questions of what may be appropriately posited about the divine nature.

### *Sin*

When it comes to discussion of theological anthropology and, more precisely, what it is that people must be saved from, Muslim critics are generally focused on what they see as Christian theology's preoccupation with sin and especially the distorting doctrine of original sin. On this calculus, the Fall narrative is irrational and deterministic, consisting of an unjust guilt transfer (to Adam's progeny) with cataclysmic consequences. Atonement in Christ is the only resolution for this tragic chain reaction with its own amplified wrongs of universal scope and yet another inappropriate guilt transfer.

Refracted through the lens of Islamic theology, sin in Christian perspective is overweighted, too ontologically fraught, too central to the system. For many thinkers it is a doctrine contrived to match the implausible flagship story of the faith – redemption through the Passion. The fruits of all of this are hardly salutary: Christians are saddled with exaggerated requirements of holiness and freedom from sin while, ironically, ending up powerless to practically counteract sin on a personal or social scale (note the alleged "law lacuna"). In effect Christianity aims higher and reaches lower than God's calling. In most presentations, this soteriological dynamic comes off poorly against Islam's simpler vision in which submission before God leads to success. The Islamic proposal is said to be grounded in a theological outlook that is more just, reasonable, and realistic about sin, humanity, and divine expectations.

### *Justice*

In terms of the moral logic of atonement, an elemental Islamic response to justification through faith in the mediation of Christ crucified is the refrain, "There is no intercessor with God." Christian theology's mediated, vicarious (not to mention bloody) atonement is assessed as unworkable because it is unjust. Islam's contrasting alternative of straight-line faith and obedience, works and reward, carries the divine imprimatur. In terms of ethical metaphysical structures, Christianity's third-party intervention is irremediably problematic.

Mediated atonement is unable to underwrite the salvation it proclaims, being intrinsically deficient both in terms of justice from above and from below. In terms of God construct – justice from above – God's own nature is maligned as he blithely shifts blame and innocence around; the picture deteriorates yet further when "justification" is achieved by his visiting violence on an innocent and exemplary Christ. The human ethics of Christian soteriology – justice from below – are equally problematic: forgiveness via the cross is tantamount to arbitrary fiat, and the recipients of this so-called grace are ever ready to exploit this "blank check" ideology, to the ethical detriment of the world.

Atonement as a *fait accompli* evacuates moral incentive, while complacency enters and ethics collapse. The concept of the death and resurrection as a finished work of grace eventuates in a harmful harvest both in terms of i) individual ethics and ii) sociopolitical ethics. In terms of the former, the product is an effete mysticism, hyper-spiritualized individualism, and anti-creational nihilism. As to the latter, one finds a gaping void at Christian soteriology's center where law should be; in turn this produces a deep malaise in its collective ethics, contributing to everything from unrealistic – and unattained – ethical ideals, prolific public immorality, imperialist oppression, and so on. Earnest Muslim interlocutors urge that attention to the requirements of justice demonstrates that effective, salvific revelation is not found in a God-human *person*, but in God's *law*; as al-Faruqi puts it, the need is not redemption but education.

### *Honor and Transcendence*

Islamic God-talk, with its supporting metaphysical instinct, generally recoils at the notion of ontotheology, exploring the essence, nature, or character of God. In all this, one risks an affront to divine transcendence, a risk intensified when Christians stake insights into the being of God on a story like that of the gospel Passion accounts. Indeed, a major preoccupation of Islamic theology is the robust guarding of the ontological frontiers between the Creator and his world, a border that Christian thought is alleged to have left all too porous in incarnation and redemption.

Common within our cadre of Islamic theologians is an aversion to framing the God–creation relationship in any way that purports to unveil his essence or which imposes obligation on him. The dyad of incarnation and Passion are accused of just such a trespass. They are construed as Christian hubris, as flirting with the seductions of polytheism. Taken as a flagrant instantiation of impossible paradox and pagan immanentization, atonement, then, is framed as inimical to God's honor, his aseity, indeed his "godness".

Viewed in abstract as the fulcrum of salvation, cruciform atonement is deleterious to divine honor because i) the crucifixion is death to a God who cannot die, nor be defeated; ii) such a death could not possibly effect salvation – it would be a loss – *whereas God always achieves his ends*; iii) any "need" for the cross represents intolerable constraint on God's freedom to forgive and condemn at will – we need not "justify" God's actions in any way; iv) the centrality of sin and redemption at the cross allegedly makes contingent historical events definitional for a God who, properly, is invulnerable and timeless.

Viewed at a more pedestrian level along a historical timeline, positioning the cross at the center of God's redemptive plans denigrates his stature, exposing him as feckless and a less than Perfect Being: i) Christian salvation history portrays a God trapped in a moral dilemma (between justice and mercy) whose "solution" appears to be one cobbled together – late in the timeline – from whatever resources he found lying to hand. ii) The complexities, pain, and inversions endemic to the Christian salvation story violate the rational symmetry and linear predictability expected of the One sovereign over human affairs. iii) The scandal of particularity: the chronological, developmental "slow burn" and geographic locatedness of the Salvation Event besmirch God's honor because they call into question the reliability and ubiquity of God's law-based prophetic call to all people at all times and in all places. iv) Quite evidently, the redemption story exposes not the honor but the earthy limits, bodily suffering, and shame and weakness of the "divine" Son. Indeed, for many Muslim respondents, the Christian metanarrative is perceived as malformed and deforming from Adam to Christ, from God to humanity.

So far I have endeavored to hear Muslim intellectuals and religious scholars as they expound ideas of salvation and particularly as they engage and critique Christian atonement thought. In the remaining chapters, I turn to distinctive, and sometimes divergent, framings of atonement by Christian theologians. As we pivot, let us tune our ears to the reverberating echo of the Islamic concerns to which we have been attending.

# 5. Anselmian Atonement

> But since our unrighteousness was fulfilled and it became perfectly clear that its reward, punishment and death, was waiting, and the time came which God had appointed to make known at last his goodness and power. Oh, the surpassing kindness and love of God! He did not hate or reject or bear a grudge against us but he was patient and bore with us, having mercy he himself experienced our sin, he himself gave his own son, a ransom on our behalf, the Holy for the lawless, the innocent for the guilty, the righteous for the unrighteous, the incorruptible for the corruptible, the immortal for the mortal … Oh, the sweet exchange! … Oh, the unexpected benefits that the … righteousness of the one should justify many lawless. (*Letter to Diognetus* 9:2-5)

## Mapping This Chapter

In this chapter we turn to the substitutionary construct of St. Anselm, a vision of salvation that is both hotly contested and of undeniable significance. Indeed, Anselm's model of vicarious suffering as reparative payment is commonly seen as the vector for later forensic and penal views (Aulén's "Latin" family) from the Reformation onward. Modern iterations of that trend concern us in the following chapter, and these two chapters together (five and six) form something of a set in our sampling of theologies of vicarious redemption. Then, in chapter seven we draw into the conversation a counterproposal from Kathryn Tanner. Chapter eight presents synthetic and summative conclusions as the in-house Christian discussions and tensions interface with the topoi, questions, and criticisms presented by Islamic scholars.

We pair, then, Anselm (and related secondary literature) in this chapter with an "Anselmian coterie" (not least, Karl Barth) in the following. This coterie accents aspects of PSA in particular. Once again, these two chapters represent a natural center of gravity for this project as notions of substitutionary suffering are prominent in my own broadly Protestant context and in contemporary debate. Furthermore, salvation by mediating death is a frequent target of Islamic comment. We might add that Anselm is particularly interesting in terms of comparative theology in that his adherence to ideas of divine perfection, divine sovereignty, and honor manifest an affinity to Islamic intuitions, but, concurrently, his meticulous detailing of salvation mediated by the death of a supposed "third party" represents, for many Muslims, all that is wrong with atonement. Thus, we turn to Anselm's thought, a theological fountainhead and locus of importance and contest.

This chapter proceeds in the following fashion: i) first comes a brief biographical overview of the principal modern scholars whose work furnishes key secondary source material for this and the following chapter.[1] ii) I then turn to Anselm, seeking to situate him with reference to the development of atonement theology, especially in terms of his seminal *Cur Deus Homo* (*CDH*). I don't attempt to recite his biography here. iii) Following that, I explore the theological challenge of parsing Anselm's thought, alongside the modern, often negative, reception of Anselm. iv) The succeeding section, then, appeals for a more nuanced and receptive mindset in the contemporary engagement with Anselm. v) Following all this, the remainder of the chapter is devoted to the threefold typology distilled from Islamic discourse, the tropes of justice, honor, and sin in various permutations.[2] vi) The chapter concludes with a summary of findings.

## The Anselmian Coterie

Besides Anselm himself, in this and the following chapter, I will be engaging a collection of thinkers who are, to one degree or another, willing "heirs" of Anselm's legacy. These scholars provide a window onto modern (mostly) Protestant appropriations and redirections of the Anselmian stream of thought on the cross and atonement.[3] I leave comments on Karl Barth for the next chapter, but here I briefly mention several, though not all, of the scholars who resource our efforts in this and the following chapter: David Bentley Hart is an American philosopher, polymath, and Eastern Orthodox theologian who has written appreciatively (!) of St. Anselm. Fleming Rutledge is an Episcopal priest and theologian, influential in terms of preaching ministry, cultural commentary, and prolific publication. Katherine Sonderegger is an Episcopal priest and theologian of considerable repute, and is the holder of the William Meade Chair in Systematic Theology at Virginia Theological Seminary. Among her competencies are the theology of Karl Barth and constructive systematics. Colin Gunton (d. 2003) was a Reformed minister and a distinguished systematic theologian at King's College, London. Adonis Vidu is a Romanian evangelical theologian at Gordon-Conwell Theological Seminary; he is noted for marshalling classical Christian sources to address questions of current theological import. Mention may also be made of Ross Hastings, an evangelical with links to Africa, Europe, and North America, who holds advanced credentials in both science and theology. Adam Johnson is a scholar at Biola University (California), who has published extensively in the arena of atonement thought. Finally, Matthew Wilcoxen is an Anglican priest-theologian whose work benefits this study.

Admittedly, not many theologians (including these) adopt "Anselmian" as their identifying sobriquet, in contrast with, for example, the many Lutherans or Calvinists. Indeed, Anselm's legacy is less comprehensive and systematic than, say, Calvin's, and thus less suited to headlining a comprehensive theological identity. Anselm's magnum opus on atonement, *CDH*, is a rather narrowly focused logical analysis rather than an attempt to explore redemption and its implications with broad-spectrum holism. Thus, my point is not that all of these collected theologians rely on Anselm as their polestar. But I offer this group as an "Anselmian coterie" in the sense that they articulate the substitutionary work of God in Christ at the cross as a non-negotiable aspect of atonement; and they generally acknowledge the constructive contribution of Anselm to soteriology – at times defending him against vociferous modern critics.

## Situating Anselm after the Fathers

Both detractors and supporters of Anslem of Canterbury generally recognize him as a theological watershed. More often than not, conceptions of the cross as substitutionary pivot of redemption, as well as logical, abstract, or legally inflected atonement constructs, are traced back to the influence of Anselm. For Rutledge, "Anselm's momentous work, *Cur Deus Homo* … has been so influential that it is impossible to study the history of Christian doctrine without it."[4]

It is natural to cast Anselm as a transitional figure between the ancient and Medieval church; for Aulén, he is the founding father of the dominant "Western" atonement modality – rationalistic and substitutionary.[5] Southern grants him a sort of moderated eminence befitting his location in the subdued "Benedictine centuries" between the Fathers and the scholastics.[6]

Debate persists as to how faithful or how innovative Anselm was with respect to inherited tradition, and whether this was to constructive or detrimental effect. Anselm does represent a major development in the history of doctrine, but exaggerating his "break" from the Fathers is unhelpful.[7] D. B. Hart warns us that the charge that Anselm radically digressed from tradition's current can only be upheld by an insistently shallow analysis.[8]

Nuance is necessary in characterizing Anselm as a change agent, but a transitional figure he is. So, for example, in his soteriology, the relations between God, humanity, and the Devil grant no reserve of "rights" to the Enemy as some Fathers seem to.[9] But even this accenting of the God–human polarity at the Devil's expense is not in *absolute* disjunction with the Fathers.[10] Arguably, Anselm's milestone *CDH* is not a cosmic salvation epic intended to replace prior patristic models, but is rather a treatise focused on narrower concerns, accounting for atonement in terms of abstracted justice, payment, human deficit, and divine honor (again, topics commanding disapproving attention from many Muslim authors).[11] Still, Anselm is a vital mile marker in the evolution of atonement theology, not least in terms of underscoring the notion of necessity. Whether or not the cross was *the only way* God could have acted, the notion "that God could not gratuitously forgive becomes a major assumption of atonement theories only after Anselm's *Cur Deus Homo* in the eleventh century."[12]

## Cur Deus Homo

We turn to an overview of the argument of *Cur Deus Homo* (*Why God Became Man*).[13] *CDH* is a tightly focused exercise in logic in which Anselm investigates redemption with "pure reasoning, without depending on the authority of Scripture, or any other authority, to support his argument at any crucial point".[14] *CDH* is an impressive rational theorization of salvation. However, in view of the considerable criticism Anselm's work has attracted, it is worth noting the modesty of Anselm's own epistemological claims.[15]

Anselm's thought exercise is aimed at showing the reasonability of the Christian story and at discovering why human redemption and blessing were in fact contingent upon the coming of the Logos among us. "By what logic or necessity did God become man, and by his death, as we believe and profess, restore life to the world, when he could have done this through the agency of some other person, angelic or human, or simply by willing it?" (*CDH* 1:1) We may grant that in the incarnation human nature was exalted, not the divine debased (*Meditation on Human Redemption* (*MHR*) 125).[16] But, nonetheless, why should this be the way in which God restores a fallen humanity?

Following Hart, we here offer a condensation of the argument of *CDH*:[17]

i) Humanity was made to partake in beatitude with God (*CDH* 1:11, 24; 2:1). But sin, passive and active disobedience, offends infinitely against divine honor and merits death (*CDH* 1:21).

ii) God's honor requires that humanity offer complete worship and obedience as well as repay the deficit it has incurred (satisfaction); otherwise, death is the requite (*CDH* 1:14-15).

iii) God in his righteous honor cannot allow sin to pass with impunity; so to do would inject injustice and disorder into the fabric of the universe and division into the being of God (*CDH* 1:12-13, 19). It is "fitting" or "necessary" then that in lieu of punishment, satisfaction be offered to restore divine honor, life to humanity, and order to creation (*CDH* 1:11, 15, 19, 24; 2:4-5).

iv) But sin is an offense against the measureless worth of God; the gravity of sin, then, is such that just reparation far exceeds human capacity (*CDH* 1:20, 23; 2:6, 11).

v) But equally it would not befit God's character to allow his good purposes to come to naught and his creatures to be destroyed (*CDH* 1:4; 2:4-5).

vi) Only God himself can possibly render a satisfaction of sufficient worth. And yet, satisfaction must be made by a descendant of Adam. Thus, only the God-man can meet the requirements, breaking an (apparent) impasse between God's justice and mercy (*CDH* 1:10; 2:6, 8, 11).

vii) In mysterious harmony with the Father, the sinless Son *voluntarily* offers perfect obedience to God unto death (*CDH* 1:9-10). As this death is not warranted, not a due punishment, it produces a superabundant merit before the justice of God (*CDH* 2:11, 17).

viii) Christ, as God, is undefeated even by death and wants for nothing. Thus, he passes on the excess merit to the faithful. The honor and justice of God is satisfied; the debt of sin remitted; and salvation accrues to those in Christ who persist in righteousness (*CDH* 2:19).

Anselm offers a summary in his own words, albeit in the mouth of Boso:

> [You, Anselm,] have thereby shown that it was not right that the restoration of human nature should be left undone, and that it could not have been brought about unless man repaid what he owed to God. This debt was so large that, although no one but man owed it, only God was capable of repaying it, assuming that there should be a man identical with God. Hence it was a necessity that God should take man into the unity of his person, so that one who ought, by virtue of his nature, to

> make the repayment and was not capable of doing so, should be one who, by virtue of his person, was capable of it ... You have furthermore proved that the life of this man is so sublime and so precious that it can suffice to repay the debt owed for the sins of the whole world, and infinitely more besides ... [Further, no one ever paid] a debt to God which he did not owe. But Christ of his own accord gave to his Father what he was never going to lose as a matter of necessity, and he paid, on behalf of sinners, a debt which he did not owe. (Anselm, *CDH* 2:18)[18]

## Debt and Honor Satisfaction vs Guilt and Substitutionary Punishment

Clearly delineating the relationship between Anselm's theory of atonement and later Protestant presentations of salvation through substitutionary suffering requires care. But there does seem to be a line of development between the archbishop and influential Protestant atonement constructs, which bear the brunt of the criticism from our Muslim interlocutors. This is one reason that we position these chapters five and six as a sort of set. *CDH* is certainly not an articulation of (the later) PSA conceptuality. Moreover, various *non-penal* atonement proposals are also heirs of Anselm.[19] Nonetheless, one can legitimately discern an Anselmian legacy in Reformation atonement theory and modern PSA.[20]

In terms of *CDH*, humanity's sin of defrauding God of all the love, honor, and obedience due to him has incurred an unpayable debt, which matures only in death. The only alternative intervention is Jesus' death, that is, his already spotless and priceless life of devotion and obedience offered up on the cross in utter freedom (*CDH* 1:8).[21] The uniquely infinite value of this gift constitutes "satisfaction" for human dishonor – arrears accounted for; salvation secured.[22]

Some writers amplify distinctions between debt and guilt, satisfaction and penal substitution (only the first item in each polarity seen as Anselmian); meanwhile, others conflate these tropes, and usually to the discredit of the so-called "objective" theories.[23] For Rutledge, "Anselm's central figure is that of satisfaction, but the idea of substitution is intrinsic to his argument and he is frequently cited as the one who introduced the motif."[24] Between satisfaction and substitution frameworks we have, I would say, distinctions within a family resemblance.[25]

Clearly, it is a commonplace of atonement debate that notions of substitution and penalty are taken, by many, to be ethically and theologically retrograde.[26] It will be part of our burden to insist that these concepts are virtually non-negotiable in a Christian confrontation with the human predicament. But there are indeed both responsible and retrograde modes of understanding and expressing these motifs.[27]

Those positively disposed to Anselm, but with an allergy to the vocabulary of punishment and substitution, often appeal to the Anselmian ethos of costly "self-donation" and of "representation".[28] But sometimes the discourse tends toward false dichotomies. Anderson, for example, commends Anselm's theology of the cross as "*the expression of the radical nature of the love that gives itself completely* ... the expression of a life that is completely being for others". This is well and good, but the consequent necessity of his exclusion of the cross "as part of a mechanism of injured right", is asserted rather than demonstrated.[29] Indeed, he even grants that Christ's violent death amounts to his "suffering the consequences of [our] crime", all the while pointedly disassociating himself from the lexicon of PSA.[30] To my mind, his rhetoric has not successfully disjoined "cost, love, and giving" from notions of substitution and penalty. I doubt that such a disjunction is truly possible.

In any case, the picture of God as debtholder over what amounts to a violent repayment remains problematic for many moderns. If dying is the cost of debt reparation, how much ground has been gained by pointing out that talk of punishment is not central to *CDH*? Certainly, we may distinguish Anselm from later theologians of "forensic" atonement, but is not some underlying forensic logic implicit, even in Anslem? Is not some such substructure required if Christ's death is to be seen as an expression of obedience or offering of worth? Whatever the nomenclature, is not Anselm operating within a paradigm that assumes an incisive role for justice? How might the cross "work" to achieve God's just and merciful ends and how is it that the price of human failing is so high? Such questions continue to press.

## Modern Problems with Anselm

Thus, Anselm's atonement theology has attracted significant questioning in modern scholarship. One may note both overlap and disjunction in the way in which modernist Western critics, on the one hand, and Muslim theologians, on the other, disapprove of Anselm or of cruciform, substitutionary atonement more broadly. (I comment further on this in the "honor" section in the final chapter.)

It is worth noting that certain underlying objections to atonements of satisfaction *or* substitution may be traced even in eras prior to modernity.[31] In any case, on grounds moral, theological, and biblical, Anselmian atonement's legal abstraction or "debt obsession" is denounced by critics for its lacunae in the relational, ethical, and ontological dimensions.[32] Anselm's salvation construct allegedly leaves us only with bare "penal suffering and remission from debt".[33]

*CDH*'s "cultural-commercial" dynamic has been blamed for a deficit of mercy, and even love, in God's own nature; for an oppressive, "feudal" rendering of justice; for underwriting patriarchy; and so on.[34] Some also decry *CDH*'s purportedly low-octane Trinitarianism.[35] Generally, critics express incredulity about Anselmian salvation's quasi-mercantile mechanism: "How can one death do all Anselm claims for it?"[36]

## Contextualizing Anselm for Our Day

Clearly, then, Anselm has been a lightning rod, attracting acerbic rebuke from those disenchanted with traditional atonement theology.[37] If we are to gain any moral or intellectual traction in engaging our medieval thinker, our reception of him will have to be carefully framed, or perhaps reframed.

### *Translating from His Theological Location to Ours*

One must be careful not to confuse the cultural and linguistic conventions available to a thinker (Anselm) with the generative and constructive use to which his thoughts may be put in our day.[38] Many of the supposed deficiencies of *CDH*'s theology are mitigated by a less suspicious hermeneutic and a sensitive recalibration of its ideas and intuitions, opening up fruitful possibilities. For Sonderegger, for example, "Anselm intends to demonstrate rationally not an ahistorical, timeless savior, but rather the Emmanuel of scripture. The Restorer of *Cur Deus Homo* is emphatically the Jesus of Nazareth of the Bible."[39] What might happen if Anselm were appreciated as one important, unique voice from the "foreign land of the past", invited to join the discussion at global theology's diverse table?[40] One might indeed find considerable fertile ground between the extremes of either categorical denunciation or naïve endorsement.

### *The Utility of a Narrow Focus*

Another common complaint about *CDH* is the narrowness of its thought – too much is left out of its vision of atonement. The objection is easy to understand, but is an all-or-nothing interpretive expectation a helpful approach to the text? It does not appear that Anselm himself couched his work as the peerless last word.[41] Must Anselm be required to "say everything" and to be impeccable in everything he says in order for us to benefit from him?

Ironically, the discourse of opponents of *CDH* can tend towards narrowness, literalism, and lack of generosity. In Hart's words:

> Anselm's argument, thus denuded [by sterile summaries] of every nuance and ambiguity that enriches the text from which it is drawn, is susceptible of every casual mis-construal the theological mind can devise; it becomes indeed a theological "theory", removed from any larger theological narrative, unable to defend itself by reference to the specific concerns that prompted it or the historical context in which it was situated.[42]

In *CDH* Anslem finetunes the logic of honor, representation, mercy, debt, and so on – pursuing a specific seam within atonement's expansive bedrock.[43] Yes, Anselm's masterpiece *is* a highly delimited, even "narrow", argument but this narrowness has its use.[44] And it certainly does not imply obliviousness to wider aspects of God's grace for the world.[45]

### CDH*: Metaphysics and Doxology*

Anselm is sometimes savaged for reducing questions of sin, redemption, and grace to an abstracted moral calculus that expunges divine mercy in the brutal mechanics of the crucifixion. But we must not miss that underlying many debates over satisfaction are incommensurable ideas about divine transcendence and creation, the metaphysical givens of humanity, the world, and sin – the substructure of reality. A knee-jerk distaste for Anselm's rhetorical mode or cultural affect must not pre-empt our patient, receptive consideration of his claims: for Anselm, the necessity of the cross goes not simply to questions of God's mercy and grace (or not) but rather to what is required to heal a broken universe.

We must not allow cultural distance to blind us to the deep structures of his logic. Visceral rejections of the inherent "violence" of Anselm may inure us to significant losses incurred when we attempt to configure redemption without any reference to genuine and ultimate "cost". Such totalizing rejections are in danger of affirming that God might forgive without rectifying injustice or calling evil to account. For Anselm, this would be "extremely unfitting ... [for] it makes sinfulness resemble God. For just as God is subject to no law, the same [would then be] the case with sinfulness" (*CDH* 1:12; cf. 1:24). Our theologizing must not inadvertently acquiesce to a world of wrong, leaving multiplied harm undisturbed all in the name of "mercy" (cf. *CDH* 1:13).

In Anselm's "objective" atonement, the cross is a function of the axiomatic, metaphysical givens of the human condition. Satisfaction is rooted in convictions about what is true, not about what we wish were true; as such, it is an "*ontological* necessity".[46] If we grant such ontological assumptions, then a strident protest – however sincere – against the "unjust violence" of satisfaction is an insufficient response to Anselm's ideas.

Of course, the objector may well differ with and dispute Anselm's intuitions about the non-fungible facts of universal reality. One may find Anselm's theorization wanting on ontological grounds. But that sort of critique cannot justly be allowed to pose as a successful indictment of his intention and moral trajectory. And, in counterpoint, if Anselm should happen to be substantially correct about the fabric of the universe, then one negates the cross as the costly and climactic act of restoration (satisfaction) only at great hazard. "If injustice goes unpunished, the universe is shown to be an unjust and so irrational place, and the God responsible for its order no longer worthy of the name God."[47]

Further, I would concede that the relentlessly logical register of *CDH* is evident and intentional. That is hardly grounds, however, for casting Anselm as architect of a cold theological system or as a thinker devoid of humility, love, or devotion. In *CDH*'s logic, salvation arrives as the "sheer gift of a God who is always who he is, a God of 'sheer "redundancy" of the good that flows from the infinite gesture of his love' with a 'generosity in excess of all calculable economy'".[48] Anslem is indeed an unrelenting *thinker*, but a thinker whose spirit marvels at the wonder of redemption (cf. Anselm *MHR* 20-30). An undeniable doxological undercurrent permeates his work (cf. *CDH* 2:16, 2:18). Anselm "prays his theology" and the currents of divine love overflow their banks, as he invokes the bounty of Christ in solidarity with his human siblings "wasting away with deprivation in the depths of misery".[49] Anselm's faith seeks understanding, a *knowing* of God that requires *love* (cf. Anselm *Proslogion* 330-80; Eph. 3:17-19).

## On Justice

### *A Fissure between Justice and Mercy?*

And so, I turn at last to consideration of our three principle themes in Anselm, beginning with *justice*. Situating the death of Jesus as a "reconciliation", in God's own being, between wrath and love, or justice and mercy, has provoked intra-Christian debate and, as we saw, flares up in Islamic rumination on the cross. Even properly locating this issue within the argument of this book presents a challenge. On the one hand, this issue goes directly to the question of God's justice. On the other hand, the alleged and implied contradiction within the divine attributes threatens to besmirch divine honor, a category of significance for both Anselm and Islamic scholars. Furthermore, does this tension relate to abstracted representations of God's nature? Or might it be more to the point to ask how these uneasily paired divine attributes (justice and mercy) impact human ethics and the experience of salvation (issues of "justice from below")?

Detractors of Anselm's "objective theory" deride the supposed incoherence of the divine character therein: this deity, it is claimed, is one who opts for the cross of Christ as the only means by which his love can achieve salvation while satisfying the unyielding demands of justice and honor.[50] (Below I comment further on the linkage between justice and honor in Anselm.) Apparently, Anselm's soteriological scheme exposes a fissure in God's own being. He comes off, they say, as a victim of the clashing demands of his various attributes, and, worse yet, his love proves subsidiary to the overdeveloped demands of his justice. Indeed, those aiming to expose the pernicious "war of attributes" allegedly endemic to Anselm's God construct will commonly pair this with a companion defect: the petulant and capricious deity eager for a vicarious propitiation by which to claw back his honor.[51]

There is then a certain instinct to decry Anselm's supposed projection of instability and ethical deficiency onto God himself. However this may be, it is clearly an etic judgment. In Anselm's discourse there is no hint of uncertainty about the fidelity or goodness of the divine nature. In all likelihood, Anselm's response would be that the problem does not lie with clashing attributes, but in a failure to rightly understand those attributes: God's virtues are one.

Alasdair MacIntyre comments that "modern tradition … holds that the variety and heterogeneity of human goods is such that their pursuit *cannot be reconciled* in any single moral order."[52] MacIntyre further asserts that for Plato, in strong counterpoint to modernity, "the virtues are not merely compatible with each other, but the presence of each requires the presence of all. This strong thesis concerning the unity of the virtues is reiterated both by Aristotle and by Aquinas … The presupposition which all three share is that there exists a cosmic order which dictates the place of each virtue in a total harmonious scheme of human life."[53] Anselm is clearly representative of this classic tradition (cf. *CDH* 1:15; 2:4).[54]

Certainly, articulating the unity of divine perfections is challenging. Max Kadushin's discussion of the integrated diversity of various thematics in rabbinic literature is enlightening. His portrayal of the integrated polyvalence of what he calls "organic concepts" may helpfully be transferred to our interest in the coinherence of divine perfections:

> Organic concepts are concepts in a whole complex of concepts, none of which can be inferred from the others but all of which are so mutually interrelated that every individual concept, though possessing its own distinctive features, nevertheless depends for its character on the character of the complex as a whole which, in turn, depends on the character of the individual concepts. Each organic concept,

> therefore, implicates the whole complex without being completely descriptive of the complex, retaining, at the same time, its own distinctive features.[55]

In the face of sin's intensification, the grace of Anselm's God abounded that much more.[56] That is how and why the donation of Christ is effective, in that it is an offering of infinite worth to be placed against the weight of human ill, loss, and dishonor. Anselm sees in this soteriological economy no contradiction between God's justice and mercy, but, rather, superabundance as they are harmoniously manifest in the death of Jesus, with destiny-shaping force.[57]

To set God's mercy against his justice is to misunderstand mercy itself. God's perfections are a unified whole, *experienced* variously depending on theological context and the disposition of the human subject standing before God. Hart puts it thus:

> [As] God's goodness cannot suffer defeat, there must be a saving initiative from God's side, and there must already be within the terms of God's changeless righteousness that dynamism that overcomes any apparent incommensurability of mercy and justice. The appearance of such an opposition is the result not only of finite human reason, but of sin: only in the rejection of God's creative mercy is his justice experienced as wrath and dereliction … When humanity fails to take up the creature's side of the divine covenant, the righteousness that condemns is also the love that restores by surmounting even human disobedience and creation's lawful subjection to death, to take up the human side on humanity's behalf.[58]

It is not as though God is at times a more merciful being, and at others a more just being. Rutledge puts it that "God's judgment is enclosed in his love."[59]

In the divine panoply of virtues, a winking sort of mercy that would skirt the holy and just, potentially leaving offenders fundamentally unchanged, all in the name of a vague compassion, is not mercy. According to Anselm, "mercy of this [permissive] kind is absolutely contrary to God's justice, which does not allow anything to be given in repayment for sin except punishment. Hence, given that it is impossible for God to be self-contradictory, it is impossible for him to be merciful in this way" (*CDH* 1:24). The cross does not represent a collision of mercy and justice, but rather the ultimate manifestation *of* them. For Anselm there could not be a "greater and juster mercy" than what God actually did for us in becoming man (*CDH* 2:20).

### *Justice and Satisfaction*

Criticisms of Anselmian atonement may be animated by concerns over both the "irrationality" and "injustice" of the template – Anselm's stark rationalism notwithstanding. Of course, these domains interlock: if what is described is unjust, it's unlikely to be rational, and vice versa. Such queries are not a late development. In *CDH* itself, Anselm's unnamed critics object to the incarnation and the cross on grounds of the deficient rationality and the ethical offense they project onto God's dignity (*CDH* 1:3). The efficacy and justice of one death for all places and times comes as challenge to many minds, and *CDH* aims to address such incredulity (*CDH* 1:4). Anselm was already sensitive to the charges of rank injustice:

> But how will it possibly be proved a just and rational thing that God treated, and allowed to be treated, in this way, the man whom he, as Father, called his beloved

> Son in whom he was well pleased, and whose nature he, as Son, took upon himself? For what justice is it for the man who was of all the most just to be put to death for a sinner? (*CDH* 1:8; cf. 1:10)

However thorny the complications of atonement theory, the Christian tradition insists on a plausibility, if partially submerged, to the Passion narrative – namely that the cross disallows "general amnesty" by fiat. In tandem with this is "the intuition that on the cross we see some sort of justice being done". One ought at least to ponder the possibility that "the event on Golgotha has something to do with God's ultimate sentence upon all the evil in the world." Rutledge's appeals here bring us into the orbit of Anselm's own logic with respect to the dying of the Incarnate Son.[60]

Whether or not one finds Anselm's argumentation compelling, *CDH* is a sustained, reasoned argument concerned for justice within a matrix oriented to order, honor, balance, and fittingness in the cosmos, an orientation consonant with prior tradition.[61] Just as death, damnation, and defeat came by way of a man's disobedience, a woman, and the Devil, so too should the obedience of a man borne of woman overthrow the Devil, bring life to the world, and save humanity (cf. *CDH* 2:8; Augustine *On the Trinity* 13:17:22). For Anselm, salvation is structured towards the restoration of beauty and order in the universe; it is no arbitrary transaction determining the fate of individual souls alone.[62]

Much like Athanasius or Augustine, Anselm finds it inconceivable that God should fail to achieve the good he intended for creation, and only *fitting* that humanity should be liberated "by its Creator in person" (*CDH* 1:5-6; cf. 2:4). A commitment to divine honor and cosmic balance is, Anselm assumes, fully consonant with the very ends of human flourishing and dignity, of justice and mercy (*CDH* 1:6). The mysteries of atonement must cohere with the perfection that is God.

For Fellipe do Vale, undergirding Anselmian atonement is his:

> perfect being theology – whatever property is superlatively perfect belongs to the divine substance. Thus, the divine substance has superlatively perfect rectitude. But one need not rely on such deductions, for Anselm simply states that God, being "the highest truth," just "is rectitude".[63]

Atonement theology inescapably raises questions of justice and sin's gravity, questions to which Anselm was hardly oblivious.[64] How and why should such a violent and shameful end be made of the innocent Jesus, and, in any case, how would it be either right or effective that his destruction should redound to the salvation of all? Why this "excessive" and "shameful" means (cf. *CDH* 1:6)? How are we to evaluate incarnation and cross in all their humility, condescension, and "great laboriousness" (*CDH* 1:6; cf. *MHR* 75-90)?[65]

Anselm raises the pressure to acute levels when he says, "What [God] wills, must be; what he wills not, cannot be. Therefore this was done by his will alone. And because his will is always good, he did this solely out of goodness" (*MHR* 75). And indeed, Anselm concludes that in becoming man, in undergoing the Passion, God's will is vindicated – comporting with the good, the true, and the beautiful on a cosmic scale. Rhetorically he asks, "Is it not fitting that man, who, by sinning, removed himself as far as he possibly could away from God, should, as recompense to God, make a gift of himself in an act of the greatest possible self-giving" (*CDH* 2:11)? The contemporary reader of *CDH* may well miss it, but to Anselm, the point of satisfaction – Jesus' death – is not simply a "pound of flesh". It is about justice measured against both God's worth and humanity's rejection of him.

For Anselm, salvation effected by the death of the incarnate Lord is not a contrivance chaotically emerging from God's opaque volition; it is not heaven's bloodlust; it is not a manifestation of the Deity's peevish ego; it is not a "ransom deal" somehow foisted upon the Creator. Painful and difficult as the Messiah's story may be, it is sourced in God's loving, just, and honorable character.

## Satisfaction and Justice: The Gift of Excess Merit

Fathers from Athanasius to the Cappadocians discerned a certain imperative in the incarnation: the resources of one who is *only* a human are insufficient to the restoration of a fallen humanity; divinity needs to assume humanity.[66] "'We need an Incarnate God; God put to death, that we might live' – to use a bold phrase of St. Gregory of Nazianzus ... It may be properly said that God dies on the Cross, but in his own humanity."[67] The redeemer must be a descendent of Adam, and one without his own deficit before God (cf. *CDH* 2:8). Yet this minimum condition is not sufficient. Anselm saw that satisfaction is only achieved by the *God*-man (cf. *CDH* 2:5-7).[68]

*CDH* is not typically forwarded as a model of "physicalist" atonement. But in it a sort of collective human solidarity seems to be assumed, alongside the solidarity of Jesus, the later Adam, with his people. One might have wished for greater explicitness, but in view of Anselm's conviction that God will not leave his original ends unrealized, the exchange effected by the cross in *CDH* does not read as mere "accounting maneuver". The ontological virtue intrinsic to the death of the God-man somehow accomplishes redemption in accord with the deep structures of reality rather than as some random decision of the divine will.

The cross represents a free offering of the sinless Jesus which he in no way "owed" to God (cf. *CDH* 1:9; 2:18; *MHR* 90-95; also, Augustine, *On the Trinity* 13:16:21). In fact, in Anselm's economy, there is virtually no way the Father could have asked for the death of the Son, for satisfaction *is* a free donation. And this free giving, Anselm insists, is ultimately a giving from *God*. Though one might have wished for greater elaboration of a Trinitarian dynamic in *CDH*, Anselm is quite explicit: salvation is a matter of God – Father, Son, and Spirit – for us in Christ (cf. *CDH* 1:9; 2:16, 18).[69] Hear Sonderegger:

> Indeed, the voluntariness of Christ's death is critical to the very notions of satisfaction, renewal, fittingness and "absolute reason". We might better translate Anselm's term satisfaction as *justificatio*, the making good or making right of the cosmos. The God-man does not simply pay back the divine loss, nor compensate for the creatures' disobedience: he does not pay a penalty. Only a sinner must pay a price. Rather, he does what the creature cannot do, make right what was wrong with human nature itself.[70]

The wounds of the world – all the worship withheld and all the evil perpetrated – must be restored; in that is a "repayment of debt" to God. For that, our resources are insufficient, and thus we die eternally as it were (*CDH* 1:23; Ps. 49:7). But satisfaction is not about God desiring death. Death simply is the inexorable human predicament. And unfortunately, neither would God's kindly indulgence on our behalf suffice to rectify (see below).

It is only the inherent worth of the hypostatic union that ensures that "[Christ's] death outweighs the number and magnitude of all sins" (*CDH* 2:14; *MHR* 110). For Anselm, Jesus' excess virtue in a fully committed life offered in lieu of humanity's unpayable deficit merits more than sufficient benefit.[71] Salvation consists in our appropriation of the supererogatory merit only Christ could supply.[72]

Jesus' unrequired death answers in mercy, but also in justice, in balance – and then some – to the gaping need, the dying soul of humanity. In the course of absolute service to the Good, in a corrupt and violent world, death would be the cost to his pure life. On Golgotha, the priceless worth of the Son of Man intersected with the truth about human darkness and indebtedness. Within Anselm's existential vortex, satisfaction is, we might say, a just way to make just.

## Satisfaction: No Impunity, Rather Restoration

Although Anselm's grammar of sin and redemption majors in the language of debt rather than law, the distinction must not be overplayed. In view of human sin – our demerit being both substantive and privative – we must either incur a strictly just punishment or make restitution, that is, *satisfaction.* So, even as justice for Anselm is grounded in God's character more explicitly than in "laws", justice remains a genuine concern. And, justice, being God's own, is "binding" upon him.[73]

It verges on cliché to highlight the "offense" of the cross. The shame, the brutality, the extremity of the cost of satisfaction for many understandably elicits caution, doubts, or resistance. But the flow of traffic may also be reversed by asking what conditions (apart from classic atonement) *would* allow for a forgiveness that is restoratively just, rather than merely permissive, and accounts for the irreparable harms of history?

For Anselm, there must not be salvation without "recompense for sin" (*CDH* 1:19). To insist on the cost of satisfaction is to strike against arbitrariness in the structuring of the world, against any trivialization of either good or evil. Contrary to caricature, Anselm's sense of sin's weight, of satisfaction "balanced to abundance", of fittingness in the economy of salvation, all gesture towards God's justice *and* mercy (cf. *CDH* 2:20; Ps. 85:10). Here we encounter again the unity of attributes – justice, goodness, and mercy must coincide, or we do not in fact have any one of them.

It must be put starkly: blithe pardon with no attention to cost or wrongs done is hardly just, and is in effect unmerciful. As Rutledge insists, "a society of impunity is intolerable. If sin is not exposed, named, and renounced, then there has been no justice and God is dishonored."[74] A simple voiding of all penalty is tantamount to leaving a universe of sin, hurt, and wounding unmended, unaccounted for. This would rend the fabric of being and besmirch the honor of God. Unfitting indeed. Now, certainly more may be said in terms of the nature of sin and a proportionately calibrated justice. But, in comprehensive perspective, Anselm's representative donation in place of penalty has to do not only with justice as retribution, but also justice *en route* to restoration.[75] God's purposes are pastoral, doggedly restorative, and so in Christ he provides the necessary resources towards that end, resources far exceeding our own reserves. *CDH* advances mercy poured out in justice, not impunity, such that the cure is correlated to the ill.[76]

## Contextualizing Satisfaction for Today

On contemporary metrics, Anselm may be cast as overly dour, pessimistic, or compulsively abstracted; worse yet he may be anti-human, a proponent of violence. On one level, the aversion is understandable; he reflects a social and rhetorical world at a great remove from ours. But, on another level, directing strident invective at him seems rather lacking in generosity – a failure to nuance one's reception of this antique thinker. There is always the danger that our engagement with Anslem will be driven by contemporary cultural contests alone and markedly lacking in the patience required for a good-faith hearing.[77]

In terms of Anselm's basic disposition to God's image bearers, he insists that humans are:

> so sublime a life-form, and with such great good as its purpose. But, if it is recognized that God has made nothing more precious than rational nature, whose intended purpose is that it should rejoice in him, it is totally foreign to him to allow any rational type of creature to perish utterly. (*CDH* 2:4)

And God's gift of satisfaction is emblematic of his dogged commitment to the good, to his unbreakable covenant with creation.

Certainly, satisfaction is liable to being cast as commodified, violent, and primitive. But to simply leave matters there would be a failure of imagination; the loss of an opportunity to translate unfamiliar thought into contemporary idiom. Can we not, for example, hear resonances of our own day in the following?

> As long as [the violator] does not repay what he has taken away, he remains in a state of guilt. And it is not sufficient merely to repay what has been taken away: rather, he ought to pay back more than he took, in proportion to the insult which he has inflicted. For just as, in the case of someone who injures the health of another, it is not sufficient for him to restore that person's health, if he does not pay some compensation for the painful injury which has been inflicted. (*CDH* 1:11)

In our age of mass atrocity, identity politics, interethnic oppression, and so on, that injustice incurs a debt requiring reparation; and that mere absolution is insufficient – these notions hardly seem alien.[78] Are we not generally aware that attempts to restore horrific evil by way of recompense are necessary, even if, in our fallen world, never existentially adequate?[79] Is there not something, after all, to the "common Medieval … intuition that a wrong can be righted only by an act that exceeds the harm done?"[80]

However much Anselm's rarefied logic hones in on the individual's debt before God, there ought not be any doubt that sin against our Maker correlates with detriment to the neighbor, the degradation of our shared world. Sin cannot be forgiven by a cavalier "wave of the hand". At varying levels, each of us is victim and victimizer. We owe reparation. We need restoration. Metaphysically mysterious, epistemologically baffling – yes, the self-donation of Christ is all this. But does not the world cry out for satisfaction?

That Anselm aims at justice must be beyond doubt. The underlying structure of Anselm's thought is oriented towards the ethical, even towards compassion.[81] His drive for a reasoned symmetry is intertwined with his commitment to rectitude, to justice.[82]

Of course, this claim does not prove *CDH* "right". Our plea is more modest. Space remains to challenge Anselm's logic, theological starting points, or metaphysical imaginary. Is the world structured as Anselm assumes? What is the nature of the Creator's intersection with creaturely reality? Can the self-donation of the Messiah-God indeed effect ontological change in the fabric of humans' "being"? If one answers in the negative, then the underlying problem is not Anselm's moral callousness but his existential assumptions; he could simply be wrong about "the way things are". If in the affirmative, there is no justice deficit in *CDH*, but rather a surfeit of hope.

## On Honor

Why the God-Man? Anselm begins with the basic deficit in the divine–human relationship. For Anselm, "everyone who sins is under an obligation to repay to God the honor which he has violently taken from him, and this is the satisfaction which every sinner is obliged to give to God" (*CDH* 1:11). Humanity's honor deficit is a throughline of *CDH* which is, for many moderns, an off-putting and misguided relic of Anselm's cultural captivity – a distorting overlay from the honor-and-shame structures of feudal society. A God so concerned with his own honor, it is thought, is tantamount to a petty feudal ruler in the heavens. Moreover, it is sometimes held that in *CDH* it is God's fixation on his own honor that drives the "necessity" of the cross. And all this comes at the expense of his freedom to act in grace, mercy, and self-donating relationship. Zeal after this "honor" is inversely related to human freedom and flourishing.

Interestingly, the polemics and counterarguments aimed at Anselm can themselves clash. Generalizing for the sake of clarity, some modern critics are intensely dissatisfied with the perceived hierarchy and lordly oppression of Anselm's God – "honor at the expense of love or, perhaps, justice". Conversely, detractors Anselm himself tried to address apparently recoiled at the dishonor of a humbled God, bound by necessity, incarnate and crucified. To simplify, for some, Anselm's honor template reveals a God who is over-grand, for others a God not grand enough. (Again, see the section on "honor" in the final chapter.)

Anselm in fact begins with the charges that incarnation and atonement besmirch the very honor and dignity of God:

> Unbelievers, deriding us for our simplicity, object that we are inflicting injury and insult on God when we assert that he descended into a woman's womb; was born of a woman; grew up nurtured on milk and human food and – to say nothing of other things which do not seem suitable for God – was subject to weariness, hunger, thirst, scourging, crucifixion between thieves, and death. (*CDH* 1:3)[83]

These sorts of ripostes are evocative of responses from our collection of Islamic scholars. And, indeed, as Rutledge reminds us, it is probable that Anselm himself writes in response to the challenge of *Jewish* thinkers in his setting. Eamon Duffy writes:

> *Cur Deus Homo* was in fact addressed to specifically Jewish criticisms of Christianity, made by learned Jews from Mainz recently arrived in London. For these Jewish intellectuals, Christianity was repellent because it dishonored God, claiming that the impassible and eternal had descended into time in a woman's womb, and had undergone the diminishment of hunger and thirst, suffering and death. Anselm's purpose therefore was to show that the Incarnation, far from dishonoring God, revealed the depths of his loving will to save suffering humanity. Anselm's insistence on "honor", therefore, is not the product of fixation with feudal hierarchy, but an *argumentum ad hominem* addressed to intelligent Jews who felt that the Christian story debased God. 'Honor' in Anselm's thought stands not for some imagined hypersensitivity by the Creator to his own dignity, but is a metaphor for the deep logic of reality, in which the balance of a universe is disrupted by the fact of death and by human alienation from others and from God, a situation which could only be rectified by divine action.[84]

R. W. Southern holds that the concept of honor is polyvalent, but

> [I]t certainly included the preservation of God's dignity against affront ... and nowhere was the dishonoring of God more conspicuous than in the supreme indignities of Christ's death. Consequently, although it was the Jews who raised the problem in its most acute form, Anselm was especially sensitive to the need for a more searching and satisfying explanation of these indignities than any so far put forward.[85]

When it comes to the importance of God's unassailable honor, the extent to which Anselm shares ground with his suspicious, contemporary interlocutors is noteworthy. He readily grants his critics' premises that God is not under any external compulsion and is not subject to change, suffering, or effort (*CDH* 1:8). Gunton points to the value of the sometimes maligned doctrine of impassibility here. God does not respond to or against human sin and offense because he is "precious", touchy, or egoistic: the impassible God is not harmed.[86] Whatever is happening in the death of the incarnate Christ, God's honor, his transcendence, is not damaged.

From where does Anselm derive his emphasis on God's honor? In the rush to critique the cleric's "feudal" mindset, an obvious starting place is often overlooked – namely its scriptural rooting.[87] The trope of the "glory" of God – and thus the peaceful, fruitful, covenantal ordering of creation itself – is profuse from the Psalms to the NT (e.g. Ps. 8; 104; Rom. 1:23; 2:7). And, commonly enough, God's "glory" is paired with attendant attributes such as "majesty" and "honor."[88] Southern offers this inductive definition of honor in Anselm:

> God's honor is the complex of service and worship which the whole creation ... owes to the Creator, and which preserves everything in its due place ... God's honor is simply another word for the ordering of the universe in its due relationship to God.[89]

### *Honor, Justice, and Restoration*

For Anslem, in the economy of salvation, it is God's commitment to the true, good, and beautiful that is at stake, not some overwrought sensitivity and fragility of Self; again, his honor is not in itself vulnerable (*CDH* 1:15). His action in holding sin to account *and* showing mercy to his creatures upholds the "order and beauty of the universe". God ought not overlook a "debt to his honor" in that he in himself is the guarantor of rightness for all creation (cf. *CDH* 1:13). Divine permissiveness would open the door to destructive potential for the cosmos, in no way benefitting the would-be objects of his mercy, and in no way befitting his honor.

> If the divine Wisdom did not impose these forms of recompense in cases where wrongdoing is endeavoring to upset the right order of things, there would be in the universe, which God ought to be regulating, a certain ugliness, resulting from the violation of the beauty of order, and God would appear to be failing in his governance. Since these two consequences are as impossible as they are unfitting, it is inevitable that recompense or punishment follows upon every sin. (*CDH* 1:15; cf. Augustine, *City of God* 11:22)

Once again, concepts of justice lie not far beneath the surface. It is not that *honor* and *justice* are synonyms *simpliciter*. But there is a gravitational field positioning them with respect to one another. In Anselm's discourse there is a connotative confluence of justice and honor within a matrix both moral and aesthetic. It is not plausible that the just and the honorable should mutually cancel, nor that their realization in the world should be anything but ordered and beautiful. Once again, Hart:

> [F]or Anselm, God's honor is inseparable from his goodness, which imparts life and harmony to creation, the rejection of which is necessarily death; as the source of all creation's beauty and order, it is the righteousness that cannot contradict itself or will anything amiss; it is justice, not wrath, and its manifestation is the *rectitudo* of God's universal government, its rightness and moral beauty.[90]

As do Vale puts it, "The picture we get here, and throughout the *Cur Deus Homo*, is that God as *creator* (and not necessarily as feudal lord) justly governs that which he has made."[91] He is "the one himself who is the only perfect Truth".[92] Once again, with sensitivity to Anselm's idiom, the "honor" being protected is not that of a contingent, preening, self-absorbed Deity. In the end, something much closer to justice or rectitude is at stake.[93]

### The Convergence of Divine Honor and Human Good

In the economy of *CDH*, *God's commitment to his honor goes to the restoration of his world, enacting the great good planned for humanity*. Honor also entails human beatitude, that is, "what God planned to give [them]" (*CDH* 1:23) – that "rejoicing in God," being made righteous, we "might be blessedly happy" (*CDH* 2:1; cf. 1:24; 2:20).[94] In pursuing "painful necessity", in the incarnation and cross, God responds to judge, set right, and heal a "cosmically disordered" universe which wounds his human creation.[95] Though God's honor is not vulnerable *in se,* humanity's debt of honor still matters because in the Anselmian architecture, salvation has an eschatological prospect aimed at nothing less than the restoration of *all* creation.[96]

Now, why should it be that Christ's innocent death is the effective response to our hapless reality, the "unpayable debt" of honor? To speak of honor and necessity is an act of truth telling, a dual estimation of human brokenness and God's divine worth, truth, and holiness.[97] Honor and shame motifs resonate in the biblical canon from the first sin to prophetic preoccupation with the honor of God's name among the nations to the Pauline congregations (cf. Gen. 3:7-10; Ezek. 36:20-23; 1 Cor. 5:1-2; 6:1-6, 19-120; 10:31-33; 14:23-25). Sin, injustice, idolatry, a defrauding of honor are both directed against God *and* detrimental to the neighbor, to creation's order. However resonant or alien the honor concept is to the modern audience, it seems fair to observe that collectively we have authored harm in this world and have not loved God with all our heart, soul, mind, and strength. In not rendering our entire orientation to the One for whom we are designed, we withhold honor.[98] In so doing, we have resisted the very conditions under which we ourselves thrive. Failure before the *Shema* is also a self-wounding. The inverse – worshipping God alone, living to his honor – then would speak to the healing of the human family.

There is a reciprocity or reflexivity when it comes to the honor of God and the good of humans, made to share in his glory (Rom. 1:21-23; 5:2; 8:18, 30). But the priority, the energy, the *telos* of honor must be situated with, in, and for God. In the words of Khaled Anatolios, "In the Scriptures, we find that God's commitment to oppose sin is not only due to his merciful love and care for creation but also bound to his own self-interest [= honor]. Of course, we should immediately reiterate yet again that God's self-interest and God's love for creation are not in competition, since the well-being of the creation strictly depends on God's own inviolable well-being."[99]

One may or may not trust Anselm's God, but if Anselm is right about the nature and identity of that God, his ways (in creation, providence, judgment, and salvation) are the only hope for securing good in the universe. His honor matters, full stop. But it also matters for human blessing. Anselm hoped to convince his contemporary opponents that in becoming man, God's honor is not suppressed but at work. This appeal might be directed at a similarly skeptical Muslim audience in our day. Then, pivoting to an opposite pole, contrary to certain modernist anxieties, I would assert that centering God's honor is actually "good for us".

### *Honor and Necessity*

A rejection of Anselm's deployment of the honor trope evidently can stem from worries that it diminishes human dignity or that it diminishes divine transcendence. The latter concern surfaces in the charge that in positing a God subject to the "necessity" of the cross, the "honor-bound" Anselm actually is threatening divine freedom, sovereignty, and honor. If the cross is *required*, then God is dishonored, portrayed as sharply limited.

God's intention in creation is ultimately beatitude, joy, and fellowship with humanity. Anselm seeks to show that this objective of the divine economy "could only happen through the agency of a Man-God; and that it is from necessity that all the things which we believe about Christ have come to pass" (*CDH* "Preface"). The motif of "necessity" infuses the spirit of *CDH.*

From different angles of attack, critics have struggled with the implications of any necessity being laid upon God. For some, the disquiet emerges from the conviction that God is in himself love. In that case, why the necessity of the reprehensible cross? Can he not simply command the good for all creation without further ado (cf. *CDH* 1:6)? For others, the concern is more narrowly directed at God's transcendence, his freedom from all obligation. "Could Almighty God not simply pardon? … Anselm's critics do not simply object to the form of God's remedy – this Roman execution – but also to the very notion of necessity that is proposed to govern the entire doctrine. Such brutality is *necessary*? *This* is the bitter kernel of complaint."[100] In Anselm's own words: "If God could not save sinners except by condemning a just man, where is his omnipotence? If, on the other hand, he was capable of doing so, but did not will it, how shall we defend his wisdom and justice" (*CDH* 1:8; cf. 1:6)?

## Necessity: Arbitrary or Fitting?

God's forgiving, restorative agenda for the world cannot be implemented without reference to restitution; the alternative is a disordered reality in which injustice itself enjoys free rein.[101] Hear Adonis Vidu:

> It would be contrary to the very nature of God to create something and then watch it be destroyed, or to destroy it himself in response to its sin. Punishment – of the kind appropriate to an infinite offense – is never an option for Anselm. His doctrine of creation and of the divine purposes commits him to a view of God as binding himself to the execution of his plans … Thus a certain necessity obtains, but it is important to understand that this necessity is tied in to the nature of God, as well as to his will: once God sets out to create such beings, he is committing himself to seeing them reach their ultimate end.[102]

On Anselm's understanding, the painful necessity of the Passion does not dent God's stature or virtue, but is, once again, simply a function of what is real. Sonderegger is trenchant: "[Sin] wrongs One who exceeds infinitely an infinite universe of worlds … [and the] work done in Atonement is by and for the sinner; it establishes the *sinner's* justice, not God's. [He is hardly] the Moloch who demands the blood of his children to salve his fury."[103] It is the justice/honor imperative – because of which God prevents a universe of moral impunity – that constitutes the "necessity" of incarnation culminating in the Passion (cf. *CDH* 1:19). Absolution and healing are not achieved by a cartoonish "wave of the wand".[104] But such "necessity" is neither arbitrary nor external to God, but rather reflective of him – the One who loves too much to allow untrammeled rot and human depredation to snowball unimpeded.

To some, Anselm's necessity may seem childishly mechanical, particularly in our complicated era of mass conflict, religious plurality, and protest atheism. But I suspect that precisely these problems (of worldly wounds or worldly vanity) would, for Anslem, underscore our stark need and the astounding character of the grace of God revealed in the God-man.[105] And it is possible to situate necessity in terms that move beyond the exclusively negative or defensive. For Anselm, his "firm conviction [is] that a Sinless Adam, the God-Man, has made the world right, restored and released it from the tomb. This can happen, *it must happen*, it has happened."[106]

Necessity Does Not Invalidate Grace

God's saving act may be portrayed as the mysterious intertwining of two paradoxical aspects of grace, a giving that is both predictable *and* utterly free (cf. *CDH* 2:5). Anselm insists on a necessity to God's good purposes in creation and redemption, all the while acknowledging that, at one level, "necessity" is misapplied to the God who is not in need and not under obligation (cf. *CDH* 2:5; 16-17).[107]

We have already intimated that God's acts derive from his aseity, from a character and will that are not dictated by anyone. But a seam of tension is apparent when Anselm speaks freely of the necessity of the cross, only to say, "it was not out of any necessity that he died but on the strength of his power alone" (*CDH* 2:16).[108] For some, locating "necessity" within the internal consistency of God's own being – his "predictable" holiness, justice, and love – undercuts his freedom, limits his transcendence, and negates the "graciousness" of God's gift. These sorts of worries dance around a sort of voluntarist–intellectualist fault line. With no pretense to final solutions, I suggest an analogy from the realm of human relations. Let us posit a markedly compassionate or sacrificial person. To denigrate the genuine graciousness of their giving or sacrifice on the grounds that "that is just their character" (such that, in some way, their generosity "doesn't count") would be most improper. Yes, redemption *is* an expression of God's nature, character, and being. But this fact does not diminish the freedom or graciousness of divine giving. It should impel us to doxology. Hear Wilcoxen:

> Why did God become man? Because, Anselm says, it was required by God's perfect being. But this is not necessity in the normal sense of external compulsion. Rather, this is an act of "free will", which is to say it has the necessity of grace – a necessity contingent upon, and only upon, God's perfection. This internal compulsion of grace [is …] the intentionality he has to put his own honor, his own perfect being, on the line in the first place. This internal compulsion denoted by Anselm, the intentionality of grace that simply is the divine being – this is the bedrock theological mystery.[109]

### *Contextualizing Honor*

Southern warns that "Those critics who have imagined Anselm's God as a jealous tyrant, greedy for recognition and honor, have failed to recognize that the feudal image, however unsatisfactory in some of its implications, stood for rationality prevailing against the inroads of self-will and chaos."[110] With sufficient nuance and receptivity as readers, we may fruitfully reappropriate Anselmian honor for our own day. As Sonderegger reminds us, "we need not reduce theological idiom to the culture out of which it springs."[111] Every possibility exists to read the honor of Anselm's God with connotations more filial and gracious than cold, rigid, and authoritarian.

Beyond the question of the attractions and aversions of contemporary, formal "Western" theology, I would suggest that we consider the continuing relevance of shame, honor, and communal categories to majority-world theology, let alone universal human experience.[112] Indeed, in scripture, sin and suffering are scarcely meaningful without an alertness to issues of communal solidarity, shame, and honor.[113] Today it is common to support a pre-emptively generous reading of "global, non-Western" theology; might we not also, then, afford a similar hospitality to Anselm? *CDH* aims to safeguard divine honor, claiming that it is intrinsically directed towards justice and the truly good, and that it operates in sovereign freedom, unimpeded by subjection to external necessity. I would suggest that, appropriated with care, Anselm's argument has a certain staying power.

## The Sin Question

### *Sin as Debt, Sin as Universal*

We have noted the accusation that Anselm's atonement is derived from an overly forensic or commercial matrix, the conceptual building blocks of which can be traced back no further than Tertullian.[114] A supposed problem is *CDH*'s framing of human sin as a *debt* to God. The intersection of i) God's honor, ii) abstracted scales of justice, and iii) sin as unpayable debt render Anselm's vision of salvation fatally unacceptable, it is said.

The assumption that the sin-as-debt construct is simply unworthy, inadequate, or even "unbiblical" can underwrite a blanket hostility to Anselm. However, there is no reason to approach Anselm's discourse as an "all-or-nothing" proposition. Gary Anderson's *Sin: A History* represents moderation in the face of such categorical dismissals. Anderson tracks the development of biblical imagery for sin from a primal sin-as-burden construct to the later sin-as-debt construct.[115] Anderson's discussion skillfully incorporates debt imagery from the biblical and post-biblical tradition on sin, thereby retrieving certain Anselmian virtues for atonement.

In *CDH,* sin is a grave matter, a gravity extending to the beginning – to original sin. But, in Anselm's thought universe, whatever universal original sin is, it is not a question of God's peremptory imputation of guilt onto the innocent. Again, one may certainly query Anselm's metaphysical assumptions, but his conviction is *not* that the Judge arbitrarily transfers a deficit onto every human born. No, for Anselm, the story of Eden is not simply about the original pair; the story of paradise is one already involving *humanity*, a humanity that was well able not to sin, yet fell under the Devil's persuasion (*CDH* 1:22). Anselm (with many before him) assumes that there is such a thing as "human nature" in which we all natively and authentically partake – it was present at the start of our story and remains with us still.

For Anselm, "original sin is the inherited lack of moral rectitude in the will of fallen humankind."[116] Since Adam, that nature, *our* nature, is twisted and accountable for the way it is and for what it does (see *CDH* 1:18; *On the Virgin Conception and Original Sin* (*OVC*) 10, 23).[117] Again, the world may not in fact be the way Anselm thinks it is. But it remains important to insist that, for him, the conundrums of salvation and the pains of human existence are not things that a tyrant inexplicably foists on passive innocents. We are all genuine participants in a shared nature, one that, with culpable volition, opposes the Good.[118] Yes, there is mystery entailed, but the mystery lies, painfully, not with "why God did this to us", but with "why the givens of reality are what they are".

### *Sin's Gravity*

On Anslem's terms, given God's limitless worth, we ought already and always to love, adore, and serve the One on whom our existence hangs without remainder (cf. *CDH* 1:20-23). This obligation to the "highest good" (to God) for its own sake is the end of humankind which results in our greatest good as well (*CDH* 2:1). However distasteful the sin miasma (allegedly) hovering over Anselm's thought may be, sin is not his starting point; God is. Anselm gravely warns that because we have not considered God rightly, we "have not yet considered how heavy the weight of sin is" (*CDH* 1:21). The proper metric for sin is the backdrop of the goodness and worth of the Creator – a worthiness calling for *exhaustive* devotion on the part of each person. Supposing then the existence of a hypothetical "mere" human (somehow) without sin – even this one would have no excess virtue to expend on behalf of others: "If, in order that I may not sin, I owe to him my own being and all that I am capable of, even when I do not sin, I have nothing to give him in recompense for sin" (*CDH* 1:20). Humanity in sin simply does not have the supererogatory resources to compensate for our sorry condition.

It may be granted that for some Anselm's discourse is unsettling. But a discomfort with his affect cannot be allowed to be the central point. Whether invariably correct in every assertion or not, *CDH* surely puts a finger on the pulse of matters of consequence. As Anselm tells us elsewhere, "all sin is injustice" (*OVC* 3). The sin issue is not a matter of idiosyncratic fastidiousness, ego, or malice on the part of the Judge. The issue is justice in the universe.[119]

I would urge that, against the tide of contemporary current, Anselm's intuitions on sin's seriousness be given a thoughtful hearing. We might perhaps ponder, for example, some of our era's intractable problems – problems ranging from the generational impact of domestic abuse to human trafficking, to genocide, land grabs, and resource exploitation. In such contexts, Yang and Davis's words are pregnant and immediate when they speak of the "almost universal human recognition that it takes a great cost to rectify a terribly wrong situation".[120]

Moreover, it is far from evident that we, merely "average" sinners, can safely project discussion outward onto the canvas of epic-scale sins, thus undermining the significance of common erring and deflecting attention elsewhere. Does not the same dark substructure of sin inform even our "diminutive darkness", the puny peccadillos of our quotidian selfishness? In this arena Anselm has often been taken to task for his apparently obsessive overweighting of the most trivial infractions, his infamous "single sinful glance" (*CDH* 1:21). But Sonderegger rightly cautions that our smallest offenses still speak to intense alienation from the God who is good: "As it is our most common and heedless gestures that most vividly characterize us, so our smallest acts of rebellion reveal the grand design that tempts and feeds our pride."[121]

However hard it may be to clear the haze clouding the mind's eye, when humans offend against the good, the true, and the beautiful in head-on collision with the Maker, stakes and costs are high. Sin harms in God's world because it ultimately is all against him. Sonderegger instructs us: "Could we not say, in more modern idiom, that certain acts take on a measure of harm or cruelty or folly in proportion to the significance and intimacy of the person wronged?"[122] I think we can. Satisfaction is necessary – necessary but not within our capacity. Restitution exceeds the value of all there is in existence besides God.[123] God became man because the gravity of the human dilemma required intervention of such a magnitude.

## Concluding Thoughts on Anselm and CDH

Anselm's voice continues to echo in atonement debate, the influence indelible, the controversy unmissable. I have urged that we take *CDH* seriously without granting it "final word" status. Sensitive to the development of atonement thought and engaged with contemporary idiom, Anselm persists as a rich resource. With respect to the three structuring tropes of this study, each is woven into the fabric of Anselm's thought, so I conclude this chapter by revisiting these themes.

Issues of justice pressure Anselmian satisfaction in several ways. First, in responding to the charge that Anselm's God is internally riven by a conflict between justice and mercy, *CDH* is best viewed through a lens refocusing the divine perfections as a unity. The cross is not the location of a war of attributes but of their confluence. Second, satisfaction is no mechanistic contrivance running roughshod over justice. Rather, at least for Anselm, it is "fitting", consonant with God's good and just nature – that is, maintaining beauty, order, and balance in his world. The redemptive effect of Christ's excess payment is not a mere notation in the ledger: quite transparently, Anselm is heavily invested in a *just* rectification. I contend that undergirding Anselm's abstracted logic are assumptions about ontological change that happens in the exchange of the cross – an exchange *freely* accomplished by God himself in Christ. From within Anselm's metaphysical matrix, satisfaction's claims to justice in *CDH* are no mere fig leaf. Fundamentally, satisfaction is a vision intolerant of unaccountable impunity, a vision of justice enacted towards restoration.

Famously or infamously, Anselm is eager to affirm divine honor throughout the economy of atonement, in the face of the seeming dishonor of incarnation, human limitation, and a shameful death. Anselm argues that the radical action of Christ crucified *is* God intervening to make creation right once again. Honor and justice mutually inform: to allow creational intent to fail truly would besmirch the divine honor in a way that the incarnation and cross do not. Moreover, one must not lose sight of the surprising fact that, for Anselm, when God is dishonored, he does not suffer ontological harm; we do. In direct contradiction to popular misreading, solicitousness for God's honor is not about the divine ego. Rather, it is entirely congruent with human beatitude. Admittedly, for some, positing *the necessity* of the cross dishonors God. For Anselm, this is to miss the point. The requirement of the cross is not a blemishing of the divine character.

Rather, it is a barometer of the facts of the created order. It is a measure of a *free and gracious* God's unwillingness to allow injustice free rein in his world. The alleged "compulsion" is not an external force applied to God but a reflection of God's good and just self.

Finally, we touch on Anselm's ominous construal of sin, particularly original sin and the depth of sin's damage. Denunciations of extremism have been cast at his sin construct, an unpayable debt supposedly distorting justice and quashing human hope. Once again, Anselm's metaphysical commitments come into play – the gravity of sin is not a measure of God's arbitrary demands and valuations, it is a measure of the ontological truth about humans before infinite God. The gravity of sin is in inverse proportion to the infinity of God's goodness and worth. From within his theological imaginary, Anselm is not motivated by a morose churlishness but by a love of God, his truth, and his world. The question, as always, is what to make of his assumptions? Turning to my own assessment, that the devastating consequences of sin are writ large in the human story seems evident; so, too, does sin's rampant ubiquity. Certainly, we may grant that various sins merit a sober and differentiated weighting on the scales of justice. Nonetheless, in accord with Anselm, I would argue the following: that all sin is against the good God to whom allegiance is always due; that sin invariably harms and "costs"; and that even minor infractions ("the sinful glance") participate in the single nexus of deceit and darkness that is sin. In the next chapter, shifting into the modern period, we yet remain on a trajectory much indebted to Anselm.

# 6. Barth and Substitutionary Atonement

> For by the sacrifice of his own body he both put an end to the law which was against us, and renewed to us a beginning of life, having given a hope of the resurrection. For since it was from man that death obtained the mastery over man, for this reason, through the Word of God becoming man, the abolition of death took place, and the resurrection of life. (Athanasius, *On the Incarnation* 10)

## Mapping the Discussion

In this chapter our concern is with modern configurations of atonement majoring on Christ's substitutionary role, vicarious suffering, and penalty. This is the arena of "objective" and/or "forensic" atonement theories. The paradigmatic type and lightning rod of debate in this domain is (versions of) PSA. And as I focus on atonement thought of this sort, the central resource upon which I draw is Karl Barth's *Church Dogmatics*.

This is the general direction of travel: I begin with the emergence of PSA with Calvin, a critical development in the Anselmian legacy. I then gesture towards ways of situating PSA with respect to other framings of salvation. I also revisit the aversion to penal theories expressed by many modern "Western" thinkers (as well as Muslims). I finally conclude this introductory overflight by contextualizing and characterizing Barth and other key voices of objective, forensic, or penal substitutionary atonement. From that point, the bulk of discussion turns to (primarily) Barthian atonement in light of the triple typology of justice, sin, and honor:

ia. The problem of "justice from below", that is, the ethics of the human impact of substitutionary atonement.

ib. The problem of "justice from above" in PSA, that is, the justice or injustice, virtue or vice, of Trinitarian relations in this soteriology.

ii. The problem of original sin or sin as the dilemma remedied at the cross.

iii. Questions of PSA's threat to divine honor. Are God's greatness and transcendence compromised if the *degradation* of the cross was *obligatory* upon God?

iv. Last, I offer a synthesis of findings with respect to PSA and the three tropes.

## From Anselm to Calvin and PSA

There are swathes of theology inveterately hostile to any atonement construct within the Anselmian legacy, and there are also heirs to Anselm who disavow any place for conceptualities of "penalty".[1] For our purposes, however, PSA is the most important current in Anselm's wake, and to it we turn. The PSA constellation is significant because of its historic importance in Protestantism, because it is a lightning rod for moral ire in the modern period, and because it is the soteriological model to which Muslim observers most often respond. The scholars most frequently engaged in this chapter, then, propose soteriologies that integrate categories of substitution and penalty, whether exclusively or not.

John Calvin is frequently taken as the classic headwaters of PSA – a systematizer and refiner of the Anselmian deposit with a marked emphasis on justice and law. Adonis Vidu highlights the following: i) In Anselmian satisfaction, God's option to accept *any* form of satisfaction is theoretically unbounded. By contrast, in PSA, fixed public law is the governing metaphor. ii) For *CDH*, Christ's death is a free offering in lieu of (our) punishment. In PSA, that death *is* the punishment. iii) Anselmian satisfaction – Christ's self-offering – is rather abstracted. In Calvin's PSA, the life and death of Christ are *relatively* more grounded in ideas of history, covenant, and law.[2]

The legal ethos of Calvin's PSA did not necessarily imply the *reduction* of divine justice to retribution and guilt transfer, but it certainly put the emphasis there.[3] For Calvin, in the atonement God has expunged guilt by way of a two-pronged satisfaction: "First, through [Christ's] active obedience, he positively fulfilled the law (Phil. 2:8). Second, in his death, he bears the punishment incumbent upon us (Gal. 3:13), the trespassers of the law."[4]

Calvin's soteriology draws fire from theologians advocating for God's priority of love as over against law and from those decrying PSA's supposed positing of a change in God's disposition. However, Rutledge counters that for Calvin there *is* no change internal to God. She insists that on Calvin's calculus, the Only Begotten on the cross is both punishment *and* a sign of God's love, *prior and continuing*.[5] Vidu also insists, that for the Reformer, grace, love, and law coexist; the *fundamental cause of our redemption is God's grace*, the instrumental cause is Christ's merit.[6]

## PSA and Other Redemption Models

A profile of salvation must account for conceptual pressures from various quarters. One must, for example, account for the myriad biblical images and tropes deployed to articulate salvation. One must attend to both the sweep of the biblical story and creedal orthodoxy's mysteries (Christology, Trinitarianism, theology proper and divine attributes). Now, whatever PSA's strengths may be, it is unlikely to do all this work in isolation from all other soteriological frameworks.

With Rutledge, I would affirm the presence of the "substitution motif" in the NT and Christian tradition; in Christ God has intervened "for us" and "in our place".[7] I would also insist that the exclusionary dichotomy sometimes posited between Jesus' *representative* and *substitutionary* roles is generally unhelpful.[8] But there is no need to make substitutionary atonement the one controlling model, or even the standalone model – better to see the substitution dynamic as congruent with a polyvalent weave of various scriptural types and tropes of salvation.[9]

Narrow presentations of PSA as the *sine qua non* of atonement are inadequate. For example, one limiting feature of common versions of PSA is a heavy lean into "negative" salvation – dealing with the sin problem – with little prospect towards the positive purposes for which we are saved. Yang and Davis remind us that atonement must deal both with "objective guilt" before the Judge and also fit us for life with God, dealing with the human "disposition or propensity to fall into sin".[10] In acknowledging the virtues of penal substitutionary thought, one need not make it exclusive, synonymous with redemption writ large. It can be, should be, nested within a more expansive atonement framework.

## Western and Islamic Issues with PSA

We have gestured previously to contemporary hostility towards PSA or theologies of vicarious suffering in general. To summarize typical criticisms:[11]

- PSA unjustifiably assumes divine justice to be retributive.
- In PSA God's love is secondary and set in opposition to his justice.
- In PSA the Father is arrayed against the Son.
- PSA is radically individualized with respect to both sin and salvation, and thus deficient with respect to the cosmic scale of atonement.
- PSA entails no redemptive necessity for the life and ministry of Christ or the resurrection.
- PSA lacks an integral link to sanctification and social transformation.
- PSA may underwrite oppressive social structures.
- PSA's mechanisms oscillate between the crude, the offensive, and the irrational.
- PSA represents an obsolete hangover from a cultic religion of "blood sacrifice."

Vidu details the modern inclination to associate PSA with legal frameworks and individualized morality, and these features of PSA are typically placed in invidious contrast with "superior" soteriologies centered on love, liberation, and social transformation.[12] Vidu characterizes the competing liberation stream as majoring on the "transpersonal and transintentional dimension of sin" with sin's "horizontal" dimension eclipsing any "vertical" considerations, and often occluding original sin.[13]

The alert reader will already have noted some overlap between these critiques and the worries of Muslim scholars. The symmetry is not, of course, complete. For example, the modern mistrust of legal categories is hardly typical of Islamic theology. But the parallels are clear. Rutledge examines critics for whom PSA's supposed violence, legal obsession, individualism, and so on are obsolete relics of its historical matrix, products of "cultural conditioning".[14] This may evoke Islamic criticisms of atonement theory as a product of historical Western cultural influences of hyper-perfectionism, unrealistic idealism, or guilt obsession. Or, when substitution thought is denounced by "progressive" critics for a history of "keeping bad company" – vested interests, colonial and otherwise – we may call to mind Muslim scholars associating atonement theology with "Western sins" ranging from the Crusades to sexual laxness.[15]

Liberal Protestant thought has viscerally reacted against vicarious suffering as unjust, irrational, and/or offensive to moral sensibility. Sonderegger asserts:

"For [ethical liberalism], the portrait of a vicarious redeemer violated moral feeling. For One to fulfill the moral law for another, and to fulfill that categorical claim of obedience through suffering, transgressed the very idea of the ethical, and elevated the heteronomous to the central moment of Christian thought."[16] Similar remonstrations against the ethical offense and irrationality of mediated redemption are already familiar from Islamic analyses.[17]

### Barth and Friends on Substitutionary Atonement

And so, we turn to positive constructions of substitutionary atonement and vicarious suffering. Throughout this chapter, the thought of Karl Barth (d. 1968) provides the better part of the discussion's infrastructure. The preponderance of emphasis on the famous Swiss theologian is a function of his inherent importance to modern theology, his relationship to substitutionary atonement, and the prolixity of his writing. Indeed, Barth is routinely referred to as "the most significant theologian of the twentieth century".[18]

Barth's agenda famously sought to deconstruct the liberal hegemony of his time, counterposing the unqualified "Godness of God", a God who offers radical grace in unconditioned love, but in contradiction to all "human religion" and natural theology.[19] Notably, a major catalyst for Barth's theological agenda was his engagement with Anselm.[20] Adam Johnson affirms that Barth lies "within the trajectory of Anselm", even as he diverged from his path and embodied many distinct developments.[21]

Barth (and the *Church Dogmatics*) is known for many things – none more so than his intensively Christological orientation. For Barth, "Christian doctrine is constructed by inference from the person of Jesus Christ."[22] Barth works outward from the revelation of God in Christ such that even the doctrine of election is "about God's choice to be himself in Jesus Christ".[23] Importantly for our purposes, Adam Johnson urges that Barth's Christocentric Trinitarianism is the grid through which to approach the various loci of his theology, not least his doctrine of reconciliation and atonement.[24]

In the first instance, our interest lies with theologies of substitutionary atonement, rather than Barth as such. However, the theologian of Basel is arguably the most important modern scholar closely associated with vicarious atonement in its forensic aspect. And so, Barth is a fitting icon for this chapter. Now, while "there is little question that Barth's account is substitutionary," there is considerable debate about Barth's stance with respect to PSA.[25] On this score, Johnson's judgment is sound: "For our purposes, regardless of Barth's specific relationship to the traditional understanding(s) of penal substitution, this debate highlights the fact that Barth develops his substitutionary account of reconciliation within a forensic/judicial framework rooted in a 'central [judicial] metaphor'."[26] As we shall see, Barth certainly does not write punishment out of his economy of salvation.

Of course, a central focus need not imply tunnel vision. Again, Johnson is helpful: "Barth's doctrine of reconciliation includes within it all that penal substitution affirms, while offering [a] larger and more encompassing account of Christ's substitutionary work."[27] So, even as Barth "argues that the theme of substitution – especially in its significance 'for us' and 'for sin' – subsumes all the others", he is far from heedless of the extended span of God's salvific action.[28] For example, he understands the dynamic of substitution as one of the overthrow of evil, sin, and corruption – accents of the *Christus Victor* (*CV*) motif.[29] Similarly, Barth's conviction that reconciliation and *revelation* are mutually informing generates space for an exemplarist strain in his objective atonement.[30]

It is also notable that Barth's signature Christocentrism can at times function to underscore the transforming effect of the mere "fact" of the incarnation, without homing in on the crucifixion. Indeed, in Barth's famous inversion of the "prodigal son" parable, atonement in Christ is comprised of "the entire story of the downward journey of the Son 'into the far country'".[31] Nonetheless, for Barth it remains the case that the story of Jesus, pre- and post-Easter, "is finally the story of his passion".[32] The cross stands at the center.

### *Barth's Atonement, Vicarious and "Objective"*

Barth as theologian of "substitutionary" or "objective" atonement commands interest in that he is not the clichéd conservative idealogue. But he is certainly a theologian of the cross. For Barth, the entirety of "theology, both that which follows and indeed that which precedes the doctrine of reconciliation, depends upon [the] *theologia crucis*."[33] Here the Lordly Christ becomes "the Judge judged in our place".[34]

Barth's atonement is an "objective" accomplishment of God, but one replete with metaphysical mystery and paradoxical effect. Indeed, his efforts at communicating the drama of atonement often elicit considerable rhetorical virtuosity:

> Why did the Son of God become man, one of us, our brother, our fellow in the human situation? The answer is: In order to judge the world ... In order to judge it in the exercise of his kingly freedom to show his grace in the execution of his judgment, to pronounce us free in passing sentence, to free us by imprisoning us, to ground our life on our death, to redeem and save us by our destruction. That is how God has actually judged in Jesus Christ. And that is why he humbled himself. That is why he went into the far country as the obedient Son of the Father.[35]

One can detect in Barth's thought features redolent of Anselm. So, for example, Christ's advent for our salvation is indicative of the fact that God was unwilling to allow his good purposes to be foiled; he "was not ready to acquiesce in the fact that while He was for us we were against Him".[36] Barth joins the chorus of Anselm and earlier Fathers, insisting that it would have been "unfitting" for God to leave the human story in abeyance or ultimate failure. "For the glory of God is threatened by man's destruction. Hence God cannot tolerate that man should perish."[37]

There also is a strong emphasis in Barth, as in Anselm, that the offering of the one who did not owe redeems the ones who did. Even if the accent is more "judicial" in Barth as compared to satisfaction categories, the architecture is very much one of unmerited and overwhelmingly powerful exchange:

> The very heart of the atonement is the overcoming of sin … It was to fulfil this judgment on sin that the Son of God as man took our place as sinners. He fulfils it – as man in our place – by completing our work *in the omnipotence of the divine Son*, by treading the way of sinners to its bitter end … in destruction … He fulfils this judgment by suffering the punishment which we have all brought on ourselves.[38]

In any case, Barth certainly agrees with Anselm that "we are debtors who cannot pay, [and] that [God's] forgiveness is the only adequate and relevant and effective work."[39] Tellingly, Johnson speaks of Barth's "reformulated satisfaction theory".[40]

And so, for Barth, in the substitutionary exchange of the Messiah's death, multiple lines converge: the justice and searing goodness of God; the expression of infinite love, worth, and righteousness in Christ; and the (otherwise) incurable wound of sin on the human soul:

> And so Christ must and is willing to stand as *the greatest robber, murderer, adulterer, thief, defiler and blasphemer etc. of all, than whom no-one has ever in the world been greater.* And it is the secret of what took place in Jesus Christ that in him there met and clashed, *highest, greatest, and only sin and highest, greatest, and only righteousness,* but in such a way that there could be no doubt as to the outcome: *In Christ, the sin of all is conquered, put to death, and buried, and righteous remains the victor and ruler for eternity.*[41]

As I examine themes in substitutionary atonement in Barth and others, contemporary uneasiness with PSA lies close at hand. I turn first to a motif that is one of the drivers of debate over "objective" substitutionary atonement, namely, divine justice. We consider questions of justice of "from below" and "from above." That is, at the cross, i) how could God possibly be just in his action towards and expectations of humanity and the created order, and ii) how might God be just both towards Christ and within himself?

## Justice "from Below": God, Substitution, and Humanity

### *Wrath and Love*

The conundrum of a perceived tension between divine justice and mercy is hardly new. This issue might have been engaged as a justice problem between the Father and his elect Messiah, or, as we saw with some Muslim objectors, as a problem internal to God's own character and attributes – thus, a denigration of his honor. However, in deference to a modern prioritization of the *human* experience of salvation, I begin the exploration of this seeming aporia, here considering questions of "justice from below". Acute questions arise when this alleged clash of divine attributes eventuates in humanity's experience of either wrath or love.

One cannot fairly escape the reality of judgment as a biblical theme. For his part, Barth works "backwards" from Christ, seeing in the cross the manifestation and concentration of God's cosmic, just judgment, his wrath – that is, a microcosm of the horrors, wrongs, and violence writ large in human history broadly and the story of Israel particularly.[42] In parallel with Anselm, this judgment is a stark measure of the truth about human nature as it stands before God's unmitigated purity.

Vidu underscores how the forensic overtone of much substitutionary atonement exacerbates debates over the compatibility of retributive justice and love and mercy.[43] Given modern hierarchies of value, divine wrath is often invoked as the most invidious feature of PSA. Wrath is paired with "violence" in zero-sum opposition to love. Ironically, God's "wrath" – which is his *judgment* – is taken to be *unjust*, or, perhaps, even justice itself is inferior to love.[44]

As we have seen, Anselm cannot allow a competition of attributes internal to God, disparate human experiences notwithstanding.[45] On classical assumptions, there is no hierarchy, no differentiated list of external, real qualities in which God participates: "he *is* his attributes."[46] The unity, hierarchy, or even conflict of divine attributes is a watershed issue, an inflection point in atonement perspectives. It is likely that such assumptions grounded in traditional ideas of the divine simplicity will evoke less pushback from Islamic thinkers than from scholars in the domain of contemporary "Western" theology.

In terms of this classical lineage, the diversity of human contexts, responses to God, and encounters with his providence do not betray a contradiction within God's being, nor the negation of either his justice or mercy. Barth, by "pairing God's holiness and righteousness under the perfection of God's loving … makes clear that there is no such thing as a cleavage between the grace and holiness of God, nor between God's mercy and righteousness."[47]

> [W]e must see, feel and appreciate His love to us even in His anger, condemnation, and punishment. For we cannot avoid the conclusion that it is where the divine love and therefore the divine grace and mercy are attested … i.e. in Jesus Christ, that according to the unmistakable witness of the New Testament itself they encounter us as a divine act of wrath, judgment, and punishment … The event of Good Friday embodies the divine No, which contains in itself the divine Yes.[48]

### *Wrath and Penalty*

The issue of divine wrath sits at a nexus of acute moral tensions and antinomies. I cannot begin to engage the myriad of relevant debates (e.g. the mystery and meaning of unexplained and unresolved pain) that spider outwards from this central node. To the question at hand, my minimal starting point seeks to contextualize God's wrath – experienced as his judgment – not as a noxious passion by which he is overwhelmed but, rather, as his "opposition to sin and evil".[49] Counterintuitively, God's wrath towards us in our recalcitrance to the good may even be an affirmation of "our status and our relationship with Him … God does not have the same attitude for rocks, trees, or puppies."[50] Faith rightly insists that across the long arc of God's dealings in his world – which none of us can comprehensively interpret – God's wrath is aimed at destroying the curse element of existence which stymies human benediction (cf. Gal. 3:13; Col. 3:5-6; 1 Pet. 2:24).[51]

Divine anger is not a definitive attribute of God, but rather "the manifestation of the presence of God in the midst of sin".[52] While God's love and justice are constants, his wrath remains *contingent* on his holiness.[53] "Love is essential to

God's character in a way that wrath is not. Love endures forever, and anger is more limited."[54] Holy anger expressed in support of those wronged and abused is in fact congruent with love, a love that even now advances "some measure of moral equilibrium in a broken and morally imperfect world".[55]

If sin is a regrettable, unescapable reality, then "penalty" is an expression of divine wrath's proper response.[56] So, in traditional theological perspective, penalty is a function of justice. But, quite evidently, in many quarters, language of penalty elicits visceral portrayals of PSA in the darkest of hues. At one level, we are driven back on metaphysical commitments. Under the surface of the atonement debate lie crucial but difficult questions about what simply *is* – questions exceedingly difficult to adjudicate in any way likely to command universal assent.

And so the questions persist. For example, even if some measure of penalty is granted as intrinsic to notions of (retributive) justice, many will wonder if (as sinners stand before their Maker) the sum total of penalty incurred is proportional. Is it measured? There is an instinctive revolt against the idea that God punishes even earnest would-be servants for their inability to live up to his demands. In Sonderegger's words,

> The pattern of exile and return, of Risen Life after affliction, of silent Bearing of those crushed by divine service: just this is the pattern many feminists describe as the cycle of abuse. The powerless punished for what they cannot carry out, then brought back to the abuser through tenderness and promise of better days, the love that an afflicted and broken victim needs desperately and will die to win [... So] it is just this cycle, and the anguish that lies at its heart, that [feminists] denounce and repudiate.[57]

Sonderegger rightly insists that we must hear the laments and indictments, really hear the *persons* making them. Certainly, if one's atonement architecture (PSA or otherwise) assumes disproportionate sanctions and derisive delight in violence, then the criticisms gain purchase. But Sonderegger wisely also cautions that ours is no universe in which such matters can be resolved on the basis of abstract analysis. Tensions, contested intuitions, and epistemic uncertainty will always dog discussions of justice and sin's gravity.

If, however, we are committed to a biblical framework, then neither abstracted debate nor ideological location – however relevant to the quest – will provide sufficient light on its own terms. Our aspiration is a scriptural faith seeking understanding, and in scripture we have to do with a personal, covenantal relation. Whatever "answers" emerge will come by way of the God known and trusted, not by an abstracted reasoning aiming to terminate all uncertainty. Particularly in the story of the cross, we must finally circle back to the Trinity – to the God who loves and calls Abraham, Israel, the least, enemies, even us. We circle back to the Judge judged for us. This is the Father who condescends not only to command but also to hear, who goes down into exile with Israel. The "exile and return" is no "abusive cycle"; it is the experience of God with his people living in suffering, faith, and hope.[58]

### Penalty Affirmed and Decentered

Thus, in the family of atonement models inflected by both justice and a legal accent, penalty cannot be abstracted away. Neither need it be redemption's central fixation. If we consider salvation in Barth, the concept of punishment as outlined in Isaiah 53 is neither evaded nor given center stage:

> My turning from God is followed by God's annihilating turning from me. When it is resisted his love works itself out as death-dealing wrath. If Jesus Christ has followed our way as sinners to the end to which it leads, in outer darkness, then we can say with that passage from the Old Testament that he has suffered this punishment of ours. But we must not make this a main concept.[59]

Rutledge puts it that "Barth, characteristically, insists on the point that Jesus has taken the place of the man of sin ('Adam', as in Rom. 5), but the emphasis is not on the penalty suffered. Surely, it is suffered – no dispute there – but Barth throws all the weight on the undoing of Sin."[60]

And it is precisely at this node of "punishment" that we must recall the principle of the non-conflicting perfections of God. "Each divine action has to be seen as exhibiting the full being of God. The crucifixion, no less, equally demonstrates God's love, not simply his justice … punishment is the form the holy love of God had to take, given the human condition of sin and liability to punishment."[61]

Barth's substitutionary atonement includes but extends beyond retributive justice. As Johnson notes, Barth articulates a fourfold typology that is comprehensively substitutionary, *not* comprehensively penal: the Lord "took our place as Judge. He took our place as the judged. He was judged in our place. And He acted justly in our place."[62] If one's atonement construct is thematized by justice, penalty cannot be dispensed with; neither, though, can it bear the soteriological load alone. The scope of Christ's life (not limited to death and penalty) is an effective, representative justice. "Barth is just as concerned with the fourth 'for us' of Jesus' work (in which he acts justly in our place) as he is in the second and third (in which he bears our judgement or punishment). To put it quite simply, Barth thinks that an over-emphasis on punishment simply cannot do justice to the justice of God manifest in the substitutionary work of Christ."[63]

Vicarious intervention is too frequently oriented towards "salvation from" to the neglect of "salvation for". This need not be the case. Even the generally narrow focus of PSA can be positioned within a soteriological arc directed at the restoration of the created order. According to Johnson, although Barth's exposition is underdeveloped, his construal of redemption logically impinges "on an ontological spectrum, touching the created order, self, family, community, institutions, nations, the angelic (and demonic) order, and the relations between these."[64]

### *Justice and the Metaphysics of Exchange*

Barth famously portrays God's downward trajectory from incarnation to the cross by inverting Luke's so-called prodigal son parable; for us and for our salvation, God in Christ has journeyed into the "far country" in which humanity languishes under sin.[65] It is important that such narrative configurations of salvation be kept before our eyes. Expositions of the abstracted logic underlying PSA are all well and good, but they must never be divorced from the "real world" story of God and humanity. This is because atonement is first and foremost a concept distilled out of tangible action by God *for us*. Salvation must not be reduced to forensic algorithms or quasi-bureaucratic conferrals of status – whatever role such abstractions may play *as aspects of the whole*. The viability and, indeed, *justice* of a "theory" (e.g. PSA) depends on a metaphysical act in the created world; redemption is more than a nicely balanced equation on the screen.

Reason must invariably be invoked, but the theological task cannot be reduced to rational control of the data. The objective is not the elimination of mystery. Anatolios tells us, "The infinite God cannot be contained by finite human knowing. Yet, human knowing and human existence in its entirety can be so contained and determined by the divine self-disclosure as to be suffused with knowledge and love and union with the divine."[66] Thus, our understanding is that the salvation of the world involves metaphysical transformation that exceeds our rhetorical, analytic, and epistemological limits. A posture of faithful receptivity is required.

The apparent linear impossibility and injustice of PSA is a familiar charge, ready to hand: "An innocent person cannot take on the guilt of another."[67] The critique seems to land telling blows when vicarious redemption is styled as a system of bookkeeping maneuvers. But Rutledge rightly warns both advocates and critics of PSA that such overly rationalistic and "literal-minded" approaches to atonement are misguided from the start.[68] If, however, we vacate unnecessarily mechanistic intellection, we may well find that both truth and utility infuse traditional substitutionary concepts.[69]

Wondrously, the exchange at the heart of PSA yields the justification of human sinners. If this exchange were limited to matters of status ("sinner" to "justified"), limited to divine decision ("judgment" to "reward"), then doubts as to justice in atonement would persist. As we discuss below, Trinitarian parameters must be invoked such that the One sinned against is seen to be the very One who forgives and bears the consequences.[70] Seeing the Passion, indeed all of redemption, as the act of the eternal Trinity – transcendent and immanent – further demands that an ethical metaphysical reality underwrite the forensics of salvation. If PSA is to "work", renewal and transformation must surpass the notional; they must be ontological and substantial.

In Barth's rather dramatic terms, this change happens in the world of created reality because redemption is underwritten by a free, sovereign "event in the life of God".[71]

> Because it was the Son of God, i.e. God Himself, who took our place on Good Friday, the substitution could be effectual and procure our reconciliation with the righteous God … Only God, our Lord and Creator, could stand surety for us, could take our place, could suffer eternal death in our stead as the consequence of our sin in such a way that it was finally suffered and overcome and therefore did not need to be suffered any more by us. No creature, no other man could do that. But God's own Son could do it.[72]

## Substitution and Representation

Jesus' life, death, and rising effect a dramatic exchange of life for death, hope for despair, wherein God sets us right by taking our place, by becoming "the object of his own severity".[73] But again, resistance to PSA has led to an insistence by some on the *representative* features of Christ's work as over against the *substitutionary*. Unsavory presentations of PSA may elicit such dichotomizing reactions. But we must not allow malformed constructs to obfuscate legitimate truths. Barth's vicarious atonement would suffer sclerotic breakdown if oppositional polarities between substitution and representation held. But the dichotomies are misapprehensions.[74]

Substitution is quite evidently an authentic NT theme, and indeed is frequently implicit in representation itself.[75] J. I. Packer is surely correct that driving a wedge between substitution and representation often produces a "distinction without a difference".[76] As Sonderegger says:

> There is, to speak doctrinally, a *substitutionary* moment in all representation: one stands in the place of the many, taking their cause and their reality for his own. He, not they, stands before the tribunal or the crowd or the Judgment Seat; even as their Leader and Spokesman. He, not they, hangs nailed to the cross; he, and not his abusers, refuses to reject the cross and save himself.[77]

At the cross, substitution, representation, and exchange fluidly converge in polyphonous concert, as Barth recognizes.[78] So too must reason, justice, love, and God's ontological power coalesce in the atonement.

## The "Exchange" of PSA: A Metaphysical Participation

The ill repute of substitutionary and forensic soteriology is often tied to construals of justification as a "legal fiction". This should not be. In the interests of both justice and efficacy, forensic declarations sourced in substitution and representation must be conjoined with metaphysical reality, a participatory movement of the Spirit. "Justice cannot be seen to be done in the forensic transactional nature of the atonement unless the Son has become one with humanity in its totality. And conversely, the vicarious humanity aspect is not complete without the objective aspect of the atonement."[79]

The exchange God effects in atonement is something that flips reality, that upends experience and ontology. In the atonement there is both "the *exinanitio*, the abasement, of God, and the *exaltatio*, the exaltation of man. It was God who went into the far country, and it is man who returns home. Both took place in the one Jesus Christ."[80] Jesus mediates between God and man as fully both – his Godliness makes uplift for the world possible, but he does it all as man, to make it actual for us.[81] Jesus stands in for his people not merely in some titular sense, but with true and vital connection (cf. Rom. 6:1-11; Gal. 2:20-21; Col. 2:11-13). In Sonderegger's terms, the Lord incarnate "*identifies* himself with [his people], the Perfect for the broken, the Whole for the partial and flawed, the Final for the frail and passing away … *This* is why he is served when a cup of cold water is given to the least, because he takes on the face of the poor so that many should become rich … He is hidden among the lost."[82]

Mercy, substitution, forensic declaration, and all the other structural aspects of PSA are to be affirmed; but they are only made actual – and only "just" – because the grounding power of the Creator's being underlies this transaction. Justification cannot be reduced to legal pretense. Barth is sure that in the cross, in Christ's reign, God is *doing* something in the fabric of the cosmos:

> There is no room for any fears that in the justification of man we are dealing only with a verbal action, with a kind of bracketed "as if", as though what is pronounced were not the whole truth about man. Certainly *we have to do with a declaring righteous*, but it is a declaration about man which is fulfilled and therefore effective in this event, *which corresponds to actuality because it creates and therefore reveals the actuality.*[83]

For justification to be actual, "alien righteousness" cannot be left external, nominal, and formal.[84]

### "Objective" Atonement: Who is Changed?

Some descriptions of PSA imply that atonement is a matter of God's anti-human hostility being mollified by a third party's reception of God's ire. In this problematic tableau, one encounters a God who waxes hot and cold, swayed by external inputs. Here we have the deficiency of divine instability matched by deficits in divine justice. Thankfully this sort of construct need not be overlayed on the logic of PSA. Once again, we are called back to Trinitarian guardrails (more below) and to convictions about the unity of divine attributes. Clearly justice from above (the just being of God himself) is at issue here; but so is justice from below, the question being, "Who is changed in atonement, God or humanity?"

The challenge lies with the assumption that in objective atonement the evident change in the God–human relationship must betray a change within God's own being. At a minimum, in vicarious intervention the believer's status before and experience of God does change. Something has changed, and that change involves God. Certainly, the reconfiguration of the divine–human relation is the product of God's energy at work. And the interchange is dynamic and interpersonal. But it is also asymmetrical. In the objective event of atonement, it is fundamentally not God who changes, it is those being saved. Vidu's analysis is congruent with Barth's grounding commitments:

> [Thus,] it is not that the crucifixion produced a change in God, from which point God was enabled to engage in another particular action. Rather, crucifixion, resurrection, glorification, as well as God's adoption of us into his Triune life – all are elements of a single, all-encompassing, utterly uncontradictable action … The crucifixion does not *enable* God to so adjust his attributes that he is now able to receive us.[85]

There is an integral parallel here with the union of natures in the incarnation: God takes on, transforms, and heals *real* humanity, but without surrendering or destabilizing his own nature. So too in redemption, the direction of travel is from up to down. Neither God's being nor disposition required a course correction; ours did. In the death and rising of Jesus this is realized, metaphysically and justly.

Barth's articulation of forensic substitution supplies that which is sometimes lacking in reductive presentations of PSA – namely, the Christ event as a metaphysical exchange between God and humanity, an exchange changing *us*.[86] Only Christ – God *and* "the brother of man" – can carry our burden of sin and death "downwards to the abyss", crying in dereliction as "האדם", being in this way *God for us*, raising us to him.[87]

From one vantage point, Christs acts for us, so "exempting" us, but from an equally necessary perspective, by the blood of the Lamb, "we *have* died in and with Him, [so] that as the people we were we have been done away and destroyed."[88] Due judgment is not evaded or misdirected, it is executed even if in the most unanticipated, world-inverting manner.[89] The death of Jesus manifests the righteous judgment of God which burns us (as humanity beholden to sin) to the ground, only thereby to offer hope and redemption in the resurrection, for the "man of sin" has been judged.[90] This is representation *and* substitution – searing, effective, redeeming.[91] Rhetorical paradox points to truth: judgment happened to us in Christ so that it might *not* happen to us.

"[A]n objective circumstance is now in place (we are now in Christ), which makes us experience God as more loving than just, even though strictly speaking nothing has changed in God."[92] This salvation is not staged, as if the Christian is an actor who for theoretical religious purposes plays the justified person but in fact goes on to live without reference to any transformation. No, Barth insists that Jesus is not the "innocent man whose patient suffering changes the temper of God, inducing in Him an indulgent sparing of all other men, so that all other men can rather shamefacedly take refuge behind his suffering, happily saved but quite unchanged in themselves".[93] *We* are changed as judgment and love converge at the cross. Objective atonement indeed.

## The Metaphysics of Exchange: Ethics and Discipleship

"Man's reconciliation with God takes place through God putting Himself in man's place and man's being put in God's place, as a sheer act of grace. It is this inconceivable miracle which is our reconciliation."[94] The initiative in reconciliation is patently from God, but a living dynamic relationship is the result. In the exchange that is atonement, Jesus draws us to share in his life, including the "smooth" and "rough" textures of that participation. Even "the irruption of [Christ's] suffering into the life of the Christian [is] the sign of [our] fellowship, and thus the manifestation of the supreme dignity of the Christian."[95]

The conduit connecting a person to new life generated by the salvific interchange is faith. And in the community of faith, "Christ crucified" becomes the template for the life of the believer – a mold for discipleship.[96] The believer's cruciform reconfiguration in virtue, obedience, power, and faithful suffering is itself a facet – not cause or foundation – of salvation.[97] Barth insists that ethical transformation is fundamental to atonement, even if articulating how all elements seamlessly interlock remains elusive. He affirms that "Sanctification cannot then be separated from justification."[98]

Indeed, NT exhortations to conformity to Christ are no optional enhancement to justification but are, rather, integral to the reality itself.[99] The ethical is both an authentic overflow from grateful hearts reconciled and also a gift of the reconciling Spirit.[100] So, good works are not "man's contribution to his reconciliation with God."[101] Barth allows for no space between the believer who works and the God who is behind all good. But, in any case, in salvation, human transformation is essential and ontological. To decouple PSA from ontological transformation is to decouple soteriology from justice. (In tactile experience, of course, our "redeemed" lives invariably fall short of the justice, the glory, the transformation that the atonement announces. I respond very briefly to this dilemma in the last chapter.)

### *Justice and Resurrection*

Discussions of PSA at times fail to adequately integrate resurrection into the discussion.[102] Theologizing the Passion without reference to the resurrection, and indeed ascension, truncates salvation's trajectory.[103] Leaving the story "half told" has damaging implications for our understanding of God's justice – whether in terms of his justice towards Christ or of his justice towards humanity (our current purview).

In Barth's terms, "What took place on the cross of Golgotha is the last word of an old history and the first word of a new. God was always the One whose condescension showed itself to be unlimited in the suffering and death of the man Jesus. He is the same God who was truly gracious to Israel in the hiddenness of His love in the form of His righteous wrath."[104] Jesus stands at the center of a very particular story, a *covenantal and Israelite* story – one whose mysterious ramifications are cosmic and universal – happening in Jerusalem so as to enfold also Greece and Rome.[105]

The Passion is indeed central to the contours of atonement, but this story of God's engagement with humanity does not terminate on Good Friday. The narrative must not terminate prematurely; it necessarily runs through to the resurrection and beyond, as Barth recognizes.

> To sum up, the resurrection of Jesus Christ is the great verdict of God, the fulfilment and proclamation of God's decision concerning the event of the cross. It is its acceptance as the act of the Son of God appointed our Representative, an act which fulfilled the divine wrath but did so in the service of the divine grace. It is its acceptance as the act of His obedience which judges the world, but judges it with the aim of saving it.[106]

God's "No" to our sin (localized on the Roman gallows) and his "Yes" to our reconciliation and rectification is vindicated – I would add, even accomplished – in the resurrection of the Messiah (cf. Rom. 4:25).[107] Reverberating through time and space, the resurrection underscores the goodness, the justice, and the vindication of God in the entirety of the Christ event.

The resurrection of the Lord is bound up with the fact of the Son's being very God of very God. His life is indestructible (Heb. 7:16). It is convergent with God's commitment to undo the damage that death wrought at the beginning (cf. Gen. 2:17; 3:19, 22-24; 12:1-3; Rom. 5:12-21; 8:9-11; 1 Cor. 15:12-28; Gal. 3:7-14). The resurrection underscores God's fidelity to his life-giving purposes in the original project of creation (cf. Gen. 1:28; Isa. 65:17-25; 66:22-23). The revelation of God to us in Christ is finally a rescue in which God acts objectively in fidelity to himself, to his law and covenant, and to us.[108] The resurrection of

Jesus – and believers with him – caps a storied symmetry and is the climactic enactment of the OT trope of covenant fidelity or חֶסֶד. It is a proleptic undoing of the Fall's depredations – not simply a fortuitous turn of events – but the tangible demonstration of God's justice (δικαιοσύνη/κρίσις) and fidelity (πίστις) to the original blessing intended in creation.

God's triumph over hell and death in the resurrection extends outward into the world. Intriguingly, J. Ralston commends resurrection, as opposed to the cross, as a potentially generative locus for engagement with Muslims, framing the resurrection as the engine for redemptive ethical action in the world.[109] According to Ralston, "The resurrection both vindicates the before of Jesus's ministry and promises ahead to the future consummation of all creation through the judge Jesus. Prioritizing the resurrection as central to salvation resists the valorization of suffering that Muslims rightly challenge."[110]

The ethic of the cross infuses the Christian life *en route* to the new creation – not a valorization of suffering and death, but rather a harbinger of their overthrow proleptically enacted in the resurrection.[111] The believer is directed along Christ's trail of travail to triumph; *through much tribulation the Kingdom is entered* (Acts 14:22; Rom. 8:29; Phil. 3:10; 1 Pet. 4:12).[112] In this way, justice rolls on.

The underlying logic of PSA is not discontinuous with the resurrection as an event underscoring and vindicating that which went before. It is not so clear, however, that the logic of PSA as such necessarily implies resurrection as the fulcrum of salvation. If one shifts horizons to a larger framework of redemption, the resurrection surfaces as the climactic development. Indeed, Barth's drawing notions of covenant, the chosen people, and the wider Gentile world into his exposition of resurrection points in this direction. PSA, it seems, is best positioned within the broader biblical mosaic of creation, redemption, and renewal, rather than taken as atonement's sufficient summation.

## Excursus: Christ Alone?

I shall soon pivot to questions of how God's justice is revealed in and for his Messiah within schemes of substitutionary atonement. But this evokes an intramural discussion of some oblique relevance, a debate associated with "Rahner's rule", which is the degree to which the economic Trinity is comprehensively revelatory of the immanent Trinity. This question is closely associated with matters of Christology and soteriology. To what degree is the action of God in Christ *for us* all we may know, all we need to know, all there is to know about the being of God himself?

One's understanding of *God for us* reveals a great deal about one's God construct in itself. It is, for example, little wonder that the implications of God revealed in Christ crucified are a fault line of contestation for Muslims; the way Christians situate Jesus concerns Muslims, not simply because of what it implies about their view of the Messiah, but also their view of God. Barth is of course well known for his Christocentrism, at times seeming to indicate that God is fully manifest in the revelation of the Son of Man *without remainder*. I want to offer here a few observations on this disputed matter of "Christoexclusivism". This detour seems appropriate to the concerns of this book given that: i) Islam is directed towards the elevation and assertion of the unique and sovereign *oneness* of Allah above all else (*tawhid*); and ii) Muslims see the "pagan" elevation of Jesus's status, the "idolatrous absurdity" of the incarnation, and the offense of salvation by the cross as severe denigrations of this exclusive worship of the One. We saw above, for example, al-Faruqi vigorously protesting the Christian subordination of the divine identity to atonement in Christ, making God-in-himself contingent upon human redemption. This, as it happens, is also a live issue between Christian theologians.

God is climactically, uniquely, and savingly revealed to us in Jesus Christ (Jn. 1:1-4, 14-18; Ac. 4:12; Col. 1:15-20). The being and nature of God is expressed to us in the Logos enfleshed. Divine ontology must necessarily be consonant with that which we know of God in the economy of salvation, and that knowledge may be relied on because God is faithful and true (Num. 23:19; Ps. 102:27; Mt. 24:35; Jn. 17:21-26; Rev. 19:11). The Son is indeed the one who ushers us into the eternal life of the Trinity.

But to speak thus does not reduce the reality of God to all that may be apprehended in the story of Jesus our savior. God certainly is "for us", but that fact does not limit the being of God to that which *we* can apprehend in the Messiah. Nor does it cosmically situate God's purposes and worth as subsidiary to ours. The eternal, uncreated One, who alone simply *is*, is the center; the "economy" of the God-and-humanity story does not exhaust the reality that is God.

Even as I modestly query Barth's nascent Christoexclusivism, I will also invoke his thought. In a fascinating passage, Barth speaks to the question of God's infinite excess, his transcendence. He insists that the mystery of incarnation not only does not contradict God's sovereign, free transcendence, but is an expression thereof. He warns that we must discern the infinite power and goodness of God from the paradox of what he has in fact done in Christ and measure his greatness by it. In fact, to construct God's greatness "from the ground up" – that is, by taking God simply to be the contradiction of all things human and creaturely – is to occlude the astounding truth about himself manifest in Christ. Such a move would be, he says, "pagan.".[113] Moreover, I would further insist that the revelation about God in the OT *and* in Christ both press upon us the realization that with God there is always "more" (cf. 1 Ki. 8:12; Isa. 55:8-9; Mt. 24:35; Jn. 17:5; 1 Tim. 6:16). The trajectory of the incarnation points truly to God, but it also self-consciously gestures beyond the borders of our intellectual capacity to a God who is more than is written on the surface of salvation's story.

An understanding of God constructed by way of rigorous tunnel vision on the economy alone can engender problems. There is some risk here with respect to Barth; might a Christocentrism become a Christomonism? The difficulties are further amplified in a theology such as Jürgen Moltmann's, when everything there is to know about God is apparently read *exclusively* from the "ground up", from the cross, resulting in a hyperbolic dereliction motif and even a potential pathology internal to the suffering God himself.[114] To insist on the ultimacy of Christ for our salvation and knowledge of God does not require that all truth about God is *limited* to the story of Jesus of Nazareth. Indeed, the extended witness of Scripture would suggest that this is not the case.

Wilcoxen helpfully unpacks Sonderegger on God's constitutive ontological humility – a divine reality conceptually prior to his "decision" to be elect in Christ Jesus (Barth's rhetoric notwithstanding). Thus, God *is* properly known in the economy of salvation without reducing the God who is to a mere replication of that knowledge:

> Yet by referring to an eternal moral disposition rather than a voluntary act of decision, Sonderegger affirms [the ontological authenticity of God's eternal condescension] without the possible entailment that God somehow constitutes his own being through his work *ad extra*. No, she says, God's work *ad extra* flows as a contingent necessity from the absolute necessity of his morally perfect being … Because [God's] being is conceived of as intrinsically intentional – morally formed through and through – this allows her to close the gap between the immanent and economic life of God, but without collapsing the former into the latter.[115]

Christ is the saving means of our knowing, but the One God is God apart from our knowledge of him in Christ.[116] Jesus is the climax of the metanarrative, but that truth does not render the preponderant and the preceding aspects of the story superfluous. (My instinct here to correct Christomonist tendencies, while hardly Islamic, may express certain harmonics with many Muslim thinkers' commitment to God's transcendence and independence from the creaturely.) Christo- and cruci-exclusivism – reading (only) backwards from the cross to the nature of God – threaten distortions in basic theology and even the possibilities for redemption. Yes, Christ is God in solidarity with humanity. But, ironically, a misguided construal of, or a misguided limitation on, this God has damaging implications for his capacity to save; it leads counterproductively to a loss of hope, vision, and transformation.[117]

Below I further engage Barth's emphasis on the *exhaustiveness* of the incarnation as *the* indicator of the very identity of God, an emphasis that threatens to inject contingency into the Creator's eternal being.[118] Admittedly, Barth has so much to say that one also finds passages that *counteract* the very threat he introduces.[119] In any case, with respect to either Christomonism or an extreme limitation of all "Godness" to that which is apprehended in the economy, Sonderegger rightly warns us that we must not identify

> the Immanence with the economy in such a way that the historical, formal elements of Holy Scripture become imported into the High Mystery of God's inner Life. That is Barth's path in *Church Dogmatics*, IV.1, and he is clear-eyed about the hazards and walks bravely toward them. But they are costs too high for a proper metaphysical doctrine of the Holy Trinity: the Lofty Inwardness of Almighty God is become too contingent, mutable, particular, and individual for a Unique, Formless, Necessary, and Tri-Personal God who is Utterly, Spiritually One. It cannot be, then, that Isaiah 53 becomes a dogmatically realist text by identifying the inner Life and Relations of Almighty God with oppression and rejection, with obedience and sin-bearing. The Pre-existence of the Son, His proper Eternity, cannot mean this. But it is equally clear that the dogma of the Most Holy Trinity will not be properly set forth by prizing it free of such texts, placing it wholly and unrestrainedly in the logician's classroom, and resolving technical problems in

technical vocabulary through puzzle cases, counterexamples, and exotic thought experiments.[120]

## Justice "from Above": Atonement and Trinity

### *Trinity Enables Redemption*

We turn now to justice from above: how it is that God is loving and, particularly, *just* within his own nature and with respect to his innocent Son, "sent" for us in atonement. Where is God's justice if the Son bears the wrath of the Father? Multiple doctrinal concerns converge, e.g. the unity of perfections, the Persons, processions, and inseparable action of the Trinity, and so on.

Sonderegger asserts that the nature of God, his incendiary holiness, his unaccountable otherness, the unified diversity of his attributes, his love and wrath – all confront us in Christ with

> a great breadth of acts, all compatible with Humility: this holy Lord can be in turns majestic and confrontational, unexpected and severe, quiet and altogether ordinary, seemingly invisible and of no account, and in all these the omnipotent Lord. *The Power of the Lord is strongly metaphysical in character.* To be sure, Omnipotence cannot be in opposition to Goodness; the Divine Nature is not self-contradictory. But Divine Power is the surpassing, gloriously effective Act and Fullness of Divine Reality.[121]

This transcendent diversity in a superheated unity necessitates a robust Trinitarianism. Prerequisite to a plausible substitutionary atonement is the understanding that in the Passion we encounter God. Unfortunately, not all delineations of PSA have been cogent on this point. Barth's Christocentric Trinitarianism leaves nothing to chance in declaring that at the cross, "God has been hard upon *himself* [… displaying a] sternness of God against *himself.*"[122]

> He is amongst us in humility, our God, God for us, as that which he is in himself, in the most inward depth of his Godhead … In the condescension in which he gives himself to us in Jesus Christ, he exists and speaks and acts as the One he was from all eternity and will be to all eternity. *The truth and actuality of our atonement depends on this being the case.*[123]

The Lord God revealed in the Nazarene is this fierce and humble God – as he is before creation, in creating, and in incarnation. But recall our cautions about Christoexclusivism. We need God incarnate, but God does not need to be incarnate to be God. He is this fierce and humble Trinity preceding all.[124] In the Messiah of our salvation, this God – hidden and resplendent – is revealed as the *One* actively loving us (Rom. 5:8).[125]

### *Trinitarian Unity Disciplines PSA: No Vengeance of Father on Son*

The articulation of the Trinity – monotheism with distinction – is something of a verbal tightwire act. Johnson describes the task as the taking together of "(1) the doctrine of perichoresis and (2) the doctrine of appropriations combined with the rule *opera trinitatis ad extra sunt indivisa.*"[126] On this diverse, unified action of God is suspended the salvation of humanity. In Barth's language this three-in-one "God is he who in this [Christ] event is subject, predicate and object; the revealer, the act of revelation, the revealed; Father, Son and Holy Spirit."[127]

The economy of salvation is expressed in congruence with God's justice and all his virtues. And, as Hastings reminds us, God's Trinitarian being enacts redemption as a matter of mind-independent reality:

> [A]part from the irreducible differentiated identity and integrity and responsiveness of the divine persons, the atonement is a nonsense, for though it is clearly not an interaction between two separate *individuals*, it does involve *persons* conveyed as such in the economy and the gospel record, and it does involve one person, in particular, who, unlike the other two divine persons, has taken on human flesh to stand in the place of humanity before his God.[128]

Only the triune God can bear the "cost" of being "righteous without annihilating us".[129] Indeed, "the Trinity is 'the ever-present, inner presupposition of the doctrine of the cross'."[130]

Balancing the holistic action of God differently appropriated to the Persons is crucial to a substitutionary intervention that is just, loving, and efficacious. Barth is virtually strident in decrying a Father vs Son atonement structure. No, the entire drama is God's own action – his heart, his initiative, his pain-bearing.[131]

> Thus we do not have [in the cross] – as in the travesty in which this supreme insight and truth of the Christian faith is so often distorted – a raging indignation of God, which is ridiculous or irritating in its senselessness, against an innocent man whose patient suffering changes the temper of God, inducing in him an indulgent sparing of all other men … But it is God's own heart which … suffers what the creature ought to suffer.[132]

The confluence of tangible distinction ("'appropriation' of roles") and irreducible oneness ("indivisibility of the works") exerts productive pressure on our understanding of the Father and Son at the cross.[133] In the Passion we meet God in action, the God of interpenetrating unity, not of three entities struggling to combine their wills. It is vital to insist on the stability of God's character (he is not changed) and his undiminished justice (the cross is not the axis of "cosmic child abuse"). The appropriation of roles in the atonement is regulated by the indivisible oneness of the only God.[134] Hear Vidu:

> [*T*]*he Father does not punish the Son as a subject would punish an object.* One cannot, in other words, distinguish sharply between the action of the Father and the action of the Son. If the *omnia opera Trinitatis ad extra sunt indivisa*, to say that the Father punishes the Son – without careful qualification – is a gross distortion of the idea of substitution … "The recognition that it is God the Son, that is to say quite simply God, who suffers and dies on the cross, settles the question finally. This is God himself bearing the consequences of sin, not the abuse of some cosmic child."[135]

Bruce Marshall holds that, for all the contemporary fascination with Trinity, much atonement theorization has not in fact allowed the doctrine to inform its reading of the divine economy. Rather, concepts extracted from the Passion narratives, as read according to prevalent intuitions of our day, have been projected upward and outward onto the canvas of the eternal being of the Trinity.[136] This move, unfettered by classical commitments and sometimes of questionable logical discipline, has not been to the advantage of either soteriology or theology proper. The doctrine of inseparable actions disallows any picture in which the cross is a locus of God's war against himself. The Trinity is not a cosmic instantiation of multiple personality disorder. Also impossible, as Anselm saw, is the passivity of Jesus in salvation. Thus, it is better to speak of Christ's bearing humanity's penalty than to speak of the Father punishing the Son.[137] Yes, divine wrath (against the deepest ills) is exposed on the cross of Christ. But language of indirection better conveys that in the cross we see *God, the One,* poured out for us, not simply Jesus getting in harm's way. "Hear, Oh Israel ..."

### *Inseparable Action: Love, Wrath, and Causality*

Mysteriously God interacts with creation in time (see below), but cause and effect relations are not immanent within God himself. The Persons in God do not act upon one another in causal sequence. Father, Son, and Spirit have roles properly associated with each in the economy of salvation. But they act together, always and everywhere. One does not manipulate a response from the other.[138] Vidu, again:

> Certain [penal substitution] proponents ... often make the cross a component of a sequential and causal structure. There, the punishment of Christ plays a part in a mechanism of exchange. God is said to dispense grace *in response* to the work of Christ. The difficulty from the standpoint of inseparable operations is that it orders divine economic operations as causal to one another and therefore obscures their unity of intention and execution in the divine counsel ... "The Father's surrendering Jesus over to death" and "Jesus' being obedient unto the cross" are not *causal conditions* of "God's reconciling the world to himself".[139]

In the Passion, God is not dependent on a historical sequence, external to himself, to enable him to love and reconcile and heal.[140] That sequence *is* God loving, reconciling, healing.[141] The temporal mechanics of the history of salvation are significant factors in the human experience of grace. But they are not signposts to be read backwards into the divine essence.

Conceived rightly, atonement is an *entirety* birthed from the one and only God with no distortion of the divine attributes. Love and righteous wrath meet at the cross, but not as an internal fissure in God. The Father is not wrath while the Son is love (Jn. 3:16; Rom. 5:8). At every stage of salvation, God is present in wholeness. Naturally, PSA "does not deny the reality of divine wrath ... [But it does say] that in Christ it is not the last word. God is *pro nobis*, for us, in Christ".[142]

## Sin in Barth's Atonement Thought

The contested points that concern us here (justice, sin, and honor) naturally interlock and inform one another, although I hope that a separated, serial focus will aid clarity. Let us now rotate our gaze to the question of sin, that from which humanity must be delivered. True to form, in his exposition of humanity under sin, Barth's accent falls not on the generic "world" or on Adam, but on Jesus Christ. He would have us begin with Jesus as exemplifying humanity under grace and then consider sin as the inverse.[143] For Barth, to understand humanity in sin one should begin with the upright *Anthropos*, Jesus. First understand the Image of God, whole and healthy, and then inquire as to how it has been marred.[144]

> As in relation to his Godhead, so also in relation to his manhood, we must not allow any necessary idea of the human situation and its need to intervene. What his manhood is, and therefore true manhood, we cannot read into him from elsewhere, but must be told by him. But then we find that it is a matter of the manhood of the eternal Son of God … In virtue of the fact that he is one with God he is free man. He is a creature, but superior to his creatureliness. He is bound by sin, but quite free in relation to it because he is not bound to commit it. He is mortal, and has actually died as we must all die. But in dying he is superior to death, and at once and altogether rescued from it, so that (even as a man like us) He is triumphant and finally alive.[145]

For Barth, the incarnation is a free expression of the goodness of God's nature. Barth here exceeds, without contradicting, Anselm's quasi-negative construal of incarnation as precondition to God's putting forgiveness into effect.[146] To rightly orient perspectives on aspirational humanity and humanity in metaphysical bondage, Barth begins with the man from Nazareth.

Beholding the Man, we confirm the plight of our condition in the light of his radiance. Concomitantly, it is also in Christ's suffering and degradation that a mirror is held before us, exposing our condition as sinners, "inescapably accused and irrevocably condemned".[147] The Messiah suspended on the grisly gibbet under the weight of sin – there we hear the "verdict [… as to] what God knows about us, and therefore how it really is with us".[148]

Even in terms of humanity "in Adam" (Rom. 5), swamped by "original sin", Barth's starting point is Christ, the Last Adam. He is the exemplar of (our) redemption via (his) obedience, the gift that outstrips the bondage and loss we all share "in Adam". It is in turning towards the true Man, in understanding what makes for our restoration, that the thing that ails us – our life in sin – is put into stark relief.[149]

The goodness of Christ and the humiliation of Christ are clarifying of and calibrated to the desperation of humanity in sin. Sin for Barth, as for Anselm, is a deadly serious matter, that requires a deadly serious response. The reason God's response to the plight of evil is so apparently "extreme", again as in Anselm, is not God's personal vulnerability or precious touchiness, but that he is unwilling to leave humanity untended, spiraling inevitably to its miserable fate:

> [In humanity's] sin there obviously takes place a menacing of the whole work of God, the whole world as created by Him, a menacing which in its impotence is quite intolerable to God Himself. It is now clear that the contradiction and opposition of man, his godlessness and inhumanity, his sin against himself, are not a little absurdity but one which is incommensurably great, provoking God Himself to direct action … [The absurdity of sin] cannot encroach upon Him … because He is the high and majestic God even in His mercy; but all the same He takes it to heart. He does not will to be God, high and majestic, without us who have fallen victim to it … What is made clear in the incarnation of the Word of God and the offering up to death of the Son of God is that evil is not an element in the orderly course of the world, but an element, indeed *the* element, which absolutely threatens

> and obscures it – the sowing of the enemy in the good field, the invasion of chaos, the nihilist revolution which can result only in the annihilation of all creatures.[150]

"Sin ... consists of 'the three moments of evil, rebelling against God, enmity with one's neighbor and sin against oneself' (*CD* IV/1, 398)."[151] Sin's three-pronged trajectory is dissected at some length by Barth under the tripartite rubric of "Sin as Pride, Sloth and Falsehood".[152] Of course, this architecture is not the only way into the topic because sin is polyvalent, the inverse of the unified diversity of the beauty of Christ – a sort of negative imaging of the unity of the divine perfections.[153] Of course, the classic articulation of the essence of sin in the Western tradition is as *pride*.[154] The depth of humiliation exposed in the Passion story acts as a foil to the false self-exaltation of humanity – a prideful aggrandizement that could only be reversed and rectified by the commensurate extreme of the *Via Dolorosa*. The cross is a placard of the unvarnished human condition.[155] (This is not the place for a dedicated examination of Barth's three movements of sin, but in light of my comparative agenda, I comment further on sloth below.)

### *Original Sin, Holy Fear, and Hope*

Possibly there is no more contested domain of hamartiology – interfaith and intrafaith – than the idea of "original sin". For Barth there is no whole and salubrious condition of humanity "in nature" apart from our restoration, reconciliation, and elevation with Christ. According to Barth there is no happy outcome possible by way of natural law or natural theology. There is no natural innocence, no *fitra*, to fall back on. Humans are "originally" sinful, wholly dependent on an ontological intervention by God:

> There is, therefore, no natural religion, no natural theology, no natural law. In all these concepts "natural" means apart from Jesus Christ, apart from the Son of God ... who in his unity with Jesus of Nazareth has also human essence. The antithesis to this "natural" is ... that of human nature once for all and definitively exalted in Jesus Christ, once for all and definitively placed at the side of the Father and in fellowship with him. Without this ... even the true God would be to us a hidden God, and therefore in practice no God at all.[156]

Barth, then, is emphatic about the inescapable reality of humanity under sin, that is "original sin". However, as indelible and universal as the imprint of original sin may be in Barth's theology, he does not have in mind notions such as transmitted guilt or inherited blame. He is more concerned about sin's universal reality and the reality of human agency than he is in the "history" of its beginnings.[157] John Webster tells us:

> Barth is little interested in original sin because alongside his concern to display sin's abolition in Christ, he is also concerned to offer a description of sin as a human reality ... Barth's anthropology betrays a deep-seated instinct to hold together agency, responsibility, and guilt, and to refuse all forms of fatalism in which sin is viewed as anything other than what we both will and do.[158]

For Barth, original sin is a matter of universal fact, of paradigm, of generic reality; it is not a matter of chronological inheritance.[159] "Adam is not a fate which God has suspended over us. Adam is the truth concerning us as it is known to God and told to us. The relationship between him and us, and us and him, is not ... one which can be explained in terms of a transmission between him and us."[160] Barth does insist that sin is an experience of negative, universal solidarity.[161]

In Barth's thought, Adam appears more as an illustration of a human reality, not a simple cause of it. He insists that:

> No one has to be Adam. We are so freely and on our own responsibility. Although the guilt of Adam is like ours, it is just as little our excuse as our guilt is his. We and he are reached by the same Word and judgment of God in the same direct way. The only difference is that what we all are and do he was and did at the very gateway of history.[162]

There is an intuitive plausibility to Barth's portrayal of sin, but with limited attention devoted to etiology.[163]

Sin persists as a basic reality, reenacted from Adam onward. We continually arrogate judgment to ourselves, usurping the Creator's role as Judge, ultimately to our own despair.[164] This usurpation is killing us. But, in Christ, the "Judge judged in our stead", we are deposed as the risen Lord assumes authority. This eventuates in the lifting of our anxiety and despair, our liberation.[165] Thus the human subject comes "in fear before the Judge on whose good and redemptive will I can already count ... in whose hands I can know that my own case and that of others is at least safe. In a fear, therefore, which at bottom is hope ... And whatever the decision may be, I have reason to look forward to its disclosure with terror, but with a terror-stricken joy."[166]

To reiterate, implicitly undergirding "forensic" atonement is a transcendent metaphysic and a narrative theology. Barth's "courtroom" is a scene within a dramatic, martial plot – *Christus Victor*:

> [I]n the battle against sin ... the passion of the Son of God who became man for us ... is the radical divine action which attacks and destroys at its very root the primary evil in the world; the activity of the second Adam who took the place of the first, who reversed and overthrew the activity of the first in this place, and in so doing brought in a new man, founded a new world and inaugurated a new eon.[167]

In our reconciling, sin is undone, and a new world rises.

John Webster provides helpful insights on Barth's construal of sin as "nothingness" (a privation). This characterization is not a dodge of human responsibility, not a denial of sin as "positive evil".[168] In its negative reality (privation) *is* a deplorable revolt. But there are more hopeful considerations attending on sin as "negative" reality – sin as a failure to hold on to God's covenant, his goodness towards us. The consequences and loss incurred are severe, but they are always subject to being undone by the covenant-keeping Redeemer; sin is antithetical to God, has no part with him, and thus cannot finally vanquish.[169] Even in Barth's devastating depiction of the sorry reality of our world, original sin is not synonymous with the complete annihilation of all creational goods.[170] Even in the desperation of the human condition, the redeemable remains.

### *The Enormity of Sloth*

> [Sin] is a matter of man's rebellion against God, of the invasion of God's good creation by chaos. God himself – and first of all – takes it in all seriousness. He takes it so seriously that he encounters it in his own person. It grieves him for our sake, his creatures and covenant partners. It offends his glory that in committing it we turn against him and therefore have to be without him.[171]

Barth paints the downward trajectory of universal sin and its evanescent reversal in Christ with persuasively bold strokes and hues. The evidence of history writ large suggests that the human condition "really is that bad". But, are there not some virtuous and exemplary individuals and yet others who are, at the least, "not all that bad"? What about our average peccadillos, sin on the level of the petty, the absurd, the banal? Sin may be universal, but is its "badness" *always* so terribly bad? Might not Barth's presentation of sin (let alone that in other iterations of PSA) be overblown? Is it in proportion? What about sin as mere sloth – is it such a cataclysm that so drastic a remedy as the cross is required? The objections of our Muslim critics echo here.

Barth is hardly apologetic in the face of such pleas for "moderation" or remonstrances against "overwrought" profiles of sin. He is straightforwardly critical of accounts that are more "moderate" in their assessments, taking sin on a sliding scale, as simply an aspect of created existence, something to be measured against natural law or theology. No, for Barth, this rationalizing approach will not do. Biblical revelation in Christ exposes the true depth of our lostness without regard to our feelings or rationalizations.[172] Here Barth is with Anselm: *Quanti ponderis sit peccatum* (how great a weight is sin).[173]

Sin is not measured by variegated human conscience or intellectualized theorization. Sin is measured by the yawning gap that opens up when we encounter God in Christ. "But the Word made flesh, the grace of God encountering man, his salvation, the Gospel, is Jesus Christ. He and his existence as the Son of God and Son of Man are the light in which man as the man of sin is made known to himself, in which he must see and confess himself as such."[174] The point is not how empirically bad any one person's sinfulness is in comparison to another. No, for Barth, the depth of our alienation from God is a scarring cosmic reality – whatever the variations in texture from person to person. The metric is Jesus, "abandoned" at the cross in shame and devastation – this is the measure of humanity lost in sin, even sin that appears trivial – sin as a slothful, shrugging decision to "go my own way".[175]

In confrontation with the Son of Man the subversive deadliness of sin as sloth is revealed. One need not be a grotesquely voracious violator to stand in painful, unpayable deficit before God (not to mention one's fellow creatures). Barth deconstructs the "smallness" of our infractions against God's good design; measured against God's rightness, and given sin's perpetration of malformation in creation, no reprobation qualifies as "small".[176] Petty acts denying God our full love and allegiance reverberate out into the universe – into our treatment of one another – as anything but small and harmless.[177] Once again this is Anselm's terrain, the domain of the "single, sinful glance".

Here, Barth is with Anselm, but he aims to surpass Anselm's "negative inferences" and to find that the weight of human guilt is to be measured *primarily* by reference to the overwhelming contrast of God's goodness, "his forgiveness in sheer mercy".[178] Sloth, our mediocrity, our selfish smallness, our triviality – these are sin. And not in the abstract, not in horizontal comparison, but before our good, loving, just Lord.[179] Sin matters. And not because God arbitrarily contrives burdens and wantonly manufactures moral obstacle courses for humanity. The standards we have violated, even in our "merely" slothful state, are simply authentic givens of existence, structures proceeding from the one made known in Christ, him who is the Good, the True, the Beautiful.

> [The cross] brings home to us how great is the absurdity of sin, and how serious it is. God Himself is affected and disturbed and harmed by it. His own cause, His purpose for man and the world, is disrupted and arrested; His own glory is called in question. He Himself finds Himself assaulted by it in His being as God, and He hazards no less than His being as God to encounter it.[180]

## Divine Honor I: God in Salvation History

I would hazard the generalization that language of honor is more at home in premodern Christian and Islamic contexts than in modern Western theology, but it does have its place in Barth's atonement thought. To start with, it seems reasonable to link the category of honor with Barth's robust and constant affirmation of God's freedom and sovereignty, that his acts are unconstrained and unobligated. However, atonement theology immediately brings conundrums to the surface. Consider, for example, the cross as "necessity", the "shameful" dimensions of incarnation and Passion, the mystery and irrationality of cruciform salvation – all these pressurize thinking about God's honor, his authority, and his freedom.

Barth is deservedly known for his repeated invocation of God's *utter freedom*. On the face of it, language of divine freedom sounds axiomatic and non-controversial. But in keeping the story of Jesus front and center, challenges emerge. In locating God's honor with Christ in his earthy humiliation, the shock and subversion of the story of redemption soon brings us to a crossroads. Can it be that in Christ crucified *God is great* (الله اكبر)?

I previously suggested that the Islamic religious aesthetic inclines to the linear, the austere and lucid, towards predictability and manifest success, especially in the logics of salvation. Truth triumphs and coincides with publicly evident victory. We have already heard disaffection with mystery, antinomy, and paradox from thinkers such as Akhtar, al-Faruqi, Rida, or Tabatabai. Conversely, without abandoning reason, Christian soteriology operates in that very terrain: mystery, complexity, and paradox. This is no late development. The "mystery of the faith" (cf. 1 Tim. 3:16) is deeply rooted in scriptural revelation. The "word of the cross" unleashed its power in inverse and subversive ways, beginning not with the great but with the lowly (1 Cor. 1:18, 20-29). The way of the cross speaks to an "upside-down" Kingdom ethic. The saving Messiah beckoned the last, the least, the lost to suffer, to stoop, to serve (Mk 10:45; Mt. 16:24-25; 19:30; 20:16, 26-27). In dying is life, in loss is gain, in condescension is elevation (cf. Phil. 2:6-11; Augustine, *Confessions* 1:4). In Christ's Passion, as with his rising and ruling, God's glory and greatness are expressed. Mystery attends the revelation of God's honor and glory (cf. Jn. 12:28-33).

*God's Freedom and the "Necessity" of the Cross*

For some, that God should resort to the cross presents an insurmountable problem for his freedom and honor. The alleged contradictions are not limited to the diminishments entailed in incarnation or the apparent failure of love or justice in the Son under wrath. Quite simply, if the cross is "required", God's honor – his untrammeled freedom – appears to be threatened. Barth himself invokes these tensions: he presents God as necessarily "true to himself" and thus liable to visit on humanity "that which they deserve", namely "the abyss". But if God were to follow through with such a judgment, how would his self-consistency in terms of his faithfulness, love, and mercy be preserved? Barth construes this as a "dilemma" whose solution "lies in [God's own] interposition for us at Golgotha".[181]

We have already encountered the assessment that the dynamic of "dilemma and solution" is in the nature of the case sufficient evidence of the theological bankruptcy of substitutionary atonement. "A free deity is not subject to dilemmas." Can any response be offered? For starters, Barth's talk of "dilemma" is partly rhetorical flourish. At the least, he must be seen as adopting the perspective of *humanity's* problem and how it is solved – the intended point never was that God himself was befuddled by a bind. Any "necessities" that inform the God–humanity–sin nexus are congruent with God himself. Any contradictions are apparent only from the side of human experience. The "requirements" of goodness, justice, mercy, retribution, honor, and so on are not *placed upon* God but are non-contradicting aspects *of* God as he is experienced in his created realm.

Indeed, if Barth consistently adverts to any theme with respect to God's own being, it is hardly his grappling with a dilemma; it is his radically free "decision" in electing incarnation and salvation in Christ.[182] Certainly, theological problems manifest (for any monotheist) when one attempts to excavate down to the origin of God's acts. Some would look to God's character, his perfections, or his love as ground zero for all that follows. Others resort to volition – God's radically free will – for the starting point. Burrell puts it that God's will to create is free in that it stems from his love, not in that it is "arbitrary".[183] Barth might well agree. From any angle of approach, though, we must insist that in a properly grounded atonement (even PSA), there is no question of a "law over God". As Barth puts it:

> The fact that God acts as he does in the justification of man proves conclusively that he could not act in this way just as well as any other but that what we have here is not whim and caprice but right, the supreme right of all. Not, of course, that God is determined and bound and limited by some law which is different from himself and therefore is forced to act in this way. God does not stand under any alien law, any general truth and possibility and presupposition embracing and conditioning and limiting both himself and the world and man.[184]

Barth evocatively puts it that atonement is "an event in the life of God".[185] At times he seems to virtually reduce God's identity to his "free decision" to be incarnate in Christ. Trenchant issues arise. There is a threat of a sort of "sting in the tail" here. If God has "freely" chosen to define himself *wholly* by the narrative events of redemption, then has he in reality made himself contingent? This could call into doubt his undefeatable capacity to save. Ironically, unintentionally, Barth could be placing divine freedom under threat. To my mind, Vanhoozer's framing is to be preferred: "As to the temporal experiences of the human Jesus, they do not constitute but corroborate his identity (i.e. they are signs). The history of Jesus neither inaugurates nor interrupts the Son's personal identity but rather graphically illustrates and enacts it."[186] Vidu also is helpful, even if somewhat tentative in his judgment with respect to Barth. He says, "If… God chooses to be this particular God in relation to salvific actions, it follows that the identity of God is constituted by contingent realities which need not have occurred (creation, the fall, redemption, etc.)."[187] I take this as a helpful caution when it comes to reading Barth on this point.

Of course, the question of the cross's necessity goes to questions not only of any "external" law or questions of God's nature, but also to the nature of sin. Put in vernacular terms, one might ask, "Why must God take sin so seriously or deal with it in this way?" The questions are understandable. But it is possible that the appropriate starting point is not the questions of why God views sin thus, but rather the need to grapple with *the fact* of his having revealed to us that he does. In any case, for both Barth and Anselm, the cross is "necessary", but not for reasons external to God. Atonement is not arbitrary. It is seamlessly, if painfully, meaningful. On the other hand, for both, salvation is the free act of God, whose lordly freedom is never under threat. Though the theological grammar differs, Anselm would seem to agree with Barth that Christians are beneficiaries of unmerited inclusion in Christ, a soteriological initiative sourced in the divine counsel.[188] God's honor is not in question.

### *God's Honor and the Strangeness of Salvation's Story*

Christian salvation history does pose a challenge to common sense notions of divine honor. The presenting stumbling block is, of course, the humiliation, pain, and indignity of the Passion itself. Moreover, we have heard remonstrances against the implausibility of God nursing a lengthy historical process towards resolution, grappling with his own internal dissonance, in order to save. Without ceding the field, we can acknowledge a certain strangeness to the Gospel storyline. The Author of all submits to untold wrongs for the sake of his violent, blind, and recalcitrant creatures. The story of the Father's grace is a strange and challenging one. Indeed, the gospels' recitations of cataclysmic manifestations around the Passion seem to indicate the cosmos's own recoil at the numinous "otherness" of it all. Hear Barth:

> [Consider] the transformation of the accuser into the accused and the judge into the judged, the naming and handling of the Holy God as one who is godless. But it could not be prevented. It had to take place, and it did in fact take place. Not by the reign of chance, nor in consequence of a human nexus of guilt and destiny … In what happens to Jesus, the participants, both Jews and Gentiles, are described in

> the factual commentary of Acts (2:23, 4:28) as – for all the obvious and supreme guilt and reprehensibility of their action – only instruments in the hand of God, agents and executors of "the determinate counsel and foreknowledge of God". It does not excuse them – but it was necessary that Christ should "suffer these things" (Lk. 24:26). No, his God had not really forsaken him. In that strange and scandalous reversal we have a necessary fulfillment of the divine purpose which the Son accepts in fear and trembling as the will of his Father.[189] (cf. Mk 15:33; Mt. 27:51)

The story of the crucifixion (through to the ascension) is a jarring reversal, an overlap of good and evil wills, "the triumph of God being concealed under that of His adversary".[190] In the Passion, the mysterious and restorative will of God envelops and infuses a genuinely human event. Subsisting in different metaphysical levels, the history of the cross is readily susceptible to misinterpretation.[191] Indeed, a recurrent refrain in the gospels is that the Passion was strangely and unexpectedly, but precisely, the fulfillment of the prophetic word.[192] And all this is taken to be mysteriously congruent with genuine human – and demonic – agency, the will to self at work even in providentially ordered events.[193]

These narrative contours seem to pressure the goodness, the immanence, the transcendence, the justice, and *the honor* of God. Disparate communities produce disparate responses. For one, in some "progressive theology", theologians will entirely disassociate the cross from God's purposes and foreordination, a tendency noted elsewhere in this study.[194] We have also met Islamic critics (such as Rida) who construe the Passion narratives as a dishonorable pseudo-solution to the sin problem – a "solution" that God stumbled onto "late in time", as it were. There are other options besides.

We may concede the epistemic and spiritual difficulties facing us as finite readers of God's designs in history, even with the benefit of revelation. Nonetheless, to my mind, at this juncture, Barth's approach is superior to the options cited above. He productively reads with the grain of the NT witness, accepting its wonder and paradox: "The passion of Christ is not for [the gospels] a catastrophe which burst unexpectedly into his life. It is the necessary result of it. It is thus essential that it should be announced in it."[195] The story of humanity's rescue is strange, surprising, subversive – and, for all that, the more tailored to reality, the more marvelous and efficacious; the more to God's own honor.

### *The Descent of the Son: God's Honor or Shame?*

Barth does not underplay the apparent denigration of God's honor entailed in the incarnation and the Passion. The nettle must be grasped:

> It is not simply the humiliation and dishonoring of a creature, of a noble and relatively innocent man that we find here. The problem posed is not that of a theodicy: How can God will this or permit this in the world which He has created good? It is a matter of the humiliation and dishonoring of God himself, of the question which makes any question of a theodicy a complete anticlimax; the question whether in willing to let this happen to him he has not renounced and lost himself as God, whether in capitulating to the folly and wickedness of his creature he has not abdicated from his deity.[196]

But Barth's strategy is not to ameliorate the severity of Christ's condescension. It is rather to flip the script, to aggressively insist that to take pious offense at the cross is to distort the scales of "spirit and truth". Any would-be ringfencing of God's sanctity is misguided and actually catalyzes a misapprehension of God. Ironically, hyper-zeal for divine transcendence may occlude aspects of God's honor. A "no" to the God manifest in the Messiah is a move towards limiting the God who has actually been true to himself in his humiliation. Occasionally, Barth explicitly has Islam in mind:

> In his eternal counsel, and then in its execution in time, he determines to address himself to man, and to do so in such a way that he himself becomes man … And this undoubtedly means – and we must not deny the fact – that he elects and determines himself for humiliation. In so doing he does not need to become alien to himself, to change himself … In distinction from that of false gods, and especially the god of Mohammed, his Godhead embraces both height and depth, both sovereignty and humility, both lordship and service. He is the Lord over life and death. He does not become a stranger to himself when in his Son he also goes into a far country … Even – and why should we not say precisely? – in this he is God in supreme constancy, in supreme affirmation of his faithfulness.[197]

For Barth, the construct of a Lord so high and remote that descent, humility, suffering, and death are definitionally ruled out belies a problem with the would-be worshipper's governing intuitions. They have failed to allow God to be who he is, as he shows himself to be. They have not honored him, but rather foreclosed on his scope. The Passion, for all its wrenching loss and shame, does not represent a loss, diminution, or change in the essence of God or his Messiah.

> [The Passion does not] have the character of a misfortune which breaks over [Jesus] either by chance or fate, so that the initiative is wrested from him and he ceases to be the Lord. On the contrary, in his suffering and dying he is still the same as he always was, although in another form. The Passion is not an alien element in his work as a whole … And the Gospels see this because they see the whole story in the light of Easter.[198]

The cross and resurrection are a shocking and subversive sign (σημεῖον) of salvation, but it is not in contradiction to God or his Christ. The goodness, and god-ness, of God are rather confirmed.

### *The God-Man and Mystery*

For many onlookers, the rational limits of atonement doctrine speak directly to its vacuity. The antinomies, the mysterious, and the inexplicable militate against the word of the cross. In part, this is the contested terrain of theological aesthetics and the function of mystery and apophatic limits in theology. I aim to productively trace Barth's (and others') exposition of atonement, penal and otherwise, in a way that resonates and informs. But this is not intended as an "explanation" in terms of a mechanistic process.[199]

At this locus, perhaps the most fitting (!) ethos for the discussion is the classic motif of "fittingness" rather than any sort of empirical proof. The NT does not attempt to downplay the extraordinary nature of God in Christ; neither must we. The gift is *indescribable* (cf. 2 Cor. 9:15).[200] Barth asserts:

> Because it was the Son of God, because it was God himself who on Good Friday suffered for us, the destruction which took place there of the suffering and death which resulted from human disobedience to God could justly satisfy and indeed fulfil the righteousness of God. As a fulfillment of the righteousness of God it necessarily meant that in the conflict between God's faithfulness and man's unfaithfulness, the faithfulness of God himself was maintained, and therefore his honor was not violated. It was only in this way that it could also be exercised as his faithfulness to man, for how could man be really helped by a God who actually surrendered his own honor?[201]

The action of God as the incarnate sufferer is, in Barth's terms, a totalizing "no" to creation and humanity *under sin*, precisely so as to revive the cosmos, to bring about God's "yes".[202] The second Adam steps into the place of the first, "the just for the unjust (1 Pet. 3:18)", so as to launch a new eon.[203] As for Anselm, so for Barth, only the God-man will do. In this way alone is a fitting balance preserved in the universe. In this way alone is God's intervention for us effective. And in all this God's honor is not somehow barely preserved; it is magnified.

## Divine Honor II: Loving Freely and Timelessly

The recondite issues of God and his relationship to time have implications for his honor. Debate about positioning a free Creator God in relationship to time proceeds unabated.[204] I will not venture definitive pronouncements, but I do acknowledge an intuitive leaning towards a sort of divine timelessness, and that sort of presupposition will inform much of what follows. Without for a moment supposing that the intractable divides over atonement are hereby resolved, it may also be worth noting that for most traditional Islamic theologizing, the timeless eternity of God presents no conceptual stumbling block.

On this question of God and time, Barth is, as so often, generative but not indisputably consistent. For example, if, as Barth indicates, incarnation and atonement are an event in the life of God, what are the implications for God's utter freedom?[205] Can this intimate connection between the salvation of the creature and the eternal being of God be maintained without a threat to God's transcendent freedom? Is there not the danger of a sort of "backflow" making the Maker dependent on the "made"? Here and elsewhere in these ruminations, al-Faruqi's complaints about Christian redemption diluting and diminishing theology proper might be called to mind.

Barth's God is famously the "One who loves in freedom".[206] And, indeed, love is costly. The pathos of "actual atonement" elicits language replete with drama, tension, and perhaps paradox. God somehow pays an ultimate price in loving humanity, but does so freely, without obligation, and without self-diminishment. He becomes a victim without victimization. God loves, but not of need. Creation is evidence not of necessity, but only free grace.[207] His honor persists untinged, because in his being God is "the absolute freedom of love, and therefore the being of the Most High who is high and almighty and eternal and righteous and glorious … but precisely in his lowliness".[208]

So far, so good. But, within Barth's matrix, coordinating God's love in freedom with traditional convictions on God's eternity, impassibility, and immutability is not simple. Of particular interest for us is how to parse Barth's relating the suffering of the Christ to God's own being. This has implications for God's independence (or not) from being time-bound and for his invulnerability (or not) to harm or change – thus, implications for his honor. Barth's exposition is a study in tensions. To some extent he exemplifies the passionate, even anthropomorphic, modern liberationist instinct towards God in solidarity with humanity. On the other hand, his debt to divine absoluteness and aseity is likewise apparent.

So, for example, Barth will insist that God indeed feels, is affected, and "is not impassible". But he is quick to qualify that God is not passive, not subject to external influence. He is moved by compassion exclusively by his own decision – there is "no suffering in himself". He is not subject to "subsequent change". All his condescension is innate to "his very life and being as God".[209] If this is "passibilism", it is a kind yet grasping after the tradition. This is not a full "Moltmannian moment" in which the trauma of the cross seems to flow backwards into the recesses of divine ontology.

But, proceeding yet further, Barth, arguably, affirms the *Father's* suffering in time:

> It is not at all the case that God has no part in the suffering of Jesus Christ even in His mode of being as the Father … The suffering is not his own, but the alien suffering of the creature, of man, which he takes to himself in him. But he does suffer it in the humiliation of his Son with a depth with which it never was or will be suffered by any man – apart from the One who is his Son. And he does so in order that, having been borne by him in the offering and sending of his Son, it should not have to be suffered in this way by man. This fatherly fellow-suffering of God is the mystery, the basis, of the humiliation of his Son; the truth of that which takes place historically in his crucifixion.[210]

This seems to move in the direction of kenotic or liberation frameworks and, perhaps, along a trajectory towards certain social Trinitarianisms. Wilcoxen warns: "Indeed, as Barth reflects the divine-human Jesus into the doctrine of God, he at least opens the door for something like Moltmann's claim of multiple subjectivities in God that are logically prior to their oneness of purpose."[211] There are genuine concerns over how far Barth's momentum might finally push bottom-line theology.[212] The difficulty lies in unpacking Barth's vivid and complex diction. Granting the questions Barth's discourse raises, my sense is that between Barth and other, even more kenotic or liberative streams a gap persists. Note, for example, Barth's characterizing the Father's suffering as "alien" and experienced (only) "in the humiliation *of the Son*" (emphasis added). This militates somewhat against positing a fissure internal to God's being.[213]

He further affirms that incarnate redemptive suffering was not obligatory upon God, not even "internally":

> We have seen that in His work and action God is primarily true to Himself; that He can do this work as the eternal Son of the eternal Father. *But not even in the being of the triune God is there any analogy for the fact that He does actually do it.* We cannot deduce and understand it even from that point, as though God were under a necessity to do it.[214]

For Barth, God "feels" in a manner appropriate to himself. He knows suffering, but not passively. He is not vulnerable to some sort of ontological bleed. Admittedly, uncertainties and antinomies persist, but, I would suggest that we do not find here a completely packaged theology of solidarity in contemporary progressive style. Indeed, counterintuitive though it may be, in his *kenosis*, in his humility, God's glory is revealed. But even as he is "with us", God's fidelity is stable, his capacity to save undiminished, his being undamaged.[215] *Action in time has not changed him. To the extent that the exposition is coherent*, Barth's God remains free and his honor impervious.[216]

### *Honor, Freedom, and Time*

A comprehensive understanding of God's freedom in which he loves sinful humanity will always elude us. Questions of necessity – implied limits to freedom – seem to impinge on God's honor. (Surely God did not *have* to do anything for his creatures?) Again, bound up with the matter of God's freedom is his relationship to time. On God and time, Barth is, as ever, compelling and difficult.[217]

At first blush, it would seem that just as God is free to be incarnate, to be great *and* lowly, he is likewise free with respect to chronological boundaries:

> His omnipotence is that of a divine plenitude of power in the fact that … it can assume the form of weakness and impotence and do so as omnipotence … The eternity in which he himself is true time and the Creator of all time is revealed in the fact that, although our time is that of sin and death, he can enter it and himself be temporal in it, yet without ceasing to be eternal, able rather to be the Eternal in time.[218]

God comprehends time in his eternity, truly enters it, and yet remains transcendent, asymmetrically engaged with creaturely time. He is "pre-temporal, supra-temporal, and post-temporal".[219] Thus far Barth would seem to advocate something like classical notions of God's atemporality.[220]

But, perhaps we speak too fast:

> For in the eternal election of God [the humanity of Christ] is with God's Son … the primary object and content of the … will of God. He is not, of course, a second God. He is not eternal as God is. He is only the creature of God – bound to time, limited in other ways too, unable in his own strength to escape the threat of nothingness. *But as this creature* … he is before all things, even before the dawn of his own time.[221]

In some elusive manner, by God's eternal election, the event of the incarnation is pushed across a boundary into the timelessness of God.[222] Apparently, this might even include the humanity of Jesus.

Barth, it would appear, suggests the projection of pre-eternity into human history and the human into God's pre-eternity. Once again, the danger arises that the Barthian convergence of Creator with creature bleeds into admixture.[223] Concurrently, though, we have seen Barth affirm the transcendence and undilute aseity of God. Is Barth guilty of trying to have and eat his cake? Or is it simply that sublime verities will always exceed linguistic capacity? In any case, all viable structures depend on tension for solidity. I suspect that Barth *intends* a

Lord whose freedom – and honor – remain intact throughout his radical embrace of the human condition; the immanent must not be reduced to the economic.[224] Neither the matter nor Barth's rhetoric are entirely clear – and beyond this, one might argue for shifts in Barth's own thought over time.

*Divine Honor, Chronology of Salvation, and the Human Predicament*

In this final "honor segment," I proceed from a Barthian foundation to further reflections on God's honor in atonement with respect to time. We are by now aware of antagonists of "Anselmian models" (especially PSA) who protest the very idea of God *pre-intending* a historically rooted salvation, hinging on Golgotha. Unable to countenance overlapping but distinct metaphysical "freedoms" for Creator and creature, such lines of thinking denounce any theology that would embroil God in Roman violence. Cruciform atonement is theologically offensive for if "God's justice on the cross is meted out through the Roman court, this legitimizes the government's use of the sword".[225] The narrow linearity of this perspective cannot but conclude that the God of PSA is in league with imperial evil.[226] On these lines, both God's justice and honor seem to be irremediably tarnished.

Likewise, we have heard Islamic scholars object to salvation unfurled along a developmental history. They allege that in traditional Christian atonement, God is being subjected to the limits of temporal chronology as he works out (or discovers!) his (deeply ignoble) salvation solution over time. Evidently, "Anselmian" or substitutionary atonement constructs have stoked anxieties tied to conceptions of God and time, and their implications for his goodness and honor. If God "took so long" to deliver salvation to Israel and the world, and if his masterplan was the crucifixion of the Lord of glory (1 Cor. 2:6-9), how limited, clumsy, and shame-laden his best efforts seem to be.

I offer no point-scoring rebuttal but attempt to articulate a counter perspective grounded in countervailing assumptions, theological and metaphysical: God's eternity is timeless, and from that vantage point he is capable of encompassing even time, itself an aspect of his creation. He penetrates the human experience of time (e.g. incarnation) without experiencing attrition in his timeless nature. His engagement with time is lively and dynamic, but thoroughly asymmetrical.[227]

Within such a framework, and prioritizing a theocentric focus, the quandaries of the earthy development of salvation-history are ameliorated. We have argued above that sovereign providence and human agency coincide, intertwine, and yet remain distinguishable, each with its own integrity. Thus, God works patiently within the human story without suffering the attrition of time himself. He is not "slow" or "late to arrive" (cf. 2 Pet. 3:8-9). As the divine author of the story, God is not *waiting* on anything. Nor, at story's climax, is God culpable for the sin, corruption, and death of the cross – even though it is preordained as the very axis of victory over the dark powers (cf. 1 Cor. 2:6-9; Eph. 3:4-6 alongside 2:14-18; 1 Pet. 1:18-20).[228] God's action in human history is a seamlessly wondrous whole.

Vidu voices a salutary reminder that divine and human justice are analogically related – commensurate within limitations.[229] The human experience matters;

ethics matter. But the ethical calculus of the cross cannot simply be processed by exclusive reference to horizontal experience – justice, mercy, and requital in human relationships. Heed again Sonderegger's reminder that our likeness to God is embedded within a greater unlikeness.[230]

The metaphysical mystery of the God of Scripture must be allowed, in faith, to exert defining pressure on our ethical judgment about the cross and redemption, as Vidu intimates:

> But simplicity counsels that while God must be seen as involved with these human acts, his agency transcends a mere one-to-one correlation between human actions and divine actions. It is not a direct divine punishment of Jesus that works its redemptive magic; but rather the full, unified, and uncontradictable action of God throughout history – which necessarily includes but is not exhausted by or reduced to an element of condemnation and retribution – should be considered redemptive.[231]

In terms of the story of which the cross (and resurrection) are the climax, extreme options present themselves: i) to unequivocally identify God's action with that of Pilate and the Sanhedrin; or ii) to deny the cross any space in the divine design. Those who assume the former to be necessary to PSA understandably demur. But, again, the canonical reportage points elsewhere. It would seem to affirm the reality of diametrically contrasting intentions (divine and human), with distinct agency and responsibility, strangely *converging* at the cross, all with a universe-inverting outflow:salvation.[232]

Prodded by Scripture's sweep, we propose that a theocentric precommitment is essential to faithfully engaging precisely these issues. Certainly, human existence is punctuated by waiting, travail, and justice apparently delayed (cf. Ps. 13; 44; 79; 80; Hab. 1:2-3; Rev. 6:9-11). However, in the presence of the faithful Lord – whose days are without end; who is before and after all things – for this God there is no painfully inept outworking of his designs; no default in either justice or mercy; and, indeed, no "waiting" (Ps. 90:4; 102:24-28; Isa. 44:6; Jn. 8:58; Col. 1:17; Rev. 1:8).

Moreover, precommitment to a theocentric framing does not entail "good outcomes" for God at our expense. It does not imply an absolute discontinuity between God's justice and human need. It certainly does not imply anything less than a God who pours out his goodness, his very self for his creatures. Yes, weeping persists, but he weeps with us (Ps. 103:13-14; Heb. 4:15-16). God's revelation – directed *to* us, but not centered *on* us – does engender restorative action now, and hope (cf. Rom. 5:1-5; 12:9-21; Gal. 6:9-10; 1 Cor. 15:58; Jas. 2). In the mystery of providence, even our experience of hope deferred is a mark of his presence, patience, and commitment to his world (2 Pet. 3:9). A faith seeking understanding continues, even with provisional and halting apprehension (cf. Rom. 8:18-39; 1 Cor. 13:9-12; 2 Cor. 5:6-10). The questions ultimately reduce to convictions about the mind-independent truths of the cosmos, as well as trust in God's unflagging fidelity. God, pre-eminent in his Son, is the central truth of the universe and, thankfully, a truth that is liberating for all God's children (cf. Rom. 8:18-39; 1 Cor. 15:19, 24-28, 49-59). His honor sustains.

## Summing Up the Discussion

Here we conclude our selective two-chapter survey of Anselm and (aspects of) his legacy, loosely, "objective atonements". For us, the leading icon of that legacy has been Karl Barth and elements of PSA in his thought. Following is a summation of challenges to PSA and related responses thereto, ordered by our triplex of themes.

First come concerns over the justice of juridical substitution. The problem of "(in)justice from below" is one of apparent ethical impasse. Situated in a certain light, PSA seems to present a God either voraciously wrathful or conniving at human sin (justification as a divine "accounting trick"), or both. A constructive response must address the false dichotomy between just wrath and love. Also important are the analogical limits (not disjunction) between human and divine virtue. One might further insist that the abstract juridical logic of PSA be underwritten by genuine metaphysical (and thus, ethical) transformation in resurrection life. Salvation is *for* a worshipping new creation.

In terms of justice from above, PSA may be vulnerable to accusations of division and injustice, even in intra-Trinitarian relations, with a vindictive Father brutalizing an innocent Son. An integral response here must ground substitutionary dynamics in a robustly Trinitarian ontology – integrating distinct appropriations with unified action such that, in cross and resurrection, God – full stop – is present for us.

Secondly, in PSA, invidious construals of sin and, particularly original sin, as the ill for which the cross is the remedy, are too common. PSA has been accused of unblushingly portraying sin as a problem arbitrarily foisted on humanity and then disproportionately weighted in the divine scales. A proper articulation of sin will affirm its seriousness and ubiquity – "salvation from". But this without overtones of divine bloodlust, a dour sin obsession, or of a sort of biogenetic determinism.

Third, presentations of redemption must be articulated with sensitivity to divine honor in the face of claims that PSA valorizes suffering and degradation as external requirements upon a God awkwardly laboring through history. A productive response will call on many dimensions of thought. i) Acceptance of epistemological limits and mystery enters here. ii) God must be understood to be genuinely *free* in salvation – any necessity is a reflection of the divine character and will, not an imposition thereon. iii) One may cultivate a theological aesthetic in which, precisely in his condescension, God's virtue, glory, and undiminished capacity are revealed, without any attrition in his being or essence. iv) Concepts of God and time must be constructed according to theocentric construals of God's good providence. God is transcendent, immanent, and honorable in reconciling the world to himself.

If we take PSA as a flagship representative of atonement in its objective and forensic dimensions, both extreme advocacy and extreme critique require moderating. With due correction of PSA's besetting malformations, it must be affirmed as a generative, non-negotiable aspect of divine reconciliation. At the same time, it may be admitted that certain vital domains of salvation are not foregrounded, perhaps even lacking, in standard PSA constructs. For example, creation theology, the story of Israel, the ministry of Christ, resurrection, and the positive, communal, cosmic, and eschatological aspects of salvation are not necessarily integral to routine PSA templates. Sin is a disruption that PSA takes seriously, but one's salvation construct must also insistently accent the hope-laden story that sin (ultimately unsuccessfully) attempts to subvert. Theology must situate the substitution at the cross within a larger metanarrative. And so, we turn in the next chapter to an alternative approach to salvation, a participatory paradigm focused less on the cross as such and more on the incarnation broadly considered.

# 7. Tanner's Participatory Atonement

> Rank on rank the host of heaven / spreads its vanguard on the way / as the Light from Light, descending / from the realms of endless day, / comes the pow'rs of hell to vanquish / as the darkness clears away. "Let All Mortal Flesh Keep Silence" (ancient hymn)

## Turning to Participatory and Incarnational Atonement

In this chapter we turn to an atonement paradigm strongly contrastive to that which has preceded. Our focus homes in on Kathryn Tanner's soteriological framework – a model competing with, and alternative to, but not diametrically antithetical to, the satisfaction and substitution approaches of chapters five and six. I first introduce Tanner and contextualize her work for this book. Then, after a discussion of how to relate our key tropes (sin, honor, and justice) to Tanner's work, I look in some detail at Tanner's presentation of *salvation by participation in God through the incarnation.* The conclusion then circles back to relating our three key themes to Tanner's atonement theology.

## Introducing Kathryn Tanner

Kathryn Tanner is a North American theologian of considerable repute.[1] She is associated particularly with Yale Divinity School and is active in Episcopalian circles. She has published on systematic theology generally; Christology, Trinity, and atonement; the connections between theology and feminism, culture, society and politics, and economic ethics; and more.

Tanner's work on atonement provides a marked contrast to the previous two chapters which, taken together, manifest a loose affinity, centering concepts of vicarious suffering running from satisfaction theory to PSA. Again, this "substitution bloc" of atonement thought has had sustained influence over time and – in one guise or another – tends to attract the most commentary from Islamic scholars engaged with Christian salvation.

By way of contrast, when I turn in this seventh chapter to focus primarily on one scholar, I home in on a rather specific modern conceptualization of atonement and redemption. Certainly, Tanner is expressive of a broader tendency: the instinct towards holism; a focus on categories of union, participation, and incarnation; and a reappropriation of the patristic legacy. But the point is simply that Tanner is taken here in her singularity rather than as representative of a "school" or movement as such.

Why situate Tanner here in this way? Her creativity and influence; her emphasis on categories of participation and *not* on penalty and judgment; her decentering of the cross by distributing soteriological resources across other domains of the Christ Event; her works' prominence; her commitment to work with the resources of classical Christian tradition – all of these make Tanner's theorization of reconciliation an attractive counter-model to the "Anselmian highway" that we have travelled thus far.

Given the dizzying array of approaches to salvation in the story of the Church, any number of atonement theories might have been called on by way of contrast with the Anselmian cadre. Tanner's model is one propitious choice in its creative energy and in the ways in which she sharply diverges from traditional substitutionary schemes, without disowning the redemptive significance of the cross. Tanner's thought provides a condensed contrast to set alongside more traditional substitutionary atonement frameworks. From that point, one can examine both in light of critical cross-examination, that is, in light of the motifs I have drawn from the Islamic ecosystem. Hopefully, the striking alternative of Tanner's "participatory atonement" will prove an invigorating infusion to our discussion, acting as a sort of "control group" for the study.

## Tanner's Atonement and Sin, Honor, and Justice

At one level, I intend to allow the discursive trajectory of this chapter to progress organically, in a manner congruent with the themes and emphases of Tanner's work. Hence, this chapter's structure will be distinct from those preceding. But, as I trace her argumentation, I remain attuned to the themes that have carried us thus far. Tanner makes explicit proposals with respect to (i) sin and human nature and also with respect to what we have termed (ii) "honor".[2]

The question of (iii) justice surfaces in her exposition in ways that are rather different than what we have seen heretofore. Justice in traditional substitutionary accounts is a contested theme that cuts both ways: issues of justice were a driver in the rise of Western substitutionary atonement theories. But, ironically, the perceived lack of justice (alongside the alleged profusion of "violence" and "oppression") in these same constructs has energized vigorous modern backlash.

Tanner is certainly not lacking in sensitivity to matters of justice, social or otherwise; indeed, some of her earlier books feature such concerns in the titles. But taking soundings on the justice theme in her atonement discourse calls for a more oblique approach. To begin with, Tanner largely endorses the validity of the ethical complaints against standard substitutionary models (satisfaction, penalty, propitiation, and so on). Thus, Tanner's atonement construct is explicitly non-forensic and non-penal in approach. But, while affirming protests against the alleged oppression and injustice of the traditional models, Tanner does not otherwise center questions of justice (one way or another) in structuring her profile of redemption.

Again, in no way can Tanner be reproached for a lack of concern for justice as such. Her thought is replete with relevant implications. But these justice issues take on an altogether different prospect in Tanner's imagining of salvation, which foregrounds the infusion of divine life into the world by virtue of the incarnation and decenters the cross. It avoids legal and punitive categories (except in criticism). Her categories are elemental and metaphysical, not judicial.

Further, her sense of sin and human nature is less severe, more neutral, than is found, for example, in common Protestant accounts of human depravity. Little surprise then that the category of justice is not the launchpad for her explication of atonement. Again, it is not that Tanner "does not care" about justice; it is more that her atonement architecture does not emerge primarily from the imperative of addressing a justice deficit.

Disputes over justice do emerge, of course, when the subjects at hand are sin and its consequences, human accountability, and divine solutions. Justice is likewise relevant in debates about the consequences of atonement – its ethical impact and transformation of human deportment. Questions include, "How can humans justly be set right?" and "If sinners are forgiven, what (if any) ethical change must spill out into the world consequent on that 'justification'?" Above we applied the locution "justice from below" to such issues. As we shall see, Tanner's contributions certainly do speak to these issues.

## Christ the Key

One of Tanner's most famous studies is the aptly named *Christ the Key* (2010). Tanner aims at a "Christ-centered theological vision", which takes the incarnation to be the essential mechanism of atonement; that is, people are saved by participating in God through the Son's union with humanity. "God must give us God's very own life and not simply some created version of it. God cannot give us everything that God has to give by merely transforming human life itself into some created approximation of divinity. God must attach us, in all our frailty and finitude, to God."[3]

Congruent with this aspect of Tanner's theology, Hastings reminds us that whatever logical dynamics of substitution and representation inform a given atonement theory, a *metaphysically actual intervention* is concurrently vital:

> Christ is far more than an intermediator … The at-one-ing mediation that Christ secures between God and men is an ontological reality defined by his person – he is the saving union between God and humanity – and so all depends on who Christ *is* … Christ constitutes, rather than merely performs, the atonement.[4]

Invoking the ancient Fathers, Tanner takes salvation to be a project of the perfecting of humanity because of (and by way of) the Word's becoming human. This is a process of God's entering the human condition and "distributing gifts" for our healing as we are united to him. While constructing her distinctive theology, Tanner draws on motifs diffused throughout the patristic tradition.[5] Von Stosch's sketch of "Eastern" theology runs along parallel tracks:

> Eastern concepts of atonement [… focused] on human development toward unification with God … God or the divine Logos will try to help the human free will in a pedagogical process to grow and flourish … through a relationship with God. The aim … is human fulfillment and this is found in the imitation of God (*mimesis*) and in the participation (*methexis*) in divine life … Hence, the aim of atonement is the dynamic-ontological participation in God.[6]

Tanner's incarnational atonement also displays features redolent of beatific exchange and might also be said to intensify the *Christus Victor* template so as to underscore *all* Jesus' biography as the engine for the restoration of fallen humanity.[7] She would have us follow the church Fathers who took

> the incarnation, understood as the Word's assumption of humanity … as the key to the salvation of humanity. It is in virtue of the incarnation that humanity is saved – first the humanity of Christ himself and then through him that of every other human being, one with him. Humanity is purified, healed, and elevated as a consequence of the very incarnation through which the life-giving powers of God's own nature are brought to bear on humanity in the predicament of sin. Humanity is taken to the Word in the incarnation in order to receive from the Word what saves it.[8]

### *Two Modes of Imaging, Two Natures of Christ*

Following certain patristic pathways, Tanner approaches issues of human nature, human destiny, and human rectification by positioning Genesis' *imago Dei* less as generic "human nature", and more as the Second Person of the Trinity himself – *that* is the image to whom humanity must cleave (cf. Gen. 1:26-27). Tanner proposes a radical Christocentrism, such that, not unlike Barth, anthropology itself begins with Christ.[9] So, if humans are "images" of anyone, it is of *the* Image, the Son (cf. Rom. 8:29).[10]

Tanner imagines two levels of imaging. Following Athanasius, Tanner insists that the Son

> is a natural image of the [… Father much like] the way the radiance surrounding a source of light manifests the light-filled nature of its source. The second person is therefore nothing like an image produced in a foreign medium … But that is all that human beings who are not divine can be – images of God produced in a medium of a radically different, indeed inferior, sort … [So] human beings image God only by participating in what they are not – God.[11]

Jesus from Nazareth hypostatically "has" the image in a robustly uncleavable way, and *that* humanity, *that* human, is the necessary object of our attachment. In his assumption of humanity, the Word who eternally and necessarily images God in the "strong" sense redeems and elevates us, who image God in a much "weaker" sense.[12] The saving union with God accomplished due to the Word's incarnation means that human participants are both "in God" ("essentially constituted" by him) and also forever "not God".[13] This Son of Man becomes as it were our umbilical lifeline to God who is life.[14] This in turn spills out into the reforming of humanity, of our character and ways of being, ultimately to restorative effect in the wider world. "In Christ, human nature, in short, is itself refashioned in the divine image so as to become humanly perfect."[15]

Following Athanasius, Tanner insists that this salvation by participation is an ongoing gift of sustenance that is intrinsically necessary to created humanity even without reference to sin or any Fall.[16] Tanner assumes that pristine, original humanity would have enjoyed both "weak" and "strong" imaging of God, but that strong imaging was losable, and lost, in the Fall.[17] It is restored in our union with Christ.

Jesus is the model of the whole union of God and human. The connection is seamless, organic, and life-giving – specifically a life generated from the creative force of God.

> The divinity of Christ cannot be specifically located, for example, in supernatural powers of an exceptional sort that stand out from among his more ordinary ones. Instead, he heals with the spit he commonly swallows and by way of the hem of the cloak he drags through dusty streets ... [Indeed,] the divinity of Christ does not start where his humanity ends, but shines through its entirety. That divinity is evident, for example, in the whole of his flesh resurrected – as the eternal life of his full, finished humanity, complete with all its wounds.[18]

"Jesus [after all] enjoys the same relations with the Father and the Spirit as the second Person of the Trinity does."[19] The divine attributes are diffused throughout the one person from Galilee. Therefore, participant in Jesus, believers participate in that life, wholeness, and healing – but in a dependent manner that does not hold for the Word. He *is* God; we are not. Still more, as it is God himself who takes on our humanity, his work within humanity calls out to everyone – it has "universal range".[20]

Conceptualities parallel to these can be found in unexpected terrain, for example, Barth's *Dogmatics*. Compared to Tanner, Barth is clearly more Passion-centric and more conventionally Reformed in his conceptualizing of atonement. But this does not preclude his integration of participatory and incarnational themes. For Barth, the an/enhypostatic humanity of the Latter Adam sweeps up humanity into "existence in and with God" through connection to the "human essence of the firstborn of his brethren".[21] In Barth's words:

> To [the extent that Jesus is fully God and man,] the reconciliation of the world with God and the conversion of the world to God took place in him. To that extent he himself, his existence, is this reconciliation ... Jesus Christ is the actuality of the atonement, and as such the truth of it which speaks for itself.[22]

Of course, Jesus' bearing our humanity begins with his assumption of humanity in the world in its ongoing brokenness and dysfunction. He takes on a fallen humanity. For Tanner, the Word's humanity was a

> humanity adversely affected by the consequences of sin and in that sense fallen. One must not identify that humanity, for example, with the pure, prelapsarian humanity favored in medieval accounts of the incarnation ... Since the humanity of the man, Jesus, who is without sin, nevertheless represents humanity in need of salvation, such an account of incarnation has every reason to stress the awful human conditions that the Word assumes in becoming incarnate. The humanity of the Word is humanity suffering from fear and distress, persecution by others, anxiety before death, betrayal and isolation, separation from God – all the qualities of death-infused, sin-corrupted life that require remedy. The cross then exemplifies in paradigmatic fashion the very character of human life that the Word becomes incarnate to reverse by making its own.[23]

### *United with the Son: Non-penal Justification and the Return to God*

Tanner underscores the deficiency of standard atonement models – moral-influence, vicarious satisfaction, or penal substitution – as models that, at best, integrate incarnation, resurrection, and the extended ministry of Christ only with difficulty.[24] Alternatively, she forwards the gravitational pull of the incarnation as a more appropriate and expansive center (than the cross, for example) for any discussion of atonement. From this platform, she holds, one may either incorporate other subordinate but salubrious approaches to salvation, or exclude compromised and problematic theories such as satisfaction and PSA.[25]

Thus, for Tanner, justification as a key feature of atonement is something rather different than most scholars have taken it to be: "What justification refers to in us is the fact of our unity with him, our incorporation within his own life, which brings about our being born again to a new identity in him."[26] And Tanner describes regeneration as a circular "trinitarian movement" of Son and Spirit down from the Father to raise us to him, and send us back reconciled and with gifts for mission.[27] This upward movement may be termed our justification.

Tanner resists justification positioned as a bureaucratic fiction. No, it is more actual, more metaphysical a matter than that. But she likewise is far from construing justification as a punctiliar, ontological *fait accompli*. She aims at an ontologically real but progressive motion in which justification is *whole* because it is not based on us, but the One who is *whole*.

> United in baptism to Christ, before we fully manifest that unity in the sort of lives we lead, and simply for that reason moving along with him in his return to the Father, we ascend to the Father by being brought back as sinners before him, into his very presence just as we are with all our faults, to be found favorable in the Father's sight because of the company we keep. Justification ... is therefore a primary aspect of this ascending movement; it brings a sense of the Father's forgiveness and free favor into our lives ... [And the] descent with the gifts of Son and Spirit from the Father can be identified with our receiving the power of the Spirit to be sanctified according to the form of Christ. The Spirit does not merely join us to Christ but, once we are so joined, enters within us as the power for new life according to the shape of Christ's own life as the Son incarnate.[28]

## Participation: A Call to Life in the Trinity

For Tanner, "The incarnation is for the purpose of humanity's entrance into Trinitarian relations."[29] This Christologically focused action is executed by God *in se*, by Father, Son, and Spirit. "Christ is by nature the divine Son who images the Father; human beings by the grace of the Holy Spirit become sons in the image of the divine image and thereby of the Father."[30] This revivifying action of God entails "the presence of Word and Spirit" to humans in a manner unique in creation.[31] Tanner holds that participation in God eventuates in "a Trinitarian way of life" which redounds to soteriological and existential impact on the people of God – we as "adoptees" by the Spirit experience the love of the Father poured out upon the Son.[32]

This economy of salvation is entirely of a piece with the being of God; no alteration is entailed:

> There are no new movements of the Trinity represented by the mission on which the one Jesus calls Father sends the Son and Spirit. The persons of the trinity just keep doing what they are always doing, but now with humanity along for the ride ... [We have] a changed relationship with ... the Trinity in virtue of Christ, whose humanity is bound to the second person of the Trinity, and all that follows from that new relationship for human life – moral righteousness, human fulfillment, eternal life, and so on ... Over the course of Jesus' life, death, and resurrection, the

> character of human life suffering under the weight of sin and death is being made over.[33] (cf. Jn. 14:2-3)

"Incarnation … for the sake of human redemption" *happens* in the Son but is an action of the Trinity.[34] Tanner insists that distinction within the Trinity is not random.[35] But she likewise assures us that all "movement" in the economy remains a *unified* movement from up to down, and back up again, by God the Father, Son, and Holy Spirit, as, in consequence of the incarnation, we are carried along *with* and *to* God our source.[36] The circle, initiated by the Father, envelops his children, bringing them home as it were.[37]

### *Trinitarian Monotheism*

In the atoning incarnation, where Jesus acts, God is acting. There is no space between what the Word does and what God may be said to do. Tanner reminds us that Jesus insists:

> "all that the Father has is mine" (John 17:10); and therefore the Son himself exercises the Father's powers of jurisdiction. The Son carries out what the Father performs, raising us, for example, from the dead, and he is able to do so himself because he has "life in himself" from the Father (John 5:26).[38]

Tanner also reminds us that, as Athanasius remarks, "there is nothing that is not originated and actuated through the Word and in the Spirit."[39]

However difficult for our minds to process, an undergirding factor in the economy of incarnation is the reality that Trinity is simply an irreducible feature of unequivocal, transcendent *monotheism*. God is present in Christ. And God, without demurral, is One. Tanner reminds us that:

> Monotheism means … that divinity is not a class term; divinity is not a kind of thing whose defining characteristics might be displayed by many things to greater or lesser degree. Given such an understanding of divinity, everything responsible for the grace that only divine agency explains is just God – the Father who sends Word and Spirit, along with the Word and Spirit sent … The very life of God itself, consequently, must be directly mixed up with suffering, conflict, death, and disease in the saving action of Christ … Jesus therefore mediates divinity and humanity because he unites both and not because he is something in between. Divinity can be in direct contact with us without needing to fear its own contamination or loss of honor … Divinity, in short, cannot be polluted.[40]

Redeeming the world by drawing it back into participation in his own life – through the life of Jesus – is *all* the work of the totality that is God.[41] In essence, "The relationship between Jesus and the Father is not one of master and subordinate (or slave) but a relationship of perfect … partnership in which the will of one naturally aligns with the other; here obedience follows from perfect fellowship (John 15:15). When our own humanity is one day fully reworked into the image of the Son, this is what we will enjoy too: in heaven no command will sound but the voice of one's own heart."[42]

In salvation, even as Jesus submits to his Father's will, the Son has no subsidiary role to be justified as one piece of an otherwise independent scheme imposed upon him. This being the case – however pressing the ethical conundrums of the salvation narrative – God's justice and honor in salvation are much less threatened than some take them to be. Whatever else is happening in reconciliation, it is not at root a narrative about God perpetrating something on a third party, still less is it about the struggle to align "the parts" of God. Further, when God acts, his own being is invulnerable to any sort of change, harm, or corrupting "backflow" from interacting with creation.

## Decentering the Cross

These comments are emblematic of Tanner's theologizing on grace, sin, and atonement:

> What justification refers to in us is the fact of our unity with him, our incorporation within his own life, which brings about our being born again to a new identity in him. *Nothing about us, in and of ourselves, therefore has to change in order for us to be justified*; it is the fact of our attachment to Christ … that accounts for God's declaring us just.[43]

This is consonant with the fact that for Tanner the cross remains part of the architecture of the atonement but is no longer clearly in the center. It would not appear that the cross was *uniquely paramount* in changing us so as to unite us to God.

The question of how, given the incarnation, we are to relate the ministry or biography of the Messiah to his Passion is critical to establishing the contours of atonement. Early Christian portrayals of salvation would often focus on the *bios* of the Messiah as redemptive, zooming in at times on episodes other than the Passion to make the point. An example would be the temptation narratives as counterpoint to Adam's failure.[44] Tanner seems to distill and amplify this dynamic. Without denying content to the death of Jesus, Tanner's impulse is to forward *the life of Jesus* – both as ontological possession of the eternal Word and as the storyline of the Nazarene – as the means and mode of salvation. Meanwhile she operates with a relatively "light touch" when it comes to cross and death.

To her credit, Tanner does seek to incorporate (rather than occlude) the cross in her redemptive vision. Further, her insistence that the cross must not be understood in isolation from a holistic vision of the incarnate reality of the Word is salutary, for example, in the face of any hyper-concentration of PSA which might reduce *all* significance in the Jesus story to an abstracted theorization of the Passion.

Even Barth may be called on as fellow witness to some of the problematics wherein theologies of justification via substitutionary atonement have failed to account for its placement within the larger canvas of creation and the life of Christ and his kingdom. In some contrast to Tanner, Barth positively thematizes judgment and the cross in justification. Nonetheless, he rightly decries a Protestant failure to embrace the joys, restoration, and creationally restorative work of the kingdom represented in the *life* of Jesus. These, too, are integral features of the grace offered in the life of the Messiah that should not have been seen as distinct from but rather as a *basis for* the doctrines of justification and sanctification.[45]

Tanner eloquently speaks of the beauty, mystery, and gift of the cross as God's action for us. "God gives everything necessary", for us at the cross, "in a sense God is both the one sacrificing and the one sacrificed."[46] But this is not with reference to the cross *alone*: "The whole of Jesus' life – before as after his death – is such a life-giving sacrifice given by God for us to feed on, for our nourishment."[47]

> An incarnational model of atonement insists upon the relationship between the cross and the rest of Jesus' life, since the mechanism of salvation on the cross is at work throughout the whole of Jesus' life. And the effects of this salvific mechanism – its point – are, indeed, *much clearer away from the cross than on it* – for example, in Jesus' healing ministry to the sick and the outcast, the advent of the new community of God, and Jesus' resurrected life.[48]

From Tanner's perspective, then, the cross certainly has its place in a sort of recapitulative redemption achieved by the incarnation. "[The cross] simply means … that the Word must take on humanity as we know it in all its horrors if the powers of the Word are to be translated to that humanity in a saving way … Jesus had to be humiliated on the cross for the sake of salvation the way one has to be sick to go to the doctor."[49]

For Tanner, the humiliation of the cross is a matter of a whole identification with the human experience to the dregs, as it were. However, categories such as obedience and reward, penalty, forensic ruling, ransom or satisfaction, and so forth are not part of the package. They are ruled out for reasons of their artificial "externality" (as compared to God's intimate, ontological engagement in our rescue); for their temporal contingency; and (as she details elsewhere) their ethical deficit. In Tanner's conceptual grid,

> Humanity is at one with the divine in Jesus. This is true on the cross as much as everywhere else in Jesus' life and that is what is saving about it … Keeping this in mind, it becomes readily apparent how an incarnational account of the cross severely undercuts legal or contractual interpretations of the saving mechanism of the cross, typical of the vicarious satisfaction and penal substitution models. If God saves by assuming the very life of suffering and death to which Jesus is subjected, God's saving response to the events of the cross is not sufficiently external to them to make sense of a forensic analogy. God's saving act does not follow Jesus' obedience the way a reward follows the doing of good works. Nor does God's saving act follow Jesus' self-sacrificial death in the way release from debtors' prison follows the payment of a debt. In sum, God's saving action can no longer be viewed, in the temporally subsequent sense required by a forensic analogy, as any kind of legally mandated response – to what Jesus does on the cross, to his obedience, self-sacrifice, or suffering unto death. Saying any of that makes God's action to save come too late…[50]

Tanner's vivid rhetoric frequently challenges the reader as she maneuvers around the fault lines and logical tensions of atonement theology. She is insistent that her "account of the incarnation" is "far from turning attention away from the cross".[51] And yet, conversely, it is at the least unusual, if not provocative, to hear a theologian allegedly expositing the (positive) meaning of the cross for our salvation to aver that: "What happens on the cross does not evoke what God does to save, in any strong sense."[52]

### *The Metaphysics of Substitution or Representation*

In light of what we have already seen of Tanner's incarnational atonement, one might not expect her construct to feature the substitution trope, but Tanner's complexity may surprise. We have already had occasion to note the presence of a "happy exchange" motif. She further maintains that:

> While we remained sinners standing apart from God in repudiation of him, Christ took our place as the one in whom God is well pleased, the one, though crucified as a sinner, whose life God vindicates, pronounces acceptable, in raising from the dead … Christ does for us all that we cannot … Christ substitutes himself for us in a way that implicates us in, rather than excluding us from, what he has achieved in himself.[53]

Not surprisingly, whatever "substitution" may be as a feature of Tanner's atonement thought, it is not a matter of forensic status; it has a peculiarly metaphysical or ontological component. With this caveat though, even a sort of "alien righteousness" is applicable. For Tanner, our righteousness in Christ "remains alien to us in that Christ is what we can never be: the unity of divine and human in a single divine person; a human being who can be identified with God … [So our being made righteous remains ever and] only in dependence upon him."[54]

Tanner's theological grammar trades in tensions; it can contribute to the liveliness of the register in which she communicates, but at times the semantic strain is considerable. In any case, while adhering to some degree of substitutionary work by Christ, Tanner self-consciously attempts to expand the daylight between her participatory or representative categories and "the usual" substitutionary categories, about which she is skeptical.

> [T]he incarnational model of the atonement undercuts the sense of vicariousness in the satisfaction and penal models. In the claim that Jesus dies for us, the primary meaning of "for us" is benefit rather than legal substitution; Jesus dies to benefit us so that we will no longer have to live as we do in a sin-afflicted, death-ridden world … It is this incarnational identification of the Word with humanity rather than Jesus' simple standing in our place before the law that makes Jesus our substitute in the prosecution of our cause. Jesus does not represent us, stand in for us, primarily by taking on the position of guilty, death-deserving persons before the law.[55]

### *Participatory Atonement, Sacrifice, and Criticism of Satisfaction and Penal Models*

Tanner believes her incarnational model provides for a rightly balanced incorporation of the cross in her salvation construct in a way that counteracts some feminists' categorical negation of the positive value of the cross while onboarding the criticisms that sacrificial, satisfaction, or penal models legitimate oppression and violence.[56]

> Here [on the incarnational framework] is a God who works unswervingly for our good, who puts no value on death and suffering, and no ultimate value on self-sacrifice for the good, a God of gift-giving abundance struggling against the forces of sin and death in the greatest possible solidarity with us – that of incarnation … All those cruel and bloody features of the cross that feminists and womanists worry

> atonement theories positively evaluate are here identified in no uncertain terms with the world from which one needs to be saved … Nothing stands in the way … of a quite realistic appraisal of the religious and political reasons for Jesus' execution, since they make all the more evident the sinful, conflictual, and death-dealing world that the incarnation of the Word works to heal.[57]

Tanner seeks to make short shrift of any attempt to integrate juridical categories into atonement. She dismisses any description of "God's saving action in legal or contractual terms".[58] The categories of the Son's obedience and self-offering to God are also negated.

> God's action on the cross to save takes center stage.[59] The sacrifice of the cross is then viewed accordingly – as a rite performed by God and not human beings. God is sacrificing there for us and our salvation. If the work is done by God, the object of that work is human existence in its plight of sin and death. The sacrifice is not directed here to God but from God to human beings. Humans are not offering anything to God; God is giving to us.[60]

Moreover, in terms of cultic or sacrificial imagery, to whatever extent the death of Jesus recapitulates OT sacrifice, Tanner emphatically rules out any legal transaction, any objective change in God, and *any sense of propitiation*.[61] In fact, Tanner is, at this juncture, so certain of her position that she seems content to insist on a seemingly arbitrary divine prerogative in employing the rite of sacrifice (in the OT or at the cross) to remove sin or impurity and restore fellowship – *it works to remove sin, apparently, just because God decided it would be so*:[62]

> The [OT rites with which the cross are associated are] not propitiatory: [the] point is not to change God's wrath to mercy, but to wipe away fault or impurity in ways that a God already desirous of communion with us institutes. Benefits do not come back to the offerer because the conditions of something like a contract have been fulfilled … Propitiation is not the reason why the rite wipes away sin; no real explanation is offered. God simply wants to reinstate God's people to full communion with God and this is what God tells God's people to do in such cases.[63]

Tanner suggests that sacrifices are about the transmission (towards us) of the "life in the blood," and, thus, expiation does not derive from "the death of the animal *per se*."[64] (cf. Lev. 17:11).

> [OT sacrifices] either celebrate or end in joyous communion – between human beings and God and among the human beings so blessed. The important point of the sacrifice is not the fact that one has given up something, since the people offering the sacrifice are often the ones who go on to eat it. Sacrifices that take the form of a holocaust – in which the animal or grain is completely lost to the worshipper by being burned – seem to suggest, not so much the renunciation of what is one's own as a return to God of what is already God's, the return to God of prior gifts on God's part to us … as an appropriate act of thanksgiving. Expiatory holocausts – in which the burning of the entire animal seems a way of wiping out sin or ritual impurity that interrupts communion with God – should therefore be understood to reinstate meal fellowship. The joy of God's presence is their presupposition and end … Atonement theories that make the death of Christ saving have the tendency to overemphasize the importance of death to sacrificial rites … Calling Jesus' death a sacrifice might indeed be a way of drawing attention to something taking place on the cross other than death. Particularly when sacrifices

are viewed as establishing and maintaining community between God and human beings by their eating together.[65]

The life-giving triumph of God at the cross Tanner takes to be a signature trait of an incarnational approach to atonement, and she sees this as necessarily in contrast to the deleterious satisfaction and penalty models. The internal momentum of her argument verges on suggesting that, *in terms of the sacrifice template, the death of Jesus is beside the point* – even as she does not quite put things in exactly these terms.[66] (Again, my primary intention in consulting Tanner is not rebuttal but resourcing my project. However, I will note that here on sacrifice, as elsewhere, I find what Tanner affirms to be helpful (life restored, communion, joy) without agreeing to that which she either minimizes or denies (e.g. the realities of death, cost, or propitiation).)

## Sin and Human Moral Disposition

In terms of sin and human nature and its relation to the Fall, Tanner proposes an understanding that acknowledges all three realities, but actually weakens the linkage between the latter two. Following certain Eastern Fathers, Tanner emphasizes human plasticity for good or ill given the freedom of the will.[67] Tanner deploys figures such as Cyril of Alexandria and Gregory of Nyssa to argue that the human capacity for virtue is in some sense a "neutral" issue, contingent on the right use of free will so as to align us with God who properly orients our faculties.[68] "[H]umans seem to have an exaggerated capacity for [relation to that which we are not-God] that opens them to a radical sort of reformation from without in the divine image."[69] Tanner takes human radical openness to good or ill, a "natural" indeterminateness, to be a shadowy aspect of our image-bearing character.[70]

Packaged with these concepts of human nature, *as it now is*, are understandings of human nature in its primal state and at the Fall – a conceptualization of the latter that is, with Tanner, milder than many a traditional Protestant option. For Tanner, although Adam's originating condition was provisional or processual, it was one in which the necessary grace of divine sustaining was experienced in its immediacy:

> In this sense of natural, existing with the grace of God was the natural state in which we were created. "Adam found [the help of God] naturally, as something normally at his disposal, and always as it were within his reach, without having to ask for it first. He did not have to seek God, because God was already near him." "The first man on earth … had for choice the [divine] good and the [divine] beautiful lying all around him in the very nature of things."[71]

The impact of sin, of the Fall, is real enough, but, on Tanner's profile, less ontologically severe.[72] She construes participatory salvation as a process of divine pedagogy and reorientation, as divine giving designed to fill structural gaps in the human constitution – rather than as a recreation of human nature which heals sin's mortal scars and embedded distortions:

> Because what we lose through sinning is something that we are not [ – the immediate participation in God – ] human nature remains as it is, however:

> essentially uncorrupted for all the utterly dire consequences of sin. What makes us totally corrupt is the loss of something that we are not – divinity – and therefore our human nature is not essentially changed for the worse in losing it.[73]

And so Tanner can claim that in receiving grace there is no need for human nature "to be in any way fundamentally reconstituted", for "nothing about our essential constitution has to change".[74] "Human beings need grace to become images of God, not because they are sunk in sin but because they cannot be images of any strong sort simply in virtue of what they are."[75]

To this point, a stalwart Protestant might be appalled at Tanner's "soft-pedaling" of sin. The debate does beckon, and questions of internal consistency do arise. But, at the least, Tanner's *intention* is clearly not a glib glossing over of the world's sorry condition, nor a flippancy about sin and evil. Somehow she would still warn of sin's devastating and tenacious claim on the human family: "[W]hat we become through sin forms a kind of second nature. What we become is knit into us in a way we cannot remove ... [W]e have so incorporated this material over time as to become inseparable from it."[76]

## Grace, Sin, and Human Nature

Tanner's positioning of grace with respect to human nature and creaturely ends has implications for her conceptualization of sin which, as we have seen, at times labors to integrate conflicting intuitions. Somehow in Tanner's panorama, sin seems less than fully devastating to "human nature" and, simultaneously, frightfully consequential. The relational rupture that is sin has entailed our loss of divine grace (in the "strong" sense); thus we lose everything, "both God and the possibility of living well ... [A]ll our acts are ruined."[77] In their meager existence after the Fall, humans – meant "to be ever-expanding containers for divine good" – make do with the ersatz, idolatrous, and bankrupt substitutes of "created goods".[78]

Tanner would somewhat redirect our thought away from sin and its impact on human nature. For her, the loss of sustaining grace (in consequence of sin) is so devastating for humanity not simply by reason of how bad sin is, but because even untainted human nature was always designed to be "insufficient" on its own – that is, wholly dependent on God himself even at its best.[79] She calls us to "shift attention from human nature itself to our functional dependence on something outside ourselves – divine inputs – now lost to us".[80] Here we return to Tanner's "neutral" human nature – "neutral" even now under sin, though always vulnerable to sin's effects: "Human nature is one thing, equally capable of opposites, in a borderland between virtue and beauty and their opposites, as Gregory of Nyssa says."[81]

In Tanner's thought, grace is fundamental to human wholeness even without reference to sin. Sin enters the scene only as a sort of secondary scar on the human subject. The addition of divine grace is required to humanize and enliven created persons. Even had we remained pristine from Adam onward, as it were, we were still "weak imagers" of God, dependent on a sustaining attachment from without.[82] Paradoxically, the addition of grace – "what we are not" – is required for the full realization of "what we are".[83]

> If God wants to give [his goodness] to humans, they have to be elevated beyond what they are themselves as creatures. In short, humans have to be given God in addition to being given themselves. Christ is the highest possible form in which the good of God's own life can be given to us: in him God and the human are one … [And] *grace is necessary to complete our nature* … [G]race becomes a requirement for simply being a human being fully alive and flourishing."[84]

For full realization, humanity has always required the adhering presence of God in all his radical disjunction to us – "a discontinuous radical leap between qualitatively different conditions".[85] "What is prone by its own nature to fall – to die and to stray – is lifted up by a power that by nature rises without fail, the divine power of eternal life. Our natural direction is thereby reversed."[86] Here the Grace–Nature binary is of even more significance than that of Grace–Sin. An intriguing antinomy surfaces: while naturalism as human self-actualization is ruled out, there is nothing more essential, more "natural", than the *external* "gift of God's own life" to human nature.[87] Grace is both intrinsically "gratuitous" and "natural".[88]

### *Grace and Union with Christ: A Restoration Exceeding Original Deficit*

Following the Fathers, atonement is, for Tanner, very much a matter of a gift in which disparate natures are brought together in such a way as to more than make up for primal loss: "The Only-Begotten was … made man … that in him … the good things returning and the grace of the Holy Spirit rooted *might be preserved securely* to our whole nature, the Only-Begotten … lending us the stability of his own nature."[89]

By design, human imaging was always dependent on our integration with Word and Spirit, a state relinquished at the Fall. Salvation's ends far exceed a wind-back to incipient innocence: "Lost through sin, the gifts of Word and Spirit that made humans the image of God at their creation would need to be restored to humanity by Christ in some new way that improves upon the original situation that permitted their loss."[90] The trajectory of atonement in Christ is to take us beyond an original pristine state to completion, beyond the possibility of sin and corruption.

> Jesus Christ, the perfect human image of God because the perfect divine image, brings human life in himself back to its perfect beginning – the perfect beginning that in a sense never was – so that it might be achieved in a way not susceptible of loss. Jesus does not just have the Spirit of God in the way a holy person might, as the gift of something that is not his own by nature; because Jesus is not just human but the Word itself become incarnate, he has the Spirit as his own … Jesus, insofar as he is divine, does not just have the divine image within himself through participation but *is* it.[91]

The devastating loss of grace due to sin and our ongoing susceptibility to detachment from the divine Source require an atonement that is consequential, radical, irreversible. Tanner's diction evokes what has sometimes been termed a "physicalist" redemption:

> The solution to all these difficulties is the *new way Word and Spirit are ours in Christ*. The attachment of humanity to the divine in Christ is of a much closer and stronger sort than anything human beings enjoy at their creation. Jesus is not simply

> a human being ... of the sort we had the capacity to be at our creation. The humanity of Jesus is instead assumed into unity with the second person of the Trinity to form a single person, a hypostatic unity.[92]

The healing and restorative effect of the incarnation *in toto* transmits restoration to a corrupting creation, like fire transmitting heat to material that is otherwise cold and lifeless.[93] The Word made flesh is the conduit by which the life of the Trinity spills out into all the cosmos, instigating a totalizing renewal beyond the merely spiritual and individual, extending beyond humanity to the creation as a whole.[94]

And so, her elusive sketch of sin notwithstanding, Tanner's construal of the entailments of salvation are quite radical: "The transition from sin to grace is therefore not simply the starkest one possible, from death to life, but itself a kind of death, a passage by way of our dying. We must die to what we have become through sin, in order to begin again, reborn."[95]

The incarnation – when applied to a person's life – is eternally, ontologically transformative. The *strong* imaging achieved in us by the *strong* experience of grace amounts to a life-endowing "new bondage"; we are not simply clothed in the Spirit as Adam was, but now that Spirit is "knit into the fabric of our humanity by way of the incarnation".[96] In union with Christ, human nature shifts from a "changeable good" to a superior "unchangeable good" with instincts reordered towards God.[97] Bound up forever with that which is not ourselves, we begin to "be" according to God's glorious design, Irenaeus' "humanity fully alive".[98] Hear Tanner:

> And humanity is only more fully itself in being thoroughly reworked by divine power. Refashioned by divine power, humans are more fully human in knowing the truth and choosing the good as they were meant to. Humans, as Thomas Torrance affirms, "are completed beyond themselves in God, so that instead of thinking that human minds and wills are crowded out by the presence of God [in Christ ...] we must think of them as reaching completeness in him ... [I]n the Incarnation the presence of the complete God does not mean the absence of man, or the presence only of incomplete man, but rather the presence of man in his completeness as man in God ... Because the presence of God is creative, instead of excluding or overwhelming what is human, it posits it, upholds, and renews it."[99]

## The Ethics of Participatory Atonement: The Sanctified Life

How is the justice of God reflected in his atonement and in his atoned-for people? Recalling our nomenclature of justice "above" and "below", some might argue that in Tanner's conceptual universe, given her decentering of the cross, the pressure of questions on justice "from above" is reduced (but not excised). The "below" questions pertain to the atonement's impact on the community of faith – again, how in fact can sinners justly be reconciled and rectified, and, more so, is no cost, response, or change to be expected? These "below" questions remain – questions of Christian ethics, transformation, and sanctification.

### *Christ (Not the "Social Trinity"): The Pattern for Ethical Community*

Participation in Christ has a transformative and reformative aspect to it, producing effects in those joined to God in Christ. But when it comes to pinpointing the source, model, and driver of this transformation, Tanner cautions against invoking a speculative social Trinitarianism that would overlay the stencil of Trinitarian relations onto human society.[100] Instead, for an ethical and relational lens, she pivots towards the Trinity as enacted *in the life of Jesus* – in the way *he* engages people.[101] This becomes the "Trinitarian" model for horizontal relationships.[102] For Tanner's vision of life in the atoned community, "the *Christ* of the Trinity is key", offering us a more constructive, less plastic, template than *generically* Trinitarian paradigms.

Incarnational atonement produces for its participants a redemptively reworked society, a wonderfully "unnatural" organism of unified diversity, with a new mode of being:

> When every human being becomes one in Christ this overrides in a significant sense forms of already established kinship that would otherwise keep people apart; this is an unnatural community one might say in much the way humanity and divinity in Christ are an unnatural community, made up of what is naturally disparate and dissimilar. More like the relationship between humanity and divinity in Christ than the Trinity, this is a community of previously diverse persons brought together only by something different from all of them that they share – Christ.[103]

Salvation by way of participation in Christ has implications for the ethical shape of the *ekklesia*. Christ becomes the engine that powers change and renewal throughout. "Our lives are to be the reflection in action of our assumption into Christ, in virtue of their taking on the mode of Sonship. Our assumption into Christ is to become visible as our lives show forth … the form of Christ's own life, the mode of Sonship. Thereby, the glory of God's own triune superabundance shines forth … from all that it is that we do for the good … of others."[104]

The incarnation as conduit of life into the human sphere is endlessly generative because God's gracious effulgence is beyond diminishing; it is sourced in love and responsive to need, not merit.[105] This movement in turn stamps an ethical pattern onto the people of Jesus – a non-diminishing, non-competitive ethic of superabundance towards the neighbor, the "poor" in all senses of the term.[106]

Moreover, in the wake of the incarnation, the Christ community's contours are distinctively non-competitive and collective – though also non-homogenizing.[107] Tanner sets this in contrast to contemporary Western consumer societies: "Christian beliefs about a shared origin and fate entail, in sum, a refusal of the privatizing of risk and reward at the heart of finance-dominated capitalism. One fails, morally and otherwise, in the company of others. And one gains salvation by God's grace alone."[108]

"Christ's human life" is the point of reference for God's ongoing agenda to rework human life in community: "The world is different because of Christ even if no one recognizes that fact and attempts to live accordingly. But one can knowingly and willingly make what Christ achieves alone the basis of one's life project now only by depending on other witnesses to its meaning for their lives."[109]

Tanner's outline of the ethics of God's people embraces certain tensions and polarities. For example, on the one hand, relational interdependence and the accompanying moral transformation are, at least aspirationally, intense. But, on the other hand, individual dependence is wholly on the Head, not on one another *in any absolute sense.*[110] The individual – directly bound to God – is never effaced or subsumed in the collective, maintaining their worth even should they "underperform" spiritually.[111]

Tanner's profile of the saved community embraces interesting ecclesial perspectives on sin, virtue, and moral models. So, on the one hand, sin remains a threat to discipleship in community. Because we are "dead" apart from our sustaining participation in Christ, we must be on constant alert against our non-eradicated sin inclination. But, on the other hand, Tanner affirms that within the ecosystem of grace, in contradiction "to a work ethic … one's value in God's eyes is not conditional upon particular achievements that distinguish one from others. One remains of value in God's eyes even if one fails completely."[112]

The gathered people who have been rescued quite literally "in Christ" form a living fellowship of diversity implausibly unified much like the unfathomable union of hypostases in the Man from Nazareth.[113]

> On a Christian understanding … the God who is nothing like any [Christian], and in that sense outside of them all, can be enjoyed as a whole by each and every one of them, through a kind of direct link in each and every case. The very same object of love and knowledge is made the basis of a common vision and desire. The community here is intense. People are united, that is, in ways that overcome all division, but such community is never predicated on the erasure of the individual [particularity] … What brings them together to unify them is simply the object upon which they all rest.[114]

### *The Moral Shape of the Atoned Community*

The fact of Christ incarnate is of categorical importance for humanity writ large: "Justification, in short, is a matter of incarnation."[115] But prior to any systemic restoration in the human family, redemption, renewal, and rectification had to be enacted for Christ's own humanity – Christ's humanity joined to the Word, thereby gaining the Spirit. Sanctification, for Tanner, happens first in Christ not only as a model for us, but as an actualized paradigm transmitted to us.[116] We are sanctified by

> the perfection and holiness of Christ's human life as that takes shape over time, by way of his active drawing on the powers of the Holy Spirit … that is the sanctification appropriate to his humanity rather than his divinity, the sanctification of his humanity properly speaking, for example, the leading of a perfectly good human life and the healing of a body, broken by the sin of others, to new life.[117]

Lives of moral difference or holiness are produced in an outflow from Christ into those participant in God through him, through his Spirit. "Even if we do lead holy human lives of love and service to God through the power of the Spirit that is ours in Christ, it is not possible to consider our abilities to do so independently of the Spirit, as if leading such lives were intelligible simply on the new human basis given to us by grace."[118]

As we have seen, the priority of the fact of incarnation and the participation of the creaturely in the Creator does not, for Tanner, obviate the subsidiary role of the death of Jesus as essential to this larger process. So, for example, Tanner speaks of the life-imparting work of *sacrifice* – the crucifixion and resurrection generating a new life pattern for Christians; however, she characteristically expounds this with as little reference to death as possible:

> The direction of these living human sacrifices becomes in this way the same as God's: toward the satisfaction of human needs, the reversal of the effects of sin on human life. Service to the neighbor becomes the reality designated by "sacrifices to God". Here we see a connection with the sacrifices of martyrs, but a connection *that now downplays their deaths* in that it calls attention to lives dedicated wholly and unswervingly to God's mission of life, as Jesus' was.[119]

But, if the union of God and man in Christ is as determinative for humanity and the cosmos as alleged, pressing questions arise with respect to the moral texture of these new communities formed by participation in Christ:

> Are those communities dedicated to anything like what Jesus was dedicated to in his relations with other people? Are they dedicated to policies ensuring the comprehensive well-being of all their members, especially the disempowered, following Jesus' own concern for the physical and spiritual well-being of the poor and suffering?[120]

Tanner's moral profile of the "community of participation" is one that militates against all forms of oppression, abuse, and deprivation, one that attends to those on the margins – even though it may be noted that, in the works consulted here, she generally does not map out this ecclesial ethic and praxis in granular detail.[121] Allowing ourselves a gesture here towards the larger context of the current project, one might argue that Tanner's insistence on the this-worldly implications of atonement might appear in some ways to answer to Islamic concerns about the "ethereal" nature of Christian salvation.[122]

Sanctification, a Spirit-driven change in today's observable world, is not anywhere near final or complete on Tanner's understanding, but it is nonetheless real. Thus, Tanner rejects the Marxist critique – the supposed "opiate effect" of Christian salvation and eschatology. The gifts of God imbued to his people in the incarnation by definition must have real-world consequences, and be distributed to good effect.[123] Just so, with discerning nuance she insists that no ideological economic agenda trumps or precisely maps onto the priorities of loyalty to God; all other commitments are relativized by a life "in Christ".[124]

> The grace that is necessary to change things radically exists and is at work in the world now, providing human beings with everything they need to live life differently. There is, therefore, a way for us now to get from here to there because the motor of that change is as much ours now as it ever will be in future – that motor being life in Christ. The future to come in this way funds the struggle for realistic proximate futures in the present. Drawing on that grace of God, one should do everything one can now to manifest it in the character of the life one leads.[125]

At the same time, Tanner's idealism and realism intersect in a way that markedly qualifies expectations of manifest success in this life: "[B]efore the world ends … we should expect defeat as much as success. One with Christ … we must prefer defeat to success everywhere that such success means being favored by death-dealing forces at work in human life … [B]etter to go to the cross in faithfulness to the mission of a gift-giving God, than to reap the riches of a kingdom of death."[126]

So, with the sort of rhetorical tension we have come to look for in Tanner, her exhortation here might be juxtaposed with our comments just above. This-worldly change is very much an entailment of incarnational atonement; even so, whether due to external threat or internal fragility, the Christian's expectation of manifest "success" in this world must be muted. (This aspect of Tanner's ethical trajectory might then appear somewhat less congenial to the Islamic program implicit in the chapters above.)

In any case, Tanner situates virtues as products of our attachment to God through Christ. Hopefully, we are formed to find all our goods in *the Good*, and to love him the more fervently. She quotes Augustine to good effect:

> The human will is so divinely aided in the pursuit of righteousness that … in addition to free will and [instruction] in how he ought to live … there is formed in his mind [through the Holy Spirit] a delight in, and love of, that supreme and unchangeable good which is God … in order that … he might conceive an ardent desire to cling to his maker, and may burn to enter upon the participation in that true light, that it may go well with him from him to whom he owes his existence.[127]

### *Justification and Sanctification*

Tanner's sense of grace and the unbounded Godward-side of atonement is constructive. So too is her sense of the moral and ethical difference the incarnation makes in the world. But, consider these two forces manifest in her writing: i) incarnational atonement as a grace fully accomplished, and that by God alone; and ii) the necessary impacts and fruits of that work evidenced in Christian lives. An attempt to articulate their convergence will expose certain ambiguities or apparent aporias. For example, justification and sanctification are helpfully distinguished for the sake of conceptual clarity. But Tanner's rhetoric threatens at times to detach them more absolutely.[128] I would suggest that this could ultimately blur atonement's reality and justice.

On the one hand, the operative principle is grace, with little reference to the quality of its human reception: "God gives unity with Godself in Christ even to sinners … The gift of union with Christ remains ours, moreover, however short we come in the effort to reflect what it should mean for the lives we lead."[129] And, similarly, "That attachment [of the believer to Christ] itself is one thing; its effect on our human lives something else. Christ can be attached to us, and we to him in virtue of his attachment to us, whether or not that attachment shows itself in the changed human dispositions and actions that are its effects."[130] Are not such assertions difficult to square with, for example, Jesus' challenge to follow him in Matthew 10:38 and 16:24-27?

But, on the other hand, Tanner can make other bracing claims about sanctification – even if they sit uneasily alongside her statements above:

"Attachment to Christ, in virtue of which one is justified, and the gift of the Holy Spirit, through which one comes to be sanctified, are very closely associated in this account of justification and sanctification. The one indeed cannot exist without the other … The gift of the divine power to live differently can therefore be considered part of what it means to be justified."[131]

Again, consider the following: "Nothing has necessarily happened to change our human character [in justification] … The impression [of the Spirit] itself is constituted by what we are not."[132] And then, few lines later, we are assured that "because we have the gift of Christ's Spirit, in being justified we are made holy in a certain sense, not just declared righteous. There is a holiness in us and not simply a holiness outside ourselves that can be considered ours through attachment to it."[133] This is not a matter of crass contradiction, but neither has Tanner sufficiently helped the reader to appreciate how these distinctive claims interweave.

Tanner uses arboreal imagery to illustrate the nuances of justification and its relation to sanctification: in Christ we become a new planting. "But becoming [a] new tree is not equivalent to its bearing fruit."[134] This is fair as far as it goes. Instantly visible sanctity may not follow every turning to Christ (although there is biblical precedent for such a trajectory, e.g. Luke 19:1-10). Nonetheless, remaining with Tanner's imagery, we might at least assume that the sap has begun flowing – a point she does not explicitly make. One *is* a new creation.

Tanner's assertion of the priority and effect of grace in justification is salutary. And, further, no thinker's attempt to comprehensively sketch out a lived theology will be absent its tensions, not least in balancing justification and sanctification. Even so, one might have hoped that, with the grain of the NT text, Tanner would have leaned harder into the expectation of change in the life of those atoned for (e.g. 1 Cor. 6:9-11; Eph. 5:8-10).[135]

### *A Patient Leaning-in to Renewal*

One repeated motif in Tanner's reflection on demonstrated ethics in the renewed community is a diminished expectation of manifest success in this life. For example, she describes one way of situating the work of the Spirit in the lives of redeemed "participants in God". This perspective emphasizes the earthy, pedestrian, and prosaic texture of "life *de facto*" in the community of faith – that is, it underscores "historical process, mediation, publicity, surprise within the course of the commonplace, and the ability of the Spirit to make do with the fallibility, corruption, and confusions of human life for its own purposes."[136]

For Tanner, "Christ saves, not by a divine life exempt from the mess, conflict, and loss of human life, but by one given over without reserve to those very features of it; he takes them, utterly and completely, to himself for his own," thereby healing them.[137] Key here is the idea that just this same messiness, hiddenness, imperceptibility of the good, and so on, is likely to linger on in the lives of those now in Christ:

> [D]ivine power only gradually makes its presence felt in reworked features of human life itself – and only very clearly in the end, the flesh resurrected, reconciled with its enemies, healed. The human is already elevated in union with Christ above itself to enjoy the very life of God, but this will be fully manifest in us only at a

> time of some unknown future reckoning. Sin will ultimately be extinguished in our lives ... But this will happen only ultimately in some disturbed, unpredictably non-linear process, comparable to the conquering of the effects of sin on Jesus' own life – what looks like final defeat, simple loss under sin's crushing weight, is not ... The Spirit's working in us is invisible in much the way divinity in Christ is invisible.[138]

Hear too this candid assessment:

> While Christians are confident that the gift of the Spirit in Christ is sufficient to enable their thorough reformation, sins, though now forgiven, remain surprisingly salient for whatever reason in most Christian lives ... Indeed, in a host of at least apparent ways, the world does not seem appreciably better after Christ's incarnation than before it. While they may be united with Christ in faith and love for him, Christians have arguably so far made no especially great moral progress toward that new manner of existence made possible in Christ.[139]

For Tanner, the incarnation, the hypostatic union, is a prism through which to understand the "making real" of the atonement, theological anthropology, the Spirit in the Community, and even eschatological hope. She holds that the mystery and tensions of the union of Word and man in Christ have their counterparts in the mottled texture of the lives of the faithful joined to him. So, is Tanner's take on the disciple's regeneration permissive, pessimistic, contradictory, realistic, hopeful, or conversant with lament? Her discourse provokes both thought and further debate.[140]

When it comes to Tanner's proposals on the ethics of participatory salvation, a generous receptivity may find there an energizing dialectic between a patient realism and a proleptic hope for atonement finally realized in the cosmos.

> [I]n and through our humanity as that participates in Christ's own, our whole lives are to gain a new character in the Spirit. From the depths of sin and death, out of the very occurrence of conflict, suffering, and loss in our lives together, which all but renders the Spirit invisible, will have to come what one would never expect and could never predict: a new human manner of existence; human lives reformed, reworked as a whole by the Spirit into a life-giving, Spirit-filled form.[141]

Tanner straddles a rather fine line. On the one hand, the fact of the incarnation "changes everything" – really, metaphysically. The atonement is no sleight of hand, no legal fiction. "The force of our assumption by Christ is felt ... in and through the ways our lives are led, in and through what happens in them, the shape they take, whereby the gifts of God come to be distributed."[142] This would seem to answer, in part, to the queries about the "justice" of a gratuitous salvation that exonerates, exculpates, and leaves the perpetrators unchanged.

On the other hand, Tanner is hardly triumphalist about the transformed quality of actual Christian lives, and assumes that often the process of conformity to Christ is lengthy, perhaps invisible, and ultimately eschatological:

> One will remain the finite creature one is, however radical the ultimate transformation of human existence itself, simply human potentials finally perfected in the end. But one's whole manner of existence will nonetheless be changed from the ground up, insofar as one will one day come to live off the very life of God already one's own in Christ. One will not simply have that Spirit of Christ for one's own, as one does now, but one's whole life will transparently manifest that fact, in

> ways that cannot be anticipated beforehand ... [That coming life] represents no simple extension of the finite human creature's own potentials but a literally God-infused life.[143]

## Preserving the Divine Transcendence

Significant space has already been devoted to God's distinction from all creation, the surpassing quality of his attributes not only in degree but in bare ontological status, and the reserve of "godness" that can only ever be his and not ours. This constellation of ideas of transcendence we have associated with God's "honor". For all her innovative theologizing, Tanner herself is quite in line with these rather traditional commitments on the nature of God.

Central to the drive to preserve divine honor is the insistence on God's originating, unconstrained freedom, matched with his limitless power. Whatever it is that God accomplishes in reconciling the world to himself in Christ, it is not done in this way because God operates in submission to some external demand. Additionally, at least two other factors must be made to cohere with the first: God's love which resonates throughout the apostolic witness to the Christ Event; and the darkness and shame of the Passion (whether reflecting human depravity, divine victory, love, or something else).

In integrating these exegetical and moral pressures, one penchant of classic theologians was to seek out a certain "fittingness" to redemption; to discern in God's action both freedom and virtue, rather than a mere exercise of raw power. If a pattern of atonement is "befitting" of God, then both divine purity or justice *and* the effectiveness of salvation will be preserved – God's honor is preserved. As various pathways of salvation are imagined, the axiomatic assumption is that God's character and intentions are trustworthy and have been adequately revealed, even as his power and being remain untainted across an unbridgeable gap from the created realm.

But, once again, in the eyes of many interpreters, the cross itself is an impediment to the harmonic confluence of all these suppositions about God. For example, many would hold that it is anything but self-evident that the incarnation or the cross are consonant with the freedom, the unbounded power, or the honor of God. How is such humility, condescension, and intimacy with human degradation to be posited of God and reconciled with his glory, honor, and transcendence?

One approach has been a transparent grasping of the nettle: to turn the spotlight back on the questioner's presuppositions and to question the skeptic's conceptualization of power, transcendence, and honor altogether. It has been argued against conventional notions that power is manifest *in God's condescending love*. (Of course, the foundational templates for this conceptual reversal are well embedded in the biblical sources, for example, Isaiah 29:14, Romans 11:32-35 and 1 Corinthians 1:18-2:5).

For example, with an eye on the world of Islam, Kenneth Cragg aims to upend conventional scales of value and their assumptions about power and honor:

> Omnipotence is not constituted by irresistible coercion or by untrammeled might. To be divine it has to be compatible with love. It must be the capacity to stand

unrivalled in the end, to outdo without remainder all that might defy or defeat its purposes or undo its consistency. Never in contradiction with itself, it out-masters all contradiction. Omnipotence is the spiritual counterpart of the sublime truth that "God is One".[144]

In this light, the incarnation must not be taken as a diminishing of divine greatness, but rather as the expression thereof. In the Nyssen's words:

> In the first place, that the omnipotent nature was capable of descending to man's lowly position is a clearer evidence of power than great and supernatural miracles ... God's transcendent power is not so much displayed in the vastness of the heavens, or the luster of the stars, or the orderly arrangement of the universe or his perpetual oversight of it, as in his condescension to our weak nature. We marvel at the way the Godhead was entwined in human nature and, while becoming man, did not cease to be God.[145]

In such efforts to draw together God's honor and transcendence along with questions of incarnation, salvation, and divine character, Tanner is for the most part a fellow traveler. This is nowhere truer than in her locating love in a God of unmitigated transcendence. Tanner is quite firm on the categorical distinction that is God. Yes, human salvation is participation in God's own being. But for God himself there is no other being or category in which he participates; he *is* being.[146] Salvation through participation in the divine nature ("deification") does not trade in a blurring of the Creator–creature distinction. For Tanner, the opposite is in fact the case. This border must be robustly patrolled both in honor of the truth about God and to ensure the possibility of human benediction.[147]

For humans to experience the "life which is true life" (1 Tim. 6:19), we must be joined to that which we are not and can never be: to God. "The goodness of God cannot be contained in any genus; it is beyond all distinctions in kind. And this is just what cannot be communicated to finite creatures."[148] Again, "divinity is not a class term".[149] God is not only different from all creation, but he is different in a way that is unlike the way any other two created realities might differ from one another.[150]

Even as Tanner takes the unity of God and man in the incarnation to be the ultimate soteriological hinge, she rigorously affirms the indelible Creator–creature divide. As Tanner is at pains to insist, the union of God and man in Christ is genuine – no half measure – providing insight into the ineffable God's engagement with his creatures. But, as Hastings reminds us, a necessary asymmetry perdures: "the concept of *koinonia* ... between the divine person of the Logos and his human nature [is] a very appropriate way of envisioning how [God] is in asymmetric and sovereign fellowship with his creation."[151]

Atonement in its fully orbed sense entails our re-reception, in the "strong sense", of the image of God, possible only because the Word first received humanness to himself:

> In a second, much stronger way of being an image through participation in what one is not, creatures would receive the divine image itself for their own, and end the futile struggle, so to speak, to approximate God in and through what they are simply in themselves. Creatures would receive from God what is beyond themselves – the divine image itself.[152]

But in all this we may not smudge the bold line separating our creatureliness from God's eternal being. Tanner insistently foregrounds the fact that it is precisely the divine distance from us that enables his saving nearness:

> Now hope is fueled by how *different* the Trinitarian relations, in which we are to be incorporated, are from anything with which we are familiar under the constraints of finitude and sin. The difference between the Trinity and us now holds out hope for a radical improvement of the human condition. The Trinity is not brought down to our level as a model for us to imitate; our hope is that we might be raised up to its level.[153]

We have had occasion previously to cite David Burrell's portrayal of the relationships of God, humanity, and providence – a reality in which the Creator's and creature's planes of being dynamically (while asymmetrically) intersect without damage to either. These realms are actually engaged one with the other, but with such a fundamental distinction that they are also "non-competitive". His characterization of a deft balance in the God–world relation (summarized by Soars) is consonant with Tanner's thinking on that relation generally and also as it is actualized in Christ:

> "Distinction", "relation", and "creation" coalesce conceptually for Burrell: if we focus on the distinction between God and world without also attending to the relation, the risk is that we characterize them as two "entities" (God + world) alongside each other; whereas if we emphasize relation and lose sight of the all-important distinction, we veer towards pantheism ... Uniquely in the case of God, God's ontological distinction from the world is God's logical relation with the world, and vice versa.[154]

### *Transcendence and the Gratuity of Grace*

Tanner explicates an important connection between God's absolute difference from all creatureliness and the effectiveness of his grace. To be fully actualized, humanity, even without reference to sin, is thoroughly dependent on the sustained gift of God's own life. Thus, "the interrupting factor [of sin serves only to make] our final end gracious in a stronger sense."[155]

> [The radical] difference between the divine and the human ... is sufficient to show that grace is gratuitous. As Augustine makes the point: "the soul itself, even though it may be always wise ... will be wise through participation in the changeless Wisdom, which is other than itself. For even if the atmosphere were never bereft of the light which is shed on it, there would still be the difference between its being and the light by which it is illuminated."[156]

Against the grain of so much modern thought, God's sovereign difference from creatures is not a threat to human dignity or freedom. The God–human bond is "non-competitive". Moreover, neither is God's difference an impediment to his solidarity with humanity. Thus Tanner counters the tendency to posit soteriological virtue in an incarnation that entails God's assuming limitation into his very "godness": "God must be incarnate in order to save, *but God must be different from us in order to save us* and it is just that difference that now seems jeopardized by kenoticism and the historicizing of God. God as an essentially historical being may now suffer along with us in Jesus, but how consoling is that?"[157]

### *Honoring God: Humility Before Divine Transcendence*

It is precisely because God so exceeds all qualifiers that attach to the created sphere that he has the resources to save, and the gifts of life to offer. Tanner's ethical thought is deeply conditioned by the idea of the unrelenting priority and superabundance of God's grace in the incarnation – all human good proceeds via Christ and the Spirit from that which we are not, i.e. God.[158] The appropriate human response then is humility and gratitude on the part of those now participant in the Son. From this proceeds humble obedience and service in the world, but not a dead end of self-loathing and world-hating.[159]

Tanner's stress on our dependency and on the God–human gap is common, of course, to garden-variety Protestantism, not to mention religious sensibilities much further afield. But more interesting for our purposes is i) Tanner's insistence on God's radical distinction from creation alongside ii) her moderating account of human depravity, including a robust affirmation of human goods.[160]

Tanner's construction of saving grace insists that any

> glory for the good we exhibit in our lives should therefore be reserved for God … [But] the primary reasons for [our] humility are not the usual Protestant ones: sin and a devaluation of any good achieved by us. Sin may make us horribly corrupt … But humility would be our proper posture toward God even if sin were totally removed by the grace of Christ or we had not fallen into it to begin with … The primary reason for humility simply stems from the strong sense of participation in God that we have stressed throughout. We are good not in virtue of what we are but in virtue of what we are not, like darkness lit up by a light that enters into it from without.[161]

### *Incarnation's "Rough Texture": A Threat to Divine Honor?*

We have encountered Islamic invective against the irrationality and especially the indignity of a salvation wrought in time through God enfleshed. The notion of incarnation as such is seen to be massively problematic, but also problematic (on this assessment) is incarnation's embedding within a plodding, contingent salvation-historical sequence. While Tanner is not addressing Muslim worries as such, her characterization of participatory atonement is relevant here.

Again and again, Tanner affirms that God's difference from us is foundational to his shocking closeness to us, the latter in no way contaminating or canceling out the former. She does not apologize for the ironies, the surprise, the mottled moral surface of the narrative of God's shepherding presence in salvation. Rather, she revels in it, taking it as grace-infused, unanticipated liberation – a hope not available in any other way to a humanity in bondage:

> Keeping the earlier unpredictable surprise of Christ's advent in mind, Christians may … be unusually resistant to the hindsight bias that so commonly afflicts … financial markets. Christians … typically tell stories about themselves and salvation history that stress just how unpredictably surprising the future looked from the standpoint of the past. They do not typically use retrospective stories about the past to smooth over discontinuous jumps in previous sequences of events but to highlight them.[162]

There are undoubtedly a myriad of antinomies and surprises when the Eternal intersects with the contingent; when the Creator expresses a radical stake in what and who he has made. Cragg, with Islam in mind, reflects on the wonder of God's intimate acquaintance with creatureliness – an intimacy that negates all forms of idolatry as the Creator yet remains distinct from worldly qualifications:

> [The] New Testament is among the most inclusive liquidators of idolatry in all history, whether the idols of the nation or of the marketplace … "God in Christ" is continuous with aspects of [Muslim] faith … with [our] common faith in creation, for creation means the Creator–creature relationship. Only in that situation can transcendence be acknowledged. The Creator has a stake in the creature. This cannot be a "compromise" of God.[163]

Tanner's situating of Christ in salvation likewise grasps both ends of a polarity. On the one hand, the radical interest of God in the creature could not be put more starkly than the Word incarnate. On the other hand, Tanner is emphatic that none of this diminishes God's otherness or his aseity – in fact it requires it. In God's gratuitous giving to us in Christ, he remains thoroughly undiminished: "God does not so much want something *of* us as want to be *with* us. God does not really need us *for* anything … In giving rise to the creature and elevating it to God's own level, God is always bringing about something less rather than something more than what the triune God already is in itself."[164]

### *Incarnation Without Temporal Indexing*

Tanner's generally traditional construal of divine attributes and perfections includes God's freedom from temporal qualification. God's atemporality, rather than distancing him from us, underwrites his ability to superintend and be present to human history – without coercion or disruption of human agency. God's relationship to human experience is radically other, seamlessly overlapping, and "non-competitive" all at once.[165] In this way he is incarnate without essential ontic change or damage; he is with us to save.[166]

Arguably, God's freedom from time implies that he can make unconstrained choices which coordinate with our own agency – and the consequences that our actions generate – without damage to his freedom, love, or essential character.

> It is true that God's free decision to create us with a particular sort of nature does not adversely affect the free character of God's decision to give us additional gifts. This is simply a consequence of the fact that God's decisions are not sequential as ours are. We find ourselves constrained by decisions we have already made because we will one thing after another with some ignorance of what our initial decisions might imply. Rather than willing one thing and then being constrained to will whatever else turns out to follow from a decision to create something of that sort, God, to the contrary, wills at once the whole of what God wants to happen: both creatures with certain natures and what follows from their having those natures … [We might best approach soteriology by way of reference] to the gracious character of *God's whole intent for us*.[167]

So, in human experience, even in the human experience of Jesus, salvation is sequential and developmental. But as an act of God, the incarnation is a whole – not something he has to wait upon or work through from one set of causes and effects to the next, as it were.

> [H]umanity suffering under the weight of sin is reworked in a process of salvation over time, from Jesus' birth up to and through his death. *The incarnation remains*

> *a constant* but its effects are not. Salvation, what the incarnation brings about, takes time, in short; salvation is a form of temporal, historical process, involving struggle with the forces of sin and death, and the sort of changes that typify any human life, sinful or not.[168]

Tanner presses the cognitive reception of the incarnation as an adamantine unit, a seamless whole. It is not especially about the nativity at the expense of the Passion (or the reverse); rather the two mutually inform each other.[169] In one sense, the time required for the story of Jesus to play out is beside the point.[170]

> One ... misunderstanding is to see the incarnation in a narrow temporally indexed way – that is, as simply referring to Jesus' birth – and therefore separated from the cross by the whole intervening span of Jesus' life. The incarnation, however, refers primarily to the fact that the Word has assumed or united the humanity of Jesus to itself ... [Thus,] verses of the Gospel of John that introduce the birth of Jesus – the light shines in the darkness (John 1), and so on – [are associated] with the death of Christ. There too, indeed especially on the cross, one finds the light coming into the darkness.[171]

### *Stability in the Grace of a Timeless God*

Divine transcendence is not on this understanding primarily about God's remoteness but about his reliability, capacity, and even nearness. We have already had occasion to consider how the timelessness of God may mitigate perceived threats to human freedom or to justice in his engagement with the world. Adequately parsing this subject matter certainly stretches epistemological limits (at least my own), but from within the boundaries of this framework, the worshipper – even now – is afforded grounds of trust, of stability, of security in the sufficiency and justice of a God beyond time.

> At every moment one is encouraged to assess the profitability of one's own life, so to speak, from its end in the eyes of someone, God, with the capacity to see the whole of it to its very depths. One imagines oneself engaged in such a task, moreover, in the company of all those similarly concerned – those who came before, the blessed dead, and all those who will in future go to make up the communion of saints before the world's end. One holds them in mind now, as if they existed concurrently with one's own efforts at the moment to make one's life over in God's image: one sings together with them, for example, before the communion table. In so doing one participates in the present in God's own awareness of time, an awareness with the capacity to hold together at once, to form into a simultaneous whole, the entirety of such past, present, and future efforts at God devotion.[172]

As the Christian lives through the process of atonement realized, participant in the divine life but facing the maelstrom of worldly instability, there is immense hope, for "the self is not fundamentally providing itself with the resources necessary for unifying the passing present. Those resources come from elsewhere, from the object [God] that orients one and is nothing like oneself."[173]

## Tanner's Incarnational Model: Concluding Thoughts

A hallmark of Tanner's theological production is a dynamic sort of simple creativity. The incarnation of the Word becomes the key to understanding every theological category with implications for humanity. This does not entail, however, an infusion of creaturely limitation into the essence of the God revealed to us in Jesus. No, that God remains the immutable Trinity. In Christ we are drawn into an asymmetrical unity with the life of that God.

In Tanner's structuring of atonement, we find an innovative reappropriation of theological topoi from scripture and Christian tradition. Her construal of participation in God through the mystery of incarnation helps us retrieve elemental dimensions of atonement, offering a holistic architecture that is lacking in some expressions of justification. Tanner's is a wide-angle perspective offering resources for thinking about both "salvation from" and "salvation for".

### *A Mild Critique*

However, her construct still suffers from some blind spots, in terms of how she selectively engages the spread of biblical data and also screens out certain potentially productive atonement perspectives. For reasons of space and the purposes of this book, I do not devote a great deal of energy to critiquing Tanner's arguments. But I will offer some commentary here. (I also make mild criticisms in some of the notes.)

There are needless losses, I believe, in the way Tanner downplays the cross as the climax of the Jesus Event. In fact, centering on the death-resurrection complex need not cut the ground out from under an incarnational framing of redemption. (Think, for example, of how central the cross is to Athanasius precisely in his *On the Incarnation*.)

By my judgment, Tanner also unnecessarily either dilutes or entirely loses the added value of, and biblical warrant for, categories such as satisfaction, penalty, and vicarious suffering. Tanner, and other theologians much more so, is inclined to downplay the intersection of personal sin, penalty, and expiation at the cross. It is, of course, possible to fixate on or over-specify penal dynamics in atonement. But there is no defensible eliding of the NT claim that Jesus died "for" sins. This cannot be reduced to the bare assertion that Jesus met his death simply identifying with human experience and because of the presence of evil out there in the world at some unspecified remove. The claim is certainly more personal and intentional than that. If Christ died "for sins", we – all of us – certainly must be included among the "unrighteous", deserving punishment, who have by this death been brought to God (cf. 1 Pet. 3:18).

I do believe – and Tanner productively pressured my thought here – that such traditional Protestant atonement tropes do need to be rightly situated within a wider reconciliation framework – perhaps one like hers! These templates (e.g. PSA) also need to be properly and sensitively articulated. But, when handled with theological nuance, they can do considerable work in terms of justice, mercy, forgiveness, and genuine *atonement*. Further, considering Tanner's own positioning of incarnational atonement *as a whole act*, not temporally indexed in the story of Jesus, it is not clear to me why she finds the sequential elements of the Passion narrative to be an insurmountable logical impediment to adopting PSA in any form.

In Tanner's evocative work there is a danger of overcorrection, an acquiescence to false dichotomies; one result might be that the cross gets pushed too far towards the margins of the picture. Florovsky's words display a better balance: "The evangelical pattern of life, as delineated in his parables and in the Sermon on the Mount, belonged to the very structure of his redemptive ministry. All events of Christ's life had a redemptive significance, including the Temptation, the Agony in the Garden, and also the miracles, which were the sign of the Kingdom. But the climax of his life was his death."[174] Sonderegger, too, is apt here:

> As impressive as have been the theologies of gift, and even more of non-competitive giving, the sacrificial cultus that stands at the very center of Israel's life is one of death and alienation, of expense and attrition, and not simply life and feasting. The "life that is in the blood" endorses the vitality and value of a living creature, certainly, but it is released, gathered, and spread about through the death of the animal: nothing less is imagined in Holy Writ. Sacrifice is food, yes, and a pleasing savor, yes again, but it is also slaughter and exile and handing over.[175]

Tanner's admirable aim of rightly integrating incarnation and cross notwithstanding, her decentering of the death of the Messiah has distorted the contours of salvation's economy. It is unfortunate that Tanner attenuates her investment in the salvific resources of the Passion, and limits the range of tropes allowed to inform its meaning – particularly judgment, penalty, payment, and, to a lesser extent, sacrifice. When such traditional "atonements" are set alongside Tanner's larger framework, she perceives incompatible dichotomies where I do not. Much that she affirms needs affirming; some of what she denies need not have been denied.

A brief note here on Tanner and our interfaith interest: Tanner's emphasis on the productive impact of the whole life of Jesus is potentially congenial to Islamic thought. And clearly, any sort of de-emphasis on the cross catches the eye when one is thinking in parallel with Muslims. There are also harmonies between Tanner's approach and Islamic complaints about the rationality of a "third party punishment", and also the problematics of the crucifixion, which they take to be a slow, sequential mechanism of salvation, "late in the story" as it were. On the other hand, Tanner retains Christian orthodoxies (incarnation, Trinity, and even the cross) which are endemic points of contention with Islam.

### *Participation and Justice*

Tanner's incarnational accent encourages us to better connect the spectrum of canonical and gospel witness to our ideas of redemption. Important here are both notions of creation and the divine purpose for humanity as well as the entire life of Jesus effective in salvation.[176] Tanner's deeply metaphysical, if not mystical, sense of reconciliation by participation answers somewhat better than merely abstracted, forensic theories to questions of how the restoration of humanity might "work". Tanner's work encourages consideration of the divine hope for all humanity, all creation, rather than myopic attention only to the spiritualized rectification of a few souls.

Tanner's repositioning of the crucifixion is a significant move relevant to claims of the inherent injustice of crucicentric atonement ("justice from above"). However, one doubts that this is enough to satisfy the most strident cross skeptics. More importantly, I am not sanguine about the biblical fidelity and practical outcomes of decentering the cross in articulations of soteriology. Be that as it may, Tanner's participatory model, especially in its breadth, offers interesting contributions to the debate on justice in God's salvation.

### *Participation and Honor*

For Tanner, Trinity *is* monotheism because "divinity is not a class term" – in mind-independent reality, there are not various types or varieties of deity on offer. Redemption is our assumption into the eternal dynamic of Trinity, all the while entailing no change whatsoever in "deity". A persistent refrain in Tanner's writing is the transcendence of God, that is, the Trinity's absolute difference, freedom, timelessness, and power, and the sheer gratuity of divine gifts. Definitionally, we are "not God". In this respect she may be said to be solicitous for God's honor. This basic theology is hardly novel, but in this arena her theologizing is incisive: counterintuitively, she frames the incarnation as the iconic instantiation of God's unsurpassed difference from us and, thus, his capacity to save. Paradoxically, incarnation exhibits transcendence.

### *Participation, Sin, and Human Nature*

Tanner approaches the issue of sin in the human condition – and the attendant assumptions about grace and salvation – from an oblique angle. A reverberating drumbeat in her thought is that externally supplied grace is vital for the realization of "natural" humanity – even without reference to sin. There is scarce space for human hubris here. In terms of sin itself, while Tanner affirms the universal scope of sin's depredations, she appears to propose a rather mild impact of sin on human nature *per se*. What exactly this implies for sin, atonement, and an ethic of sanctification ("justice from below") is not easy to determine across the complexity, diversity, and tensions of her discourse. At times one may detect a distinctively hopeful prospect for actualized human renewal flowing from the atonement; but, conversely, Tanner's realism or pessimism appears to dilute any resolute commitment to sanctification as a non-negotiable feature of atonement.

Tanner's theorization of atonement is compelling for the breadth and freshness of her vision, the unique manner in which she centers incarnation. Interesting for our own purposes is the notable degree to which the atonement models with which Tanner is discontent are similarly problematic for many Muslim intellectuals (if not always for the same reasons). In our concluding chapter, I press towards a convergence between a broad incarnational framework and a relatively traditional emphasis on atonement through vicarious suffering. All this with thoughts attuned to the worries of the Muslim coterie that featured so prominently in chapters three and four.

# 8. Tying the Strands Together

> Who, then, is Jesus, the miracle of life, of love, and of healing? He is the Word of God and the servant of God and the messenger of God. He is the savior of us all, for what is salvation but healing? A savior is not simply one who dies for the sins of others but also one who heals the sickness of the human soul; one who infuses life into dead spirits by his own life and spirit. The original meaning of salvation is "to be healed", "to be made wholesome", "to be truly restored to life". This, according to the Qur'an, was the mission of Jesus. (Ayoub, *A Muslim View of Christianity*, 115)

## Synthesizing the Research

The engagement with Muslims in this study has significantly been aimed at "ourselves", a Christian audience. An undergirding agenda has been that we refine our contemplation of the wonder of salvation, that our doxology be elevated. In reductionist perspective, then, this book is "theological" rather than "missional". But to absolutize that dichotomy would be an error for "mission" is integral to Christian theology. Be that as it may, in terms of mission, this project clearly is not utilitarian, perhaps not even "strategic". The reader will not discover here "the keys" to persuasive proclamation to Muslims. This is not a pragmatic manual of intercultural outreach.

But I do hope that missional implications are not lost on the engaged Christian reader. To listen across a religious boundary before speaking, to fortify and examine one's own Christian conviction even as one seeks to communicate to the "religious other", and so on; surely these are both theological and missional gains. This "theological" study has consciously been carried out within the ambit of God's mission to all the peoples of his world.

In concluding this study, I hope to tie together the various threads we have been following. In general, I have been assuming more-or-less usual Protestant emphases such as the centrality of the cross and substitution themes (*à la* Anselm and Barth) as the platform from which to initiate discussion of atonement. With that starting point in mind, this chapter proceeds in three movements: first, I consider how critically onboarding Kathryn Tanner's contributions can helpfully inform our conceptualization of salvation. Second, I draw in potentially constructive influences from our coterie of Muslim theologians, refracted through the tripartite typology of sin, justice, and honor. This process is not, however, exclusively a matter of accepting and incorporating; in some domains, refining, redefining, or counter-challenging are appropriate. Finally, I conclude this journey by articulating an atonement synthesis that integrates a range of important concerns, emphases, and inflections emerging from this endeavor in comparative theology.

## Contributions of Tanner and Participatory Thought

This study has interrogated atonement taking vicarious redemption at the cross (including the penalty motif) as the starting point. The challenge has been to clarify, refine, broaden, and even correct various expressions of substitutionary atonement by way of questions emergent from an Islamic milieu and also by way of comparison with Kathryn Tanner's very different Christian angle of approach. Let us consider for a moment the contributions that Tanner has made.

Within the boundaries of my purposes here, I am primarily interested in what may be fruitfully derived from Tanner's incarnational theology and applied to the project at hand. Her work offers considerable resources. Now, it is true that I also find much to query in Tanner's proposals, but debate and critique of what I take to be the gaps in her theology is not my leading purpose here. In my response to her work, let me suffice with a general observation: Tanner often deploys dualities taken to be substantially mutually exclusive: love vs wrath; forensic penal satisfaction vs relational participatory holism; sacrifice as death vs sacrifice as life. Most of these I find unnecessary and unhelpful. Much Tanner affirms, I would; much she feels compelled to deny, I do not.[1]

Madigan, a Jesuit scholar of Islam, expresses matters in terms congenial to this study and to Tanner's thought:

> The mutual self-giving of the Father, the Son, and the Spirit is, of course, an eternal interrelation. However, in the incarnation, life, death, and resurrection of Jesus Christ, humanity is drawn into this action and relation of mutual self-giving. Here at last is a human life lived completely according to the *fitra* (nature) God intended; here at last is one who does not treat God as a rival; who resonates completely and seamlessly with the Word through which all is created (Jn. 1:3); who does "not consider equality with God something to be exploited for himself" (Phil. 2:6).[2]

I take the central challenge in addressing Muslim concerns to be clarity of thought and fidelity to scripture and tradition – rather than finding clever "proofs" to overturn Islamic objections. On this score, Tanner's focus on incarnation as constitutive of salvation raises important and sensitive issues. Any invocation of "incarnation" is vulnerable to allegations of *shirk* (associating the created with God) from Muslim opponents of traditional Christian doctrines. With Tanner, it is vital for Christian communicators to understand and to underscore that this doctrine is not predicated on the divinizing of the mere man Jesus – a theological heresy already warded off in the early church (see more below).[3]

Tanner's repeated drumbeat on the entire life of Jesus, the very "fact" of the Savior, might answer to some Islamic complaints about reductive PSA-style portraits of salvation which elide the *life* of Prophet Jesus and the relevance of virtuous, ethically powerful living. In this sense, a participatory salvation model entails emphases and commitments that helpfully converge with some Islamic worries over ethically permissive "grace theology" and salvation by proxy. Now, it is also true that this sort of emphasis in incarnational thought *can* be taken in an exemplarist direction with obvious affinities for the preferences of many Muslim thinkers. The utility of all of this for communicating atonement "to Islam" or for a pacifying dialogue of religions has limits, of course. I would not claim (nor would Tanner) that exemplarism captures the essence of the salvific moment. Indeed, Tanner's profile of Jesus is not simply that this prophetic Galilean lived a singular life, but that that life was indeed *the* life of the incarnate Son and thus of the world itself. Her claim that Jesus saves because he "has" the Spirit as an ontological given, rather than as an extrinsic gift – by nature rather than by grace – moves her Messiah well beyond the realm of Islamic prophetology.

### *Tanner, Transcendence, and Honor*

There are, at first blush, certain convergences between conventional Islamic commitments and Tanner's aggressive profiling of God's honor or transcendence. This dynamic is quite interesting – and for Muslims, complicating – in a theologian like Tanner who simultaneously is heavily preoccupied with the incarnation. She clearly feels no compunction to restrict her theorizing of Jesus to a "low Christology".

Indeed, Tanner is quite convinced – as are most Muslims – of God's absolute difference, freedom, timelessness, and the sheer gratuity of his gifts. But God's changelessness and category-defying timelessness can only be expressed, for Tanner, in terms of Trinity. (This is, of course, no less true for Anselm or Barth, though Anselm has on occasion been chided for under-integrating this theological fundamental in *CDH*.) Redemption is the assuming of humanity into this eternal triune dynamic without the admixing of categories nor any erosion of God's being. For Tanner, Trinity is monotheism because "divinity is not a class term" – there are not a variety of iterations which may be categorized under the heading "God". Trinity is who he is. So, once again, even where certain opening gambits in Tanner's thought suggest overtures to Islam, incompatibilities present themselves as soon as "flesh" (as it were) is put on her grounding axioms.

### *Tanner and Sin*

With respect to the topic of sin, it is difficult to articulate Tanner's contributions to the atonement debate in terms of Islamic concerns. A real difficulty here lies with the complexity, if not contradictions, of her own theorization. On the one hand, Tanner's sin construct is apparently less ontologically totalizing than many common Protestant depictions (including those of Anselm and Barth). This may indicate a degree of opening to the Islamic protests against Christian pessimism and sin obsession. Nonetheless, her Protestant fingerprints have hardly been effaced. Tanner's presentation of the ubiquitous necessity of grace (even for un-sinning humanity) is a challenge to all human hubris, and at times her description of humanity under sin is sketched in darker and more ominous hues than in most Muslim presentations.

### *Tanner on Justice and Holism*

The participatory emphases of Tanner's atonement portend a certain convergence with Islamic concerns when it comes to salvation, justice and holistic impact. We have seen Islamic charges of ethical derogation, individualism, and other-worldliness leveled at Christian salvation. For my part, I have argued that justice in properly framed PSA models is central and is anything but a sham or a legal fiction. Be that as it may, Tanner's redirection of soteriology onto the whole pattern of Jesus' life and the restoration of all creation by participation in the healing virtues of incarnation is also on point and productive.

The ontological bent in Tanner's construct may better help us to account for the positive trajectory of salvation, a salvation "for" many things in this world. Incarnation clearly affirms God's providential momentum for the good of humanity and all creation, not limited to a spiritualized rectification of a few souls as some Muslims have understood Christian doctrine. There are potential openings here for those concerned that salvation should impact all of life, should bring justice to bear on the world, should be, in a word, "earthier".

But, once again, one must also qualify. For one thing, Tanner is not terribly granular in her depiction of the actual life of atoned humanity either now or in the eschaton. (I say this as a relevant observation, not necessarily a major criticism.) Furthermore, as strong as Tanner may be in her ethical *aspiration* – after all, Christ himself is the key – she is somewhat ambivalent in her actual ethical *expectation* of believers. And, once again, Tanner yet adheres to core commitments that Muslims generally find insurmountable: Trinity, incarnation, and even cross. Conversely, on my accounting, some of her moves come at too high a theological cost, no matter how congenial they might first appear in conversation with Muslims (e.g. the decentering of the cross or negation of substitutionary tropes).

Traditional Protestant salvation tropes and theories require proper articulation so as to avoid contradiction or failure on ethical, logical, and biblical grounds. I contend that this can be done, must be done, without a wholesale abandonment of key facets of traditional atonement thought. Indeed, I would argue that both Anselm and Barth, rightly read, can be conscripted as allies in this endeavor. But even with due nuance and care in expression, soteriologies such as PSA do not "say it all". And here, in the face of a world of questions and queries, Tanner can be helpful. Her theologizing is hardly the only entrée to these vital discussions, but her creative and eloquent discourse can contribute substantively. In the domain of atonement thought, she productively pushes us to integrate the lived ministry of Jesus with all his soteriological impact; to position atonement in terms of its metaphysical and, to some extent, ethical transformation; and to ground the Messiah's "saving" not only in Jesus' death but in the all-enveloping reality of the incarnation itself.

## Integrating Islamic Critique and the Triple Themes

We have been considering salvation in terms of interventions centered on sin and the human condition, divine justice, and divine honor. My aim has been to attend to these pressures originating from an external nexus – Islamic thought – while maintaining prior, non-negotiable Christian commitments. Thus, however my mapping of salvation ideas may account for these pressures, it will not be by way of decentering the Passion or peripheralizing Trinity and incarnation. The reader will judge the productivity of this venture.

### *Sin*

A prominent line of demarcation between Christians and Muslims debating ultimate eschatological blessing arises over matters of sin and human nature. Barth and al-Faruqi represent a somewhat explicit contretemps on this score.[4] Their respective theologies transparently clash over (Barth's) prioritization of Christology and atonement as key to a proper theological anthropology and doctrine of sin. The divide appears to be irreducibly basic. As we have seen, for al-Faruqi, Christian atonement theory is an exercise of cart before horse, an "ideological presupposition" that distorts Christian theology, hamartiology, anthropology, and eschatology, and drains the Christian outlook of any this-worldly hopefulness.[5]

For Barth, though, virtually all considerations *must* begin with the *kerygma* of Christ crucified and risen. (A Christocentric vision is no less characteristic of Tanner.) Of course, to notice this prioritization does not itself settle the debate. Yes, the lens of incarnation and soteriology inform so much Christian thought on all else. But is that vision enlightening or distorting? Does the centrality of atonement lead Christians to a destructive pessimism? On this I would affirm Madigan's insight that "*Pace* al-Faruqi, a lively sense of human sinfulness is not just an 'ideological presupposition' upon which to construct an elaborate theory of atonement; rather it is the concomitant of a vivid sense of God's mercy."[6]

#### Sin: Original and Weighty

So, as a fundamental commitment, we must aver, in the face of some Islamic resistance, that sin is a matter whose dark seriousness is congruent with the dark seriousness of the crucifixion. This perspective is commensurate with divine justice for it is commensurate with divine worth. The offense of sin – being against God – is impossibly weighty, as Anselm saw. For us, this is congruent with God's *aseity*, a dogmatic affirmation congenial to many Muslims as well: We are dependent and owe him *all*, certainly not the other way around (cf. Q 47:38; Job 41:11; Ps. 24:1; 50:10; Lk. 17:10; Rom. 11:33-36; Ac. 17:25). What do we have that is not a gift (1 Cor. 4:7)?

To take sin seriously because we take God seriously is not, however, to invest all depictions of hell with a garish and gruesome literality; nor to validate an implication that God is a fiend delighting in torment; nor to doubt the balance and proportionality of all his judgments; nor to underweight the preponderant power of his grace. To take sin seriously *is* to assume that justice requires that goodness finally expunge all that is harmful, destructive, arrogant, and oppressive. It *is* to assume that unrepentant rebellion must not be left unaccountable, and that – coming into contact with God's searing mercy, white-hot love, and zealous purity – it simply is judged. It is to affirm the unity of God's attributes and the goodness of his creational purposes. All these pertain not to why God *had* to use the cross as much as to why in fact he did. This is the "necessity".

Original sin presses important but elusive questions. Muslim complaints of ethical malpractice centered on "transferred guilt" in Protestant atonement constructs are hard to miss. And yet, at this point of tension, it is worth recalling the scholarship (noted above) that highlights a strain in the Qur'an and Islamic discourse that asserts the gravity and universality of sin.[7]

In any case, the concerns about an original sin that negates human agency and drowns us in fatalism's arbitrary waters are not vacuous. Hear John Webster:

> That curiosity about the causes of evil carries ... dangers is amply illustrated by the history of Christian doctrines of original sin. To put the point simply, there are serious religious *objections* to the idea of *peccatum originale*. At heart, these objections concern the ease with which such an idea may undermine our sense that we are responsible agents accountable for our deeds. Language about the origin of our sinfulness in some anterior act by a predecessor appears to suggest that we are fundamentally passive, that which is most determinative in human persons is involuntary.[8]

A construal of the mystery of original sin and the human condition must respond to the critics' demurrals with at least this affirmation: the fallen condition of human nature is as serious as it is empirically ubiquitous, but it is not a matter of arbitrary guilt transfers, still less an imposition of a desiccating determinism.[9] It is a tangible, undeniable reality of human nature.

## Ontological Redemption: The Implications for Allegedly Sin-Obsessed Soteriology

At this juncture, an atonement inflected in terms of ontology or participation may be helpful. "Helpful" not in the sense of sidestepping or occluding debates about the seriousness of sin or the need for atoning sacrifice – these, we contend, must be maintained but argued with sensitivity and nuance – but, rather, "helpful" in that a broadened perspective can both sharpen a Christian apprehension of the wonders of salvation and answer to certain criticisms of atonement's supposed sin-focused pessimism, ethereality, and social uselessness.

Above we encountered Crisp's Athanasian-influenced thought: on this outline, rather than imputed guilt, the accent in "original sin" is on the organic link and empirical solidarity between us and Adam, *and* the Latter Adam. The ultimate "human" extends a sort of vicarious therapy to Adam's sin-sickened family.[10] Of course, this by no means diminishes mystery or turns the economy of salvation into the straight-line "works accounting" that some Islamic theorists desire. But it is arguably resonant with existential realities. And this vision does set the issues of sin and (allegedly arbitrary) guilt–merit transfer in a different light.

When soteriology is not reduced to an algorithm for the attainment of pardon but takes into account creation's purposes and metanarrative sweep, then, as serious as sin is, the disruption it represents is neither definitive for, nor constitutive of, the Christian story (counter to al-Faruqi, Rida, and others). For patristic thinkers like Irenaeus and Athanasius, God's activity in creation is unified, coherent, and continuous.[11] In meeting Jesus, we meet Creator and Origin, Irenaeus' "First" who appeared last.[12] We must remember that, from the start, the business of the Logos was creation, not to mention *new* creation.

Salvation is not narrowly about sin but rather the construction and reconstruction of the cosmos.

### Sin as Violation of Law

In certain Islamic assessments, the Christian construal of sin is both exaggeratedly dark and also strangely vital to the true revelation of God. And then, tragically bereft of a legal remedy, Christians are left ill-equipped to counter sin's effects.[13] Here enters the category of law or *Shari'a*. Interestingly, PSA – the theory most subject to opprobrium – is arguably the soteriological vision most beholden to legal categories. Within wider visions of salvation, however, a Christian theologizing of sin certainly extends beyond the exclusively legal. Sin is not merely violation of rules; in marked distinction from conventional Islamic framing, sin vitiates an interpersonal bond with the Creator.

Wrapped up with the breaking of divine command is the scarring of "the image" such that a human–divine relationship, even "partnership" of dependence, is violated. The interchange – now, the pure with the impure – has been sullied, issuing in death. So, for Barth (as for Anselm) sin is so grievous to God, not because his own being is vulnerable to harm – still less because a mere "regulation" has been violated – but because *our relationship to him* is thus vulnerable.[14] And God is unwilling to let matters so to stand. Sin simply is that grievous. Indeed, again for Barth, it is measured in terms of the gap between fallen humanity and Christ. Thus, God's remedy at the cross is serious enough, loving enough, powerful enough to match. (Legal aspects of salvation command further comment below.)

### The Cross as the Prism for Sin

Finally, then, questions arising from the Islamic sector, alongside contributions from incarnational templates, can apply productive pressure on conceptualizations of sin typically associated with atonements of vicarious suffering. Even so, after appropriate qualifying and repositioning has been implemented, we are driven back to the Passion, to the verity, the offense, and the hope of the cross. In final assessment, the Christian as liberated captive glories in the strangeness and power of the crucifixion. The cross remains our most honest vantage point on sin, as Barth intones. (Thus, he reminds us, even sloth must not be sloughed off as trivial digression.)

At Golgotha we encounter the unvarnished apocalypse on sin, on the decay and despair that haunt humanity (cf. Rom. 1:18). This is the node where our need is met head-on. As Madigan puts it:

> Golgotha ... is a place accessible to all ... The point where, in the Christian understanding, God opens the divine life fully to humanity is not a place delimited by the sacrality of a temple, the perfection of law observance, the learning of a synagogue, or the power of a palace. Humanity at its worst is at home there: jeering and cursing, brutalizing and violating, fickle and arrogant, as the gospels attest. There humanity does its worst, but its worst is not enough to vanquish divine love.[15]

### *Justice*

Prods from the Islamic ethos foreground tensions and questions around justice in "objective" constructs such as PSA. Tanner's thought can also add to the conversation, but I would suggest that the "head-on" encounter between Islamic and traditional Protestant thought is potentially more productive in penetrating the justice issue. Why so? Not because Tanner is unconcerned for justice as such, but because (partly in response to the justice attack on vicarious suffering) she cedes too much ground in her own rejection of PSA. Thus, repairing to defensive ramparts in the face of liberationist, anti-substitution critiques, Tanner's thought contributes less than it might have to our understanding of the judicial and justice aspects of the cross.

The profile of justice in objective atonement constructs is indeed liable to distortion. But, equally, the juridical, the forensic, and the "justice overtones" of substitutionary suffering must not be surrendered or deflected. They must be sensitively parsed. They remain vital and hopeful in that they speak to the convergence of the radical love and justice of God precisely at the point of human deficit.

#### Justice from Above

Certain flat readings of PSA – assuming a very mechanistic, linear, and sequential relationship between all the parties to salvation (God, Jesus, and humanity) – generate seemingly unbearable contradictions and disjunctions. These disjunctions touch on the integrity of God's own being – problems of "justice from above". How can God punish and justify the "wrong" parties and remain just? For Muslim theologians, interjecting a third party into the simple binary of Sovereign and subjects deeply distorts the moral aesthetic. Further, the cross would seem to be a rather crude resolution to the unseemly clash of justice and mercy within the being of a God who in fact should not be depicted as experiencing internal discord and who is subject to no warring impulses in any case (see further under "honor" below).

Part of the Christian response must be to cast the net wide enough so that atonement is expressed in both its objective and subjective aspects, such that justice is seen to be both retributive and restorative. But even more fundamental to the questions of justice from above are definitive confessions as to the nature of God, confessions that Muslims will invariably find problematic. We speak, of course, of Trinity and incarnation. At this juncture in Christian–Muslim dialogue – setting to one side the possibility of epiphanic conversion – the most to which we may aspire is winsome communication and a probable parting of ways.

But to revisit the matter of a clash between God's justice and mercy allegedly entailed in cruciform atonement: here a classic crux text is Romans 3:26. That is, God's sacrificial presentation of the Messiah "was to show his righteousness at the present time, so that he might be just and the justifier of the one who has faith in Jesus" (ESV). The exegetical flashpoints in this larger pericope are multiple. Among the questions are: "Is Paul in fact deploying cultic language here?" "Is τὸν ἐκ πίστεως Ἰησοῦ referencing 'faith in Jesus' or 'the faith of Jesus'?" These cannot detain us here.

I merely submit that an experiential conflict between justice or judgment and mercy or love is a common creaturely instinct. For example, in a given situation, a penalty exacted by a judge may well be just, even necessary. But the recipient of that just consequence would very infrequently *experience* that justice as an act of love, to say the least. Nonetheless, to state matters this way amounts to little more than a topographic survey of the subject's psychological or emotional landscape. Granting the uncomfortable and commonly perceived antinomy between justice and mercy, nothing in the moral structure of the scenario invoked here actually demonstrates an absence of love or mercy on the part of the judge.[16]

Back to Romans 3:26: at a minimum, we have here the assertion that in God's action in the death of the Messiah, both God's justice (as such) and his mercy (his saving justice) are unveiled and made effective. Apocalyptic? Unexpected? Subversive? Undoubtedly. Might the human subject grapple with the apparent tensions and marvel at the mystery? Surely. But nothing Paul has said encourages us to import a conflict into God's own being. Nothing here suggests a fissure within God's own nature that requires patching up. At the cross we meet God's justice and mercy in confluence. His "justness" is never absent love. His love never absent justice.

Despite some unfortunate portrayals of the logic of the Passion story, the cross is not the site of the resolution of a conflict intrinsic to God. For all that, it is mysterious; it is the numinous unleashing of God's love, power, justice, and mercy all at once; it is the powerful liberating expression of God for us. Assuming all this, we certainly may yet grant that in the atonement the ineluctable intersection of God's attributes and his transcendent essence strains the limits of human knowing.

Certain signature features of Christian theology seem to be more a militarized frontier than an open crossing point between the competing monotheisms. Nevertheless, however one grapples with such divides, it remains essential to Christian soteriology and to questions of justice that God, the One author of reconciliation, is Trinity. Furthermore, the Trinity's activity *ad extra* is unified, not in conflict or fragmented. PSA must be situated as itself a manifestation of this truth – at the cross we see God at work in one seamless motion.

At ground level, the Gospel narrative in all its earthy texture is a striking wonder, sometimes a conundrum. But we hold that in the story of Jesus we encounter *God* at work, Father–Son–Spirit in the single act of redemption. Justice from above is secure for the Father is mistreating neither the Son nor a prophet; rather, God himself is present to us in Christ. Vidu's stance on inseparable action undercuts any sense of one member of the Trinity punishing another, any fracture or opposition within the immanent being of God. In this move, he also very interestingly positions PSA within the broader doctrine of incarnation:

> I regard the penal sufferings of Jesus (in his human nature) as a created effect of the mission of the Son. As a created effect, they do not go into the ontological constitution of the work of redemption itself, but are a consequent condition. The basic act of God is a particular kind of unitive action. What turns redemption's wheel, so to speak, is the incarnation itself.[17]

The revelation of God and the experience of God display a Trinitarian structure. Bringing in Trinity as a defense of God's just atonement is not simply a matter of marshalling one more peculiar doctrine in a series of Christian–Muslim dogmatic disputes. With the Trinity, the commitments and entailments are rather "all or nothing". These are the waters in which we swim, the light that illumines the way ahead. The Trinity is the God we know.[18] A formidable interfaith disjunction it may be, but there is no pathway around, only through.

### Justice from Below

There is also, of course, the problem of justice from below. Some malformed articulations of objective atonement seem to leave little room for, or expectancy of, human agency, change, or transformation. The unjust are simply declared just and then left to wallow in (or enjoy?) their ongoing vice-laden existence under a form of cosmic "diplomatic immunity". This is the complaint about the ethically enervating impact of a "*fait accompli* redemption". So, Joshua Ralston states:

> The central problem in Christian talk of redemption is its already completedness. Christianity, unlike Islam, proclaims that atonement has already occurred, that the most important thing has already been done. What remains for humanity is to accept God's action on their behalf. However, al-Faruqi avers that if redemption is accomplished once and for all in Jesus, apart from any human effort or action, it leaves human beings largely unchanged and offers little impetus for moral transformation.[19]

Does not human wrong, to be righted, require more than a deposit to our account by a white-knight investor with limitless resources? How can the existential bearing of punishment, and (for violators) the escaping of it, justly be executed on such bureaucratic terms? Cragg evokes this Muslim aversion to substitutionary atonement as a "revulsion against 'shuffling the cards' of guilt, against false exoneration, and incrimination".[20]

But, as we have seen, the necessary truths of the forensic and quasi-numeric logic of PSA (and even satisfaction, for that matter), need not stand alone. Indeed, they do not. The truth of atonement does involve a "status" freely granted to repentant sinners, but *as they are in fact joined to Christ.* The truth of atonement must be metaphysical and substantive, a participation (even if proleptic) enabled by union with Christ. The change of status comes about as in Christ the marred image is healed, as we participate in *the* Image. In Hastings' words:

> The biblical authors believe Jesus can, with perfect justice, die physically and suffer spiritually for the sins of the world. How? On the basis of his hypostatic union with humanity. And that on this basis, humans can, by the work of the Spirit, appropriate the atoning work of the Son by entering into the reality of that union. And that this includes *both* justification forensically, *and* sanctification or transformation into the image of Christ.[21]

### Objective and Subjective Together

The "objectivity" of PSA clearly foregrounds the issue of retributive justice. But, despite demurrals, there is no implicit incompatibility between classic objective models and the wider vistas we have been encouraging – notions of participation, for example. And in these wider vistas, the subjective experience of redemption is more readily brought to the fore – the restorative justice of lived ethics and eschatological expectation both. This answers in part the question of justice from below. In an encompassing view of salvation, we have to do with the objective and the subjective, salvation from and for (cf. Heb. 9:28).

On this point, Madigan's work is instructive as Christian theologizing attuned to the Islamic realm. His insights are valuable, even if not, in my judgment, entirely sufficient.

> It was not Jesus' killing that God willed, but rather Jesus' complete faithfulness to expressing mercy and compassion even when it was clear it would almost certainly lead to his death. It makes little sense to say that God willed the murderous rejection of his Word, as Muslims are not slow to point out.[22]

To an extent, I would stand with Madigan here. But questions linger both in the realm of "objective" vs "subjective" frameworks and in terms of the mysteries of time, providence, and human agency (with which we have grappled above). Indeed, the cross is the narrative of what happens when a self-giving God encounters a rapacious and consumptive world – *it is the ultimate expression of God's love for us*.[23] For Madigan, "The death of Jesus is an essential element of atonement not because it was the price demanded by God, but because in that death Jesus was enacting the unconditional love that is the very nature of God."[24]

I am convinced, however, that the oppositional binary he constructs ought rather to be a mutual affirmation. The wording too might be adjusted yielding the result that the cross represents God's bearing of the cost of our redemption, and, in that, he enacts the unconditional love of his nature. Still, a cost there is (cf. Rom. 6:23).

I discern an implicit omission here underlying both Madigan's and Ralston's thoughts.[25] I would argue that, on their terms, it is hard to see how the cross itself is the fulcrum finally ushering in the Kingdom. It appears here that, though the cross was the actual *outcome* of Jesus' ministry, it needn't necessarily have become the center of Gospel proclamation that throughout the NT it clearly is. It is hard to see how (on their accounting) the cross was not just an unfortunate, "accidental" consequence of the nature of the world and the nature of Jesus. I would argue, rather, that the NT insists that the cross *was* the "cup" given to Jesus by the Father (Jn. 18:11). It is hard to see how (on their terms) the cross is, as in the NT, the actual fulfillment of a prophetic pattern of redemption that "had" to be this way (Mt. 3:15; Jn. 12:27; 19:24, 36-37; Ac. 13:27; Mk. 8:31-33: "…δεῖ τὸν υἱὸν τοῦ ἀνθρώπου…").[26]

Recall again Burrell's invocation of Alter on biblical narrative: "the omnipresence of the divine actor in no way suppresses … the poignancy of human initiatives and failures."[27] Through what humans freely and culpably intend for evil, God concurrently can intend and effect good (cf. Gen. 50:20; 45:4-8). In the final accounting, God's purposes prevail, but, with both their loss and liberation, neither human nor divine agency cancel the other. The divine economy is perplexing and restorative at once.

Certainly, the cross represents the unconditional love of God. But, to be effective, it must also be the mystical, surprising, and justice-enacting work *of*

*God.* Yes, this happens in a manner beyond our ken such that the divine and human planes overlap without coercion. But, the point is, at the cross, a metaphysical transformation must be intended and unleashed in the act. Otherwise, however sincere and grand our rhetoric, we still have not moved past the realm of "example" alone; and example alone is inadequate to the challenges of the human drama.[28]

Objective atonement is the necessary foundation. But, equally, classic objective models need to be articulated with a panoramic vision and language that exceed their sometimes narrow expressions. The dynamics of redemption must not be reduced to logic chopping, account shifting, and mathematical balance; redemption must be (as Barth himself insists) underwritten by metaphysical resources. These generators of ontological change, we might add, are the Spirit and Son on mission.

Little good happens in the cosmos, ethically or eschatologically, if being pardoned, we remain as we are. Substitution, representation, and participation coinhere, so that in Christ sinners both are "saved" from judgment and also are themselves judged, they die and rise to new, just, living. Atonement is actual, is mysterious, is *not* a conniving fiction. Justice in the world depends on these *realities*. Metaphysical transformation and the exertion of divine power are required to "justify" justification. A viable hope depends on it. But if this power of union with Christ be granted as essential to salvation, the underlying logic of PSA also stands.

## Resurrection and Justice

Barth, as descendent of Anselm, may be commended for exceeding him in more explicitly rejecting a valorization of suffering and death, even as he propounds the vicarious suffering of the Savior. He also exceeded Anslem's (intentionally) more constricted gaze in emphasizing resurrection as engrained in the meaning of the cross. Resurrection is no mere addendum, nor even simply a reversal of the cross's "loss", but is actually integral to the singular saving act of the Lord (the "inseparable action" of the Trinity). Thus, speaking to the hope of new life, the resurrection also speaks to the basic justice of God's action in and for humanity.

In any accounting of salvation, creational purposes must be borne in mind. Salvation's agenda is after all recreation. That is, even in the word of the cross, the telos must be resurrection. As Ralston says, "Following Paul … it is only because of the resurrection that we rightly and foolishly call the cross 'saving'. Without this act of divine vindication, we Christians are fools but to be pitied."[29] Hope, change, and transformation are bound up with the unlikely story of the cross, and only because of the unlikely, but true, story of the rising of the King.

The Passion speaks to justice in the world but does so as stamped by the resurrection. Ralston positions Jesus' resurrection as the crown of salvation, so rebutting the skeptics' claim that atonement theology is world-despising and pain-valorizing.[30] However, as genuine and tangible as Christians assert that the resurrection *kerygma* is, it is also admittedly the basis of a life lived now *in eschatological prospect*. Cruciform redemption announces justice in the real world. Perhaps participatory lenses (in particular) on redemption can help us to sharpen our view of the intersection of creation, resurrection, and new creation. But all of this is a present ethic only partially and imperfectly enacted, sustained by an eschatological hope (Rom. 8:23-25). This is the hopeful realism of the Gospel, and in that News of resurrection there is justice (Rom. 1:1-4, 16-17). Once again, Ralston:

> Reading atonement as the divine vindication of the innocent Jesus [in resurrection] is an affirmation of God's solidarity with and commitment to a justice not of this world's making. The exposure of injustice on the cross, and the vindication of those crushed by unjust power, remains, however, an eschatological hope. The already-ness of the atonement as divine vindication is a promise, one that sends human beings outward by the same Spirit who raised Jesus into acts of mercy and justice.[31]

### *Honor*

When it comes to the honor of God in salvation, the doxological sensibilities of Christianity and Islam are quite incongruous but, for all that, it must be granted that both theological visions *aim to be* solicitous for the glory of God. Conventional Christianity and Islam, as theistic faiths, converge on the premise that the creature is to live life oriented towards and in dependence on the surpassing greatness, worth, and limitless capacity of the Creator. God's honor is an uncontested presupposition.

However, equally definitive for the Christian is the revelation of that selfsame Creator in the Jesus of the NT. Thus, the Christian and Muslim religious aesthetics diverge in terms of the tangible outworking of God's honor, his greatness, and his transcendence. For Christians, however counterintuitive, the confession is sure that from the face of the lowly Nazarene, acquainted with sorrow and familiar with grief, radiates the glory of God triumphant (2 Cor. 4:6). The Messiah's apparent weakness is an unnerving cosmic surprise, but in the confession of that Lord rebellion and idolatry are overthrown and God's greatness revealed.[32]

### The Cross as the Intersection of Incompatible Divine Perfections

We have seen Muslim misgivings about the cross positioned as a resolution to dissonant virtues (justice and mercy) within God's being. While Islamic tradition is not entirely univocal, a common strain would entirely avoid holding God to any standards of "virtue". Virtues are God's expectations of *us*. Inflecting God in voluntarist terms, many would strongly assert that we are in no position to associate any sort of virtue, attribute, or ethic with God's essence. However that may be, Muslim thinkers certainly balk at the suggestion of any contradiction to attributes within God.

There is an admonition here for any theorists of PSA who would set the free authority of God, or the justice of God, in atonement over against other attributes (e.g. goodness, mercy, or love). Too easily a false dichotomy may emerge. The justice of God simply "is". It is not undermined by or in opposition to these other qualities, even if fallen human interaction with that justice may be difficult or painful in consequence. A certain analogy may be discerned in Paul's description, in Romans chapters six and seven, of the severe impacts of the Torah when it interfaces with fallen humanity; these "negative" impacts in no way gainsay the goodness of the Law itself. Its goodness stands. It simply "is".

A "Western" modernist metaphysic will often place God in a zero-sum relationship to humanity and will thus dilute divine transcendence in an effort to affirm divine love, mercy, and justice; and to enhance human freedom and dignity. In other words, it is claimed that the cross cannot be the pre-eternal sovereign design of God for that would make him unjust and unmerciful, and humans less free. (This is true of Anselm's fiercest critics, though contemporary detractors also find many other targets besides our Medieval monk.) To put this intellectual trajectory in crassly reductionist terms, there must be an incompatibility between a good God's exhaustive sovereignty and the cross. Since the cross undeniably stands as a historical, if not theological, fact, then God's sovereignty, his capacities, and his transcendence must be redefined in order to exculpate him with respect to the crucifixion. Crudely: *God did not intend the cross, it just happened.* Progressive theologians go on from there to make of it whatever they can. But the Muslim intuition on this supposed economic trade-off between the limitless transcendence of God and the ignominy of the cross travels in the opposite direction. Muslims are generally inclined to affirm the transcendent sovereignty of God in such a way that the reality or meaning of the cross is negated. *For very traditional Muslims, indeed, the cross did not happen.*

In certain "Western" modernist visions, then, given the crucifixion, God's "honor" (his transcendence) is diminished to save his reputation (!). Conversely, in a conventional Islamic vision, it is the crucifixion that is abolished in deference to God's honor. Charting a path oblique to both instincts, I would appeal for a balanced affirmation of the radical transcendence of God in strange harmony with his perfections – manifest savingly, mysteriously, precisely in the crucifixion, resurrection, and ascension. There is no ontological clash between the justice and mercy of God. The cross does not *resolve* these two virtues; it reveals them. God is holy, and as such, his love is just, his justice loving. As with the persons of the Trinity, God's attributes are many and are one.

### God's Honor in Timeless and Non-competitive Relations

The recondite issues of God's relationship to time and to human agency have ever been a theological "pebble in the shoe". This study has generally been happy to acquiesce to traditional notions of God's timelessness and has invoked the concept with respect to God's justice in atonement. On this there is much to debate, which, presently, we must foreswear. But the powerful contestation of divine atemporality in our day must at least be acknowledged.[33] Nonetheless, in considerable convergence with Tanner, Burrell, Sonderegger, and others, I have appealed to God's non-competitive interface with his creatures. He subsists both "beyond" time and, as he chooses, within it. As the Life of God on its own level of existence intersects with ours, no agency is lost to either party. God's purposes may both overlap with and upend retrograde human intentions, with no loss to God's justice, freedom, and dignity *or* to human agency. In other words, his relation to us – even in the mysteries of the Passion – is dynamic and reciprocal, but also asymmetrical. His honor is unperturbed.

In their own distinctive grammars, both Barth and Tanner advert to a God who is dynamic in his timeless transcendence. This construction of God and time answers, then, to the chronological sequence of humiliation and injustices through which Jesus proceeds for our salvation. This also addresses the scandal of particularity – complaints about salvation history's delayed gestation until an event outside Jerusalem two millennia ago. Incarnation (including the cross) viewed from the "godward side" is a whole cloth; it is, in Tanner's terms, an "event" not indexed to chronology. So, even as God acts sequentially in our world, he is not subject to time's vicissitudes. Nor is his justice contingent, subject (as it may seem) to a sequence of "injustices" before arriving at resolution. We can concede, of course, that something like this is our temporal, fallen *human* experience. But as Vidu has reminded us, Trinitarian relations are not immanent and sequentially causal – they are one and whole. Furthermore, then, the human wrongs entailed in the story of Jesus remain *human* failings, not God's.

And so, even as humanity must experience history along an often rocky timeline, atonement is a design preceding creation's causal continuum. For God, that continuum is not closed; rather, he upholds it. And his design is ultimately for the blessing of the nations (cf. Gal. 3:13-14, 22-29; 4:4-5; 1 Pet. 1:19-20). God's ways are beyond our searching out (cf. Rom. 11:33-36). Admittedly, if such theocentric framings are privileged, the tensions of our lived experience do not evaporate, but God's honor and limitlessness persist undeterred. As such, this suggests grounds for faith and hope even amidst the continued ambiguities of "life on the ground".

To be sure, I make no breezy claim that all problems are solved, and all contestation silenced as, in droves, Muslim (or other) critics acquiesce to the ideas I propound here. Recall, this book is more theology than apologetics or even "contextualized theology", as commonly understood. The central effort in this book has been to draw Islamic discourse into a Christian conversation; to do so in concord with prior theological commitments; and to do so with as much discipline and hospitality as can be mustered. To the extent that this refining of Christian articulation enhances both clarity and effective Gospel communication back into a Muslim context, that would be a gain.

However, my working assumption has never been that this "clarifying" or "honing" will necessarily lead to converging theologies or will necessarily prove persuasive to Muslim devotees. Any moves I make here remain embedded within the mysteries of incarnation and substitution at the cross. In most cases, the incompatibility of basic Christian and Islamic commitments will persist. My fundamental hope has been to constructively develop our understanding *as Christians*. The aspiration is a fruitful portrait of the saving economy of a particular God – the all-surpassing I Am uniquely known in Jesus. In all this, God's honor is accounted for; indeed, it is on display.

### Necessity as a Challenge to Divine Honor

We have seen the charge against substitutionary atonement that such constructs subject God to extrinsic constraint. The cross becomes a mechanism God must contrive in order to save. Such "need" offends against divine honor. Atonement theory contradicts the freedom and sovereignty of God who can forgive at will. In contrast, the remonstrant insists, God simply says, "be," and it is so (Q 40:68: فَإِنَّمَا يَقُولُ لَهُ كُنْ فَيَكُونُ). Ralston's distillation of al-Faruqi is familiar: "al-Faruqi claims that substitutionary models of atonement end up giving something, in this case retributive justice, purchase over God and therefore constraining divine freedom."[34]

Anselm's *CDH* has long been a storm center of the "necessity" debate. However, as argued above, in *CDH* the contours of "necessity" are not so crass and lacking in complexity as is often made out. It is hardly self-evident that *CDH*'s conceptual architecture invalidates divine freedom. In *CDH* the "constraints" of justice are neither external to God nor coercive, but God acts authentically, freely, in love, *and* at great "cost". He acts in accord with the justice that he himself is, in accord with his own honor.

As Muslim and Christian proclaim versions of God's salvation across boundaries of incomprehension, there is irony in the fact that each construes the stance of its interlocutor as "arbitrary". On Christian terms (as I understand them), justification by sheer pronouncement is arbitrary. (In view of ubiquitous human failing, I am convinced that this is so even if judgment were solely according to works.) Meanwhile, we have already seen the Islamic charge that God's honor is diminished if he must resort to the arbitrary mechanism of a Roman gallows to secure forgiveness for sinners. The impasse persists.

Conventionally, Muslims understand sovereign command to suffice for forgiveness, particularly if in response to repentance and works. "Necessity" is repugnant. But in Christian conviction, "necessity" is simply a way of saying that forgiveness is according to God's holiness and virtue. It is not by *fiat*; it is neither random nor an exercise of raw force. Such would be the case if God's forgiveness were simply a matter of unmoored decision. In the face of sin's unrelenting reality, intervention will be just and must be on a cosmic scale – this is the cross. On these grounds, worries about God's freedom (which is assumed) are simply not on point. Salvation involves a metaphysical excess that God brings into our rescue. The sacrifice of the cross – implemented ultimately in resurrection and ascension – is an apocalyptic revelation, an overwhelming surplus of divine resource.[35] Shocking? Perhaps. But if it is understood as the power of God unto salvation, then God's honor is not diluted but amplified.

Sin has not foisted a dilemma onto God. Any "necessity" in atonement is a free expression of that which is intrinsic to him. The cross is not the solution to a problem to which God is subject. It is a *revelation of* God and the solution to a problem to which *we* are subject. Not surprisingly, revelation and solution coincide, for the One whom we need simply is God, the God of all honor.

## Religious Aesthetics and Divine Honor: The Direction of Travel in Incarnation

Perhaps the most ready-to-hand indictment of Christian soteriology for Muslim respondents is the evident shame, limitation, and dishonor of the hardscrabble reality of incarnation and the consequent suffering and humility of the Passion; on this, Rida's protest is particularly florid. The moral aesthetics of the two religions are manifestly incommensurable, displaying yawning gaps as to how

God's glory, virtue, and greatness are, or are not, compatible with Christian atonement.

This research is principally devoted to atonement rather than incarnation *per se*. But, on any reasonably orthodox construct, incarnational presuppositions are unavoidable at this juncture. Certainly, consensus Christian doctrine is adamant as to the impermeability of the Creator–creature distinction. But Muslim thought is inveterately suspicious that the doctrine of incarnation violates this defining commitment. And, of course, participation-inflected soteriologies such as Tanner's are unlikely to assuage that anxiety.

In other words, any theorization of salvation via incarnation is liable to trigger motion sensors guarding the boundaries of Islamic terrain; at stake are *tawhid* and the concomitant threat of infidelity or idolatry – *shirk* or "associationism". Thus it is important here to be abundantly clear that incarnational soteriology is not "adoptionist". Incarnation is not a matter of deifying an ordinary man or of positing the appearance of an "elevated" creature who came to rescue us in some fashion. On Qur'anic terms, God did not "take a son by adoption" [لَمْ يَتَّخِذْ وَلَدًا].[36] The direction of travel is rather the reverse.[37]

Furthermore, Jesus does not mediate salvation between God and humanity as some sort of "third entity", as David Burrell reminds us:

> Christian Scripture and theology speak in countless ways of Jesus Christ as "mediator between God and human beings". Now the ordinary use of *between* makes it sound as though Jesus operates in a space between the Creator and the creatures. Yet that would be an Arian view, explicitly repudiated in the early councils, so in orthodox Christian belief Jesus's mediation operates theandrically – that is, as something intrinsic to Jesus' divine-human constitution … So while the actions of Jesus can effect an immediate relation to God as Father, Jesus does not mediate as a "go-between". So the very feature of mediation which Muslims deny to the Prophet, thinking that to be Jesus' manner of mediating, represents a distortion of Christian thought … [J]ust as Jesus could not be construed, thanks to the *Shema*, as a "being alongside God" (which is the meaning Muslims attach to *shirk* …), so Christians falsify their own faith if they conceive of Jesus's mediation … as situated "between" the Creator and creatures. As the Word who is God, Jesus's mediation effects that immediate relation to God as Father, which Christians presume in their recurrent prayer: "Our Father."[38]

*From a Christian perspective then*, onboarding incarnation at the heart of atonement talk answers to issues highlighted by Muslim observers and others. Integrating the whole life of Christ with salvation speaks in some manner to the ends of that salvation and the ethics of the "saved life". Further, incarnation touches on another Islamic worry – the immediacy (or not) of God's saving act. As we have just seen with Burrell, Jesus the Mediator is no "third-party actor". God's salvation is "immediately" present in him. Of course, from a traditional Islamic perspective, these responses come prepackaged with an irreducible problem: *they fundamentally entail incarnation.*

Yes, a Muslim may well complain of irrationalism if they cannot accept the counterintuitive possibility of God himself assuming humanity to restore the cosmos. But, taking the Christian confession on its own terms, the complaint ought not to be that incarnation diminishes divine transcendence or greatness. As for the Christ: Jesus' humanity remains human, and the Logos is ever God.

With transparency and internal coherence, Christian doctrine holds that deity is not diminished in contact with humanity, but rather that consequently *we* are elevated and "saved". And any elevating that happens to those "in Christ" does not transform them into objects of worship or sovereign autonomy. God's honor is intact; Creator and creature remain ever distinct. For a Muslim ready to grapple receptively with a theology of incarnation, it seems more fair to protest not that the doctrine dishonors God – it certainly does not intend to – but rather that it is simply impossible.[39] If a Muslim were willing to listen but remained, at last, unconvinced, then (to my mind) the fairer charges against incarnational atonement would be "unreason" or "incomprehensibility" more so than "blasphemy".

### The "Risk" in Salvation

One semantic field that attempts to sharpen the contours of what is at stake in incarnation and salvation is the "risky" language of risk. Once again, we are intruding on territory that many, not least Muslim theologians, will perceive as deleterious to a theology of honor and glory. But I would submit that the rhetoric of risk can sometimes open up constructive avenues of approach.

Explicit recourse to "God's risk in redemption" is not typical of most of the authors we have consulted. In the discussion above I have myself worried about certain "risky" speculation when it comes to the implications of God's supposed "suffering" in incarnation (say by Barth or Moltmann). But here I invoke a slightly different theological imaginary, a different angle on "risk". Adam Johnson, for example, ventures some bold diction:

> Irenaeus helps us see how God's wisdom was at stake in binding himself to his creatures … God had put himself forward, binding himself to his creatures through his purposes and covenants, so that in a very real (though limited) sense, he had put himself at stake.[40]

Johnson employs daring language to highlight that God himself is implicated in the consequences of atonement, though not as any sort of passive or derivative recipient of action. Without implying God's uncertainty or loss of sovereignty, it is appropriate to speak of his involvement, entailment, and, quite vividly, "risk" in the human project. He ties himself to relation with humanity, a humanity with the capacity to rebel and ruin. In this context God commits to a salvific trajectory in which he prevails, but all the while allowing an apparent challenge to his glory, at some cost or seeming risk.

Certainly, divine resources remain more than sufficient, but the radical nature of God's covenant fidelity is writ large in the biblical story. At the primordial stage, in the face of humanity's bitter harvest, instead of "wiping the slate clean", God irrevocably determines to remain engaged with the human condition (cf. Gen. 6:6; 8:21–9:17; Isa. 59:14-21). The canonical narrative often situates God as the bearer of pain or loss – even indignity – pre-eminently, *but not only*, in the gospels' Passion (cf. Ezek. 16). The sheer enormity of this grace may be termed "fitting" but also perhaps "radical" and "risky".

Of course, all this is a bridge too far for consensus Islamic theology. It is all the more interesting, therefore, that the *ambience* of risk is one candidly embraced by a Christian theologian who spent most of his career in the environs of Islamic thought, namely, Bishop Kenneth Cragg. Cragg acknowledges the Islamic concern for the preservation of transcendence, of the Creator–creature divide. But, he insists that Christian convictions about the Son are not only compatible with Islamic intuitions about the God–human relationship, but in fact follow their trajectory to a proper conclusion.

> That divine "interest" in us is embodied and enjoined in prophethood and proceeds within the given structures of … "religion according to God" … Only if [prophethood and humanity's religious nature] "compromise" God could the faith as to Christ also "compromise" him, for that faith only carried forward into its own perspectives that divine "interest" in man which creation, law, and prophethood express.[41]

Yes, the incarnation is, as it were, a quantum leap beyond prophecy, but, for Cragg that leap is congruent and necessary. Still further, he insists, the Creator–creature *distinction and entailment* stands in both faiths. Whether or not the terminology of risk is the most appropriate, we must strain after dynamic, even fraught, ways of communicating that God *has a stake* in the human story. God's radical interest and stake in humanity is vocalized at high decibel and in distinctive keys by all three of our primary theologians. This wonder, I would assert, is only to his glory.

#### Transcendence Persists in Incarnation

In line with the tradition, we argue that the reality of incarnation, the reality of redemptive suffering, is not an ontological threat to God's glory or transcendence. It is important to articulate these elusive truths as lucidly as possible for the sake of theological integrity, more so than for the sake of apologetic scorekeeping. Tanner is particularly helpful here in her full-bodied embrace of both poles of the mystery of incarnation. On the one hand, the radical "interest" of God in the creature could not be instantiated more starkly than in the Word incarnate. On the other hand, Tanner is emphatic that none of this diminishes God's otherness or his aseity – in fact, a *saving* intervention requires precisely that otherness. The gratuity of God's giving to us in Christ leaves him thoroughly undiminished.

In Tanner's participatory paradigm, God is transcendent and *therefore intimately present to human life* (cf. Q 50:16). This is possible because divine–human relations are non-competitive – dynamic, reciprocal, and yet asymmetrical at once. On these terms, we do not relate to God along a sliding scale of inverse gains and losses. Being "full of God does not equate to a diminishing of the creature's own existence and dignity".[42]

Arguably, under the conceptual umbrella of each of the iconic theologians studied here, we may sustain the notion of God's impassible suffering – his transcendence is not infringed on the cross, even as the God-man suffers death. Tanner's recourse to the classical tradition (not least the Eastern Fathers) strengthens such convictions further in that the Logos provides the grounding, power, and uplift necessary to the anhypostatic humanity of Christ. A full union of integral, unmixed natures is asserted, but the priority and initiative always remain with God. God is both in union with humanity and ever non-contingent.

However little anyone may have anticipated God in Christ, as Cragg intimated, the incarnation is not even "unlikely" if God is understood to be the superabundant source of all good, the lavish sustainer of all he has made, and a Person not reducible to "category" or "class" like all other objects in the universe. "With Tanner's principles in place, the incarnation is not a freakish exception to the normally extrinsic relation between God and creatures … Tanner's principles establish precisely that *in principle* there is nothing impossible about the coinherence of divinity and humanity in one person."[43]

In other words, incarnation is not God "overdoing" his nearness to us, but it is paradoxically his very "otherness", brought into our humanness, which funds our redemption. Adam Johnson insists:

> While the otherness within God is the principle for the negative aspect of Christ's work (focused on that which he saves us from …), it is also the basis of that for which God saves us: "Himself, fellowship and intercourse with Himself" (*CD* I/1, 444), and "eternal life as the continuance of man in fellowship with God Himself" (*CD* IV/1, 72).[44]

In reconciling humanity, God's honor is not imperiled but, rather, magnified.

### Downward to Glory: Pondering What is Possible for God

We have had several occasions to comment on the disjunction between the moral aesthetics of Christianity and Islam, even as both faiths intend a doxological posture towards the transcendent Creator. That God's glory, and hope for humankind, should travel along the course charted in the NT, that is, the downward path of the suffering Servant – all this raises acute antinomies for many audiences, Islamic and other. The atonement seems to say that the way up is first the way down. One can hardly fail to see that the arc of Jesus' story, of redemption, is not one of ease, of manifest victory, or of dominance and success. The Christ Event, with apparent shame and loss foregrounded, hardly communicates that straying humanity simply requires improved "guidance" for its rectification. In Sonderegger's words:

> No, but the victory cry that escapes from the dying lips of our Lord itself *conforms* to this anguished shape of sorrow and rejection. It is in this dying, this death of humiliation and scandal, the *stumbling block*, that Christ proclaims to us as His Telos, His Perfect Victory. Isaiah 53 served the early church as a prophetic text just because it followed that contour: the anonymity and rejection that *in a hidden way* is the intercession for, the making righteous, of the many.[45]

To embrace atonement on NT contours will require, for most of us, a reframing of our understanding of God's honor and glory. The pattern is one of power expressed, in the first instance, in surrender, weakness, and self-emptying. It is a subversive dynamic, thematically expressed, for example, in Paul's manner of invoking Isaiah throughout Romans and 1 Corinthians: God's hidden, subversive, and unanticipated ways at first offend and repel even his own people; he comes in weakness, humility, and service but, in the end, God's greater wisdom, power, and love redound to the liberation and rescue of the humble, even as the wicked and arrogant are overthrown.

This is the way of the Savior. Jesus with his face set as flint towards Jerusalem is an embodiment of fidelity to his mission and a zeal for God's honor. With respect to this mindset of the Messiah, Cragg points out, both Muslims and Christians can agree that Jesus was impelled for the honor of God *as he approached Golgotha*.[46] But, of course, the Gospel course down to the tomb by way of bloody execution, and then to the splendor of ascension, this pathway Islam will not tread. And precisely here Cragg exhorts us to allow the self-emptying profile of Jesus to communicate the heart, the attributes, and even the true honor of God. His appeal to us, to the Muslim, is not to foreclose on *how* God may reveal his honor and what the Messiah's story may expose about the Almighty himself.[47] He would have us attend to the story with receptivity to the unexpected glory of God rather than to pre-decide what is "unworthy" of God. Barth's Christological window on deity is richly harmonic at this juncture as well.

Long before, Gregory of Nazianzus also responded to attacks centered on the "unworthy" implications of the cross about the Father. Gregory's "Arian" or "Eunomian" interlocutors were concerned that if one were to accept the consubstantiality of Christ and Father, then the Passion would be trumpeting an intolerable suffering, degradation, and humiliation of God himself. Gregory, boldly staking out a Trinitarian *terra firma*, flips the script: there is no doubt that the suffering of Jesus is a window onto the character of God (the Father) himself. However, the suffering and death of the divine Christ is *not* "a 'terrible injury' to the dignity of the Godhead. For Gregory this 'cause of dishonor' is actually cause for the greatest glorification … The humility of God is not a shame, but a source of wonderment and glory, that the Lord himself should stoop so mercifully to repair the pain of death."[48]

The clash over what is or is not congruent with God's own glory can become a displaced contest over *human* status, over *our* pride and what *we* find acceptable or imaginable. Recall that in his *City of God*, as Augustine laments Porphyry's rejection of the incarnation, he insists that taking on flesh is not unthinkable for God; *having any part in sin is* (*City of God* 10:24; cf. 24-29). Augustine says that the humiliation of enfleshment is not beneath divine dignity as the Platonists assume; it is rather the shoals upon which human pride comes to grief.

This revelation of divine glory may be a hard pill to swallow, but it is what is prescribed. If we are willing to surrender preconceived limits on how God might reveal himself – on how he might act in shocking ways to save and to upend our hubris – then, perhaps, we will see the honor of God revealed in Christ and him crucified.[49] Paul Gavrilyuk says:

> The Word made human experiences his very own by transforming them from within: that which was violent, involuntary, tragically purposeless, and fatal for an ordinary human being was made voluntary, soteriologically purposeful, and life-giving in the ministry of the Word. The Word who is above suffering in his own nature suffered by appropriating human nature and obtained victory over suffering.[50]

We have had occasion to see the reciprocal incomprehension in Barth's and al-Faruqi's mutually cancelling notions of "pagan" vs "monotheistic" thought (solicitous for divine transcendence). Indeed, on those rare occasions in which Barth directly addressed Islam, we saw him aver that its hyper-transcendence is an impious diminishment of divine glory. Meanwhile, for al-Faruqi, the entailments of incarnation are a "pagan immanentizing", an "apotheosizing of nature", and an "objectifying of the transcendent God". There is little scope for compromise here. For my part, I can only affirm Barth's assertion that to construct God's greatness "from the ground up" – that is, by taking God simply to be the contradiction of all things human and creaturely – is to occlude the astounding truth God has manifest about himself in Christ.[51]

Of course, our attempts to grapple with the Creator's trajectory downward to glory is no charm that simply dispels Akhtar's warning above about the incomprehensibility of the "weakness trope" to Muslim and secular critics. The least we must aspire to, however, is careful, clear, and faithful Christian communication, even as we rely on the Spirit and acknowledge that final judgment is with God. Further, as Christian thinkers and disciples, we must be clear that the inversion represented by the cross is no mere artifact for theorization; the action of God in reconciliation must be seen to establish reconciled communities of audacious humility, love, and stubborn service in the world. Herein lies tangible witness to the atonement. And, finally, the *telos* of God's inverse intervention in incarnation and Passion must remain integral to the annunciation of salvation. Cross and resurrection hope are mutually interpreting. Power in apparent weakness is challenging, paradoxical, and confounding, but *power* it remains. Salvation's trajectory is not acquiescence in hurt, but rather overcoming and healing.[52] God's honor is burnished, not tainted.

## Christoexclusivism and God's Honor

Sometimes inputs from Muslim interlocutors may hone Christian self-understanding and theological expression. Sometimes they simply clarify innate interfaith impasses and aporias. At other times, the Islamic voice acts as a sort of call to retrieve elements of our own tradition too easily neglected. I conclude this overview of the honor motif with just such a reminder.

The surpassing greatness of God and exclusivity of devotion to him is something of a signature trope intrinsic to Islam's theological grammar. This is, of course, congruent with Scripture's own orientation. But Christian theory and praxis may occasionally benefit from reproaches issuing from unexpected quarters. Islamic zeal for "no god but God" may harbor instruction for us as Christians, even if not in the manner the Muslim plaintiff assumes. As absolutely basic and non-negotiable as the revelation of God in Christ is, one must nonetheless exercise vigilance to forestall any drift from a theology that is Christologically inflected, towards a theology that is, for all intents and purposes, Christomonist. Left undisciplined, such a trend may in fact contribute to the derogation of the honor of God Almighty.

Of course, I am in no way calling for the surrender of central convictions or the relinquishing of hermeneutical or epistemological reins to Muslim respondents. Obviously, as Christians we will not accede to al-Faruqi's rejection of the revelation of God in Christ; but there is potential value in at least attending to his chiding.[53] The point here is really quite simple: the Islamic drumbeat on the transcendence of God can be a reminder to us that the God truly and necessarily revealed in Jesus is always and only the Creator God, uncontained by even the "heaven of heavens" (1 Ki. 8:27; 2 Chron. 2:6). Yes, we enter into the gift of his own life through Christ, the one who came out of Nazareth. But this does not mean that all that may be said or thought about him is delimited to the "first-century history" of the Galilean. Indeed, Jesus himself called us to the God already known in Israel's history (even as Jesus himself was in some mysterious way ensconced there). Yes, Jesus is the climax of revelation, the *telos* of the Torah. But God's capacity to speak of himself in his ineffable reality is not limited exclusively to the texts in which Jesus is patently read off the surface.

The Islamic concern for God's greatness, for his freedom from the limits and boundaries of human definition, can be salutary. In Christ, it is graphically clear that God loves and that he pursues the well-being of his recalcitrant creatures. Yes, we affirm that God's honor is properly refracted through a Christological lens. But, the Islamic penchant for the "magnification" of God (*takbir*) may serve as a salutary reminder to properly Christocentric believers: the encounter with the heart of God in Christ, with our Lord as "friend" (Jn. 15:14-15), need not and must not dilute our orientation toward God's mastery, or towards his own glory.

Certainly, "God is for us". But we do well to remember that a God construct *that limits itself* to the ways in which God is "for us" in Jesus, and only in the first century, says not enough about God and in that way diminishes him. Indeed, I am not advocating any negating of Christ but, rather, a renewed confession of the Trinity, including the Son *in his fullness*. Recall the danger of a sort of Christomonism we have already grappled with in our chapter on Barth. My appeal, in part, is that when it comes to Jesus, the incarnate Son, we must dare to affirm the glory of the Logos *asarkos*.[54]

But, even more simply, let us insist that there is a fundamental rightness to the notion that the universe is oriented to God and his glory. God is surely "for us". But this does not indicate that existence itself is "all about us". Indeed, a christological lens on Scripture and salvation does not indicate otherwise. Jesus' own sustenance was the will of the Father. We have been made for him and his glory – and that to our own great gain (cf. Dt. 6:4-9; 8:3; 30:11-20; Ps. 19:7-14; 63:1-4; Ac. 17:28; Rom. 11:36; 1 Tim. 1:17; Heb. 4:13; Rev. 4:11; 15:3-4).

## Reaffirming Transcendence

In distinct ways, virtually all of our chosen interlocutors (Muslim and Christian) have underscored God's transcendence, aseity, otherness, and independence. This affirmation of God's honor must inform theology proper, Christology, and soteriology. This, for example, was a key concern in the discussions above of God's timeless freedom, of Trinity, and of the problems of "Christoexclusivism". Even as Trinitarian orthodoxy and the centrality of Jesus are vigorously maintained, it turns out that certain Islamic assertions are worth a critically open hearing as we contemplate God, Christ, and redemption. How so?

i) A robust proclamation of the Gospel will certainly entail significant surprise, subversion, paradox, suffering, humility, hiddenness, and apparent shame. But, at the very same time, Jesus must be proclaimed as *Lord.* The Messiah is not passive or diminished; he has authority to lay down his life and to take it up. The man from Galilee is himself the category-shattering inbreaking of the boundless Creator on the human scene. That is, the honor of the transcendent God must remain an abiding concern even as we tell the story of the suffering and saving Jesus.

ii) Again, there are related concerns about preserving the honor and transcendence of God highlighted in the previous discussion of "Christoexclusivism". Yes, the revelation of God in Christ – the Father active in his world by Son and Spirit – is vital, true, and even *the* truth about God. Nonetheless, the tangible economy of salvation is not exhaustive of all that God is. He remains always "more", above and beyond our (intellectual) control – even as he dwells with us. Let us affirm the mystery. The Three in One revealed to us in the Messiah's loving sacrifice is – before, after, always – the ineffable, uncorruptible, uncontainable God. Attending to Islamic concerns, I want both to affirm the mystery of incarnate redemption and to insist that theology does not reduce to soteriology.

Thankfully, the glory of God is not at odds with human well-being. Once again, there is a reflexivity of sorts when it comes to the honor of God and the good of humans. But the foundational good, the energy of initiative, the *telos* of honor, must be situated with, in, and for God.[55] God in Christ is love, is humble, is disorienting, is surprising, is powerful, and … he is great.

### *Penultimate Issues: Atonement in Comparative Perspective*

As a final summation, further below, I wish to sketch a meta-orientation towards atonement, which, I believe, is implied in the ground we have covered. I am attempting to roughly profile what I believe to be an edifying orientation and affect when it comes to atonement theology. I do not claim to present a free-standing, comprehensive atonement theology in granular detail. In terms of the preceding research, I forward here key dimensions not to be overlooked in one's theorizing of salvation. In this dialectic, I firstly aim at an intervention in Christian atonement; but I secondarily hope that these refined conceptions of salvation may fruitfully be communicated back into an Islamic setting.

One of the gauntlets thrown down both by Muslim thinkers and certain "Western" theological modernists is to question the crucifixion's centrality. Emerging from the foregoing, I would counter that in a well-grounded atonement the cross may well remain central, but not isolated: it must be integrated with a salvation enacted across an expansive canvas. The cross must not be an anomalous appendage to the OT story or, indeed, to the incarnation itself. But, bound to resurrection, it certainly is the fulcrum of ontological rescue and metaphysical transformation. It is not reducible to example or instruction, still less to an unfortunate, unintended outcome of the Messiah's love and fidelity. The cross is indeed an expression of human darkness and moral malaise. On intersecting levels, it is many things at once. But one's portrait of the Passion must certainly incorporate it as the wrenching, raw, and restorative intentionality of God in Christ.[56]

So, we may say that God's intention to reconcile all things to himself is an incarnational movement dramatically enacted, accomplished, and sealed in death and resurrection.[57] It is an act of divine revelation, not an act that causes change in God; the change happens in his created realm. Some of these claims are consonant with Tanner's exposition. All the more, then, do I find it unfortunate that she seems unwilling to trade very much in the gospel mystery that the cross is climactically Christ's glorification (cf. Jn. 12:27-33). To speak on these terms *is not* to celebrate abusive hierarchy. Rather, in the Passion such evils are exposed and, in the strange power of God, overthrown and judged. Yes, *judged.* Again, in some contrast to Tanner, I would insist that just penalty is an aspect of wrong's undoing.

All this is for our good and restoration, brought to empirical fruition in the resurrection of Jesus. This rising in fact vindicates the subversive purposiveness of the cross – creation-wide purposes of restoration underwritten by the Spirit of God himself. These outlines are "incarnational" but incline not at all towards marginalizing the Passion. Here we may revisit Athanasius, icon of "incarnational theology", who speaks of the death of the Messiah as "the main point of our faith".[58] Dysfunctional and mutually excluding oppositions must be avoided, for the soteriological inflection point of the Word's incarnation is the death to session of the Messiah.

## Coordinating Confessionally Contested Salvations: My Christian Perspective

This study has assumed objective atonement constructs, including common Protestant intuitions on vicarious suffering, as a starting point. Taking Anselm and Barth as leading symbols of this foundation, their thought was engaged in some depth and set alongside Tanner's rather different intervention. And all of this theological probing was catalyzed and informed by concerns arising from Muslim commentary, concerns ordered under the headings of divine justice, divine honor, and sin and human nature.

Giving particular attention to the Muslim–Christian intersection, the theological interface contrived by this research can be sorted into three effects:

i) From certain angles, classic nodes of dispute between Islam and Christianity must simply be clarified, better articulated, and left to stand (e.g. the cross, Trinity, and incarnation).

ii) In some cases, the criticism, questions, and cross-pollination between these disparate theological imaginaries suggested avenues of correction or refinement in a Christian representation of salvation. Questions asked of and charges levied at "Christian salvation" called for renewed attention to the following fields:

- Ethics and transformation
- Balanced, sharpened theologizing of sin
- Justice issues: the avoidance of framing justification as arbitrary
- Divine immutability and honor throughout the economy of redemption
- Affirming God's attributes, essential stability, and oneness (via a Trinitarian lens)

iii) Occasionally, zones of partial, potential, or quasi-convergence between Islamic and Christian reflection were highlighted. For example:

- Drawing in the *entire life* of Christ as salvific (though of a piece with his cross)

- Embedding the value of creation – both now and to come – within soteriology
- Learning to articulate *salvation for* as forcefully as *salvation from*

By correlating the life and cross of Christ with resurrection and the formation of a justice-seeking community, *salvation must be presented as the triumph of Almighty God*.[59] Thematically, there is much here that Muslims and Christians might agree on, even as one must also grant that in terms of underlying dynamics, historical expression, and core theological commitments, divides will persist.

## Sidebar on Sin: Spotlight on a Zone of Shared Concern

With respect to our three rubrics, then, at any of the interfaith intersections there may be domains of incomprehension and miscommunication, domains of diametrical opposition, and domains of partial rapprochement. Take the "sin" theme as an example. We have already addressed the sin question above, but our point here is to highlight the "hybrid" features typical of a constructive Muslim–Christian interface. Such an interface will be a complex interweaving of both convergence and disjunction. So, Islamic deconstruction of Christian hamartiology, especially original sin, provides momentum by which to correct or hone some of our thinking; it can also clarify that not every discrepancy is as stark and disjunctive as purported; and yet it also confirms that unbridged chasms persist.

As we have seen, Muslim critics commonly perceive objective atonements (including both satisfaction and PSA models) as tightly bound up with a dour sin obsession and the supposed infelicities of original sin doctrine. At one level, there need be no reflexive retreat on the part of Christian theology. Substitutionary models operate under no illusions: in centering the cross we do center God's "foolishness", a stumbling block, *and* his wisdom towards a world in deep darkness. In accord with the Gospel, then, traditional atonement thought has much to contribute in terms of justice and the seriousness of sin in the very face of Islamic protest.

Classic atonement constructs profile sin as an acid corroding the divine–human umbilical cord; or as unpayable deficit, a bankrupting "cost" proportional to the worth of the bondholder. There is no good reason to dilute the weighty prophetic challenge of such images. Original sin is deeply penetrating, destructively corrupting, and ubiquitous in the human family. There is a severity to sin that vitiates the presumption that moral effort and divine law are sufficient responses to its depredations.

Nonetheless, an attunement to Islamic critique can constructively steer Christian characterizations of humanity in sin away from unhelpful extremes. As we have asserted, *salvation is not only about sin but is embedded in a much larger God–human arc directed to creational goods and eschatological restoration*. Dour disproportion is neither constructive nor theologically faithful. Further, yes, all are sinners; but, no, all are not as horrifically depraved as possibly could be.

Neither is original sin an arbitrary and oppressive dispersal of guilt across an otherwise innocent humanity. Rather, to requisition Tanner's term, sin is, tragically and mysteriously, humanity's "second nature". Sadly, original sin simply "is". Moreover, God's judgment *is* as deadly serious as sin is. But this is not to say it is spiteful, petty, or an exercise in blood sport. It is mediated in accord with holiness, justice, and love. Sin is serious, but it is no match for God, no impediment to his covenant fidelity.

In Christian engagement with Islamic interlocutors, unbridged discontinuity cannot be denied or avoided. But, also, Christian theology may be strengthened by listening before responding. False dichotomies as well as aspects of Christian misrepresentation can be corrected. Disagreements with our critics may press upon us creative retrieval of resources already resident in Scripture and the historical tradition.

Certainly, then, the Muslim–Christian interface over various *topoi* will often manifest hybridity, that is, both affirmation and negation. If an "aside within an aside" might be permitted, consider once again the Islamic claims about the "degradation" that incarnation and Passion foist upon the honor of God. In light of these anxieties, we do well to sensitively develop the NT's own surprising *kerygma* in which it is precisely divine humility, condescension, and love which both i) speak to the verities of the human condition and ii) astoundingly unleash the saving power *and glory* of God into the world. The signature Islamic concern for God's honor, then, may serve to remind us that this is equally a Christian concern. This, even though realism may suggest that the stunning inversion intrinsic to the Gospel will remain unpalatable to the Muslim interlocutor. Once again, we find partial convergence and persisting disjunction.

### The Legal Lacuna and the Law of Christ

Above we encountered a classical Muslim–Christian impasse that impinges on notions of salvation, namely the matter of divine law. The question of law was typically seen as a gaping and deleterious lacuna in Christian soteriology. Unlike some of the other "hybrid" zones we have noted, "law" would seem to represent a more absolute disjunction between the faiths, but even here there may be more to say.[60] A terse way of sharpening the Muslim–Christian divide is to say that, in Christian thought, God's highest revelation is a person; in Islamic thought, a book (read: "law" or "command").

Conventional Islam is unabashedly a religion of divine command, of obedience to *Shari'a* issues in salvation – a rescue from punishment and enjoyment of good. Islamic scholars commonly promote a positive prospect on the efficacy of law in terms of both social uplift and personal eschatology. Conversely, the Gospel of the Kingdom, as expounded in the NT, simply does not generate a legally bounded community in any way comparable to the Islamic *umma*. Certainly, the popular, embedded stereotype, which aligns the Christian gospel with grace and *against* "the Law" or Torah, is in fact theologically and biblically quite problematic. But still, it does seem a fair generalization to describe the contours of Christian soteriology as more salvation-historical than juridical.

Nonetheless, the contours of "the saved life" – how the atoned community should live – still matter. Our Christian–Muslim interface *has* clearly underscored the necessity of addressing justice and ethics as relevant to soteriology. I have repeatedly acknowledged the need to accent even PSA in terms of justice from above and below. And, again, controversial though the results may be, objective atonement constructs were often birthed out of concerns for ultimate justice and righteousness.

Granted, Christian atonement theology may not be ensconced in a legal matrix in a way comparable to the Islamic theorization of divine judgment and the final fate of humans. But this is not to say that justice is in any way an alien category. Legally oriented or not, Christian atonement does have a stake in questions of justice. So, for example, on matters such as the *Shari'a* and the Pauline "Law of Christ" further productive comparison can be imagined.[61]

### Metaphysics and Mystery

Another dimension of interfaith encounter with which we are familiar by now is the difference in terms of theological ethos or epistemological environment, difference which may precede and inform divergences in particular doctrines. I have in mind categories such as mystery, paradox, and the religious aesthetic. What are the proper imaginative preunderstandings or theoretical bounds imposed upon us by the correct theological grammar? Sometimes the answers to these queries are zero-sum. Monotheism, it turns out, cannot in fact be rightly expressed as both *tawhid* and Trinity. Certain realia intrinsic to Christian soteriology are definitionally disallowed in the Islamic matrix. In Christian thought, for example, categories deemed problematic by Muslims (incarnation, the cross) are not bugs but features of the system. And such commitments have been *from the start* sources not only of power and hope, but also offense (cf. Mk. 14:61-64; Jn. 5:18; 8:58-59; 10:31-39; 1 Cor. 1:18-25). Little has changed.

Again, one may discern a pattern in which Islamic and Christian scholars acquiesce to or reject the invocation of "mystery", but usually at very different loci. Thus, our Islamic intellectuals (al-Faruqi, Akhtar, Tabatabai, Rida, and others) would take God to be absolute and unlimited (think, for example, of divine names such as المتكبر / الجبار / العزيز ). In Islamic thought, God is in many respects utterly mysterious; it arguably prohibits attempts to describe the divine essence even more aggressively than any Christian theologizing would. And yet, when it comes to the mysteries and antinomies of Christian salvation dynamics, there is a visceral aversion (on the part of many Muslim intellectuals) to any appeal to paradox or mystery. Christian invocations of mystery in soteriology are generally dismissed as indulgence in irrationality, injustice, and the derogation of divine transcendence.

In harmony with Cragg's observations, I am struck by how absent in al-Faruqi's theological imaginary is any acknowledgment of the anguished vagaries of human life "in Adam", its compounded scars writ large in a fallen world. Missing is the sense of sin as encroaching power; absent, too, is the mystery of the transcendent God's self-involvement with the pain of the human story; and missing is the palpable interplay of "tragedy" and hope in the metanarrative of salvation.[62] For al-Faruqi, of course, this is all to the good. Much to be preferred is the simple divine command template for human destiny. I am convinced otherwise. To my mind, the allegedly elegant simplicity of that paradigm is in fact more problematic and uncertain than is usually acknowledged. Even more to the point, I find it inadequate to account for the mottled splendor *and* depravity of human life and ill-matched to the human heart's thirst to know the transcendent-immanent God.

Some of the most critical divides between Islamic and Christian conceptualizations of salvation, eschatology, and human destiny will remain irreconcilable. But, still more, *even in terms internal to each faith*, these matters will never be reducible to mechanistic explanation or empirical proof. Much of theology's terrain is made up of the vitally important, the contestable, but also the finally irresolvable. These are the arenas of religious aesthetics and moral imaginary, the attempts to confess transcendent, ontological (and thus mysterious) truth. To be sure, thought and reason are non-negotiable, but they cannot take us the entire distance. Mystery remains. We have here not the irrational, but the supra-rational.

So, for example, speaking from the Christian vantage point, I would hope that Christians speaking into the Islamic context will affirm divine honor and justice in salvation with some eloquence and sensitivity. Journeying together with Muslims in the same direction where possible is valuable. Clarity is valuable. Clearing away misconceptions is valuable. Persisting in faithful, integral relationships is valuable. Let all parties to the conversation remain hopeful and engaged, persevering to the end, witnessing, and "pointing in the right direction". Let our recourse as Christians be to the Spirit of Christ, not to individual rhetorical art, still less to clever manipulation. But as long as the auditor remains within established Islamic parameters, basic features of Christianity's soteriological narrative will remain to them fundamentally opaque and disqualifying. May all parties to the conversation think, listen, speak, love, and pray. But in the final analysis, certain mystery remains with God, and to him is each one's recourse.

## Conclusion: A Call to Integrative Atonement

And so we come to the end of this discursive journey. To reiterate, my concluding statement is not an effort to verbalize the full contents of atonement theology or of a doctrine of reconciliation and restoration. I will be content if I have usefully sketched certain contours and considerations that should inform a soteriological proposal that is theologically balanced, biblically whole, and contextually sensitive.

If atonement is understood in terms of tightly circumscribed "systems" or "theories" (e.g. PSA, ransom, satisfaction), an exclusive allegiance to any one system as a totalizing expression of salvation is sure to produce unfortunate gaps and disproportions. Our theologizing is most hopefully and helpfully directed when we pursue an integrative or composite approach to atonement, an instinct evident in many of my preferred interlocutors (e.g. Crisp, Hart, Hastings, Johnson, Rutledge, Sonderegger, and Vidu). Recall Matthew Baker's helpful admonition that "vicarious representation, sacrifice, and legal vindication" at the cross are only a part, but nevertheless a vital "dimension of that multi-faceted plan of the Creator to save his fallen creatures … and to raise them up into union with him".[63]

Influenced by thinkers like Anselm and Barth, it is therefore appropriate, on the one hand, to take the logic of substitution, vicarious representation, and even penalty as informative and constructive, while, on the other, to insist that such substitutionary paradigms are too narrow to encapsulate the entire theology of reconciliation. One may argue for the "truth" of PSA without likewise requiring that it be adopted as the comprehensive archetype of salvation. Better to align it with broader dynamics (e.g. exchange) which themselves must nest within even more capacious frameworks such as incarnation, salvation history, and union with Christ. A pattern of embedding our ideas of redemption within ever-widening conceptual circles should help us attend to various important contextual challenges that may emerge (e.g. the typology of justice, honor, and sin), and thus to articulate any narrower or more focused aspect of our theorizing (e.g. PSA) with more accuracy and fidelity.

In light of the course I have pursued here, this suggests a pattern that i) centers objective atonement and ii) affirms (a version of) PSA, while iii) situating it within an expansive canvas and soteriological metanarrative. This "expansive canvas and soteriological metanarrative" is further guided by orthodox, classical theological infrastructure. This requires operating from Trinitarian premises that emphasize modalities like union with Christ, incarnation, and participation – emphases prominent in Tanner's oeuvre.

Describing *how* these grounding themes work within a composite modeling of atonement is challenging. For example, on the one hand, consider Tanner's Trinitarianism, which is vital to her participatory atonement. This is clearly an emphasis that can productively inform one's theorizing of salvation. On the other hand, however, Trinitarianism is already at least nominally a given for *any* Christian theologizing. It can and must be affirmed in PSA whether one bothers to further reflect on "participation" or not. (Indeed, it is implicitly integral to *CDH* and explicitly vital in Barth.) All this is simply to concede that while I argue for the importance of a broad, integrative approach to atonement theology, crisply and clearly verbalizing the contours of such a project is not easy.

In any case, an emphasis such as saved humanity's union with the incarnate Son better accounts, than does PSA in isolation, for several key concerns of this research: i) justice from above and below; ii) integrating resurrection with atonement; iii) "salvation for"; iv) a metaphysics of transformation and sanctification; v) the ethical model of Christ's life; and vi) integrating robust doctrines of creation, incarnation, and the entire biblical storyline with cross theology.

The point is certainly not that all one needs to do is invoke "participation" and all conundrums are instantaneously resolved. But it seems clear that incarnation ought to be fundamental to structuring and enacting atonement, and not merely a perfunctory precondition thereof. Jesus came as Last Adam to complete salvation's trajectory – the defeat of death and the reintegration of Adam's family into the life of God. If our atonement models suffer from a weak Trinitarian substructure; if they content themselves with pardon and justified "status"; if they lack the ontologically restructuring vindication of resurrection; then God's creational agenda is truncated and left in abeyance. (And, depending on how God and Christ are positioned, such models may also transmit disturbing implications about the character of God himself.) Salvation "from" and "for" require the defeat not only of sin, but also hell and death. We must be remade.[64]

In speaking about salvation, then, it can be appropriate for specific purposes to offer compressed summaries structured around an objective atonement with a Crucicentric core (e.g. tropes of vicarious suffering, PSA, etc.). There is certainly no need to forswear the death and resurrection of Jesus (perhaps even extending to his session in glory) as the climax of the biblical story. Indeed, the weight of the Passion narratives in the Gospel, the Last Supper symbolism, the emphasis on the cross in the NT generally, the reference to the death and rising of Jesus as summaries of the good news (Rom. 1:1-4; 1 Cor. 1:18; 15:3-4; Gal. 2:20-21; Col. 1:20) – these affirm this instinct. And, for specific reasons and settings, the salvation message articulated with such a sharp and narrow focus may be useful. But the story of our redemption and of God's glory in Christ extends – prior and post – beyond the compressed kernel of Jesus' vicarious suffering in first-century Roman Judea.

So, even such "compressed expressions" must account well for issues such as divine honor, justice and ethics, and the realities of the human condition. They must emerge from and make explicit the Trinitarian matrix, and must assume and articulate that even juridically inflected explanations of redemption are underwritten by ontological action – atonement must be "actual".[65] And, finally, they must at least gesture towards the greater dimensions of salvation; a widening out into a larger story which draws on the OT, Israel's history, incarnation, and eschatological hope. In this manner, multiple classic images and metaphors will enter the frame (from *CV* to exemplarist impulses), and salvation will evince both its negative and positive aspects.

Again, to decouple PSA from ontological transformation is to decouple soteriology from justice. It would be a death knell for faith. Even so, honesty must admit that in any generation, empirically verifying the soteriological sanctification of Christ's people is challenging to say the least. The ethical and creational renewal anticipated in the resurrection is less than self-evident throughout the lived experience of the church, as critics of the cross readily point out. Barth, too, is well aware that we do not now see "all things subject to Christ".[66] How shall we respond? We can lament. We can attempt to discern those remarkable tokens of grace in which the Spirit *is* at work in our day. And we can look ahead in hope. Our hope is not *only* future, but it is necessarily so, and is grounded in the only place in which judgment and restoration are manifestly complete, in the Christ Event (cf. Rom. 8:22-25).[67]

Redemption is more than, though not less than, suffering substitution, a removal of demerit, and a "salvation from". All these elements nest in a more cosmic agenda – (re)union with God, a "salvation for". Salvation is expressly restorative, congruent with creation's original purposes and humanity's regency therein – the latter emphasis is familiar also in Qur'anic thought (Q 2:29-30; 6:165). On this score, without reference to Islam, Khaled Anatolios's recent work has been influential for me. In many ways I resonate with his atonement construct as one informed by Trinitarian commitments and a soteriology of ontological transformation. That spirit tends towards a broad-spectrum view of God's ends in human redemption, one that still centers the cross while drawing in harmonics relative to our three themes – concerns pointing to human contrition; holistic, creational restoration (beyond punishment and forgiveness); and the glorification (honor!) of the God of all perfections (justice, mercy, and more).

So, in concluding this itinerary, I take my leave echoing Anatolios's apt words: if creation is understood as a purposive project of the Trinity and if "humanity is thus 'represented' by the Son within the Trinity, beginning with the very act of creation … [Then, w]hen the Son becomes incarnate and goes to the cross on behalf of humanity, he is therefore doing nothing more than following through, in the face of human sin, with faithfulness to that original representation."[68] Throughout this spiritual excursion, I have called us to hear voices not only within but also without our Christian tradition. The undergirding agenda has been to refine our contemplation as Christians of the wonder of salvation, to elevate our theology, that is, our doxology. I hope that end has in some small measure been achieved.

# Bibliography

## Christian Theology Sources


Accad, Martin, and Jonathan Andrews, Eds. *The Religious Other: A Biblical Understanding of Islam, the Qur'an and Muhammad.* Carlisle: Langham Global Library, 2020.

Anatolios, Khaled. *Retrieving Nicaea: The Development and Meaning of Trinitarian Doctrine*. Grand Rapids: Baker Academic, 2011.

– – – . "Creation and Salvation in St. Athanasius of Alexandria". In *On the Tree of the Cross*. Jordanville: Holy Trinity Seminary Press, 2016, 59–72

– – – . *Deification Through the Cross: An Eastern Christian Theology of Salvation*. Grand Rapids: Eerdmans, 2020.

Anderson, Gary A. "Sacrifice and Sacrificial Offerings: Old Testament". In *The Anchor Yale Bible Dictionary*. Ed. D. N. Freedman. New York: Doubleday, 1992, 5:870–86.

– – – . *Sin: A History*. New Haven and London: Yale University Press, 2009.

– – – . *Christian Doctrine and the Old Testament: Theology in the Service of Biblical Exegesis*. Grand Rapids: Baker Academic, 2017.

Anselm. "Meditation on the Mystery of Human Redemption". In *Prayers and Meditations of St. Anselm with the Proslogion.* Trans. Benedicta Ward. Rev ed. London: Penguin, 1973, 230–37.

– – – . "Proslogion". In *Prayers and Meditations of St. Anselm with the Proslogion*. Trans. Benedicta Ward. Revised edition. London: Penguin, 1973, 238–67.

– – – . "On the Virgin Conception and Original Sin". In *Anselm of Canterbury: The Major Works*. Eds. Brian Davies and G. R. Evans. Reissue. Oxford and New York: Oxford University Press, 2008, 357–89.

– – – . "Why God Became Man". In *Anselm of Canterbury: The Major Works*. Eds. Brian Davies and G. R. Evans. Reissue. Oxford and New York: Oxford University Press, 2008, 260–356.

Athanasius of Alexandria. *On the Incarnation of the Word of God*. Trans. T. H. Bindley. 2nd rev ed. London: The Religious Tract Society, 1903.

Augustine. *Augustine: The City of God Against the Pagans*. Ed. R. W. Dyson. Cambridge and New York: Cambridge University Press, 1998.

– – – . *On the Trinity*. Trans. Arthur West Haddan. Veritatis Splendor Publications, 2012.

– – – . *Confessions*. Trans. Sarah Ruden. New York: Modern Library, 2017.

Aulén, Gustaf. *Christus Victor: An Historical Study of the Three Main Types of the Idea of Atonement.* Trans. A. G. Herbert. New York: Macmillan Company, 1986.

Baker, Mark D., and Joel B. Green. *Recovering the Scandal of the Cross: Atonement in New Testament and Contemporary Contexts*. 2nd ed. Downers Grove: IVP Academic, 2011.

Baker, Matthew. "In Ligno Crucis: Atonement in the Theology of Fr Georges Florovsky". In *On the Tree of the Cross: Georges Florovsky and the Patristic Doctrine of Atonement*. Jordanville: Holy Trinity Seminary Press, 2016, 101–26.

Baker, Matthew, Seraphim Danckaert, and Nicholas Marinides, Eds. *On the Tree of the Cross: Georges Florovsky and the Patristic Doctrine of Atonement*. Jordanville: Holy Trinity Seminary Press, 2016.

Barclay, John M. G. *Paul and the Gift*. Grand Rapids: Eerdmans. 2015.

Barth, Karl. *Church Dogmatics*. Ed. T. F. Torrance. Trans. G. W. Bromiley. 5 Vols. London: T&T Clark, 2004.

Bauckham, Richard. *Bible and Mission: Christian Witness in a Postmodern World.* Grand Rapids: Baker Academic, 2003.

– – – . "Moltmann, Jürgen." In *New Dictionary of Theology: Historical and Systematic*. Eds. Martin Davie, Tim Grass, Stephen R. Holmes, John McDowell, and Thomas A. Noble. 2nd ed. Downers Grove: IVP Academic, 2016, 586–88.

Behr, John. *Formation of Christian Theology, Vol. 2: The Nicene Faith.* Crestwood: St Vladimir's Seminary Press, 2004.

– – – . "Irenaus on 'Atonement'". In *On the Tree of the Cross*. Jordanville: Holy Trinity Seminary Press, 2016, 43–58.

– – – . "Irenaus of Lyons". In *T&T Clark Companion to Atonement*. Ed. Adam J. Johnson. Bloomsbury Companions 5. London and New York: T&T Clark, 2017, 569–75.

Bennett, Matthew Aaron. *Narratives in Conflict: Atonement in Hebrews and the Qur'an*. Eugene: Pickwick Publications, 2019.

Bennett, Thomas Andrew. "Reconciliation". In *T&T Clark Companion to Atonement*. Ed. Adam J. Johnson. Bloomsbury Companions 5. London and New York: T&T Clark, 2017, 713–18.

Boersma, Hans. Violence, *Hospitality, and the Cross: Reappropriating the Atonement Tradition.* Grand Rapids: Baker Academic, 2004.

Brannan, Rick, trans. "Letter to Diognetus". In *The Apostolic Fathers in English.* Bellingham: Lexham Press, 2012.

Bray, Gerald. *The Attributes of God: An Introduction.* Wheaton: Crossway, 2021.

Davies, Brian and Evans, G.R., eds. *Anselm of Canterbury: The Major Works.* Oxford; New York: Oxford University Press, 2008.

Burrell, David. *Knowing the Unknowable God: Ibn-Sina, Maimonides, Aquinas.* Notre Dame: University of Notre Dame Press, 1986.

– – – . *Freedom and Creation in Three Traditions*. Notre Dame: University of Notre Dame Press, 1993.

– – – . "Dialogue between Muslims and Christians as Mutually Transformative Speech". In *Criteria of Discernment in Interreligious Dialogue*. Ed. Catherine Cornille. Eugene: Cascade Books, 2009, 1:87–99.

– – – . *Towards a Jewish–Christian–Muslim Theology*. Chichester: John Wiley & Sons, 2011.

– – – . "Perceptions of God in Christianity and Islam". In *Routledge Handbook on Christian–Muslim Relations*. Ed. David Thomas. London: Routledge, 2017, 304–10.

Campbell, John McLeod. *The Nature of the Atonement*. Pickerington: Beloved Publishing, 2015 (1856).

Carbine, Rosemary P., and Hilda P. Koster. "Introduction: The Gift of Kathryn Tanner's Theological Imagination". In *The Gift of Theology: The Contribution of Kathryn Tanner*. Eds. Rosemary P. Carbine and Hilda P. Koster. Minneapolis: Fortress Press, 2015, xxv–xxxix.

Castelo, Daniel. *The Apathetic God: Exploring the Contemporary Relevance of Divine Impassibility*. Milton Keynes: Paternoster, 2009.

– – – . "Impassibility (Divine)". In *T&T Clark Companion to Atonement*. Ed. Adam J. Johnson. Bloomsbury Companions 5. London and New York: T&T Clark, 2017, 563–68.

– – – . "Qualified Impassibility". In *Divine Impassibility: Four Views of God's Emotions and Suffering*. Eds. Robert J. Matz and A. Chadwick Thornhill. Downers Grove: IVP Academic, 2019, 53–74.

Chua, How Chuang. "Japanese Perspectives on the Death of Christ: A Study in Contextualized Christology". PhD diss. Trinity Evangelical Divinity School, 2007.

Clooney, Francis X. *Hindu God, Christian God: How Reason Helps Break Down the Boundaries between Religions*. Oxford: Oxford University Press, 2001.

– – – . *Comparative Theology: Deep Learning Across Religious Borders*. Chichester and Malden: Wiley-Blackwell, 2011.

Clooney, Francis X., and Klaus von Stosch, Eds. *How to Do Comparative Theology*. New York: Fordham University Press, 2017.

Cole, Graham A. "Expiation/Propitiation". In *T&T Clark Companion to Atonement*. Ed. Adam J. Johnson. Bloomsbury Companions 5. London and New York: T&T Clark, 2017, 489–92.

Cone, James H. *The Cross and the Lynching Tree*. Maryknoll: Orbis, 2011.

Cornille, Catherine, Ed. *Atonement and Comparative Theology: The Cross in Dialogue with Other Religions*. New York: Fordham University Press, 2021.

Crisp, Oliver D. *Approaching the Atonement: The Reconciling Work of Christ*. Downers Grove: IVP Academic, 2020.

– – – . *Participation and Atonement: An Analytic and Constructive Account*. Grand Rapids: Baker Academic, 2022.

Cyril of Alexandria. *On the Unity of Christ*. Ed. John Behr. Trans. John McGuckin. Vol. 13. Crestwood: St. Vladimir's Seminary Press, 1995.

Davidson, Ivor J. "Atonement and Incarnation". In *T&T Clark Companion to Atonement*. Ed. Adam J. Johnson. Bloomsbury Companions 5. London and New York: T&T Clark, 2017, 35–56.

de la Trinité, Philippe. *What Is Redemption?* Trans. Anthony Armstrong. Vol. 25. Twentieth Century Encyclopedia of Catholicism, Section II. New York: Hawthorn Books, 1961.

Deng, Natalja. 2018. "Eternity in Christian Thought". In *The Stanford Encyclopedia of Philosophy*. Ed. Edward N. Zalta. [accessed online] https://plato.stanford.edu/archives/fall2018/entries/eternity/.

do Vale, Fellipe. "Anselm on the *Rectus Ordus* of Creation". *Saint Anselm Journal* 14:1 (2018), 93–109.

– – – . "On Thomas Aquinas's Rejection of an 'Incarnation Anyway'". *TheoLogica: An International Journal for Philosophy of Religion and Philosophical Theology* 2:3 (2019), 144–64.

Fairbairn, Donald. "Cyril of Alexandria". In *T&T Clark Companion to Atonement*. Ed. Adam J. Johnson. Bloomsbury Companions 5. London and New York: T&T Clark, 2017, 457–60.

Feinberg, John S. *No One Like Him*. Wheaton: Crossway, 2001.

Florovsky, Georges. "In Ligno Crucis: The Church Fathers' Doctrine of Redemption Interpreted from the Perspective of Eastern Orthodox Theology". In *On the Tree of the Cross*. Jordanville: Holy Trinity Seminary Press, 2016, 143–52.

Garcia, Mark A. "Union with Christ". In *T&T Clark Companion to Atonement*. Ed. Adam J. Johnson. Bloomsbury Companions 5. London and New York: T&T Clark, 2017, 781–86.

Gavrilyuk, Paul L. *The Suffering of the Impassible God: The Dialectics of Patristic Thought*. Oxford: Oxford University Press, 2004.

Girard, René. *Violence and the Sacred*. Trans. Patrick Gregory. Baltimore: Johns Hopkins University Press, 1977.

– – – . *I See Satan Fall Like Lightning*. Trans. James G. Williams. Maryknoll: Orbis, 2012.

Gockel, Matthias. "Constructive Theology, the Cross of Christ, and the Praxis of Liberation". *Dialog* 56:3 (2017), 228–32.

Gomes, Alan W. "Socinus". In *T&T Clark Companion to Atonement*. Ed. Adam J. Johnson. Bloomsbury Companions 5. London and New York: T&T Clark, 2017, 754–57.

Graham, Jeannine Michele. "Substitution and Representation". In *T&T Clark Companion to Atonement*. Ed. Adam J. Johnson. Bloomsbury Companions 5. London and New York: T&T Clark, 2017, 749–52.

Grebe, Matthias. "Jürgen Moltmann". In *T&T Clark Companion to Atonement*. Ed. Adam J. Johnson. Bloomsbury Companions 5. London and New York: T&T Clark, 2017, 651–54.

Green, Joel B. "Theologies of Atonement in the New Testament". In *T&T Clark Companion to Atonement*. Ed. Adam J. Johnson. Bloomsbury Companions 5. London and New York: T&T Clark, 2017, 115–34.

Gregory of Nazianzus. "Select Orations of Saint Gregory Nazianzen". In *S. Cyril of Jerusalem, S. Gregory Nazianzen*. Ed. P. Schaff and H. Wace. Vol. 7. New York: Christian Literature Company, 1894.

Gregory of Nyssa. *St. Gregory of Nyssa: The Lord's Prayer, The Beatitudes*. Trans. H. C. Graef. Vol. 18. New York and Mahwah: Paulist Press, 1954.

– – – . *Catechetical Discourse: A Handbook for Catechists*. Trans. Ignatius Green. Vol. 60. Popular Patristics. Yonkers: St Vladimir's Seminary Press,

2019. (Note: also known as *Catechetical Oration*, and can be presented with traditional section [rather than page] numbers.)

Gudmundsdóttir, Arnfridur. "Crucified – So What? Feminist Rereadings of the Cross-Event." In *T&T Clark Companion to Atonement*. Ed. Adam J. Johnson. Bloomsbury Companions 5. London and New York: T&T Clark, 2017, 335–54.

Gunton, Colin. "*Christus Victor* Revisited. A Study in Metaphor and the Transformation of Meaning". *The Journal of Theological Studies* 36:1 (1985), 129–45.

– – – . *The Actuality of Atonement: A Study of Metaphor, Rationality and the Christian Tradition*. Edinburgh: T&T Clark, 1988.

Hart, D. Bentley. "A Gift Exceeding Every Debt: An Eastern Orthodox Appreciation of Anselm's *Cur Deus Homo*". *Pro Ecclesia* 7:3 (1998), 333–49.

Hasker, William. "Eternity and Providence". In *The Cambridge Companion to Christian Philosophical Theology*. Eds. Charles Taliaferro and Chad Meister. Cambridge: Cambridge University Press, 2009, 81–92.

Hastings, W. Ross. *Total Atonement: Trinitarian Participation in the Reconciliation of Humanity and Creation*. Lanham: Fortress Academic, 2019.

Heim, Erin M. *Adoption in Galatians and Romans: Contemporary Metaphor Theories and the Pauline Huiothesia Metaphors*. Biblical Interpretation Series Vol. 153. Leiden: Brill, 2017.

Heschel, Abraham Joshua. *The Prophets*. New York: Perennial Classics, 2001.

Holmes, Stephen R. "God". In *New Dictionary of Theology: Historical and Systematic*. Eds. Martin Davie, Tim Grass, Stephen R. Holmes, John McDowell, and Thomas A. Noble. 2nd ed. Downers Grove: IVP Academic, 2016, 369–73.

– – – . "Penal Substitution". In *T&T Clark Companion to Atonement*. Ed. Adam J. Johnson. Bloomsbury Companions 5. London and New York: T&T Clark, 2017, 295–314.

Hunsinger, George. "The Chief Point of Our Faith: Christ's Saving Death in Selected Greek Fathers". In *The Gift of Theology: The Contribution of Kathryn Tanner*. Eds. Rosemary P. Carbine and Hilda P. Koster. Minneapolis: Fortress Press, 2015, 99–114.

Hurlbert, Brandon. "*René Girard and the Nonviolent God*, Scott Cowdell, University of Notre Dame Press, 2018". *Reviews in Religion & Theology* 27:4 (2020), 496–98.

Irenaeus of Lyons. *The Demonstration of the Apostolic Preaching*. Trans. J. A. Robinson. London and New York: Society for Promoting Christian Knowledge, 1920.

Johnson, Adam J. *God's Being in Reconciliation: The Theological Basis of the Unity and Diversity of the Atonement in the Theology of Karl Barth*. London: Bloomsbury, 2013.

– – – . *Atonement: A Guide for the Perplexed*. Guides for the Perplexed. London: Bloomsbury T&T Clark, 2015.

– – – . "Peter Abelard". In *T&T Clark Companion to Atonement*. Ed. Adam J. Johnson. Bloomsbury Companions 5. London and New York: T&T Clark, 2017, 357–60.

– – – . "René Girard". In *T&T Clark Companion to Atonement*. Ed. Adam J. Johnson. Bloomsbury Companions 5. London and New York: T&T Clark, 2017, 505–508.

– – – . Ed. *T&T Clark Companion to Atonement*. Bloomsbury Companions 5. London and New York: T&T Clark, 2017.

– – – . "Violence". In *T&T Clark Companion to Atonement*. Ed. Adam J. Johnson. Bloomsbury Companions 5. London and New York: T&T Clark, 2017, 791–96.

Kärkkäinen, Veli-Matti. *Christ and Reconciliation: A Constructive Christian Theology for the Pluralistic World*. Vol. 1. Grand Rapids: Eerdmans, 2013.

– – – . *Christian Theology in the Pluralistic World: A Global Introduction*. Grand Rapids: Eerdmans, 2019.

– – – . *Doing the Work of Comparative Theology: A Primer for Christians*. Grand Rapids: Eerdmans, 2020.

Klawans, Jonathan. *Purity, Sacrifice, and the Temple: Symbolism and Supersessionism in the Study of Ancient Judaism*. New York: Oxford University Press, 2009.

Kotsko, Adam. "Exemplarism". In *T&T Clark Companion to Atonement*. Ed. Adam J. Johnson. Bloomsbury Companions 5. London and New York: T&T Clark, 2017, 485–88.

– – – . "The Persistence of the Ransom Theory of the Atonement". In *T&T Clark Companion to Atonement*. Ed. Adam J. Johnson. Bloomsbury Companions 5. London and New York: T&T Clark, 2017, 277–93.

Kraemer, Hendrik. "Extracts from The Christian Message in a Non-Christian World". In *Routledge Reader in Christian–Muslim Relations*. Ed. Mona Siddiqui. London: Routledge, 2013,163–75.

Lam, Joseph. *Patterns of Sin in the Hebrew Bible: Metaphor, Culture, and the Making of a Religious Concept*. New York: Oxford University Press, 2016.

Lowe, Walter. "Christ and Salvation". In *Christian Theology: An Introduction to Its Traditions and Tasks*. Eds. Peter C. Hodgson and Robert H. King. Updated ed. Minneapolis: Fortress Press, 1994, 222–48.

Luy, David. "Simplicity and Language: Bonaventure's Semiotic Asymptoticism". *Modern Theology* 35:3 (2019), 481–95.

Lynch, Matthew J. *Portraying Violence in the Hebrew Bible: A Literary and Cultural Study*. New York: Cambridge University Press, 2020.

Macchia, Frank D. *Introduction to Theology, Declaring the Wonders of God*. Grand Rapids: Baker Academic, 2023.

MacIntyre, Alasdair. *After Virtue: A Study in Moral Theory*. 3rd ed. Notre Dame: University of Notre Dame Press, 2007.

Madigan, Daniel A. "People of the Word: Reading John with a Muslim". *Review & Expositor* 104:1 (2007), 81–95.

– – – . "Who Needs It? Atonement in Muslim–Christian Theological Engagement". In *Atonement and Comparative Theology: The Cross in*

*Dialogue with Other Religions*. Ed. Catherine Cornille. New York: Fordham University Press, 2021, 11–39.

Matz, Robert J., and A. Chadwick Thornhill, Eds. *Divine Impassibility: Four Views of God's Emotions and Suffering*. Downers Grove: IVP Academic, 2019.

McFarland, Ian A. "Present in Love: Rethinking Barth on the Divine Perfections". *Modern Theology* 33:2 (2017), 243–58.

McGowan, A. T. B. "Substitution, Penal". In *New Dictionary of Theology: Historical and Systematic*. 2nd ed. Downers Grove: InterVarsity Press, 2016.

McGuckin, John. "Theology of Salvation in St. Gregory the Theologian". In *On the Tree of the Cross*. Jordanville: Holy Trinity Seminary Press, 2016, 73–88.

– – – . "St. Gregory of Nyssa on the Dynamics of Salvation". In *T&T Clark Companion to Atonement*. Ed. Adam J. Johnson. Bloomsbury Companions 5. London and New York: T&T Clark, 2017, 155–73.

McNall, Joshua M. *The Mosaic of Atonement: An Integrated Approach to Christ's Work*. Grand Rapids: Zondervan Academic, 2019.

Meconi, David Vincent. "Augustine". In *T&T Clark Companion to Atonement*. Ed. Adam J. Johnson. Bloomsbury Companions 5. London and New York: T&T Clark, 2017, 381–87.

Mingana, Alphonse, trans. *Woodbrooke Studies, Christian Documents in Syriac, Arabic, and Garshuni*, Edited and Translated with a Critical Apparatus. Vol. 2. Cambridge: W. Heffer & Sons, 1928.

Moffitt, David. *Rethinking the Atonement: New Perspectives on Jesus's Death, Resurrection, and Ascension.* Grand Rapids: Baker Academic, 2022.

Moltmann, Jürgen. *The Crucified God: The Cross of Christ as the Foundation and Criticism of Christian Theology*. New York: Harper & Row, 1974.

– – – . *God in Creation: A New Theology of Creation and the Spirit of God*. Minneapolis: Fortress Press, 1993.

– – – . *The Trinity and the Kingdom: The Doctrine of God*. Minneapolis: Fortress Press, 1993.

Morris, Leon L. *The Atonement: Its Meaning and Significance*. Downers Grove: IVP Academic, 1983.

Mouw, Richard J., Douglas A. Sweeney, and Willie Jennings. *The Suffering and Victorious Christ: Toward a More Compassionate Christology*. Grand Rapids: Baker Academic, 2013.

Mullins, R. T. "Simply Impossible: A Case against Divine Simplicity". *Journal of Reformed Theology* 7 (2013), 181–203.

– – – . *The End of the Timeless God*. Oxford: Oxford University Press, 2016.

Myers, Benjamin. "The Patristic Atonement Model". In *Locating Atonement*. Eds. Oliver D. Crisp and Fred Sanders. Grand Rapids: Zondervan, 2015, 71–88.

– – – . *The Apostles' Creed: A Guide to the Ancient Catechism*. Bellingham: Lexham Press, 2018.

Neder, Adam. "Sin". In *T&T Clark Companion to Atonement*. Ed. Adam J. Johnson. Bloomsbury Companions 5. London and New York: T&T Clark, 2017, 749–52.

Netland, Harold A., and Keith E. Yandell. *Spirituality Without God?: Buddhist Enlightenment and Christian Salvation.* Milton Keynes: Paternoster, 2009.

Newbigin, Lesslie. *Foolishness to the Greeks: The Gospel and Western Culture.* Grand Rapids: Eerdmans, 1986.

Nicole, Roger R., Charles E. Hill, and Frank A. James, Eds. *The Glory of the Atonement: Biblical, Historical & Practical Perspectives: Essays in Honor of Roger Nicole.* Downers Grove: InterVarsity Press, 2004.

Oord, Thomas Jay. *The Uncontrolling Love of God: An Open and Relational Account of Providence.* Downers Grove: IVP Academic, 2015.

Packer, James I. "What Did the Cross Achieve: The Logic of Penal Substitution". *Tyndale Bulletin* 25 (1974), 3–45.

Placher, William C. "How Does Jesus Save? (An Alternative View of Atonement)". *The Christian Century* 126:11 (2009), 23–27.

Provan, Iain. *The Reformation and the Right Reading of Scripture.* Waco, TX: Baylor University Press, 2017.

Ralston, Joshua. "The Way(s) of Salvation: The Function of the Law in John Calvin and Abu Hamid al- Ghazali". In *Comparing Faithfully: Insights for Systematic Theological Reflection.* Ed. Michelle Voss Roberts. New York: Fordham University Press, 2016, 255–73.

– – – . *Law and the Rule of God: A Christian Engagement with Shari'a.* Cambridge: Cambridge University Press, 2020.

– – – . "Judgment on the Cross, Resurrection as Divine Vindication". In *Atonement and Comparative Theology: The Cross in Dialogue with Other Religions.* Ed. Catherine Cornille. New York: Fordham University Press, 2021, 214–38.

Ricoeur, Paul. *The Rule of Metaphor: The Creation of Meaning in Language.* 3rd ed. London: Routledge, 2003.

Roberts, Michelle Voss, Ed. *Comparing Faithfully: Insights for Systematic Theological Reflection.* New York: Fordham University Press, 2016.

Rutledge, Fleming. *The Crucifixion: Understanding the Death of Jesus Christ.* Grand Rapids: Eerdmans, 2015.

Sanders, E. P. *Paul and Palestinian Judaism.* 40th Anniversary Ed. Minneapolis: Fortress Press, 2017.

Sanders, Fred. *Fountain of Salvation: Trinity and Soteriology.* Grand Rapids: Eerdmans, 2021.

Schendel, Joshua. "'That Justice Might Not Be Infringed Upon': The Judgment of God in the Passion of Christ in Irenaus of Lyons". *Scottish Journal of Theology* 71:2 (2018), 212–25.

Smythe, Shannon Nicole. "Karl Barth". In *T&T Clark Companion to Atonement.* Ed. Adam J. Johnson. Bloomsbury Companions 5. London and New York: T&T Clark, 2017, 237–55.

Soars, Daniel. "From David Burrell CSC to Sara Grant RSCJ: The Distinctive Relation between Creature and Creator in Christian Theology". *Scottish Journal of Theology* 74:2 (2021), 123–34.

Sonderegger, Katherine. "Must Christ Suffer to Redeem? The Doctrine of Vicarious Atonement in Schliermacher and Baeck". *Zeitschrift Für Neuere Theologiegeschichte* 2:2 (1995), 175–92.

– – – . "Anselm, Defensor Fidei". *International Journal of Systematic Theology* 9:3 (2007), 342–59.

– – – . "Theological Themes in the Passion". In *Engaging the Passion: Perspectives on the Death of Jesus*. Ed. Oliver Larry Yarbrough. Minneapolis: Fortress Press, 2015, 387–404.

– – – . *Systematic Theology: The Doctrine of God*, Volume 1. Minneapolis: Fortress Press, 2015.

– – – . "Anselmian Atonement". In *T&T Clark Companion to Atonement*. Ed. Adam J. Johnson. Bloomsbury Companions 5. London and New York: T&T Clark, 2017, 175–93.

– – – . *Systematic Theology: The Doctrine of the Holy Trinity: Processions and Persons*, Volume 2. Minneapolis: Fortress Press, 2020.

Southern, R. W. *Saint Anselm, A Portrait in a Landscape*. Cambridge: Cambridge University Press, 1990.

Spjuth, Roland. "Gustaf Aulén". In *T&T Clark Companion to Atonement*. Ed. Adam J. Johnson. Bloomsbury Companions 5. London and New York: T&T Clark, 2017, 389–92.

Stevenson, P. K. "Campbell, John Mcleod (1800–72)". In *New Dictionary of Theology: Historical and Systematic*. Eds. Martin Davie, Tim Grass, Stephen R. Holmes, John McDowell, and Thomas A. Noble. 2nd ed. Downers Grove: IVP Academic, 2016, 149–51.

Stott, John R. W. *The Cross of Christ*. 20th Anniversary ed. Downers Grove: IVP Academic, 2012.

Takács, Axel Marc Oaks. "'An Interpreter and Not a Judge': Insights into a Christian–Islamic Comparative Theology". In *How to Do Comparative Theology*. New York: Fordham University Press, 2017, 98–121.

Tanner, Kathryn. *God and Creation in Christian Theology: Tyranny and Empowerment?* Minneapolis: Fortress Press, 1988.

– – – . *The Politics of God: Christian Theologies and Social Justice*. Minneapolis: Fortress Press, 1992.

– – – . *Jesus Humanity and the Trinity*. Minneapolis: Fortress Press, 2001.

– – – . "Incarnation, Cross, and Sacrifice: A Feminist-Inspired Reappraisal". *Anglican Theological Review* 86:1 (2004), 35–56.

– – – . *Christ the Key*. Current Issues in Theology series. Cambridge: Cambridge University Press, 2010.

– – – . *Christianity and the New Spirit of Capitalism*. New Haven and London: Yale University Press, 2019.

Tennent, Timothy C. *Theology in the Context of World Christianity: How the Global Church is Influencing the Way We Think About and Discuss Theology*. Grand Rapids: Zondervan, 2007.

Thiel, John E. "Foreword". In *The Gift of Theology: The Contribution of Kathryn Tanner*. Eds. Rosemary P. Carbine and Hilda P. Koster. Minneapolis: Fortress Press, 2015, xxi–xxiii.

Treier, Daniel. *Lord Jesus Christ*. Eds. Scott R. Swain and Michael Allen. Grand Rapids: Zondervan Academic, 2023.

Vanhoozer, Kevin J. *The Drama of Doctrine: A Canonical Linguistic Approach to Christian Doctrine*. Louisville: Westminster John Knox Press, 2005.

– – – . *Remythologizing Theology: Divine Action, Passion, and Authorship*. Cambridge: Cambridge University Press, 2010.

– – – . "Atonement". In *Mapping Modern Theology: A Thematic and Historical Introduction*. Eds. Kelly M. Kapic and Bruce L. McCormack. Grand Rapids: Baker Academic, 2012, 175–202.

– – – . "Putting on Christ: Spiritual Formation and the Drama of Discipleship". *Journal of Spiritual Formation & Soul Care* 8:2 (2015), 147–71.

– – – . "Love of God". In *New Dictionary of Theology: Historical and Systematic*. Eds. Martin Davie, Tim Grass, Stephen R. Holmes, John McDowell, and Thomas A. Noble. 2nd ed. Downers Grove: IVP Academic, 2016, 535–36.

– – – . "Love Without Measure? John Webster's Unfinished Dogmatic Account of the Love of God, in Dialogue with Thomas Jay Oord's Interdisciplinary Theological Account". In *Love, Divine and Human: Contemporary Essays in Systematic and Philosophical Theology*. Eds. Oliver D. Crisp, James M. Arcadi, and Jordan Wessling. New York: T&T Clark, 2019, 7–26.

Vanhoozer, Kevin J., Craig G. Bartholomew, Daniel J. Treier, and N. T. Wright, Eds. *Dictionary for Theological Interpretation of the Bible*. London: SPCK and Grand Rapids: Baker Academic, 2005.

Vidu, Adonis. *Atonement, Law, and Justice: The Cross in Historical and Cultural Contexts*. Grand Rapids: Baker Academic, 2014.

– – – . "The Place of the Cross among the Inseparable Operations of the Trinity". In *Locating Atonement*. Eds. Oliver D. Crisp and Fred Sanders. Grand Rapids: Zondervan, 2015, 21–42.

– – – . "The Missions of the Divine Persons". In *T&T Clark Companion to Atonement*. Ed. Adam J. Johnson. Bloomsbury Companions 5. London and New York: T&T Clark, 2017, 645–50.

von Stosch, Klaus. "How Q 5:75 Can Help Christians Conceptualize Atonement". In *Atonement and Comparative Theology: The Cross in Dialogue with Other Religions*. Ed. Catherine Cornille. New York: Fordham University Press, 2021, 61–77.

Ward, Benedicta, Ed. *Prayers and Meditations of St. Anselm with the Proslogion*. Rev ed. London: Penguin, 1973.

Weaver, J. Denny. *The Nonviolent Atonement*. 2nd ed. Grand Rapids: Eerdmans, 2011.

Webster, John. "The Firmest Grasp of the Real: Barth on Original Sin". *Toronto Journal of Theology* 4:1 (1988), 19–29.

– – – . "Barth, Karl (1886–1968)". In *New Dictionary of Theology: Historical and Systematic*. Eds. Martin Davie, Tim Grass, Stephen R. Holmes, John McDowell, and Thomas A. Noble. 2nd ed. Downers Grove: IVP Academic, 2016, 103–107.

Weinandy, Thomas G. "Impassibility of God and Human Suffering". In *New Dictionary of Theology: Historical and Systematic*. Eds. Martin Davie, Tim Grass, Stephen R. Holmes, John McDowell, and Thomas A. Noble. 2nd ed. Downers Grove: IVP Academic, 2016, 445–48.

– – – . "Athanasius' Incarnational Soteriology". In *T&T Clark Companion to Atonement*. Ed. Adam J. Johnson. Bloomsbury Companions 5. London and New York: T&T Clark, 2017, 135–54.

Wilcoxen, Matthew A. *Divine Humility: God's Morally Perfect Being*. Waco: Baylor University Press, 2019.

Willard, Dallas. *The Divine Conspiracy*. New York: Harper Collins, 1998.

Wright, N. T. *The Day the Revolution Began: Reconsidering the Meaning of Jesus's Crucifixion*. San Francisco: HarperOne, 2018.

Wright, William A. "On Making Christology Look Too Easy: A Dialectical 'Rejoiner' to Tanner's Lineage". In *The Gift of Theology: The Contribution of Kathryn Tanner*. Eds. Rosemary P. Carbine and Hilda P. Koster. Minneapolis: Fortress Press, 2015, 115–38.

Wynne, Jeremy J. "Wrath." In *T&T Clark Companion to Atonement*. Ed. Adam J. Johnson. Bloomsbury Companions 5. London and New York: T&T Clark, 2017, 807–11.

Yandell, Keith E., and Harold A. Netland. *Buddhism: A Christian Exploration and Appraisal*. Downers Grove: IVP Academic, 2009.

Yang, Eric T., and Stephen T. Davis. "Atonement and the Wrath of God". In *Locating Atonement*. Eds. Oliver D. Crisp and Fred Sanders. Grand Rapids: Zondervan, 2015, 154–67.

## Islamic and Islam-related Sources

Adang, Camilla. *Muslim Writers on Judaism and the Hebrew Bible: From Ibn Rabban to Ibn Hazm*. New York: Brill Academic Pub, 1997.

Akhavi, Shahrough. "Qutb, Sayyid". In *Oxford Encyclopedia of the Islamic World*. Ed. John L. Esposito. Rev ed. New York: Oxford University Press, 2009, 4:493–98.

Akhtar, Shabbir. *The Final Imperative: An Islamic Theology of Liberation*. London: Bellew Pub, 1991.

– – – . *The New Testament in Muslim Eyes*. London: Routledge, 2018.

Algar, Hamid. *Jesus in the Qur'an: His Reality Expounded in the Qur'an*. Oneonta: Islamic Publications International, 1999.

al-'Aqqad, Abbas Mahmud. *The Genius of Christ*. Trans. F. Peter Ford. Binghamton and Provo: Global Academic Publishing, 2001.

Aquinas, Thomas. "Reasons for the Faith against Muslim Objections". Trans. Joseph Kenny. *Islamochristiana* 22 (1996), 31–52.

Arnaldez, Roger. "Ibn Hazm". In *Encyclopedia of Religion*. 2nd ed. Gale Virtual Reference Library. Detroit: Macmillan Reference, 2005, 6:4267–69.

Asad, Muhammad. *The Message of the Qur'an*. Trans. Muhammad Asad. Bristol: The Book Foundation, 2003.

Awad, Najib George. "'If His Crucifixion Was Figurative as You Claim, Then So Be It': How Two Christian *Mutakallims* from the Abbasid Era Used *an-Nisā* 4:157-158 in Dialogues with Muslims". *Journal of Eastern Christian Studies* 68:1–2 (2016), 53–80.

Ayoub, Mahmoud. *Redemptive Suffering in Islam*. The Hague: De Gruyter Mouton, 1978.

– – – . "Towards an Islamic Christology, II: The Death of Jesus, Reality or Delusion". *Muslim World* 70:2 (1980): 91–121.

– – – . *A Muslim View of Christianity: Essays on Dialogue*. Ed. Irfan A. Omar. Maryknoll: Orbis Books, 2007.

Azaiez, Mehdi, Gabriel Said Reynolds, Tommaso Tesei, and Hamza M. Zafer, Eds. *The Qur'an Seminar Commentary / Le Qur'an Seminar: A Collaborative Study of 50 Qur'anic Passages / Commentaire Collaboratif De 50 Passages Coraniques*. Bilingual ed. Berlin: De Gruyter, 2016.

al-Azhar Islamic Research Group. *Tafsir Al-Wasit Lil-Qur'an al-Karim*. Vol. 2. Cairo: al-Matba'at al-Mashaf al-Sharif, 1992.

Azumah, John. "Jesus as God's Revelation in Christian-Muslim Relations". In *Theological Issues in Christian–Muslim Dialogue*. Ed. Charles Tieszen. Eugene: Pickwick Publications, 2018, 66–75.

Beaumont, Mark. *Christology in Dialogue with Muslims: A Critical Analysis of Christian Presentations of Christ for Muslims from the Ninth and Twentieth Centuries.* Oxford: Regnum, 2005.

– – – . "Debating the Cross in Early Christian Dialogues with Muslims". In *Jesus and the Cross*. Ed. David Singh. Eugene: Wipf and Stock, 2008, 55–64.

Beaumont, Mark, and Maha El Kaisy-Friemuth, Eds. *al-Radd al-Jamīl – a Fitting Refutation of the Divinity of Jesus: Attributed to Abu Hamid Al-Ghazali*. Bilingual ed. Leiden and Boston: Brill, 2016.

Behloul, Martin-Samuel. "The Testimony of Reason and the Historical Reality: Ibn Ḥazm's Refutation of Christianity". In *Ibn Ḥazm of Cordoba: The Life and Works of a Controversial Thinker*. Eds. Camilla Adang, Maribel Fierro, and Sabine Schmidtke. Leiden and Boston: Brill, 2012, 457–84.

Bertaina, David. Christian and Muslim Dialogues: *The Religious Uses of a Literary Form in the Early Islamic Middle East*. Piscataway: Gorgias Press, 2011.

Brown, Daniel W. *A New Introduction to Islam*. 3rd ed. Oxford: Wiley, 2017.

Brown, Jonathan A. C. "Sin, Forgiveness, and Reconciliation, A Muslim Perspective". In *Sin, Forgiveness, and Reconciliation: Christian and Muslim Perspectives*. Eds. Lucinda Mosher and David Marshall. Washington: Georgetown University Press, 2016, 13–20.

Cook, David. *Martyrdom in Islam*. Cambridge: Cambridge University Press, 2007.

Coward, Harold G. *Sin and Salvation in the World Religions: A Short Introduction*. Oxford: Oneworld Publications, 2003.

Cragg, Kenneth. "Isma'il al-Faruqi in the Field of Dialogue". In *Christian–Muslim Encounters*. Ed. Yvonne Yazbeck Haddad and Wadi Z. Haddad. Gainesville: University Press of Florida, 1995, 399–410.

– – – . *Jesus and the Muslim: An Exploration*. Oxford: Oneworld Publications, 1999.

Crowther, Daniel J., Shirin Shafaie, Ida Glaser, and Shabbir Akhtar, Eds. *Reading the Bible in Islamic Context: Qur'anic Conversations*. London and New York: Routledge, 2017.

Cumming, Joseph. "Did Jesus Die on the Cross? Reflections from Muslim Commentaries". In *Muslim and Christian Reflections on Peace: Divine and*

*Human Dimensions*. Eds. J. Dudley Woodberry, O. Zümrüt, and M. Köylü. Maryland: University Press of America, 2005, 32–50.

Darwaza, Muhammad 'Izzat. *al-Tafsir al-Hadith Tartib al-Suwar Hasab al-Nuzul*. Vol. 8. Beirut: Dar al-Gharb al-Islami, 2000.

Davids, Adelbert, and Pim Valkenberg. "John of Damascus, The Heresy of the Ishmaelites." In *The Routledge Reader in Christian-Muslim Relations*. Ed. Mona Siddiqui. London and New York: Routledge, 2013, 18–32.

Droge, A. J., Ed. *The Qur'an: A New Annotated Translation*. Bristol: Equinox Publishing, 2013.

Elmi, Mohammad Jafar, and Reza Shah-Kazemi. "Ṭabāṭabā'ī, 'Allāma". In *Encyclopedia of Religion*. Ed. Lindsay Jones. 2nd ed. 13:8945–46. Detroit: Macmillan Reference USA, 2005.

Esposito, John L., and John O. Voll. *Makers of Contemporary Islam*. New York: Oxford University Press, 2001.

Esposito, John L., Ed. *The Oxford Encyclopedia of the Islamic World*. Rev ed. 6 Vols. NY: Oxford University Press, 2009.

Euben, Roxanne L., and Muhammad Qasim Zaman, Eds. *Princeton Readings in Islamist Thought: Texts and Contexts from Al-Banna to Bin Laden*. Princeton: Princeton University Press, 2009.

al-Faruqi, Isma'il R. *Islam and Other Faiths*. Leicester: Islamic Foundation, 1998.

– – – . *Christian Ethics: A Historical and Systematic Analysis of its Dominant Ideas*. Kuala Lumpur: A. S. Noordeen, 1999.

– – – . "Islam and Christianity: Diatribe or Dialogue". In *Routledge Reader in Christian–Muslim Relations*. Ed. Mona Siddiqui. London: Routledge, 2013, 198–220.

Fatoohi, Louay. *The Mystery of the Crucifixion: The Attempt to Kill Jesus in the Qur'an, the New Testament, and Historical Sources*. Birmingham: Luna Plena Publishing, 2008.

– – – . *The Mystery of the Messiah*. Birmingham: Luna Plena Publishing, 2009.

Ford, F. Peter Jr. "The End of Jesus' Mission and the Honor of God in the Qur'an: The Search for Common Ground between Muslims and Christians". *Islam and Christian–Muslim Relations* 24:1 (2013), 15–26.

al-Ghazali, Abu Hamid Muhammad. "The Beginning of Guidance (Bidayat al-Hidaya)". In *The Faith and Practice of Al-Ghazali*. Trans. W. Montgomery Watt. Chicago: Kazi Publications, 1982, 86–152.

– – – . *Al-Ghazali's Path to Sufism: His Deliverance from Error (al-Munqidh Min al-Dalal)*. Trans. R. J. McCarthy. 2nd ed. Louisville: Fons Vitae, 2000.

– – – . *Mukhtasar Ihya' 'Ulum ad-Din*. Trans. Marwan Khalad. 2nd ed. Cyprus: Spohr, 2014.

– – – . *The Principles of the Creed: Book 2 of the Revival of the Religious Sciences*. Trans. Khalid Williams. Louisville: Fons Vitae, 2016.

Goddard, Hugh. *A History of Christian-Muslim Relations*. 2nd ed. Edinburgh: Edinburgh University Press, 2020.

Griffith, Sidney H. *The Church in the Shadow of the Mosque: Christians and Muslims in the World of Islam*. Princeton: Princeton University Press, 2008.

Haddad, Yvonne Yazbeck, and Wadi Z. Haddad, Eds. *Christian–Muslim Encounters*. Gainesville: University Press of Florida, 1995.

Haddad, Wadi Z. "A Tenth-Century Speculative Theologian's Refutation of the Basic Doctrines of Christianity: Al-Baqillani (d. A.D. 1013)". In *Christian–Muslim Encounters*. Eds. Yvonne Yazbeck Haddad and Wadi Z. Haddad. Gainesville: University Press of Florida, 1995, 82–94.

Hamzah, Dyala. "Rida, Muhammad Rashid". In *The Princeton Encyclopedia of Islamic Political Thought*. Ed. Gerhard Bowering. Princeton: Princeton University Press, 2013, 472–73.

Hermansen, Marcia. "Acts of Salvation: Agency, Others, and Prayer Beyond the Grave in Islam". In *Between Heaven and Hell: Islam, Salvation, and the Fate of Others*. Ed. Mohammad Hassan Khalil. Oxford and New York: Oxford University Press, 2013, 273–87.

Howard, Damian. "The Nature of the Human in Contemporary Christian–Muslim Relations". In *Routledge Handbook on Christian–Muslim Relations*. Ed. David Thomas. London: Routledge, 2017, 320–28.

Ibn Taymiyya, and Muhammad Khalil Harras. *Sharh Al-Aqeedat-Il-Wasitiyah*. Trans. Muhammad Rafiq Khan, Hafiz Muhammad Tahir, and Abdul-Qaadir Abdul Khaaliq. Riyad: Dar-us-Salam Publications, 1996.

Islamic Foundation (Khurshid Ahmad, et al, Eds). *Christian Mission and Islamic Da'wah: Proceedings of the Chambésy Dialogue Consultation*. Leicester: Islamic Foundation, 1982.

Khadduri, Majid. *The Islamic Conception of Justice*. Baltimore: Johns Hopkins University Press, 1984.

Khalil, Mohammad Hassan. *Islam and the Fate of Others: The Salvation Question*. New York: Oxford University Press, 2012.

– – – . "Divine Forgiveness in Islamic Scripture and Thought". In *Sin, Forgiveness, and Reconciliation: Christian and Muslim Perspectives*. Eds. Lucinda Mosher and David Marshall. Washington: Georgetown University Press, 2016, 83–89.

Kueny, Kathryn. "Tafsir". In *Encyclopedia of Islam and the Muslim World*. Ed. Richard C. Martin. New York: Macmillan Reference, 2004, 2:672–74.

Lange, Christian. "Ibn Hazm on Sins and Salvation". In *Ibn Hazm of Cordoba: The Life and Works of a Controversial Thinker*. Eds. Camilla Adang, Maribel Fierro, and Sabine Schmidtke. Leiden and Boston: Brill, 2012, 429–55.

Lawson, Todd. *The Crucifixion and the Qur'an: A Study in the History of Muslim Thought*. Oxford: Oneworld Publications, 2009.

Lazarus-Yafeh, Hava. *Intertwined Worlds: Medieval Islam and Bible Criticism*. Princeton: Princeton University Press, 2014.

Leaman, Oliver, Ed. *The Qur'an: An Encyclopedia*. London: Routledge, 2005.

Leirvik, Oddbjørn. *Images of Jesus Christ in Islam*. 2nd ed. London: Continuum, 2010.

McAuliffe, Jane Dammen. *Qur'anic Christians: An Analysis of Classical and Modern Exegesis*. Cambridge: Cambridge University Press, 1991.

Merad, Ali. "Christ According to the Qur'an". *Encounter: Documents for Muslim–Christian Understanding* 69 (1980), 1–17.

Michel, Thomas F., Ed. *A Muslim Theologian's Response to Christianity: Ibn Taymiyya's Al-Jawab Al-Sahih*. Delmar: Caravan Books, 1985.

Moosa, Ebrahim. "Foreword". In *Major Themes of the Qur'an*. 2nd ed. Chicago: University of Chicago Press, 2009, ix–xiv.

Mosher, Lucinda, and David Marshall, Eds. *Sin, Forgiveness, and Reconciliation: Christian and Muslim Perspectives*. Washington: Georgetown University Press, 2016.

– – – . Eds. *Monotheism and its Complexities: Christian and Muslim Perspectives*. Washington: Georgetown University Press, 2018.

Mourad, Suleiman A. "Does the Qur'ān Deny or Assert Jesus' Crucifixion and Death?". In *New Perspectives on the Qur'an: The Qur'an in Its Historical Context 2*. Ed. Gabriel Said Reynolds. New York: Routledge, 2011, 349–57.

– – – . "The Death of Jesus in Islam". In *Engaging the Passion, Perspectives on the Death of Jesus*. Ed. Oliver Larry Yarbrough. Minneapolis: Fortress, 2015.

Nasr, Seyyed Hossein. "Response to Hans Küng's Paper on Christian–Muslim Dialogue". *The Muslim World* 77:2 (1987), 96–105.

– – – . "Comments on a Few Issues in Islamic–Christian Dialogue". In *Christian–Muslim Encounters*. Eds. Yvonne Yazbeck Haddad and Wadi Z. Haddad. Gainesville: University Press of Florida, 1995, 457–67.

– – – . "Tabātabā'ī, Muhammad Husayn". In *Oxford Encyclopedia of the Islamic World*. Ed. John L. Esposito. Rev ed. New York: Oxford University Press, 2009, 5:288–89.

– – – . Ed. *The Study Quran: A New Translation and Commentary*. New York: HarperOne, 2015.

Neely, Brent. "At Cross Purposes: Islam and the Crucifixion of Christ, a Theological Response". *Transformation* 34:3 (2017), 176–213.

Netton, Ian Richard. "Theology and Christian–Muslim Relations". In *Routledge Handbook on Christian–Muslim Relations*. Ed. David Thomas. London: Routledge, 2017, 311–19.

Newman, N. A., Ed. *Early Christian–Muslim Dialogue*. Hatfield, PA: Interdisciplinary Biblical Research, 1993.

Nickel, Gordon. "Islam and Salvation: Some On-site Observations". *Direction* 23:1 (1994), 3–16.

al-Nowaihi, Mohamed. "Religion of Islam: A Presentation to Christians". *International Review of Mission* 65:258 (1976), 216–25.

Parrinder, Geoffrey. *Jesus in the Qur'an*. Reprint edition. London: Oneworld Publications, 2013.

Pink, Johanna. "Rida, Rashid". In *Encyclopedia of the Qur'an*. Ed. Jane Dammen McAuliffe, Online ed. Vol. IV. Leiden: Brill, 2016.

Poorthuis, M., B. Roggema, and P. Valkenberg. *The Three Rings: Textual Studies in the Historical Trialogue of Judaism, Christianity and Islam*. Leuven and Dudley: Peeters Publishers, 2005.

Qarai, Ali Quli. *The Qur'an: With a Phrase-by-Phrase English Translation*. Independently published, 2019.

Qutb, Sayyid. *Fi Zilal al-Qur'an*. New ed. Combined vols. Cairo: Dar al-Shuruq, 2003.

– – – . *In the Shade of the Qur'an*. Trans. Adil Salahi. 18 vols. Markfield: Islamic Foundation, 2009.
Rahman, Fazlur. *Major Themes of the Qur'an*. 2nd ed. Chicago: University of Chicago Press, 2009.
Reeves, John C., Ed. *Bible and Qu'ran: Essays in Scriptural Intertextuality*. Atlanta: Society of Biblical Literature, 2003.
Renard, John, Ed. *Islamic Theological Themes: A Primary Source Reader*. Oakland: University of California Press, 2014.
Reynolds, Gabriel Said. *A Muslim Theologian in the Sectarian Milieu: Abd al-Jabbar and the Critique of Christian Origins*. Leiden and Boston: Brill, 2004.
– – – . "The Muslim Jesus: Dead or Alive?". *Bulletin of the School of Oriental and African Studies* 72:2 (2009), 237–58.
– – – . *The Qur'an and the Bible: Text and Commentary*. Trans. Ali Quli Qarai. New Haven: Yale University Press, 2018.
– – – . "Original Sin and the Qur'an". *Islamochristiana* 46 (2020), 197–218.
Ricks, Thomas W. "The Doctrine of the Incarnation in Dialogue with Islam: Four Lines of Argumentation". In *Heirs of the Apostles*. Ed. David Bertaina, Sandra Toenies Keating, Mark N. Swanson, and Alexander Trieger. Leiden: Brill, 2019, 179–93.
Rida, Muhammad Rashid. *Tafsir Al-Manar*. Vol. 6. Cairo: Dar al-Manar, 1948.
– – – . *The Muhammadan Revelation*. Trans. Yusuf Talal DeLorenzo. Alexandria: al-Saadawi Publications, 1996.
Rizvi, Sajjad H. "Oneself as the Saved Other? The Ethics and Soteriology of Difference in Two Muslim Thinkers". In *Between Heaven and Hell: Islam, Salvation, and the Fate of Others*. Ed. Mohammad Hassan Khalil. Oxford: Oxford University Press, 2013, 180–205.
Roberts, Nancy. "A Muslim Reflects on Christ Crucified: Stumbling-Block or Blessing?" *Islam and Christian-Muslim Relations* 24:3 (2013), 313–31.
Robinson, Neal. *Christ in Islam and Christianity: Representation of Jesus in the Qur'an and the Classical Muslim Commentaries*. Albany: State University of New York Press, 1991.
– – – . "Sayyid Qutb's Attitude Towards Christianity: Sūra 9.29-35 in Fī Zilāl Al-Qur'ān". In *Islamic Interpretations of Christianity*. Ed. Lloyd Ridgeon. New York: St. Martin's Press, 2001, 159–78.
– – – . "Jesus". In *Encyclopaedia of the Qur'ān*. Ed. Jane Dammen McAuliffe. Leiden: Brill, 2003, 3:7–20.
Ryad, Umar. *Islamic Reformism and Christianity: A Critical Reading of the Works of Muhammad Rashid Rida and His Associates (1898–1935)*. History of Christian–Muslim Relations Vol. 12. Leiden: Brill, 2009.
Saleh, Walid. "A Fifteenth-Century Muslim Hebraist: Al-Biqa'i and His Defense of Using the Bible to Interpret the Qur'an". *Speculum* 83 (2008), 629–54.
– – – . "Al-Biqāʿī". *Encyclopaedia of Islam, THREE*, October 2010. [accessed online] https://referenceworks.brillonline.com/entries/encyclopaedia-of-islam-3/al-biqai-COM_23717.
– – – . "Quranic Commentaries". In *The Study Quran: A New Translation and Commentary*. Ed. Seyyed Hossein Nasr. New York: HarperOne, 2015, 1645–58.

Samir, Samir Khalil. “The Earliest Arab Apology for Christianity (c. 750)”. In *Christian Arabic Apologetics During the Abbasid Period (750–1258)*. Eds. Samir Khalil Samir and Jorgen S. Nielsen. Leiden: Brill, 1994, 57–114.

Sarbah, Cosmas Ebo. “Sin and Redemption in Christianity and Islam”. In *Theological Issues in Christian–Muslim Dialogue*. Ed. Charles Tieszen. Eugene: Pickwick Publications, 2018, 77–90.

Shabana, Ayman. “The Concept of Sin in the Qur’an in Light of the Story of Adam”. In *Sin, Forgiveness, and Reconciliation: Christian and Muslim Perspectives*. Eds. Lucinda Mosher and David Marshall. Washington, DC: Georgetown University Press, 2016, 40–65.

Shahin, Emad Eldin. “Rashīd Rīdā, Muhammad”. In *Oxford Encyclopedia of the Islamic World*. Ed. John L. Esposito. Rev ed. New York: Oxford University Press, 2009, 4:508–10.

al-Sha‘rawi, Muhammad Mitwalli. *Tafsir Al-Sha’rawi*. Vol. 5. Cairo: Dar Akhbar al-Yawm, 1991.

Shepard, William E. “Sayyid Qutb”. In *The Qur’an: An Encyclopedia*. Ed. Oliver Leaman. London: Routledge, 2006, 568–71.

– – – . “Sayyid Qutb”. In *The Princeton Encyclopedia of Islamic Political Thought*. Princeton: Princeton University Press, 2013, 488–89.

Siddiqui, Mona. *Christians, Muslims, and Jesus*. New Haven: Yale University Press, 2013.

– – – . Ed. *The Routledge Reader in Christian–Muslim Relations*. London: Routledge, 2013.

Sirry, Mun’im A. “Early Muslim–Christian Dialogue: A Closer Look at Major Themes of the Theological Encounter”. *Islam and Christian-Muslim Relations* 16:4 (2005), 361–76.

– – – . *Scriptural Polemics: The Qur’an and Other Religions*. Oxford: Oxford University Press, 2014.

– – – . “QS1 Q1:1–7”. In *The Qur’an Seminar Commentary / Le Qur’an Seminar: A Collaborative Study of 50 Qur’anic Passages / Commentaire Collaboratif De 50 Passages Coraniques*. Eds. Mehdi Azaiez, Gabriel Said Reynolds, Tommaso Tesei, and Hamza M. Zafer. Bilingual ed. Berlin: De Gruyter, 2016, 53–54.

Smith, Jane Idleman, and Yvonne Yazbeck Haddad. *The Islamic Understanding of Death and Resurrection*. New York: Oxford University Press, 2002.

Stefanidis, Emmanuelle. “QS2 Q2:30–39”. In The Qur’an Seminar Commentary / Le Qur’an Seminar: A Collaborative Study of 50 Qur’anic Passages / Commentaire Collaboratif De 50 Passages Coraniques. Eds. Mehdi Azaiez, Gabriel Said Reynolds, Tommaso Tesei, and Hamza M. Zafer, Bilingual edition. Berlin: De Gruyter, 2016, 64.

Swanson, Mark. “The Cross of Christ in the Earliest Arabic Melkite Apologies”. In *Christian Arabic Apologetics during the Abbasid Period (750-1258)*. Ed. Samir Khalil Samir and Jorgen S. Nielsen. Leiden: Brill, 1994, 115–45.

– – – . “Ibn Taymiyya and the *Kitab Al-Burhan*: A Muslim Controversialist Responds to a Ninth-Century Arabic Christian Apology”. In *Christian-Muslim Encounters*. Eds. Yvonne Yazbeck Haddad and Wadi Z. Haddad. Gainesville: University Press of Florida, 1995, 95–107.

– – – . "Folly to the *Hunafa*': The Crucifixion in Early Christian–Muslim Controversy". In *The Encounter of Eastern Christianity with Early Islam*. Eds. Emmanouela Grypeou, Mark Swanson, and David Thomas. Leiden: Brill, 2006, 237–56.

– – – . "Folly to the *Hunafa*': The Crucifixion in Early Christian–Muslim Controversy". In *The Routledge Reader in Christian–Muslim Relations*. Ed. Mona Siddiqui. London and New York: Routledge, 2013, 72–85.

Sweetman, James W. *Islam and Christian Theology, Part I*, Vol. 2. Library of Ecclesiastical History. Cambridge: James Clarke & Co, 2002.

– – – . *Islam and Christian Theology, Part II*, Vol. 1. Library of Ecclesiastical History. Cambridge: James Clarke & Co, 2002.

– – – . *Islam and Christian Theology, Part II*, Vol. 2. Library of Ecclesiastical History. Cambridge: James Clarke & Co, 2002.

Tabatabai, Muhammad Hussein. *Al-Mizan Fi Tafsir al-Qur'an*. Vols. 3 and 5. Beirut: Mu'asasa al-'alami lil-Matbu'at, 1997.

– – – . "Tafsir al-Mizan (English): Discourse on 'Jesus and Christianity', p. 134–172." Trans. Tawheed Institute Australia, 2020. [accessed online] https://www.almizan.org/index.php.

– – – . "Tafsir al-Mizan (English): Discourse on 'Judaism and Christianity from a Historical Point of View', p. 172–175." Trans. Tawheed Institute Australia, 2020. [accessed online] https://www.almizan.org/index.php.

– – – . "Tafsir al-Mizan (English): Discourse on 'Jesus and the Gospels', p. 175–202." Trans. Tawheed Institute Australia, 2020. [accessed online] https://www.almizan.org/index.php.

– – – . "Tafsir al-Mizan (English): Commentary on Q 4:153–169." Trans. Tawheed Institute Australia, 2020. https://www.almizan.org/index.php.

Talia, Shawqi. "Muslim Views of the Cross as a Symbol of the Christian Faith". In *Heirs of the Apostles*. Eds. David Bertaina, Sandra Toenies Keating, Mark N. Swanson, and Alexander Trieger. Leiden: Brill, 2019, 194–213.

al-Tayyib, Ahmad Muhammad. "The Quran as Source of Islamic Law". In *The Study Quran: A New Translation and Commentary*. Ed. Seyyed Hossein Nasr. New York: HarperOne, 2015, 1695–1718.

Thomas, David. "Denying the Cross in Early Muslim Dialogues with Christians". In *Jesus and the Cross*. Ed. David Singh. Eugene: Wipf and Stock, 2008, 49–54.

– – – . Ed. 2017. *Routledge Handbook on Christian–Muslim Relations*. London: Routledge.

– – – . "The Doctrine of the Trinity in Early Islam: Misperceptions and Misrepresentations". In *Heirs of the Apostles*. Eds. David Bertaina, Sandra Toenies Keating, Mark N. Swanson, and Alexander Trieger. Leiden: Brill, 2019, 214–27.

Tieszen, Charles. *A Textual History of Christian–Muslim Relations: Seventh–Fifteenth Centuries*. Minneapolis: Fortress, 2015.

– – – . *Cross Veneration in the Medieval Islamic World: Christian Identity and Practice under Muslim Rule*. London: I.B. Tauris, 2017.

– – – . Ed. *Theological Issues in Christian-Muslim Dialogue*. Eugene: Pickwick Publications, 2018.

Van Ess, Josef. "Mu'tazilah". In *Encyclopedia of Religion.* Ed. Lindsay Jones. 2nd ed. Detroit: Macmillan Reference, 2005, 9:6317–25.

van Koningsveld, P. S. "The Islamic Image of Paul and the Origin of the Gospel of Barnabas". In *The Routledge Reader in Christian–Muslim Relations*. Ed. Mona Siddiqui. London and New York: Routledge, 2013, 33–48.

Voll, John O. "Salafiyya". In *Encyclopedia of Islam and the Muslim World.* New York: Macmillan Reference, 2004, 2:608–10.

Wensinck, A. J. *The Muslim Creed: Its Genesis and Historical Development.* 2nd ed. New Delhi: Oriental Books Reprint Corp, 1979.

Wessels, Anton. *The Torah, the Gospel, and the Qur'an: Three Books, Two Cities, One Tale*. Grand Rapids: Eerdmans, 2013.

Wood, Simon. *Christian Criticisms, Islamic Proofs: Rashid Rida's Modernist Defence of Islam.* Trans. Simon Wood. Oxford: Oneworld, 2008.

Yusuf, Hamza. "Death, Dying, and the Afterlife in the Quran". In *The Study Quran: A New Translation and Commentary*. Ed. Seyyed Hossein Nasr. New York: HarperOne, 2015, 1819–55.

Zahniser, A.H. Mathias. *The Mission and Death of Jesus in Islam and Christianity*. Maryknoll: Orbis Books, 2008.

# Appendix A: Considering Comparative Theology

This book is a venture in comparative theology, one of many types of comparative theology. No single work was the originating model for this project, but there are many comparative works in Christianity and Islam, and some of them have influenced me. Here I offer a non-exhaustive sampling of certain types of comparative religious studies.

Several edited volumes feature chapters in which Christians and Muslims address a given theme or theological topic.[1] There are, of course, a variety of works in which Muslims directly criticize Christian concepts or address areas of shared concern, whether or not the works are "comparative" in any thoroughgoing sense. Many of the authors in this book's third and fourth chapters fall into this category.

There are also many studies that investigate themes, tropes, characters, or community experiences across the major monotheisms.[2] Most of these are not works of systematic theology but are of a more historical, textual, "biblical", or philological bent. Example topics might be the creation account in three traditions, or the tracing of the Joseph or David profile in Jewish, Christian, and Muslim tradition. Among the many exemplary efforts, I would commend the generative work of Madigan (2007) on the Gospel of John and Islam.[3] A relevant series is Routledge's "Reading the Bible in Islamic Context" (eds. Glaser and Akhtar). Also worth considering are De Gruyter's two series "Key Concepts in Interreligious Discourses" and "Judaism, Christianity, and Islam – Tension, Transmission, Transformation".

Publications by Christian authors with an eye on Islam appear in many different styles. Zahniser's *The Mission and Death of Jesus in Islam and Christianity* (2008) is an example of an academic *and* apologetic Christian response to Islam focused on Jesus, his history, and his role in redemption. Zahniser examines the Islamic rejections of the crucifixion and death of Jesus. He also addresses Muslim objections to substitutionary atonement.[4] Beaumont's *Christology in Dialogue with Muslims* (2005) examines church Christology (ancient and modern) targeted towards Muslims. And Sweetman's *Islam and Christian Theology* (2002; orig. 1945) is an older, erudite exploration of Christian doctrines set alongside major texts and theological categories of classical Islamic theology. See, too, *The Religious Other*, which presents diverse Christian approaches to Islam, Muhammad, the Qur'an, and mission (eds. Accad and Andrews, 2020). Kenneth Cragg (d. 2012) is also important in such discussions. Cragg was an Anglican bishop and prolific author, and was a towering figure of Christian scholarship on Islam.

Timothy Tennent's *Theology in the Context of World Christianity* (2007) intends to broaden, refine, and challenge standard "Western" configurations of theology by way of global case studies.[5] In the two chapters touching on Islam, Tennent largely provides *his own* assessment of the challenge presented by the Islamic context, rather than engaging deeply with Islamic texts.[6] At some remove from Tennent's evangelical sensibilities, Anthony Wessels' work explores the confluence of the Christian and Islamic realms. His *The Torah, the Gospel, and the Qur'an: Three Books, Two Cities, One Tale* (2013) is a free-flowing, discursive and thematic essay on the "Abrahamic religions". Wessels' theological grammar inclines to pluralism, perhaps even relativism.

Edited multi-author volumes can be useful samplings of comparative theology across various traditions and topoi. For example, Clooney and von Stosch's *How to Do Comparative Theology* (2017) touches on a broad range of religions and theological topics with an emphasis on method. In *Comparing Faithfully* (2016), edited by Michelle Voss Roberts, different religions are made to intersect across domains such as divinity, theodicy, soteriology (e.g. Ralston 2016), and so on. Close to the interests of this study is Catherine Cornille's *Atonement and Comparative Theology* (2021), a collection of articles, across a range of traditions, authored primarily by Christian and/or "Western" academics, with a few chapters highlighting Islam (see below).

Francis Clooney is a comparative theologian of impressive erudition whose interest beyond the bounds of Christianity lies particularly with Hinduism. His *Hindu God, Christian God* (2001) innovatively brings key Christian thinkers (Barth, Rahner, and von Balthasar among others) into conversation with Hindu thought on topics including incarnation and revelation. This approach clearly resonates with mine here. Now, at first blush, Clooney's discourse suggests an instinct towards a theological pluralism that I do not share. But this is counterbalanced by Clooney's avowed intention to produce a work of "Christian theology", not philosophical relativism – a work both "comparative" and "confessional".[7]

Axel Takács' work aims to address a relative deficiency in sophisticated Christian engagement with Islam.[8] His "An Interpreter and Not a Judge" (2017) deftly models learning from Ibn al-'Arabi's (d. 1240) ontology, hermeneutics, cosmology, and theology of religions for the sake of constructive Christian theology – "to be an *interpreter* rather than a *judge*".[9] Takács' learning from "the other" is positioned against (what he sees as) too "universalizing" a commitment to creed, which, being too controlling and dogmatic, precludes an *agapic* epistemology.[10]

Unfortunately, Takács' discourse seems to me to founder on his resistance to "exclusivity", a concept I believe to be a necessary – though not solely sufficient – aspect of any workable conception of truth. I would insist that the virtue of epistemological humility before God and others does not require my denying that a given (say, "Christian") revelation properly affirms certain claims to the exclusion of other contradictory ones.[11] Humility before the untamable breadth of God's truth is vital; but to learn from Muslims, for example, I need not first accept, as he does, the fundamental, equal, and "*infinite* self-disclosures of God in various beliefs or religious traditions".[12] If inspired revelation is indeed so radically and effectively dispersed across all boundaries ("infinite"), one could conceivably do without any number of world traditions picked at random, for presumably all the truth one could need and more would remain accessible elsewhere. God's truth is "infinitely" disbursed, he seems to say, across many or even all faiths. This is unconvincing.

Also deserving recognition is Matthew Bennett's *Narratives in Conflict* (2019), which overlaps with my concern for comparative soteriology, Christian and Islamic. Our methods and aims are, however, quite distinct. Focusing quite narrowly on holy writ and aiming at missiological impact, Bennett's work argues that the Book of Hebrews represents a more coherent salvation-historical fulfillment and expression of Levitical *yom kippur* concepts than does the Qur'an, and thus the New Testament's claim to complete former revelation is to be preferred to the Qur'an's similar claims.[13]

Above I noted the Islam-oriented chapters in *Atonement and Comparative Theology* (2021). Here I will comment on only two of them:[14]

Madigan's article, "Who Needs It?", shares many of my own concerns. This is particularly true with respect to his aims "to identify and acknowledge valid Muslim critiques of some Christian understandings of sin and salvation; to sketch a theology of sin and atonement that steers its way between the various pitfalls to which the Islamic critique points and yet remains true to Christian tradition."[15] In my judgment he is largely successful.

Joshua Ralston's excellent "Judgment on the Cross" (2021) surveys Islamic disapprobation of "standard" Christian atonement theory (whether *Christus Victor* or "objective") through the lenses of two thinkers, ʻAli al-Tabari (ninth century) and the redoubtable Ismaʻil al-Faruqi. Ralston then proceeds to "consider how shifting the theological focus of the import of the atonement to the resurrection – and not placing the primary explanatory power of salvation on [*sic*] first and foremost on the incarnation, the crucifixion, or the imitation of Jesus – provides a framework from within which Muslim concerns around propitiation, morality, and eschatology might be re-thought."[16] My book harmonizes significantly with Ralston's aims, albeit with a somewhat different approach and length.

Also resonant with my comparative agenda is Ralston's book, *Law and the Rule of God* (2020). Ralston draws in Islamic thought insightfully and respectfully, while affirming that both "learning from" and "critique of" are valid.[17] Although my focus is not Ralston's political theology, I too aspire to examine "specific elements of the Christian tradition … in comparison with elements of another religious tradition" and hopefully in an edifying manner.[18]

Ralston himself praises another interlocutor whose comparative theorizing has been helpful in my own research: David Burrell. Burrell has written at the intersection of Judaism, Christianity, and Islam, most often in a sophisticated philosophical register and with special attention to Medieval masters.[19] In much sympathy with these scholars, my aim is a comparative modality that is "open" in the sense of a concerted effort to listen and learn. Simultaneously, I offer no apologies for a foundational commitment to Christian tradition with its own universalizing metaphysical claims. As Ralston puts it:

> The danger of both Enlightenment modernity and contemporary advocates of a theology of religious pluralism is that their quest for human harmony and unity comes at the cost of particularity and what is most central to many religious

> traditions. For Burrell, "The fact that all religions make totalizing claims is a constituting feature of such faiths; it is not up to us to relativize them from some purportedly superior perspective." However, the fact that religious claims exist within distinct linguistic communities does not foreclose the possibility of learning and reasoning across traditions.[20]

Although I would not concur with him at every juncture, Veli-Matti Kärkkäinen's comparative theology (note his works in the bibliography) is often close in spirit to my own aspirations.[21] Kärkkäinen says:

> Only careful attention to the details of investigation, respectful honoring of the otherness of other traditions and their representatives, as well as bold but humble arguing for one's deepest convictions make such a multifaceted enterprise feasible … What matters is the capacity to listen to the distinctive testimony of the other, to patiently wait upon the other, and to make a safe space for him or her.[22]

# Appendix B: Brief Notice on Atonements of Liberation and Non-Violence

In the atonement debate, the sacrifice trope has become a site of agonistic encounter, often paired with disputation over the question of divine wrath. That sacrifice metaphors undergird many scriptural portrayals of Christ's mission is hardly in doubt. How to understand ancient Levitical sacrifice and how to evaluate the death of Christ in that light – these questions are greatly contested. The issues are tangled. Dispute hangs over whether to associate sacrifice with wrath and penalty; over the nature of the sin and/or impurity addressed by OT sacrifice; and even over whether or not death itself is to the point in animal sacrifice.

Here I will simply suffice to say with respect to divine wrath, it is mischaracterized if taken as a surging bile and vindictiveness. But, equally problematic is to disassociate God from "wrath", root and branch. The point is hardly that God simply must have a victim, any victim, to be appeased.[1] Rather, the severity of the cure goes to the severity of the disease. For Barth, the atonement "is the only place from which we can see and judge from the Christian standpoint what sin is".[2] The searing reality of the Passion must be carefully, and firmly, foregrounded as God's restorative answer to the otherwise insoluble human condition – a response drastic, fitting, and loving altogether.

With respect to sacrifice, wrath need not be taken as the exclusive category of relevance. Neither do animal sacrifices fall comprehensively under juridical categories. And, yes, the giving or renewing of *life* is a central trope in sacrificial thinking. But neither is it realistic to disassociate all sacrifice (for sin or impurity) from the notion of sin's very real cost, namely, "death". In a very specific sense, then, the distance from there to "wrath" is not overly great.

## Liberation Models

Theologians disaffected with traditional atonement configurations – objective, substitutionary, and satisfaction or penalty based – have pursued constructive agendas of their own. Two loose headings under which many of these variegated models may be placed are the "liberationist" and the "non-violent", with these arguably being contrasting, not contradicting, emphases within a larger stream. Emblematic motifs here include divine relationality and reciprocity, dismantling of hierarchy, solidarity with the disenfranchised, and a "praxis" arising from contemporary social concerns. Some of the more famous iterations of this larger phenomenon include Latin American, African American, feminist, and other theologies.[3] And some of these liberationist modes are marked by influences from the famous Jürgen Moltmann whether or not he is labeled a liberation theologian in his own right.

We take a moment here for a brief, merely illustrative, consideration of the feminist theorization of atonement. In view of the ills attributed to objective constructs in which a violent Patriarch abuses his submissive Son, some theorists have abandoned the theological legitimacy of the Passion altogether.[4] According to Baker and Green, D. K. Ray pursues another course of feminist liberation, retaining the value of the cross *reinterpreted.* In contrast with the "lordly" hierarchies of Anselmian thought, Ray commends *Christus Victor* frameworks directed away from personal morality and towards God's overthrow of Satan as "the sum total of [systemic, cosmic] evil".[5]

So, it seems that even with common aspirations, feminist theologians can espouse diametrically opposed approaches to the cross and human liberation.[6] In any case, as a whole, feminist proponents of cruciform liberation reject the "passive" stencil of the Passion – one which arguably leaves the condition of the oppressed unchanged – moving towards a more "activist" portrayal of Jesus who died in solidarity with the abused, resisting and ultimately overthrowing patriarchy's "unjust powers".[7]

## Non-Violent Atonement

Whether one's horizon is general human experience or the biblical tableaux, violence presents a stark ethical, theological, and existential challenge. For both proponents and detractors of a cross-borne salvation, the crucifixion is difficult and unsettling. For some, the moral calculus is simple: "violent acts are morally objectionable, so that bringing about reconciliation or atonement through violent means is morally unsustainable."[8] Once again, some vehemently object to this supposed Anselmian vision of redemption, "the sadomasochism of Christian teaching at its most transparent".[9]

There is a soteriological trend here that goes under the banner of "non-violence". These trajectories commonly fit comfortably within a typically modern instinct in which "bondage [to 'sin'] is [seen as] epistemologically mediated, one might say gnostically mediated. What enslaves us is a failure of vision. Consequently, what would liberate us is a removal of the cataract, a defogging of our vision of the good."[10] In harmony with this, pacificist or non-violent theologians often reduce the crucifixion to a travesty perpetrated by "the powers" and entirely disassociate it from God.[11]

Without the vitriol of the most radical pacifist theologians, social theorist René Girard unleashed an influential and highly creative project in "non-violent" atonement, contesting the old orthodoxies' insistence upon divine intention behind the crucifixion.[12] At the heart of Girard's system is the notion of society's "scapegoat": throughout human history, in aid of community cohesion and managing the impulse towards envious total warfare, a subsection of society has been unjustly designated as the source of all ills – the scapegoat – and violently pursued. According to Girard, this universal human dynamic is uniquely subverted in biblical revelation: climaxing in the crucifixion of Jesus, humanity's eyes are opened to the rank falsity of substitutionary violence, injustice is overturned, and redemption arises in a community of peace. On a Girardian typology, PSA in particular "appears to be a profound *misreading*" of New Testament theology.[13] Perhaps PSA becomes the scapegoat of choice![14]

Is Girard's creative thinking tenable?[15] Once again, if atonement is reduced to Girardian terms, we are left with an epistemic enlightenment-dependent model. Again, bondage and redemption are "gnostically mediated". Kärkkäinen's assessment is apt: "It is far from certain that men and women, just having realized that violence is a vicious circle, will stop resorting to it."[16]

*Appropriating and Critiquing Non-Violent Proposals*

Non-violent models draw attention to the character of God; the motivation of divine love; the embedded harms of violence; and the unparalleled example of Christ facing down webs of human interest, cynicism, and power in the event of the Passion. Rightly so. But all this ought not to exclude, *but should recenter*, the "primary constitutive rationale: this fleshly death occurs for our *sins* (1 Cor. 15:3; Rom. 4:25; Gal. 1:4), for *us* (1 Thess. 5:10; cf. 1 Pet. 3:18), and for a *sin-offering* (Rom. 8:3) … the action of the God who is and must be just in justifying … In this fleshly sacrifice … God['s] mercy, tenderness, and compassion exist in no tension with holiness, wrath, and justice … they are expressed at once *as* he acts."[17] Precisely through the pains of the cup *not* withheld (Mt. 26:39) God intersects with the brutality of our fallen world, overthrows our sin, and heals the nations. Contrary to "non-violent" proposals, the cross as powerful paradox, as the mysterious but intentional expression *of* God's love, is not a misreading.

Parsing questions of violence in atonement requires a deft treatment of metaphor.[18] Sensitivity must be applied to the traffic between the human and the divine, discerning the likeness and unlikeness in analogies. And further, lexical tools must be astutely deployed, avoiding facile semantic totality transfers. Consider, for example, the ambiguous or equivocal ways the term "violence" may be employed, such that "violence" can be used to characterize both an instance of child abuse and an armed rescue of victims of human trafficking.[19]

Certainly, one may wonder if cruciform reconciliation "works". Can God in this way carry our sin, guilt, and violence so as to heal us? The question is real. But however that may be, the analogies ought not start from the bottom (from abusive and distorted human experience) and work upwards (portraying such deformations of "sacrifice" as the essence of the thing itself). Rather, "the mystery of human redemption [is] made possible by the mystery of God's Trinity: The One who was offended bears the burden of the offense."[20] No properly articulated understanding of the Passion (including PSA) entails anything like a "divine child-abuse" archetype.

Let us be quick to admit that many of the protests from non-violent theologians do emerge from our world's intractable ills and injustices. As Sonderegger says, "The rebuke of what is taken to be an Anselmian account of the atonement – a strong misreading, I would say – rests on the proper horror Christians should take toward a god who would demand innocent blood as an appeasing meal."[21] But the legitimate aspects of a prophetic, "non-violent" exposé must not be given carte blanche to proceed on the basis of questionable hermeneutics – vitiating traditional doctrines of the cross as though they depict and seek to legitimate a god who bludgeons the vulnerable.

A "non-violent" denial that the death at the cross is divine action for us not only sidesteps the biblical witness but also threatens to muzzle God's disarming of the powers. At the cross God acts forcefully – yes, forcefully – against sin, hell, and death, in an inverted expression of the power of love.[22] As Gunton says, a well-articulated objective atonement "draws attention to the fact that the human condition is too enmeshed in evil to be able to be restored by its own agency. Forgiveness is not, therefore, simply a matter of omnipotence: something God can do simply because he wants to."[23] The claim that "substitutionism" imparts violence into the very character of God is to direct traffic in the wrong direction. Violence as a brutal, unyielding reality of the world is a tragic given. But in dying *for the world* the Lord – actively and according to plan – takes our violence onto himself, and leads us out, repentant, into peace, reconstruction, and reconciliation. The evil action of humanity at the cross mysteriously, subversively, effectively coincides with the power and aims of God unleashed for his world. This the NT clearly insists upon. (See again my reflections above on the non-competitive but intersecting metaphysical planes of Creator and creation.) This is our hope, affirmed and accomplished not only in the death but also in the undefeated life of Jesus.

# Appendix C: On Islamic Authors

Following here are brief biographical comments on key Muslim authors and works consulted for this project.

Muhammad Rashid Rida (1865–1935) authored what was probably the most influential "modernist" commentary of the first half of the 20th century, *Tafsir al-Manar*.[1] Rida was a seminal anti-colonial and anti-missionary activist, modernist reformer, and scholar in late-colonial Egypt.[2] Fittingly for a disciple of Muhammad 'Abduh (d. 1905), Rida's commentary and other works are imbued with a modern spirit that seeks to defend and articulate a sophisticated and productive Islam in the face of European culture, technology, and (fading) colonialism. His wide influence may be traced to subsequent movements both "radical" and "liberal".[3] McAuliffe casts Rida as "one of the pre-eminent exegetes of [the 20th] century".[4]

Sayyid Qutb, executed for sedition under President Nasr in 1966, was the leading ideologue of the Egyptian Muslim Brotherhood in the middle of the 20th century. He was to become a prominent intellectual architect of Islamic radicalism, but his thought is formative for swathes of the global Muslim community well beyond that circle.[5] Not surprisingly, in certain communities, Qutb's status as a martyr has lent "considerable moral authority to his writings".[6] Qutb's commentary, *In the Shade of the Qur'an* (2009), continues to enjoy wide global distribution, and Lawson thinks that it might possibly be the "most widely read Qur'an commentary of our time".[7]

Muhammad Hussein[8] Tabatabai (d. 1981) was a renowned Iranian Shi'i scholar, philosopher, and mystic. Scion of a family of religious scholars, he straddled the worlds of traditional Islam and modern thought, not least in his commentary, *al-Mizan Fi Tafsir al-Qur'an.*[9] In this commentary, Tabatabai comments on Jesus and Christianity in a number of excurses, including a rebuttal of Christian atonement thought.[10]

Isma'il al-Faruqi (d. 1986) was a prolific Sunni Muslim scholar, active in both Islamic studies, Muslim–Christian relations, and comparative religions. al-Faruqi's scholarship and activism have been influential internationally and within American Islam in particular.[11]

Fazlur Rahman (d. 1988) was a Pakistani scholar with a distinguished career in Islamic studies at the University of Chicago and elsewhere. His breadth of engagement with Islamic philosophy, theology, and history is generally considered modernist, accenting "freedom from hierarchy and localized bonds", "scientific advancements", and a "progress" paradigm of history.[12] His theologizing may be characterized as "Qur'an heavy" and "Hadith light." See Rahman, *Major Themes of the Qur'an* (2009).

Seyyed Hossein Nasr is a distinguished Iranian professor of religion, based at the George Washington University since the 1980s. He is widely published in philosophy, Islamic studies, comparative religion, philosophy of science, Sufism, and more. He is the lead editor of *The Study Qur'an*.[13] I have occasionally drawn on the commentary or essays by contributors to this volume.

Mahmoud Ayoub is a contemporary Shi'i scholar who has pursued his career primarily in the U.S. He is among a coterie of Muslim academics in the West whose theological stance vis-à-vis the Christian Scripture and the crucifixion is distinctively bold and relatively positive. Ayoub has reflected extensively on the notion of redemption in Christianity and Islam.[14] Ayoub holds in tension Islamic conviction and an epistemological pluralism which takes the varieties of religion as authentic but partial expressions of the cosmic Truth.[15]

Shabbir Akhtar (d. 2023) was a British Pakistani scholar of Islam, Muslim–Christian relations, philosophy, and more. His *The New Testament in Muslim Eyes* (2018) is a highly unusual, critical but appreciative, commentary on Paul's letter to the *Galatians*. Such a comprehensive engagement with New Testament scripture by a Muslim scholar is rare indeed. Akhtar is intent on thinking as a fair-minded but convinced Muslim who tries to delve into Paul and the Galatian letter in a contextually aware manner, all the while addressing theological issues of shared concern and contention.

Mona Siddiqui is a British Muslim scholar of Islam and interreligious studies. In the sixth chapter of *Christians, Muslims, and Jesus*, Siddiqui offers wide-ranging thinking on the meaning of the cross. In a manner reminiscent of Ayoub, she seeks to explore a Christian apprehension of the cross "from within", even as she stops well short of endorsing Christian theology.[16]

# Appendix D: Muslim Authors Receptive to "Atonement" – An Aside on Paths Not Taken[1]

It should be clear that the conventional Islamic assessment of Christian soteriology is hardly positive. But, for the sake of breadth and balance, I take a little space here to acknowledge a few ostensibly *positive* Islamic framings of a "redemptive" role for Jesus – even if these presentations stop short of positing unique atonement in Christ.

Shabbir Akhtar bears mentioning here, even though he features above primarily in the role of critic. Even so, he is not a critic wholly devoid of empathy, totally unable to imagine the viewpoint of "the other". Glimmers of this disposition occasionally appear above in my citations of Akhtar. Here is another example of his writing tenor, which can be at times sharp, at times winsome, at times wistful or even receptive:

> The scandal of the cross is embraced with irreversible and irresistible zeal. Paul preaches its ever-widening significance: Jesus is crucified, Paul is co-crucified, Paul and other followers of Christ are crucified to the world – and a reverse cosmic crucifixion. It is a vision with no Islamic or Jewish analogue.[2]

A few modern Muslim scholars attempt to "redeem" the term "redemption" for a licit soteriology, sometimes associating this redemption specifically with Jesus – even as they eschew the category of vicarious sacrifice for sin (cf. Q 9:111).[3] The tendency is to construct redemption in terms of the *example* of Jesus' piety and fidelity in the face of idolatrous opposition and through intense suffering. There is a marked "gnostic" emphasis once again – Jesus' teaching and model enlighten our pathway to salvation.[4] Parallels with Christian exemplarist or "moral-influence" soteriology come immediately to mind. Consider this assessment by a Muslim intellectual:

> The Christian scheme of salvation is not only morally and rationally unsound, but also has no support of the words of Jesus. Jesus may be said to have suffered for the sins of men in the sense that, in order to take them out of darkness into light, he incurred the wrath of the evildoers and was tortured by them; but that does not mean that his death was an atonement for the sins of others and that only those who believe in his blood would be forgiven. Jesus had come to rescue men from sin by his teaching and the example of his godly life, and not by deliberately dying for them on the cross and offering his blood as a propitiation for their sins.[5]

At times the malleability of symbolic and metaphorical language is perceived to allow for bold theological speech which, at the same time, preserves the requisite boundaries around divine ontology and transcendence. Thus Jesus may "redeem", "ransom", or "purify" without associated ideas of vicarious sacrifice or incarnation.[6]

Mahmoud Ayoub and Mona Siddiqui are among the most sympathetic Muslim thinkers who have made concerted efforts to read Christian theology on its own terms. Even so, in summing up her perspective on cruciform redemption, Siddiqui is forthright:

> It is not the language of redemption which I cannot understand, it is the necessity of God's self-revelation for this act of redemption. Why does the fall become the paradigm of human life, making the cross the ultimate paradox of death and new life? There are other ways to come to redemption even if this means looking at the world in a dramatically different way. This is a world in which the intimacy of human relations with God does not rest on an event that has occurred but on our constant movement towards him.[7]

Ayoub for his part pictures Jesus as in some way saving and reconciling, seeming to infuse life almost on a cosmic scale, all the while holding to strictures against "expiatory sacrifice" and the "divinizing" of Christ; he allows for the "special humanity" of Jesus who likely died on the cross and may serve a "general redemptive role in human history".[8] Ayoub works to narrow the chasm between Christianity and Islam through the *example* of Jesus and a call to experience the "godness" of God over all creation and our individual lives.[9]

This more positive Islamic configuration of "redemption" presents a Christ faithful "towards" the cross (whether or not he died there). Here the "redeemer" embodies a paradoxical model of suffering and fidelity in the face of evil, pointing believers to like perseverance in hopes of divine vindication. To the extent that such appropriations of redemption terminology resonate with paradigms of salvation as "revealed information" or as "moral influence," they are interesting, but their importance to this study is oblique. Certainly, the ethical import of atonement theology ("moral influence") is significant. But relatively few Christian soteriological imaginaries *center* the moral influence trope, especially not as the exclusive lens on salvation. And the paradigms centered in chapters five through seven certainly are not reducible to exemplarism. Jesus' entire ministry, life, and death is integral to atonement, but moral influence models are inadequate *as the fundamental or exclusive* lens on the Christ Event.[10]

# Appendix E: Hart's Summary of *CDH*

i) Every rational creature is created to partake of beatitude in God, so Anselm asserts, in return for which the creature owes God perfect obedience, by withholding which humanity offends infinitely against the divine honor and merits death.

ii) Inasmuch as humanity has sinned against God, to God's "dishonor", God's honor requires that humanity restore what it has taken away, and indeed give still more, in order to make satisfaction for its offense; otherwise humanity must suffer its condign penalty and be handed over to death.

iii) Nor can God merely remit the penalty, as it would contradict his own righteousness and sovereignty over creation were he to allow sin to pass with impunity, and thereby raise injustice (sin) to his own level (transcendent of any higher law), erase the distinction between good and evil (in the latter's favor), and create division within his own immutably righteous will; and so, through restitution or punishment, satisfaction or damnation, humanity *shall* restore the divine honor and the beauty of the created universe.

iv) But humanity possesses nothing by which it might satisfy divine justice; as it is God himself against whom the gravity of every transgression is measured, the slightest sin is an infinite offense, calling for an infinite and "more than infinite" restitution.

v) But it is also contrary to God's goodness and honor that his gracious purpose in creation should come to nothing and that he should abandon his creature to destruction.

vi) One is called for, then, who can of his own render to God a payment that surpasses in worth all things under God. But this is possible for God alone; and yet satisfaction must be made by one of the race of Adam. And so that divine righteousness remains inviolate, the beauty of creation be preserved, and the divine purpose be fulfilled, the God-man must come among his own, in order to make satisfaction on humanity's behalf: a high Chalcedonian Christology is a "necessity" for understanding how God has resolved this apparent *impasse* between his justice and mercy.

vii) Christ, as a man, owes God his perfect obedience, which he gladly proffers, but as he is a sinless man, he does not owe God his death; when Christ voluntarily surrenders his infinitely precious life for God's honor, and the Father accepts it, the superabundance of its worth calls forth some gracious recompense from God's justice.

viii) But Christ, being also God, wants for nothing; and so, lest God's righteousness be defeated by the injustice of no recompense being given, the benefits of Christ's death pass on to those on whom Christ would bestow them. God's infinite honor being more than infinitely satisfied, humanity's debt before

God is remitted and salvation is accomplished in such measure as persons approach God in Christ's name and live righteously.[1]

**Chapter One Notes**

[1] See Ayoub 2007, chapter thirteen; Cragg 1999, chapter six; Cumming 2005; Lawson 2009; Mourad 2015; Reynolds 2009; Zahniser 2008.
[2] Lawson 2009, 95. Ralston quotes S. H. Nasr to the effect that "the meaning of the crucifixion and the idea of redemption it signifies are perhaps the most difficult of all aspects of Christianity for an ordinary Muslim to grasp" (Ralston 2021, 215).
[3] Rutledge 2015 explores at least nine distinctive motifs or models of atonement.
[4] Cf. Kärkkäinen 2020, 12–13.
[5] Madigan 2021, 11.
[6] The image of "on ramps" for discussion was suggested to me by Dr. David Luy.
[7] Holmes 2016, 372.
[8] Moffitt 2022, 5.
[9] Kärkkäinen 2020, 22.
[10] Ralston 2021, 227 n 43.

**Chapter Two Notes**

[1] Cf. Holmes 2017, 305.
[2] Kärkkäinen 2013, 296–97; cf. Stott 2012, Kindle Locations 2938–3074. For "redeem," the lexical constellations around פָּדָה and λυτρόω /ἀπολύτρωσις also are relevant.
[3] M. Bennett 2019, 69.
[4] Moffitt 2022, 2; cf. 1–3.
[5] Cf. Kärkkäinen 2013, 296–97; see also Klawans 2009 on the dynamics of sacrifice and purity.
[6] Cf. McGuckin 2016, 73–74.
[7] Compare Johnson 2015, 11.
[8] Johnson 2015, 38; cf. Vanhoozer 2012, 176.
[9] Johnson 2015, 41.
[10] Cf. Johnson 2015, 49–50. One theme of David Moffitt (2022) is that sacrificial atonement necessarily entails purificatory and vivifying action well beyond the victim's death—in the case of both the Levitical system and the death, resurrection, and ascension of Jesus.
[11] Tanner 2010, 247–48; cf. Vidu 2014, "Introduction".
[12] Cf. Kärkkäinen 2013, 292, and sources cited.
[13] I recall Hastings articulating these ideas in an audio interview. In any case, in his book he speaks of participation as "the 'theory' behind all the models" (Hastings 2019, 4; see too 6 and chapter four).
[14] Johnson organizes his thought into "aspects" of the atonement in an ontological sense, while the more or less structured witness to these aspects by the Church through time are "theories" (Johnson 2015, 37).
[15] Cf. Hastings 2019, 6; Rutledge 2015, 9.
[16] Hastings 2019, 74–75, 79.
[17] Dr. David Luy made a point along these lines in a personal conversation.
[18] Kärkkäinen 2013, 298.
[19] See Kärkkäinen 2013, 296; cf. 297–98. Compare Gal. 3:10-14.
[20] As possible ways into the conversation on metaphor, consider the work of biblical scholar Erin Heim in chapters two and three of her *Adoption in Galatians and Romans* (2017); philosopher Paul Ricoeur's *The Rule of Metaphor* (2003); and the section on "models, metaphors, and analogies" in chapter eight of Moffitt's *Rethinking the Atonement* (2022).
[21] Dr. David Luy suggested the term "austere" to me in a discussion about comparative theological aesthetics.

[22] Sometimes the argument centers on *the locus* of mystery. For example, while most Muslims will balk at an "irrational" soteriology of incarnation and cross, there are other theological conundrums quite basic to standard Islamic theology (e.g. the relation of essence and attributes in the unitary God; the co-eternity of God and Qur'an; and the mystery of *qadar*).
[23] Hastings 2019, 14, citing A. Johnson.
[24] Crisp 2020, 25–26.
[25] Compare Sonderegger 2015 *Systemic Theology*, 392–95; 2020, 102–103, 253–54; also Hastings 2019, 3–4.
[26] Cf. Castelo 2009, 108; Sonderegger 2020, 383.
[27] 1986; first English translation, 1931.
[28] Aulén 1986, 4.
[29] Spjuth 2017, 390.
[30] Cf. Kärkkäinen 2013, 304.
[31] McGowan 2016, 876.
[32] Cf. Kärkkäinen 2013, 306–07.
[33] Cf. Kärkkäinen 2013, 298–307.
[34] Cf. Aulén 1986, 158–59.
[35] Cf. Kotsko 2017 "The Persistence of the Ransom Theory of the Atonement", 277–79, 284; Aulén 1986, 53; Gunton 1988, 62–64; Gregory of Nyssa, *Cat. Or.* 23; Augustine, *On the Trinity* 13:13:17, 13:17:22.
[36] Cf. Kotsko 2017 "The Persistence of the Ransom Theory of the Atonement", 279–82. In my view, Kotsko's positioning of liberation from "the powers" as over against regressive "objective" and "subjective" theories trades in false incompatibilities and tends to makeover the church Fathers according to a modern, progressive template. Intriguingly, McGuckin's analysis of Gregory of Nyssa's "baited hook" analogy at times reads as virtual counterpoint to Kotsko's (see McGuckin 2017, 159–73).
[37] Cf. Crisp 2020, 41; Athanasius, *On the Incarnation*, 20; Myers 2015, 76–82. Gregory of Nazianzus specifically attacked the notion of "rights" of the Devil (McGuckin 2017, 166 n 25). See Gregory of Nazianzus, *Oration* 39:13, 45:22.
[38] McGuckin 2017, 167; cf. 170–71.
[39] Cf. McGuckin 2017, 157.
[40] McGukin 2017, 159.
[41] Cf. Matthew Baker 2016, 122–23; Hunsinger 2015; McGuckin 2017, 158. I would, however, differ with McGowan's overly strong claim that from "the early Church Fathers, penal substitution has been the controlling model" (McGowan 2016, 876).
[42] Cf. Anatolios 2020; Matthew Baker 2016, 122–23; Hart 1998, 341–42, 347; McGuckin 2017, 158–59; Schendel 2018.
[43] Johnson 2015, 3.
[44] See Johnson 2015, 4, 32; cf. Hart 1998, 342; Spjuth 2017, 390–91; compare Aulén 1986, 157–58. Also, Kärkkäinen 2013, 301, 308. Note the remarkable sequence of themes in Augustine's *On the Trinity* book 4, chapters thirteen and fourteen.
[45] Placher 2009, 26–27.
[46] Johnson 2015, 37; cf. 28.
[47] See Crisp 2020, 5–6, 31–33, 51–53; Anatolios 2020, 10–17, 27–30; Hart 1998, 342.
[48] Vanhoozer 2012, 177–78.
[49] Lowe 1994, Kindle Locations 3097–98; cf. Kärkkäinen 2013, 326.
[50] Sonderegger 2015, 394–96.
[51] Cf. Gunton 1988, 158–59; Barth 2004, 2:1:396, 4:1:176; N. T. Wright 2018.
[52] Cf. Willard 1998, 36–37. I believe I encountered similar phrasing in a blog post by Nijay K. Gupta.
[53] Cf. Willard 1998, chapter two.

[54] Crisp 2020, 93, 80; Johnson 2017 "Peter Abelard", 358; Kotsko 2017 "Exemplarism", 486–87.
[55] Kärkkäinen 2013, 304.
[56] Cf. Crisp 2020, 84–89; Sonderegger 2015, 402; Kärkkäinen 2013, 314.
[57] Cf. Crisp 2020, 85–88, 91.
[58] Cf. Stott 2012, Kindle Locations 3907–84; Crisp 2020, 88.
[59] Cf. Crisp 2020, 92–93.
[60] Sonderegger 2015, 399.
[61] Gunton 1988, 160.
[62] Gunton 1988, 163; cf. 184.
[63] Baker and Green 2011, 98; cf. 98–101.
[64] Sonderegger 2015 "Theological Themes in the Passion", 401; cf. Gregory of Nazianzus, *Oration* 45:29.
[65] In terms of "proponents" see Morris 1983, esp. chapters six to eight; Stott 2012, esp. chapters five and six; and Packer 1974.
[66] Whether "penalty" and legal inflection are appropriate or not to the world of Israelite sacrifice, there is a "deadly cost" implicit in the blood offerings of Tabernacle and Temple, even if one wishes to affirm the *life-oriented character* of these offerings.
[67] Cf. Crisp 2020, 75, 148–49; Baker and Green 2011, 158.
[68] Cf. Hastings 2019, chapters eleven to thirteen; Crisp 2020, chapter six.
[69] Crisp 2020, 110–11.
[70] Baker and Green 2011, 174; see 170f.
[71] Cf. Baker and Green 2011, 79, 175–76.
[72] Cf. Baker and Green 2011, 180, 190; Holmes 2017, 305; Rutledge 2015, 489–506.
[73] Cf. Baker and Green 2011, 188–91, on Vanhoozer.
[74] Crisp 2020, 104.
[75] Cf. Crisp 2020, chapters six and ten.
[76] Holmes 2017, 314; cf. 297, 307, 313.
[77] Cf. Holmes 2017, 301–302; Johnson 2015, 41, 176; Rutledge 2015, 492–93, 502–503.
[78] Gunton 1988, 104.
[79] Cf. Gunton 1988, 157.
[80] Gunton 1988, 156.
[81] Burrell 1993, 165.
[82] Sonderegger 2020, 383 (language evoking the Fourth Lateran Council).
[83] Sonderegger 2020, 80–81.
[84] Burrell 1993, 85, referencing R. Alter. But see Burrell's own exposition throughout his work. Consider too God's providential "handing over" people in their genuine oppositional agency, even as he "pronounces" outcomes (cf. Isa. 6:9-10; Mt. 13:13-16; Rom. 1:24-32; 2 Thess. 2:10-12). Consider the cases of Judas and also Peter's denial (both "free" and "foreordained").
[85] Cf. Burrell 1993, 70–71.
[86] Cf. Burrell 1993, 92–93, 124.
[87] Burrell 1993, 6; cf. 82, 97.
[88] Cf. Burrell 1993, 2, 6, see also 86–94, 149; Behr 2016, 48–50; cf. Crisp 2020, 140 44.
[89] Cf. Burrell 1993, 12. In chapter five I note Anselm's contention that the atonement is a sign of God's love precisely because it is *not* a matter of his own self-enhancement or vulnerability to dishonor.
[90] Burrell 1993, 22; cf. 166; Stott 2012, Kindle Locations 2152–2260.
[91] Cf. Davidson 2017, 49–50.
[92] Crisp 2020, 42.
[93] Cf. Green 2017, 119; Baker and Green 2011, 58, 63; Tanner 2010, 262.

[94] Matthew Baker *et al* 2016, 10.
[95] Crisp 2020, 43–44; Davidson 2017, 35, 39; Florovsky 2016, 144; Weinandy 2017, 140–43.
[96] Davidson 2017, 54; cf. Weinandy 2017, 149–50.
[97] Crisp 2020, Chapter Nine; see too Johnson 2015, 19; Kärkkäinen 2013, 324.
[98] Baker and Green 2011; Green 2017. With respect to "mosaic", see McNall 2019.
[99] Cf. Baker and Green 2011, 36. Green delineates five key metaphors of redemption in Paul (see Green 2017, 130; Baker and Green 2011, 41, 123–37; cf. chapters two to four).
[100] Cf. Green 2017, 130, 134; Baker and Green 2011, 124–26.
[101] Cf. Crisp 2020, 155, 159–60; contrast Baker and Green 2011, 125, 139–40.
[102] Cf. Crisp 2020, 157–58.
[103] See Crisp 2020, 166–71, 173–75, 178. I was not able to consult Crisp's most recent proposal, *Participation and Atonement* (2022).
[104] Johnson 2015, 5–6, citing von Balthazar.
[105] Cf. Hastings 2019, 2–8.
[106] Cf. Johnson 2015, 41, 176.
[107] I appreciate Dr. David Luy discussing these ideas with me.

**Chapter Three Notes**

[1] Cragg 1999, 178.
[2] See, for example, al-'Aqqad 2001, 3–20 (P. Ford's comments); Ayoub 2007, chapter thirteen; al-Azhar 1992, 2:966–68; Darwaza 2000, 8:274–75; Cragg 1999, chapter six; Cumming 2005; Droge 2013, 60, n176; Fatoohi 2008; Haddad 1995, 90–91; Ibn al-'Uthamin 2008, 2:438–50; Lawson 2009; Michel 1985, 236–37, 255–325; Mourad 2011, 2015; Nasr, ed., 2015, at Q 4:157–58 (commentary by M. Dakake); Qutb 2009, 1:339–41; 3:317–18, 336–37; 4:54–57, 167–72; 8:104–107, 113–14; 13:140–41; Reynolds 2009; 2018, 181; Rida 1948 at Q 4:153–59; N. Roberts 2013; Robinson 1991, chapter thirteen; Robinson 2003; al-Sha'rawi 1991, 5:2793–99; Siddiqui 2013a, 231–43; Swanson 1994, 1995, 2013; Tabatabai 2020 (sections noted in reference list); Zahniser 2008.
[3] I consult some important Shi'i thinkers (e.g. Tabatabai and Ayoub) because they have offered significant reflections on Christian atonement theory. I do not, however, front Shi'ism as a discreet focus as such; nor do I develop the potential parallels between Shi'i and Christian motifs of redemptive suffering.
[4] The point is not that all of these authors are uniformly and strictly "Qur'an-only"; for example, Tabatabai certainly knows and uses the hadith, but, notably, such traditions are often addressed in a section separated from his primary commentary on the Qur'an.
[5] Cf. Kueny 2004; Saleh 2015, 1657–58.
[6] Hermansen 2013, 283.
[7] Cf. Nickel 1994, 3.
[8] Rahman 2009, 106; see too Nickel 1994, 4.
[9] Yusuf 2015, 1837.
[10] Cf. Smith and Haddad 2002, 146.
[11] Cf. al-Ghazali 2000, 19–20. See too *Sahih Muslim*, Kitab al-Qadar 46:40 available at: https://sunnah.com/muslim/46/40 (accessed 13 November 2019). Also see Q 30:30.
[12] al-Faruqi in Chambésy 1982, 37. Chambésy 1982 is, in the reference list, "Islamic Foundation 1982". This is a published summary of the proceedings of a conference held in 1976 in Chambésy, Switzerland.
[13] Sweetman 2002 *Islam and Christian Theology, Part I,* Vol. 2, 184; cf. Coward 2003, 63; Zahniser 2008, 232–33.
[14] Cf. Shabana 2016; also see note 16 below.

[15] Stefanidis 2016, 64.

[16] An intriguing prophetic hadith reports that Satan somehow "touches" every child entering the world, with the exceptions of Jesus and Mary (e.g. Bukhari 6:60:71, accessed 18 October 2021 at http://www.sahih-bukhari.com/Pages/Bukhari_6_60.php). Christian scholars have highlighted areas of partial and overlooked convergence in hamartiology between the Qur'an and Christian thought. The Catholic scholar, Gabriel Reynolds argues that while universal guilt may not be "on the table" for the Qur'an, a universal "disordered desire and ignorance" certainly are (Reynolds 2020, 215, 217). See too Madigan 2021, 26; Zahniser 2008, 230–33; cf. Q 20:123.

[17] Cf. Rahman 2009, 20–22, 25–30, 128.

[18] Rahman 2009, 21.

[19] Rahman 2009, 107; see too Yusuf 2015, 1847.

[20] al-Faruqi 2013, 205.

[21] Cf. K. Ahmad in Chambésy 1982, 42.

[22] Cf. Rida 1996, 6–8.

[23] Quoted in M. Bennett 2019, 160.

[24] al-Faruqi 2013, 208; cf. 198, 210; M. Bennett 2019, 158, 161–63.

[25] Rahman 2009, 21. Cf. Reynolds 2020, 204.

[26] Cf. al-Ghazali 1982, 113.

[27] Akhtar 2018, 64. See too al-Tayyib 2015, 1714; see also Q 2:286; *Sahih Muslim* 125 (Available at: https://sunnah.com/muslim/1, accessed 9 October 2019).

[28] Rahman 2009, 9; cf. M. Bennett 2019, 165.

[29] Qutb 2009, 1:57–58.

[30] Rahman 2009, 107.

[31] Rahman 2009, 30–31; cf. Q 23:115.

[32] Cf. Akhtar 2018, 251; also 64, 258–59.

[33] Akhtar 2018, 105.

[34] Akhtar 2018, 261–62. At times Akhtar expresses a semi-wistful admiration for the dynamism of the grace trope in Christianity, even if he sees it finally as an overreach: "The Christian offer appears morally more robust and indeed impossibly demanding … Christians, by contrast [with Muslims], see the unconditional forgiveness of others as a commandment of the new covenant of grace since God forgave them in the same manner. For true disciples of Christ—and alas how few are these in any age!—forgiving even one's enemies is a direct dominical demand" (Akhtar 2018, 251).

[35] Cf. Rahman 2009, 31–32.

[36] Rahman 2009, 31.

[37] al-Faruqi 2013, 213.

[38] Seyyed Hossein Nasr quoted in M. Bennett 2019, 162.

[39] Compare Akhtar 2018, 147; J. Brown 2016, 16; for an Islamic take on Jesus and ethics and law, see al-'Aqqad 2001, 172–77, 228, chapter eighteen.

[40] Qutb 2009, 3:256; cf. 15:392, 431; Q 47:34.

[41] Rahman 2009, 30.

[42] On this Rahman highlights Q 6:160; cf. Q 4:31; 42:37; 53:32; see too, J. Brown 2016, 14 on Q 39:35. God says in a famous hadith: "My mercy overwhelms my anger" (J. Brown 2016, 15 quoting *Sahih Bukhari*).

[43] Rida 1948, 6:30; cf. Ryad 2009, 289; Q 2:286

[44] Rida 1948, 6:29–30. Translations of Rida (1948) are my own, although *some lines* from the expansive section of his *tafsir* examined here have been translated by others and were thus available for comparison. Wood 2008 is (among other things) a translation of Rida's *Shubuhat al-Nasara wa Hujaj al-Islam* (*The Criticisms of the Christians and the Proofs of Islam*) first published in 1905. The sources al-Azhar 1992,

Darwaza, al-Sha'rawi, and Ibn al-'Uthamin are only in Arabic. I have examined Tabatabai in the Arabic original and in translation.

[45] *Islam and Christian Theology, Part I*. Vol. 2., 58; cf. 49, 54–55, 58–59; Coward 2003, 65, 75; Q 7:72; 11:66; 39:62.

[46] See al-Ghazali 2016, 101.

[47] Cf. Rida 1948, 6:30–31.

[48] Cf. Sweetman 2002 *Islam and Christian Theology, Part I*, Vol. 2., 213.

[49] Cf. Ayoub 2007, 94–96.

[50] Sirry 2016, 53–54; Q 2:62; 5:69.

[51] Cf. Nickel 1994, 6. The data on the bare requirements for salvation is rich, variegated, and difficult to coordinate. One tradition is particularly fascinating. In it, salvation appears to depend heavily on right faith (as over against deeds), and among the requisites of faith, acknowledging the status not only of Muhammad but also of Jesus is included. See *Sahih Bukhari* 4:55:644, available at https://www.iium.edu.my/deed/hadith/bukhari/055_sbt.html (accessed 11 May 2021).

[52] The tradition is available at https://sunnah.com/muslim/1 (accessed 15 January 2020). For Ibn Taymiyya (d. 1328) on the critical eschatological import of the "six articles" see Ibn Taymiyya and Harras 1996, 27–28; see also al-Ghazali 2000, 18; al-Ghazali 2016, 115–16; Q 23:53; 30:32.

[53] Cf. D. Brown 2017, 202.

[54] Accessed at https://sunnah.com/muslim/1 (November 23, 2020).

[55] Cf. D. Brown 2017, 196–98, 200–210.

[56] Sweetman 2002 *Islam and Christian Theology, Part I*, Vol. 2, 199. See D. Brown 2017, 206 for Ash'ari's famous parable of the three brothers on the conundrum of predestination (cf. al-Ghazali 2016, 81).

[57] In *Sahih Muslim's* "Book of Destiny", God's decisions frequently seem to be predetermining for and overwhelming of all human agency (https://sunnah.com/muslim/46 [accessed 23 November 23, 2020]). See, for example, *Sahih Muslim* 46:20 as expressed by J. Brown 2016, 18. Of course, this is not the end of the matter. The Ash'ari doctrine of *iktisab* construes human action as a secondary agency "taking on" acts pre-created by God (see Renard 2014, 326–27; cf. Khadduri 1984, 58–64, 95–97; D. Brown 2017, 207–208; see too Sweetman 2002 *Islam and Christian Theology, Part II*, Vol. 2, 299–303; also 2002 *Islam and Christian Theology, Part I*. Vol. 2, 188–89).

[58] Khadduri 1984, 108. This sentence is a paraphrase of Khadduri, but some of the diction follows his very closely. Further, see Khadduri 1984, 107–109. Incidentally, Khadduri uses the term "voluntarism" in reference to nearly absolute freewill on the part of humanity (cf. *qadariyya*) whereas it is used in this study to refer to the doctrine of the all-determining nature of *God's* will.

[59] Akhtar 2018, 147.

[60] D. Brown 2017, 210.

[61] Cf. al-Ghazali 2016, 76–77; Q 14:4; 21:23.

[62] Compare Van Ess 2005, esp. 6323–24; Wensinck 1979, 62; Khadduri 1984, 41–53.

[63] Akhtar insists that there are no questions to answer in that God remains in "perfect control of his creation". But he also wonders whether "[i]n rejecting the cross" Muslims are choosing "to ignore the riddle of evil" (Akhtar 2018, 232).

[64] Cf. Q 29:69; al-Ghazali 2016, 27.

[65] Additional complexifying dynamics include concepts of purgatory (aligned with intercession); reward grounded in *Shari'a* observance vs mystic; Sufi models of union with God; the link between martyrdom and salvation; and so on.

[66] Rida 1996, 106.

[67] Rida 1948, 6:31; cf. 29–30.

[68] Cf. Rida 1996, 10, 80–103; also see Rida in Wood 2008, 142; Qutb 2009, 15:192–93; Q 7:201; 4:17.

**Chapter Four Notes**

[1] Cragg 1999, 178.

[2] Roberts 2013, 327–28.

[3] Tabatabai 2020 "Discourse on 'Jesus and Christianity'", 150; cf. 150–68.

[4] A spread of assertions and criticisms are often intertwined within a single passage. For example, Muhammad Hussein Tabatabai's summary of Christian atonement theory stresses its "problematic" concepts such as Adam's original sin, incarnation, and the conflict of attributes in the being of God (2020 "Discourse on 'Jesus and Christianity'", 150–51; 1997, 3:335–36). Similarly, as we shall see, many of Rashid Rida's sharp rhetorical flourishes eviscerate Christian thought on multiple fronts at once.

[5] Here see Sweetman 2002 *Islam and Christian Theology, Part II*, Vol. 1, 290 on (pseudo) al-Ghazali.

[6] Rida 1948, 6:24; cf. Darwaza 2000, 8:276–77.

[7] Cf. al-Faruqi 1999, 118, 188.

[8] al-Faruqi 1999, 152; cf. 148–53 (including the qualifiers "extreme" and "absurd"). Not surprisingly, al-Faruqi is quite happy to align "the real Jesus" with Pelagian ethics (1999, 149–50).

[9] Cf. Qutb 2009, 1:57–58.

[10] See Tabatabai 2020 "Discourse on 'Jesus and Christianity'", 152–53/Arabic, 1997, 3:337; cf. Q 2:35–39. The diminishing of the seriousness of Adam's fault is further supported by Tabatabai in this context by underscoring Adam's sinlessness as a prophet.

[11] Cf. Tabatabai 1997, 3:339/2020 "Discourse on 'Jesus and Christianity'", 154–55; also Q 4:31, 48. Again, as to Adam, Tabatabai thinks that on any reasonable accounting, eating from a forbidden tree is not recalcitrant infidelity (الكفر بالله) and should not merit punishment followed by eternal torment (عقابه وتبعته هو العذاب المؤبد).

[12] al-Faruqi 2013, 208. In the same context al-Faruqi insists that for all the mysterious loss that is death, it is neither "moral" nor is it "the consequence of sin" (2013, 208).

[13] al-Faruqi 2013, 209; cf. 198, 206, 213; also, 1998, 15.

[14] See al-Faruqi 1999, 144, 188.

[15] See al-Faruqi 1999, 128. al-Faruqi sees Pauline portrayals of sin as entailing "utterly powerless" humanity; a thoroughly corrupted world; and a universe full of evil spirits. Such a schema is for him "sheer contrivance" (al-Faruqi 1999, 145). We may add that the Islamic tradition is no stranger to notions of overwhelming divine determinism and a well-populated spirit world.

[16] Cf. al-Faruqi 1999, 144, 188; Rom. 5:20.

[17] For Austrian convert to Islam, Muhammad Asad, the pious Muslim redeems himself: "As there is no hereditary sin, there is also no universal redemption of mankind in the teaching of Islam. Redemption and damnation are individual. *Every Muslim is his own redeemer*; he bears all possibilities of spiritual success and failure within his heart" (cited in Nickel 1994, 9, emphasis added).

[18] Rida 1948, 6:31.

[19] Akhtar 2018, 110; cf. 93. Interestingly, Akhtar at this location states in passing that the Qur'anic denial of the crucifixion "is hard to verify".

[20] Akhtar 2018, 65. Akhtar, here and elsewhere (p. 259–60) references a range of models or imagery of salvation in atonement theology, including cultic sacrifice, PSA, satisfaction, and ransom and *Christus Victor*.

[21] Akhtar 2018, 64.

[22] Akhtar 2018, 64–65, emphasis added. Akhtar argues that the annual sacrifice at the end of the *hajj* is not "propitiatory". Similarly, see M. Bennett 2019, 141.

[23] See Tabatabai 2020 "Discourse on 'Jesus and Christianity'", 166–67; Arabic, 1997, 3:349–50.
[24] Nowaihi 1976, 221.
[25] Cf. Sweetman 2002 *Islam and Christian Theology, Part I*, Vol. 2, 50–52; Sarbah 2018.
[26] Rahman 2009, 19.
[27] Rahman 2009, 19.
[28] See Sweetman 2002 *Islam and Christian Theology, Part I*, Vol. 2, 53.
[29] Cf. al-Nowaihi 1976, 217.
[30] Rida 1948, 6:27.
[31] Akhtar 2018, 260.
[32] Akhtar 2018, 260.
[33] al-Faruqi 1999, 163.
[34] al-Faruqi 1999, 163.
[35] see al-Faruqi 1999, 163–64.
[36] On all this see al-Faruqi 1998, 15.
[37] Qutb 2009, 3:257; cf. 9:95–96; 17:83.
[38] In concert with many Muslim thinkers, Fatoohi puts the blame of erroneous "Cross-ism" (atonement theology) squarely on Paul, thus by comparison partially exonerating the Gospel portraits of Jesus (cf. Fatoohi 2008, 62, and chapter five).
[39] Ibn al-'Uthamin 2008, 2:438.
[40] See Rida 1948, 6:24. Cf. Rida 1996, 87; Ryad 2009, 294–95. Also, "Islam is the religion of Muhammad, Christ, and the prophets. It is not possible to combine the religion of the Qur'an which falsehood cannot approach from any side [cf. Q 41:4] with the Paulinist religion based on '3=1 and 1=3' and on the doctrine of crucifixion and pagan redemption. There's no combining Islamic monotheism and Trinity; [no combining] the doctrine of salvation and benediction of humanity by knowledge and deed (وبين عقيدة نجاة الإنسان وسعادته بعلمه وعمله) and the doctrine of salvation through believing in the curse of the Lord against himself (بإيمانه بلعن ربه لنفسه), tormenting [that one] by his servants—and in which the Lord in any case failed to achieve what he wished thereby" (Rida 1948, 6:56).
[41] Cf. Rida 1948, 6:27–28; Ayoub 2007, 175; Ryad 2009, 266–68.
[42] Rida in Wood 2008, 136–37. I have adjusted the generic "he" in this quote to "they". For Rida, antinomian license is one of the ways Christian mission "lures" Muslim inquirers (cf. Wood 2008, 141–42; cf. Ryad 2009, 202–203).
[43] Rida offers examples, from the Pauline corpus and otherwise, intended to demonstrate the antinomianism of justification by faith (see Ryad 2009, 186).
[44] Cf. Tabatabai 2020 "Discourse on 'Jesus and Christianity'", 162–64; Arabic, 1997, 3:346–47. In this section, according to Tabatabai, in Christian soteriology, good works have always been viewed as utterly flaccid. Previous to Christ, both the most pious (أتقى الأتقياء) and most reprobate (أشقى الأشقياء) were damned; after the Messiah, both equally forgiven, receiving mercy so long as they believe. Tabatabai contends that Christocentric salvation necessitates insupportable condemnation of worthy priors (e.g. prophets) and the denigration of revealed law. After all, the Torah itself is innocent of redemption doctrine.
[45] al-Faruqi in Chambésy 1982, 30.
[46] al-Faruqi 2013, 210. The invocation of the notion of *fiat* is interestingly double-edged. Above we saw Akhtar suggest that God's forgiving by *fiat* is valid and rightly negates the need of the cross.
[47] Cf. Ralston 2021, 222.
[48] al-Faruqi in Chambésy 1982, 35.
[49] al-Faruqi 2013, 212.

[50] al-Faruqi 1999, 220.
[51] al-Faruqi 1999, 160. See page 189, atonement thought as socially atrophying and pages 195–96, as such in Barth where refuge is sought in paradox and eschatology. al-Faruqi holds that "the ethic of gratitude that emerged out of the notion of redemption as a *fait accompli* devaluated space-time as an unfortunate, insignificant interlude, the end of which was eagerly awaited" (al-Faruqi 2013, 212).
[52] Upon conversion, a Muslim is "conscious mainly of the fact that the greatest task lies ahead in the test of ethical conduct, [but] the Christian comes out … satisfied, relieved that the greatest task is behind him … reassured that [his] new status will favorably affect anything he may do" (al-Faruqi 1999, 159; cf. 2013, 198, 210).
[53] al-Faruqi 1999, 166. See similar citations of al-Faruqi on this theme in Madigan 2021, 32–33. Qutb and Rida also comment profusely on the corruption of Western "Christian" imperial ambition (cf. Qutb 2009, 4:192–93; Ryad 2009, 171–74, 310–16).
[54] Interestingly, the Christian Joshua Ralston (2016 and 2020) attempts to constructively and critically onboard insights from Islamic legal thought in terms of political theology, soteriology, and ethics.
[55] Akhtar 2018, 268.
[56] Cf. Rida 1996, 124–35; Tabatabai 2020 "Discourse on 'Jesus and Christianity'", 159–62.
[57] Akhtar 2018, 147–48; see too 94, 136, 147–50.
[58] Akhtar 2018, 65–66.
[59] Cf. al-Faruqi 2013, 211–12.
[60] Cf. al-Faruqi 2013, 208–209; cf. 210, 213.
[61] Cf. al-Faruqi in Chambésy 1982, 47.
[62] al-Faruqi in Chambésy 1982, 39; cf. al-Faruqi 2013, 199; 1998, 132; al-Nowaihi 1976, 216–17. The words and conceptual claims in the quote come directly from al-Faruqi, though I have adjusted the grammar and syntax to the needs of my sentence.
[63] Tabatabai 2020 "Discourse on 'Jesus and Christianity'", 157.
[64] Arabic Tabatabai, 1997, 3:341–42; 2020 "Discourse on 'Jesus and Christianity'", 157.
[65] Tabatabai 2020 "Discourse on 'Jesus and Christianity'", 157; Arabic, 1997, 3:341.
[66] Tabatabai 2020 "Discourse on 'Jesus and Christianity'", 158; Arabic, 1997, 3:342.
[67] Stipulating the possibility of the incarnation would, for Tabatabai, be tantamount to allowing for the union of God with any form, any type of creation: He might as well have taken on the being of a bird or any other species—perhaps several at once (Tabatabai 2020 "Discourse on 'Jesus and Christianity'", 158)!
[68] Algar 1999, Kindle Locations 315-319; cf. Tabatabai 2020 "Discourse on 'Jesus and Christianity'", 159; Arabic, 1997, 3:343.
[69] "Whoever accepts this story is obligated to accept that which every independent mind rejects, namely that the creator of the universe might indwell a woman's womb on this earth which compared to the rest of his possessions and the heavens which one sees from it is less than a portion of an atom. And then he becomes human, eating, drinking, tiring, and suffering whatever else humans suffer. Then his enemies subjugate and insult him (ثم يأخذه أعداؤه بالقهر والإهانة) and crucify him with the thieves and make him accursed according to the rulings of *his* book (by some of his messengers). Far be such unworthy excess from God" (Rida 1948, 6:26, emphasis added; cf. Ryad 2009, 266–68)!
[70] Rida 1948, 6:25.
[71] Arabic 1997, 3:343.
[72] Tabatabai 2020 "Discourse on 'Jesus and Christianity'", 158–59.
[73] Ali Merad 1980, 15, quoted by Ford 2013, 23; cf. al-Azhar 1992, 2:968.
[74] Among the multiple problematic influences on early Christian thought mention is often made of paganism (Roman and global), Paul, Constantine, and Judaism. The

mutual reinforcement between pagan ideas and Paul's or Constantine's agendas is easily asserted, but merits challenging.

[75] Cf. Tabatabai 2020 "Discourse on 'Jesus and Christianity'", 168–71.

[76] Cf. Akhtar 2018, 64–65.

[77] Tabatabai 2020 "Discourse on 'Jesus and Christianity'", 152; Arabic, 1997, 3:336–37.

[78] Tabatabai 2020 "Discourse on 'Jesus and Christianity'", 167–68.

[79] Rida 1948, 6:24; see too Wood 2008, 81–82, 93–96; Rida 1996, 9, 82, 87; Ryad 2009, 183, 189, 289, 294–95.

[80] Qutb 2009, 4:167–72; cf. 4:54–57; 8:104–106 [quoting Rida]; 13:140–41.

[81] Qutb 2009, 8:97; cf. Q 9:31; Qutb 2009, 3:338–41; 4:57; 8:118–20; 9:95; Robinson 2001, 168–69.

[82] See too Awad 2016.

[83] al-Azhar 1992, 2:968 commenting on Q 4:158.

[84] al-Sha'rawi 1991, 5:2793.

[85] al-Azhar 1992, 2:968; cf. Imam Chirri in Zahnizer 2008, 235.

[86] See Arabic, Tabatabai 1997, 3:349.

[87] Cf. Tabatabai 2020 "Discourse on 'Jesus and Christianity'", 165–66.

[88] Tabatabai 2020a, 166.

[89] Arabic, Tabatabai 1997, 3:348; cf. 2020 "Discourse on 'Jesus and Christianity'", 164–65.

[90] Arabic, Tabatabai 1997, 3:348; 2020 "Discourse on 'Jesus and Christianity'", 165. My translation varies somewhat from the published English version here.

[91] Arabic, Tabatabai 1997, 3:338; cf. 2020 "Discourse on 'Jesus and Christianity'", 153–4. Here Tabatabai insists that, contrary to Christian theology, Adam's sin did not remain with him, but he received mercy and guidance (cf. Q 20:122; 2:37).

[92] Cf. Akhtar 2018, 64.

[93] Cf. Rida 1948, 6:26–28.

[94] Cf. Rida 1948, 6:55. Rida is certain that God was free to spare Jesus and substitute another victim; moreover, to reward or punish, God requires no such contrivance as the Passion for "God guides those he wills onto the 'straight path' (صراط مستقيم)" (Rida 1948, 6:55).

[95] Khalil 2016, 84. Khalil illustrates his point thus: "For instance, in the *Sahih al-Bukhari* hadith collection, we read about a prostitute who used her shoe to collect water for a thirsty dog on the verge of death; on account of this good deed, God forgave her of her sins. We also read about a man who murdered ninety-nine people before seeking to mend his ways. When a monk asserted that he would not be forgiven, the monk became—to put it crudely—victim number one hundred. Eventually, the murderer encountered a man who advised him to seek guidance in a particular village. On the way to the village, the murderer passed away. With the angels disputing whether he should be punished or rewarded, God determined that he would be saved if he had passed away closer to his destination than to his starting point. As it turned out, he had not. Nevertheless, God, out of His mercy, physically moved the destination closer to him so that he would attain salvation" (Khalil 2016, 84).

[96] Akhtar 2018, 221.

[97] Akhtar 2018, 40, emphasis added.

[98] Akhtar 2018, 55, emphasis added.

[99] Of course, any theological argumentation employs reason, but dynamics such as logical tensions, epistemic mystery, complex ontology, and so on do not feature in the same way in Christian and Islamic soteriologies.

[100] al-Faruqi 1999, 19.

[101] al-Faruqi 1999, 20–21; cf. 1998, 311–12.

[102] Cf. al-Faruqi 2013, 208–209.

[103] Cragg 1995, 400, citing al-Faruqi 1999, 20; cf. 205, 211; al-Faruqi 2013, 203. There are, of course, Muslims with differing and unusual metaphysical architectures. M. Ayoub holds to Islamic conviction alongside a pluralism in which the various religions are authentic but partial expressions of cosmic Truth (cf. Ayoub 2007, 135–36; Q 49:13). In S.H. Nasr we find the suggestion that in God's mysterious volition, he *intends* Muslims to deny the crucifixion of Christ while Christians, in parallel, are meant to affirm it (Nasr 1987, 99–101).

[104] Akhtar 2018, 56; cf. 65–66.

[105] al-Faruqi 2013, 199. To many this will seem like a call to Christians to abandon Christianity, all in aid of mutual convergence. Once again, Ayoub's interreligious overture differs. Perhaps surprisingly, Ayoub tells us that "reason has not been considered, even by Islam, as the final arbiter of faith … Christians have insisted from the start that the cross is an obstacle to human wisdom and rationality. Faith is not logic but the divine gift to man transcending and transforming human wisdom and rationality" (Ayoub 2007, 175; cf. 171–72).

[106] Cf. Rahman 2009, 170.

[107] Akhtar 2018, 149.

[108] Above, I suggested the term "Islamic gnosticism" (to be understood in a manner very specific to this study). For a window onto the kind of religious sensibility I have in mind, see the words of Abu Bakr al-Razi (d. 924) cited in Khadduri 1984, 106; cf. 115 n 25.

[109] Tabatabai 2020 "Discourse on 'Jesus and Christianity'", 161; Arabic 1997, 3:345.

[110] See Tabatabai 2020 "Discourse on 'Jesus and Christianity'", 164; Arabic, 1997, 3:347.

[111] "God knew very well that, unless the problem of Adam's sin was solved, no promulgation of law would benefit at all. Yet He went on promulgating those laws by way of caution, in hope that one day he might resolve the problem and harvest the fruit of his legislation—achieving his goal and winning his object. Thus he legislated laws while hiding this truth of the matter from prophets and people. He hid the fact that there was a problem which—if remaining unresolved—would nullify the efforts of prophets and believers together, rendering the laws void. But rather he presented the revealed laws and (prophetic) missions as though serious and true (وإظهار أن التشريع والدعوة على الجد والحقيقة)" (Arabic, Tabatabai 1997, 3:346/2020a, 162). I consulted but altered the translation of the published English version.

[112] cf. al-Faruqi 1999, 160.

[113] al-Faruqi 1999, 161, emphasis added.

[114] al-Faruqi 1999, 138; cf. 188; 154–57.

[115] cf. al-Faruqi 1999, 138.

[116] Again, al-Faruqi 1999, 144, 188.

[117] al-Faruqi 1999, 139; see page 156 for his chiding of Reinhold Niebuhr. Fatoohi links original sin and redemption theology, taking them to be inversely related and misdirections of justice and reason: in original sin, innocent humanity suffers in consequence of the guilt of Adam, while in vicarious atonement, the innocent Messiah suffers in consequence of the guilt of humanity (cf. Fatoohi 2008, 126).

[118] Rida 1948, 6:25. Cf. Ryad 2009, 266–68; Darwaza 2000, 8:276–77; Ayoub 2007, 174–75.

[119] Rida 1948, 6:26.

[120] Cf. Rida on "The Sending of Prophetic Missions to Every Community" (Rida 1996, 104; cf. Q 7; 16:36; 26; 35:24).

[121] Tabatabai's complaints are similar (cf. Tabatabai 2020 "Discourse on 'Jesus and Christianity'", 155–57; Arabic, 1997, 3:339–41). He decries Christianity's "paganized" construal of a God beset by limits and commends the alternative "Perfect Being" God of

the Qur'an (cf. Tabatabai 2020 "Discourse on 'Jesus and Christianity'", 156; Arabic, 1997, 3:340; Q 37:159). The deity of Christianity is limited and immanent, "physical, embodied, subject to laws of movement, change, and completion … not the Un-Obligated, Creator of all (ماديأ جسمانيأ واقعأ تحت ناموس الحركة والتغير والاستكمال... وليس بالواجب تعالى الخالق لكل شيء)" (Arabic, Tabatabi 1997, 3:340; 2020 "Discourse on 'Jesus and Christianity'", 156).

[122] Daniel Madigan does not deploy the same tripartite rubrics (sin, justice, honor), but he offers a very useful wide-angle summary of Islamic discomfiture with Christian theology around atonement, humanity, and sin (see Madigan 2021, 13; cf. Ralston 2021, 224–25).

**Chapter Five Notes**

[1] Barth himself is discussed in the following chapter, which is, of course, centered on his thought.

[2] In discussing Anselmian atonement, a "focus triage" is necessary for reasons of space and relevance. Thus, certain critiques of Anselm by "Western" theologians are afforded limited attention. An example might be the idea that Anselm's salvation scheme fatally underweights the initiative of divine love. The reason for our lack of emphasis on this point is that the issue of divine love is not the most prominent category in Islamic discussions of salvation.

[3] Naturally, this cadre of thinkers is not internally homogenous. For example, Sonderegger warns of the danger that in Barth, the theologian of divine freedom, God becomes dependent on creation and comprehensively defined by the incarnation (see further in the next chapter).

[4] Rutledge 2015, 146.

[5] See Aulén 1986, 1–9, 38–39, chapter five. However, note Sonderegger's cautions with respect to delineating Anselm's ideological heirs (cf. Sonderegger 2007, 349–50).

[6] Southern 1990, 441–42.

[7] "Anselm's insights are anticipated by Ambrose, Hilary of Poitiers, and Victorinus, among others … not to mention Isa. 53:4-6; Rom. 5:12-21; 8:3-4; 2 Cor. 5:21; Gal. 3:10-14; 1 Pet. 2:24; 3:18" (Rutledge 2015, 146 n 1; cf. Aulén 1986, 81–82; Kotsko 2017 "The Persistence of the Ransom Theory of the Atonement", 286–88; Kärkkäinen 2013, 309).

[8] He insists that the patristic "physical" vs Western "moral" atonement dichotomy is not in fact absolute but more a matter of emphasis (Hart 1998, 342; see too 347; cf. Vidu 2014, 23).

[9] *CDH* 1:7, 22; cf. Vidu 2014, 60. The Adversary has not disappeared; he stands overthrown (*CDH* 2:8, 11, 19; cf. Southern 1990, 305). Kotsko's "non-violent" theologizing apparently rejects Anselm's decentering of "Satan and the powers", a trope that Kotsko aims to redeploy in a modern register as quasi-amorphous and oppressive social and political forces (see Kotsko 2017 "The Persistence of the Ransom Theory of the Atonement", 287-88). But, to my mind, Anatolios is on point to insist that "[t]he drama of salvation takes place primarily between God and humanity" (Anatolios 2020, 112).

[10] For example, the weighting of emphasis in Augustine, Anselm's most significant non-biblical resource, is relatively similar (cf. Vidu 2014, 29; also, Southern 1990, 71–87).

[11] Cf. Vidu 2014, 16, 33–34.

[12] Vidu 2014, 2.

[13] Or, Why a God-Man?

[14] Davies and Evans, Eds., *Anselm of Canterbury, the Major Works*, xviii.

[15] "Finally, I consider that the understanding which we gain in this life stands midway between faith and revelation. It follows, in my view, that the nearer someone comes to

attainment of this understanding, the nearer that person approaches to revelation, for which we all pant in anticipation" (Anselm *CDH* "Commendation to Pope Urban II").
[16] In Anselm's *Meditation on Human Redemption* these are the section or line numbers (not the page number).
[17] This summary is a close paraphrase, at times verbatim, taken from Hart 1998, 336–37. To compare the exact quote, see the relevant appendix.
[18] Many components of Anselm's atonement thought are rooted in Augustine (cf. *On the Trinity* book 13: chapters ten to sixteen).
[19] See for example the works by de la Trinité and. J.M. Campbell in the bibliography.
[20] Cf. Vanhoozer 2012, 177–78.
[21] Cf. Anderson 2009, 197.
[22] Cf. Hastings 2019, 215; cf. 217.
[23] "But crucially, for Anselm, this payment [at the cross] is one of satisfaction rather than substitution. Christ's obedience and thankfulness to God expressed in his offering to the Father is of infinite worth and by far supersedes any debt owed for the sin of humanity, defined primarily as a deficit in obedience and thankfulness … My own reflection would suggest that in Anselm, punishment is averted not because every sin has been punished in Jesus as in a guilt offering, but because positively, the offering of the Son seen perhaps best as a burnt offering, the offering up of positive obedience and thanks, is more than sufficient for every sin's debt" (Hastings 2019, 215–16). One can sympathize with Hastings' agenda here, but one might question the easy linkage between the "whole burnt offering" (עֹלָה) and debt payment. Arguably, other categories of sacrifice are more readily connected to a notion of debt or obligation (e.g. נֶדֶר or אָשָׁם).
[24] Rutledge 2015, 467 n 9.
[25] Distinguishing between payment and punishment or between satisfaction and substitution is reasonable at one level. But the significance of these distinctions can also be exaggerated. In *CDH*, Christ bears sin's consequence or cost (death), and gains a "surplus" for our benefit. Perhaps death is a "punishment" for sinners but not for Christ in whose case it is an "excess donation". But, in all this, one must surely admit at least the shadowy outlines of a payment that mirrors punishment, and more still the dynamic of substitution.
[26] See, for example, Anderson 2009, 197–99.
[27] Cf. Rutledge 2015, 488.
[28] Cf. Anderson 2009, 198.
[29] Anderson 2009, 199. (Both quotations relate to this citation.) Of course, if "injured right" situates God as the great Toddler in the Sky, then the point may be granted. But this is wholly unnecessary. Would not Anselm, whom Anderson seems to appreciate, agree that the cross *is* the costly and subversive "mechanism" for God's setting a wounded world right, of loving and judging, of being both just and the one who justifies (Rom. 3:26)?
[30] Anderson 2009, 198.
[31] For example, on the Reformation-era heterodox thinker Socinus, see Gomes 2017.
[32] Cf. Baker and Green 2011, 157; Hart 1998, 338–40.
[33] Hart 1998, 334; see too Johnson 2015, 142.
[34] Cf. Vidu 2014, 52; Hart 1998, 340; Kärkkäinen 2013, 309; see too Tanner 2010, 250. Blame has even been extended to include supposed after-effects of Anslem's thought such as the Crusades and the Iraq War (see Rutledge 2015, 146, 161–63).
[35] Baker and Green 2011, 159; cf. Kärkkäinen 2013, 345. The complaint is not without basis, though, in my estimation, Baker and Green don't sufficiently credit Anselm's explicit recourse to the Trinity in *CDH*. See Anselm *CDH* 1:9; 2:18; cf. Gunton 1988, 92–93; Rutledge 2015,162–65.

[36] "For modern readers of Anselm, with our more secular and autonomous anthropologies, it is hard to see how the death of a single innocent creature could redeem the human race—or indeed, should redeem it—nor is it clear how the human *polis*, with its history of tragedy, suffering, and malice, could be reconciled to God by a work called 'satisfaction', nor is it persuasive to us that God should need it. Redemption, if it is to triumph over a worldly history of sin and loss, must correlate with creation in some more radical, corporate, and explosive fashion than this" (Sonderegger 2007, 347). Cf. Gunton 1988, 92–94.

[37] Though considerable moral ire is also reserved for later developments such as PSA, much of it *is* vehemently directed at our Medieval scholar (e.g. Kotsko 2017 "The Persistence of the Ransom Theory of the Atonement"; Weaver 2011, 236–46; cf. Sonderegger 2017, 175–76, 178). Weaver is unrelenting in his animus towards Anselm's objective atonement, fatally implicated, he thinks, in the "Godward" violence of the cross and structures of oppression. See appendix on "non-violent" atonement. See too Sonderegger's critique of the tenor of the "left–right" debate on this issue: 2007, 342–43.

[38] Cf. Vidu 2014, 56; Southern 1990, 221–27.

[39] Sonderegger 2007, 352.

[40] Cf. Kärkkäinen 2013, 309.

[41] Adam Johnson draws attention to Anselm's own statement in *MHR* "that while his focus on satisfaction is indeed important to him, there is more to the work of Christ than he has explained" (Johnson 2015, 34–35). Throughout Anslem's oeuvre, the accompanying themes of love, gratitude, repentance, participation, and renewal are not hard to come by.

[42] Hart 1998, 337; cf. Rutledge 2015, 146.

[43] Cf. Hart 1998, 344–46; Hastings 2019, 184.

[44] Hart 1998, 344; cf. Hastings 2019, 184.

[45] For example, see Sonderegger on exemplarism in *CDH*: 2007, 352; cf. Anselm *CDH* 2:11, 2:18.

[46] Rutledge 2015, 156.

[47] Gunton 1988, 89; cf. 90; 163, and especially 113; *CDH* 1:15; 1:12.

[48] Hastings 2019, 186, citing Hart 1998, 348.

[49] Anselm *CDH* 2:19; cf. Ward 1973, 78–79.

[50] This question of a "divine dilemma" at the heart of objective substitutionary atonements will follow us into the next chapter. According to some readings, such a predicament is traceable as far back as Irenaeus. For Schendel, however, Irenaeus' recapitulation narrative is indeed meant to demonstrate the solution to a problem, but the problem is not God's, not internal to him. It is ours and is resolved with subversive, mysterious, and sublime wisdom. "We are not meant to read the dilemma back into [Irenaeus'] doctrine of God, as if God really were in a quandary and had to devise some clever plan in order to get out of it. Rather, by introducing the dilemma, Irenaeus is able to emphasize the wisdom of God in his one, eternal plan for the world" (Schendel 2018, 223–24, n 61).

[51] Cf. Rutledge 2015, 163–65.

[52] MacIntyre 2007, 142, emphasis added.

[53] MacIntyre 2007, 142.

[54] Assumptions rooted in this metaphysical vision fund his frequent appeal to "fittingness".

[55] Kadushin quoted in E.P. Sanders 2017, 113.

[56] Cf. Gunton 1988, 92.

[57] Cf. Mann 2019 on *Proslogion* 8–11.

[58] Hart 1998, 343–44; cf. Hastings 2019, 185–86.

[59] Rutledge 2015, 164; cf. Isa. 54:8.
[60] For all these quotes in this paragraph, see Rutledge 2015, 148–49.
[61] Even the tree in Eden is counterbalanced by God's paradoxical offensive on the "tree" of the cross (cf. *CDH* 1:3). Such structural balance is redolent of earlier thinkers, for example, Augustine, *City of God* 11:2. On "fittingness" see do Vale 2018.
[62] Cf. Sonderegger 2007, 354.
[63] do Vale 2018, 100, citing Anselm's *On Truth* 10; cf. *CDH* 1:12.
[64] Cf. Rutledge 2015, 146–58.
[65] Anselm insists that the divine nature of Christ could not suffer (Anselm *CDH* 1:8).
[66] See Lowe 1994, Kindle Location 2991 on Athanasius, *Against the Arians* 2:67 and Kindle Locations 3005-3007 on Gregory of Nazianzus' famous axiom from his *Letter to Cledonius (I)* [p. 440] (see also McGuckin 2016, 82).
[67] Matthew Baker 2016, 115, quoting Florovsky; cf. Florovsky 2016, 148–49. Baker here quotes two separate sentences from a work by Florovsky to which I have no access. See also Sonderegger 2007, 348–51; Green 2017, 13, on the efficacious Savior of Hebrews.
[68] "[Jesus] had what was above all beings that are other than God, and he took on himself all the debt that sinners ought to pay, and this when he himself owed nothing, so that he could pay the debt for the others who owed it and could not pay" (*MHR* 105–10).
[69] Nor must one forget the treatise's title; it is *God* who takes on humanity.
[70] Sonderegger 2007, 359; cf. 354.
[71] Cf. Vidu 2014, 61; Anselm *CDH* 2:11.
[72] Cf. Vidu 2014, 52; *CDH* 1:25.
[73] Cf. Vidu 2014, 51–52.
[74] Rutledge 2015, 152–53.
[75] Cf. Rutledge 2015, 152–53.
[76] Cf. Vidu 2014, 51.
[77] Again, Sonderegger 2007, 342–43.
[78] Cf. Rutledge 2015, 151.
[79] Cf. Vidu 2014, 59–60; Sonderegger 2007, 347.
[80] Sonderegger 2007, 359.
[81] "Anselm defines 'eternal punishment' as 'inconsolable need'. It can't be emphasized strongly enough: Anselm understands punishment with a pastor's heart. He is saddened by our predicament. He is not in love with the idea of punishment; rather, like Paul the apostle, he simply observes that we reap what we sow ('God gave them over' to the power of Sin—repeated three times, in Rom. 1:24, 26, 28)" (Rutledge 2015, 154).
[82] Anselm's logic of excess merit is consonant with scriptural tropes, e.g. the Pauline "how much more" and the contrastive superabundance of grace juxtaposed with sin (Rom. 5:9-10, 15-21; cf. Heb. 9:13-14). This is not to say that Anslem provides granular exegesis or an explanation of how this excess merit must result in God's gracious gift of life to sinners. Of course, the fact of a gracious gift of life from God is clearly a biblical datum (Jn. 10:10, 28).
[83] One is reminded of Islamic objections to incarnation even at the level of human digestion (cf. Q 5:75; von Stosch 2021, with whose argument I differ). Anselm goes on to ask why "the Most High should stoop to such humble things … the Almighty … do something with such great laboriousness" (*CDH* 1:8)?
[84] Duffy, "A Deadly Misunderstanding" cited and quoted in Rutledge 2015, 156 n. 22; cf. Southern 1990, 198–202.
[85] Southern 1990, 200.
[86] Cf. *CDH* 1:15; Gunton 1988, 96.
[87] Cf. Anatolios 2020, 272–73 and note 21. Vidu redirects focus away from feudal concepts towards Anselm's commitment to the hierarchy of "the 'ontological

difference' between God and humanity" (Vidu 2014, 54). Of course, many strands of modern theology are invested in radically narrowing even that gap and stand hostile to all hierarchies whatsoever.

[88] The Hebrew terms behind "honor" include, at the least, כָּבוֹד and הוֹד depending on the Bible version being consulted (cf. Ps. 96:4-9).

[89] Southern 1990, 226.

[90] Hart 1998, 346; cf. Hastings 2019, 185.

[91] do Vale 2018, 103.

[92] do Vale 2018, 101.

[93] Cf. Rutledge 2015, 156–57.

[94] We might well have preferred that full, embodied restoration were not, for our scholar-monk, wholly displaced to the world to come (cf. *CDH* 2:1-3, 20). It is true that resurrection and a total restoration of creation are not fleshed out in great detail in *CDH*. But even though Anselm's attention to these matters is brief, it is affirmative. Indeed, for Anselm, "absolute *corporeal* freedom is one of the rewards of heaven" (Southern 1990, 170, emphasis added).

[95] Cf. Gunton 1988, 96.

[96] Cf. Gunton 1988, 103, citing Athanasius; also, *CDH* 2:4; 1:15. "For it were not worthy of God's goodness that the things he had made should waste away" (Athanasius, *De Incarnatione* 6). As to Paul, for example, in Romans, the redeeming justifying God may be shown to be acting in and for creation (chapter eight); history, Israel, and the nations (chapters nine to eleven); and the communal life of his people (chapters twelve onwards). See Gunton 1988, 102.

[97] Cf. Meconi 2017, 383.

[98] "I think, therefore, that you will not say that God ought to tolerate something which it is the greatest injustice in the universe to tolerate, namely: that a creature should not give back to God what he takes away" (*CDH* 1:13). Cf. Jn. 17:3; Rom. 6:23. In terms of "owing" God, it may also be worth reminding ourselves of the repeated biblical emphasis on the limitless worthiness of the holy God (e.g. Isa. 6:3; 1 Tim. 1:17). The implication of the rightness of complete human praise, obedience, and devotion is clear. The idea that a relational rift, rend, or "debt" would result not only from "active wrongs" but from "withholding" that which is due is also quite reasonable (cf. Jas. 4:17; Mt. 18:23-35). And, indeed, while *we* owed God "all", he has in fact given precisely that to *us* (Ac. 17:25; Rom. 8:32).

[99] Anatolios 2020, 307; see too 313–16.

[100] Sonderegger 2017, 187.

[101] *CDH* 1:12; Vidu 2014, 57–58.

[102] Vidu 2014, 56–57.

[103] Sonderegger 2017, 183; cf. 359.

[104] See again Gunton 1988, 159.

[105] Cf. Sonderegger 2017, 189.

[106] Sonderegger 2017, 189, emphasis added; cf. 192.

[107] "[God acts] out of a necessary obligation to uphold what is honorable. The necessity to which I am referring is plainly nothing other than the unchangeability of God's honor, which he possesses of himself, and from no one apart from himself. For this reason, 'necessity' is a misnomer. Let us say, nevertheless, that it is a necessity that the goodness of God should bring to completion what it has begun with respect to mankind, because of his unchangeability, although the whole of what he does is grace" (*CDH* 2:5).

[108] Rutledge is surely right that "Anselm's writing is as much doxology as it is logic" (Rutldege 2015, 156).

[109] Wilcoxen 2019, 188–89.

[110] Southern 1990, 227.
[111] Sonderegger 2017, 182. See too Wilcoxen 2019, 188–89. Kärkkäinen 2013, 365–66, tries to be sympathetic, but falls prey to an over-easy critique.
[112] Kärkkäinen 2013, 309.
[113] Cf. Kärkkäinen 2013, 295.
[114] Cf. Anderson 2009, 44, 190; Aulén 1986, 81–83.
[115] See, for example, Anderson 2009, 10, 192–93. Lam 2016 is a useful accompaniment to this discussion, surveying a wider spectrum of the biblical imagery of sin.
[116] Vidu 2014, 55.
[117] For Anselm, "original sin is such that nothing can be shown to be graver" (Anselm *OVC* 2). Vidu comments that "Anselm restricts retribution to temporal sins. For the sins we commit in our lives we can be punished. Not so for original sin, for which there is no adequate punishment short of complete annihilation" (Vidu 2014, 56).
[118] "'The line [separating good and evil] runs through each person.' Allowing for shadings of difference between Anselm's time and ours, we can read him to say that it is this universal human person, both needy and unjust, that Christ died to save, for 'in order that man may attain happiness [blessedness], remission of sin is necessary'" (Rutledge 2015, 150-151; *CDH* 1:10). On the "line running through each person" Rutledge is citing Václav Havel; Aleksandr Solzhenitsyn is credited with a similar statement.
[119] Many have wondered how God's honor can ultimately be ontologically impervious to human slight, and yet, at the same time, how it is that the honor of God offended is what makes sin so infinitely weighty. By way of response, Anatolios' insights may be of help: "The weight of sin is infinite precisely because sin distorts and misrepresents the infinite glory of God and thus, in a real sense, amounts to an infinite distortion of that glory. In saying this we can still affirm that … God's intrinsic glory … does not suffer ontological injury from human sin … Insofar as God has allowed the intra-Trinitarian glorification to be represented also through humanity's participation in that eternal exchange, he puts his own glory at stake in humanity's representation of that glory. The glory of the Trinitarian 'name' is thus made vulnerable to profanation by human beings, and this profanation is indeed an 'infinite' offense inasmuch as it misrepresents and distorts … the infinite glorification of the Father, by the Son, in the Holy Spirit" (Anatolios 2020, 306).
[120] Yang and Davis 2015, 165.
[121] Sonderegger 2007, 357; cf. 357–59; 2017, 181.
[122] Sonderegger 2017, 182.
[123] *CDH* 2:6; Vidu 2014, 61.

**Chapter Six Notes**

[1] For example, John McLeod Campbell (d. 1872) developed a Protestant model which, while vicarious, was inimical to Christ's bearing of punishment. As commonly interpreted, he parsed Christ's representative work as one of "vicarious confession/repentance" (cf. Stevenson 2016; Campbell 2015 (1856); Hastings 2019, 150). On another front, one may consider the Catholic Philippe de la Trinité's (1961) non-penal substitution concept.
[2] On this paragraph, see Vidu 2014, 118–19. He offers more commentary, relying significantly on Berkhof.
[3] Cf. Vidu 2014, 120–21, 127; also Rutledge 2015, 487, quoting Calvin's *Institutes* 2:16:6.
[4] Vidu 2014, 126–27. Calvin asserts the saving impact of the obedient *life* of Christ, but it remains, arguably, an underdeveloped theme (cf. Vidu 2014, 125–27).
[5] See Rutledge 2015, 486, quoting *Institutes* 2:16:2; cf. Rom. 5:8-10.

[6] Cf. Vidu 2014, 130–31.
[7] Cf. Rutledge 2015, 470. There is a logical substructure to the idea of atonement by substitute, as Rutledge insists. This substructure is supported by non-negotiable, if sometimes unpopular, affirmations: "1. the horror, disgust, and shame of crucifixion. 2. the repeated New Testament declaration that Christ died 'for sin'. 3. the condition of the world, the hellish suffering of many, and the predicament of humanity" (Rutledge 2015, 468).
[8] Speaking of Romans 6, Rutledge insists that "[t]he principal theme here is that of assimilation to Christ in baptism, but if we are indeed 'crucified with him', then isn't it obvious (since the only crucifixion that actually took place was his) that in some sense he substituted himself for us, so that he alone received the full impact of Sin and its deserts, protecting us from them?" (Rutledge 2015, 472; cf. 469–73).
[9] Cf. Rutledge 2015, 466.
[10] Yang and Davis 2015, 162.
[11] Hastings 2019, 209–10. Though I have distilled this enumeration, it is derived from Hastings' work in conversation with other thinkers.
[12] Cf. Vidu 2014, 125–26, 175–76, 193–204; also, chapters four and five. Again, this modern intuition may extend to a totalizing rejection of any linkage between the cross and violence and divine intentionality (cf. Vidu 2014, 177–78, 215). See too, appendix on "non-violent" atonement.
[13] Vidu 2014, 183; 188; cf. 183–86.
[14] Rutledge 2015, 491.
[15] Rutledge 2015, 490. One might also cite parallels between modernist and Islamic aversion to blood sacrifice and preference for forms of exemplarism (cf. Vidu 2014, chapter five). I am the one drawing the parallels. Islam is not the focus of Rutledge or Vidu.
[16] Sonderegger 1995, 176; cf. Gunton 1988, 24; Rutledge 2015, 489, 500–502.
[17] The complaint that Anselm's heirs have inadvertently "glorified suffering" and "encouraged masochism" may remind us of complaints about "extreme" Christian assumptions about sin and virtue and/or al-Faruqi's remonstrance with the Christian valuation of "pain" as judgment (cf. Rutledge 2015, 494–95).
[18] Webster 2016, 103.
[19] Webster 2016, 104.
[20] Cf. Webster 2016, 104–105.
[21] Johnson 2013, 94 n 6, including comments on Barth 2004, 4:1:253.
[22] Webster 2016, 105.
[23] Webster 2016, 105.
[24] Johnson 2013.
[25] Johnson 2013, 94 n 7; cf. 93–94.
[26] Johnson 2013, 94.
[27] Johnson 2013, 94 n 7; cf. Smythe 2017.
[28] Rutledge 2015, 512. Adam Johnson is a theologian of "comprehensive atonement". Given that Barth's is a "consistently forensic interpretation of the cross", some may be surprised that Johnson finds in him a most congenial conversation partner (Johnson 2013, 14). But Johnson believes that developing Barth's "theology proper" can lead to an integrative and broadly nuanced construal of atonement in its many aspects (cf. Johnson 2013, 10).
[29] Cf. Barth 2004, 4:2:232, 244. Barth might here be set alongside Anselm in that his soteriology is drawn around the God–human polarity; Satan is not centered (cf. Barth 2004, 4:484). Although Barth does not heavily develop the theme of "bondage to Satan and the powers", that sensibility is not altogether absent in his discourse (cf. Johnson 2013, 154–56; Barth 2004, 4:1:272).

[30] Cf. Johnson 2013, 90; 85–91.
[31] Rutledge 2015, 514; cf. 508.
[32] Barth 2004, 4:2:249–50.
[33] Barth 2004, 4:1:273.
[34] Cf. Barth 2004, 4:1:211–83. "In the prepassion part of the four Gospels' narratives, [Jesus] is 'the divine subject of the judgment on man', for in his ministry Jesus speaks and acts as one with power to judge and dispose. From Gethsemane onward, however, he becomes the object of this judgment, the one who is himself disposed of—the Judge judged in our place" (Rutledge 2015, 520; Barth 2004, 4:1:238; see too 4:1:93–94, 226–27).
[35] Barth 2004, 4:1:222.
[36] Barth 2004, 4:1:89.
[37] Barth 2004, 4:2:226; cf. Athanasius, *On the Incarnation* 6.
[38] Barth 2004, 4:1:253, emphasis added; cf. 222, 226.
[39] Barth 2004, 4:1:486.
[40] Johnson 2013, 94 n 6. See too Smythe 2017, 238; Barth 2004, 2:2:168.
[41] Barth 2004, 4:1:238; cf. 2:1:399. The italicized sections are quotations from Luther. In the body of the text they are in Latin; I have replaced them with the English translations that were furnished in the footnotes.
[42] Cf. Barth 2004, 2:1:396.
[43] Cf. Vidu 2014, 2–4.
[44] Again, it is notable that the uneasiness of Islamic scholars with Christian atonement generally centers more on the issue of justice than on the nature of divine love.
[45] Cf. Vidu 2014, 58; *Proslogion* 9.
[46] Vidu 2014, "Introduction"; cf. 30.
[47] Smythe 2017, 239. This without at all claiming that Barth endorses classical ideas of the divine essence or philosophies of substance and form, etc.
[48] Barth 2004, 2:1:393–94; cf. Augustine, *On the Trinity* 13:16:21.
[49] Yang and Davis 2015, 155. On divine (im)passibility, passions, and affections, see Yang and Davis 2015, 155–60; Augustine, *City of God* 14:9; Castelo 2009; 2017; Gavrilyuk 2004; Heschel 2001; Matz and Thornhill 2019; Vanhoozer 2010.
[50] Yang and Davis 2015, 160; cf. Pr. 3:11-12; Heb. 12:5-6.
[51] Cf. Yang and Davis 2015, 163.
[52] Vidu 2014, 270.
[53] Vidu 2014, 269.
[54] Hastings 2019, 232, quoting Hindmarsh; cf. Ps. 30:5.
[55]Yang and Davis 2015, 160.
[56] Cf. Vidu 2014, 269.
[57] Sonderegger 2015 *Systematic Theology*, 240.
[58] Sonderegger 2015 *Systematic Theology*, 240–46.
[59] Barth 2004, 4:1:253.
[60] Rutledge 2015, 517–18; cf. Vidu 2014, 261. Barth does not allow "a rigidly schematic concept of penal substitution to become an idée fixe, crowding out all the other biblical models" (Rutledge 2015, 516).
[61] Vidu 2014, 262.
[62] Barth 2004, 4:1:273; Johnson 2013, 123.
[63] Johnson 2013, 123–24.
[64] Johnson 2013, 152.
[65] Cf. Barth 2004, 4:1:157–210.
[66] Anatolios 2011, 282.
[67] Rutledge 2015, 493.
[68] Rutledge 2015, 493.

[69] Cf. Rutledge 2015, 493–94.
[70] Cf. Cragg 1999, 180–82.
[71] Johnson 2013, 22.
[72] Barth 2004, 2:1:403.
[73] Barth 2004, 2:1:398.
[74] "The seeming 'injustice' of an agent being punished in the place of another is answered in part by the representative nature of this Man, the *eschatos* Adam. It would seem to be the case that recapitulation is necessary to the participatory and substitutionary nature of the atonement in Karl Barth" (Hastings 2019, 33).
[75] That Christ's death was "*for* us" or "*for* sin" (ὑπὲρ/περὶ) can hardly be gainsaid (e.g. 2 Cor. 5:21; 1 Pet. 3:18). But for some, such action, though *to our advantage*, is never intended to mean "in our place" (Rutledge 2015, 468–69). Exegetically, this simply cannot hold. See Rutledge 2015, 469; she also notes the dynamic of "exchange", in 1 Pet. 2:24.
[76] Packer 1974, 34, 17.
[77] Sonderegger 2015 *Systematic Theology*, 409.
[78] Cf. Barth 2004, 4:1:516.
[79] Hastings 2019, 162.
[80] Barth 2004, 4:2:21.
[81] Cf. Barth 2004, 4:1:135.
[82] Sonderegger 2015 *Systematic Theology*, 410; cf. 409–10.
[83] Barth 2004, 4:1:95, emphasis added.
[84] Cf. Barth 2004, 4:1:283.
[85] Vidu 2014, 260; cf. Barth 2004, 4:1:94; Hastings 2019, 42.
[86] Cf. Barth 2004, 4:2:141.
[87] Barth 2004, 4:1:215; cf. 4:1:550; 4:2:612–13.
[88] Barth 2004, 4:1:295, emphasis added; cf. 4:1:94; Gunton 1988, 111–12.
[89] Cf. Barth 2004, 4:1:296; 253–54.
[90] Barth 2004, 4:1:392–96.
[91] Barth 2004, 2:1:396; cf. 4:1:92, 551–56.
[92] Vidu 2014, 263; cf. 123. Vidu insists that both Augustine and Calvin were convinced of the immutability of the God whose love has ever been the basis of redemption (cf. Vidu 2014, 35–36, 121–22).
[93] Barth 2004, 2:1:402. Further: "Judged in Him we cannot be tomorrow the proud men we were yesterday. Those men are no longer there, for yesterday we were delivered up to the divine judgment. As those who are freed from our past in Him, we no longer have the freedom (the false freedom) to return to our old pride" (Barth 2004, 4:1:554).
[94] Rutledge 2015, 508, quoting Barth's *Dogmatics in Outline*; cf. Barth 2004, 4:1:92.
[95] Barth 2004, 4:2:611.
[96] See Barth 2004, 4:2:599–601, 604–605.
[97] Cf. Barth 2004, 2:1:405–406.
[98] Barth 2004, 4:1:101.
[99] Cf. Barth 2004, 4:1:295–96, 627. Adonis Vidu argues that holding together the "divine missions" of Son and Spirit alongside the "inseparable action" of the Trinity strengthens the ethics of atonement. It avoids an "artificial dichotomy between objective and subjective soteriology, between the work of the Son and the work of the Spirit, between justification and sanctification" (Vidu 2017, 648).
[100] Cf. Barth 2004:4:2:584–98.
[101] Barth 2004, 4:1:101. So far, so good. But it often appears as though, for Barth, the transformation of the believer's character and works are a virtually inevitable outcome (cf. Barth 2004, 4:2:585). We must concede that balanced descriptions of the disciple's moral exertion under the umbrella of grace are not easily expressed. Nonetheless, in

terms of sanctification, Barth's strong rhetoric—where he is emphatic and where he is cursory—flirts with questioning the reality of human agency at any level. "[I]n the ethical sections of *CD*, particularly before volume four, [Barth] is interpreted as having so grounded man's agency in Christ that the impetus for human obedience is removed, and sanctification is not recognizable as a human process" (Webster 2016, 106).

[102] Cf. Tanner 2010, 250.

[103] In its own register, this is a key concern of Moffitt 2022.

[104] Barth 2004, 4:1:176.

[105] Barth 2004, 4:2:262; see too 4:1:166; 4:2:204.

[106] Barth 2004, 4:1:309; see too 4:2:141, 144.

[107] Cf. Barth 2004, 4:1:310–11, 355–56.

[108] Cf. Barth 2004, 4:1:83.

[109] Cf. Ralston 2021, 232.

[110] Ralston 2021, 230.

[111] Cf. Barth 2004, 4:2:603, 606. "In themselves and as such, pain, suffering and death are a questioning, a destruction, and finally a negation of human life. The Christian especially cannot try to transform and glorify them … He cannot be a lover of death" (Barth 2004, 4:2:602).

[112] See Barth 2004, 4:2:607.

[113] See Barth 2004, 4:1:186. The sharply inverse depictions of what is or is not "pagan" by Barth, on the one hand, and Islamic thinkers (from al-Faruqi to Qutb to Rida), on the other, is remarkable.

[114] Jürgen Moltmann is a theologian whose work might creatively overlap with certain concerns of our Islamic critics. However, at the same time, prominent features of his work (so-called "social Trinitarianism", "panentheism", "extreme dereliction") are more problematic than Barth's exactly at this juncture and would not augur well for his reception in an Islamic ethos. On Moltmann and/or in reaction to him and related theologies, see Moltmann 1974; 1993; Bauckham 2016; Grebe 2017; Castelo 2009; Vanhoozer 2019, 19–25, 491; Weinandy 2000, 160; Wilcoxen 2019, 150–53.

[115] Wilcoxen 2019, 186–87.

[116] "Christ is epistemologically determinative, but ontologically the divine perfections must rule" (Wilcoxen 2019, 192, following Sonderegger).

[117] Sonderegger appeals strongly to God's Oneness, transcendence, simplicity, and perfections; his is a "fiery" reality extending even beyond Christology and not reducible to "method" (cf. Sonderegger 2015 *Systematic Theology*, 392–95).

[118] We have more to say below, for example, on Barth 2004, 4:2:32–35.

[119] For example, contrasting trends emerge within the same discourse unit in Barth 2004, 4:1:179–84; cf. Barth 2004, 2:1:402; 4:1:253; 4:2:252. In various places throughout the *Dogmatics*, Barth certainly would seem to deny anything like contingency in the eternal Father, to strongly affirm his aseity. See, for example, Barth 2004, 1:1:389, 392-393. See further Castelo 2009, 108; Hart 2002, 188; Hastings 2019, 41; Sonderegger 2020, 231–34, 246, 413; Swain and Allen 2013, 92–93; Vanhoozer 2010, 425; Vidu 2015, 32. Not all of these references are directly concerned with Barth, but they bear in some degree on our topic.

[120] Sonderegger 2020, 209; cf. 200; also 2015 *Systematic Theology*, 392–95.

[121] Sonderegger 2015 *Systematic Theology*, 162, emphasis added.

[122] Barth 2004, 2:1:397, emphasis added.

[123] Barth 2004, 4:1:193, emphasis added; cf. 197; Rutledge 2015, 518.

[124] Cf. Wilcoxen 2019, 167, following Sonderegger.

[125] Cf. Johnson 2013, 69; Rutledge 2015, 518.

[126] Johnson 2013, 78; 78–83.

[127] Barth 2004, 2:1:262–63; cf. 1:1:295; 4:2:33–34; Johnson 2013, 31–32.

[128] Hastings 2019, 49.
[129] Barth 2004, 2:1:399; cf. Johnson 2013, 73, 75 n 42.
[130] Anatolios 2020, 299, quoting von Balthasar. The statement is helpful, but note again the warning from Bruce Marshall: it is important that the Trinity is not simply read out of the Passion narratives alone (and according to the instincts of the Zeitgeist) in a sort of back projection. The direction of travel matters. See too Johnson 2013, 124.
[131] Cf. Vidu 2015, 37–38, 41.
[132] Barth 2004, 2:1:402.
[133] Cf. Hastings 2019, 112.
[134] In the mystery of Trinity, there are distinctive appropriations, for example the Son alone is incarnate and crucified. But where one is present, all are. God himself is present in each saving moment. For example, to say that God in Christ bears our shame at the cross does not imply that at that moment he (the Son) then fails also to rule in glory. See Athanasius, *On the Incarnation* 19 (cf. 17). The eighth-century Patriarch Timothy I (living under ʻAbbasid rule) argued "that while [Christ] was hanging on the cross, he moved the heavens, shook the earth, darkened the sun, blood-reddened the moon, rent the stones, opened the graves, and gave life to the dead that were in them" (*Apology of Timothy*, translated in Mingana 1928, 45).
[135] Vidu 2014, 261, citing I. Howard Marshall.
[136] Bruce Marshall has published extensively on Christology and the Trinity in classical and modern theology, but I refer here to an audio lecture he delivered for the Angelicum Thomistic Institute on 12 May 2021. Theologies that may in varying degrees be susceptible to Marshall's critique include those of Barth, von Balthasar, and Moltmann.
[137] Hill and Jedwab have collected expressions of PSA entailing language of "God punishing Christ" (Hill and Jedwab 2015, 150–53). Such terminology is a part of the penal-substitutionary heritage, but, they aver, the majority tendency is *not* language of "the Father punishing the Son".
[138] Cf. Augustine, *On the Trinity* 15:3:5.
[139] Vidu 2015, 39–40.
[140] Cf. Stott 2012, 173–74.
[141] Compare Augustine, *On the Trinity* 13:11:15.
[142] Hastings 2019, 243.
[143] Cf. Barth 2004, 4:1:142.
[144] Cf. Barth 2004, 4:1:389
[145] Barth 2004, 4:1:131; cf. 135.
[146] Barth 2004, 4:1:487.
[147] Barth 2004, 4:1:390.
[148] Barth 2004, 4:1:391; cf. 403–407.
[149] Cf. Barth 2004, 4:1:512–14. There is a gentle resonance here with E.P. Sanders' exposition of Paul's "discovery" of justification in Christ as a movement backwards "from solution to plight" (E.P. Sanders 2017, 572; cf. 572–76).
[150] Barth 2004, 4:1:411.
[151] Johnson 2013, 151.
[152] Cf. Johnson 2013, 141f. On sin as falsehood, the negation of the fidelity and truthfulness of God, see Barth 2004, 4:1:143–44; also, volume 4:3.1:434–61. On sloth, see below.
[153] Cf. Johnson 2013, 147.
[154] Cf. Barth 2004, 4:1:143.
[155] Cf. Barth 2004, 4:1:358f.
[156] Barth 2004, 4:2:101.
[157] Cf. Webster 1988, 21.
[158] Webster 1988, 21; cf. 28.

[159] Cf. Webster 1988, 25–26.
[160] Barth 2004, 4:1:511.
[161] Webster points out that Barth (in a posthumous publication) rounds out his ideas on the causalities of sin by invoking the impulses, forces, and evil influences that transcend solitary human agency (see Webster 1988, 26–27).
[162] Barth 2004, 4:1:509–10. Interestingly, as Gary Anderson points out, Barth delves rather deeply into the apostasy of the golden calf (Ex. 32) as a microcosmic "original sin of Israel", revealing in concentrated form what is true of all humanity from Genesis 3 onward (Anderson 2017, 73; Barth 2004, 4:1:427–28).
[163] Athanasius displays *certain* similarities when it comes to Adam and humanity in sin and Christology as the lens for anthropology. On Athanasius see Behr 2004, 197–98, 204–206.
[164] Cf. Rutledge 2015, 518–20.
[165] Cf. Barth 2004, 4:1:234.
[166] Barth 2004, 4:1:234.
[167] Barth 2004, 4:1:254.
[168] Webster 1988, 22–25.
[169] Cf. Barth 2004, 4:1:139-141, 408–409.
[170] Cf. Barth 2004, 4:2:491.
[171] Barth 2004, 4:1:533.
[172] Barth 2004, 4:2:380–81.
[173] Barth 2004, 4:2:380.
[174] Barth 2004, 4:2:381; cf. 385–90.
[175] Cf. Barth 2004:4:487.
[176] Barth 2004, 4:2:493. "Every sin, even the smallest, is mortal sin to the extent that it is worthy of death and involves our mortal sickness. How, then, can we restrict the term to the seven deadly sins, as though a venial sin not in this list could not be just as great as any of these, and even greater than all of them put together? Which supposedly little sin, even the smallest, is not committed in an inner conflict of man and the will of man, so that it is not at one and the same time voluntary sin and involuntary" (Barth 2004:4:2:493)?
[177] Barth's position is not, however, that God's judgment is homogenous and without nuance. It is just that no one stands pure and free on a flawless record. God's judgment is justly universal, for sin is; but it is also specific, calibrated, and personal as we all fail with a particular "shade of darkness" (Barth 2004, 4:2:492).
[178] Barth 2004, 4:1:487.
[179] Cf. Barth 2004, 4:2:378–93, 403–83. "If, then, [Jesus] is very different from us, if there is this distinction between him on the one side and all other men on the other, if we all confront him in our ordinariness, we cannot excuse and vindicate and justify ourselves against him in this ordinariness, or try to accuse him because he is so different. In and with the existence of this One the ground is cut away from under our feet as those who are ordinary men. In and with this One who has taken our place there has come to us grace and liberation" (Barth 2004, 4:2:392).
[180] Barth 2004, 4:2:401; cf. 400–401.
[181] Barth 2004, 2:1:401.
[182] Cf. Barth 2004, 4:2:32–34.
[183] Cf. Burrell 1993, 166.
[184] Barth 2004, 4:1:529; cf. 2:1:402.
[185] Cf. Barth 2004, 4:2:33–35; cf. Hastings 2019, 41–42, 136, 145. Consider here Wilcoxen's observation: "Augustine's doctrine of Trinitarian processions, seen in his exegesis of John 5:19-30 [makes] the case that God's condescending mercy toward creatures in the incarnation of Christ cannot be something accidental to God, but rather

is somehow rooted in the life of the Holy Trinity. The outstanding question Augustine now faces is how God shares his life with contingent creation" (Wilcoxen 2019, 105).
[186] Vanhoozer 2010, 425.
[187] Vídu 2015, 32. See too the excursus on Christoexclusivism.
[188] Barth 2004, 4:1:213–14; cf. 221–22.
[189] Barth 2004, 4:1:239.
[190] Barth 2004, 4:1:271.
[191] Cf. Barth 2004, 4:1:300.
[192] Cf. Barth 2004, 4:2:259–60.
[193] Cf. Barth 2004, 4:2:260–63. Note the previous discussion on distinct but converging metaphysical planes.
[194] See my general discussion of atonement above for brief and implicit nods in this direction as well as my various comments on the "Western" critics of Anslem and/or PSA; see too the appendix on "non-violent" atonement.
[195] Barth 2004, 4:2:253. Further, Barth insists: "The little word δεῖ must not escape our notice. It dominates the first of the predictions in all three versions: 'The Son of man *must* suffer many things.' This 'must' was and is decisive" (Barth 2004, 4:2:255; see too 255–58).
[196] Barth 2004, 4:1:246; cf. 239.
[197] Barth 2004, 4:2:84; cf. 4:1:159; 4:2:41. Barth's thought here resonates with that of Kenneth Cragg (cf. Chambésy 1982, 48–51; Cragg 1999, 180–82, 197–205). Consider too Gregory of Nyssa's radical insistence that incarnation *most* reveals God's power and that God's interface with birth, body, reproductive organs, and so on is no diminishment of his honor (Gregory of Nyssa, *Catechetical Discourse* 24, 27–28).
[198] Barth 2004, 4:2:251.
[199] Cf. Packer 1974, 26–27.
[200] See Barth 2004, 4:2:148.
[201] Barth 2004, 2:1:400.
[202] Barth 2004, 4:1:256–57.
[203] Barth 2004, 4:1:257.
[204] See Deng 2018.
[205] Cf. Barth 2004, 4:2:33–35.
[206] Barth 2004, 2:1:368; cf. p. 406.
[207] Barth 2004, 4:1:201.
[208] Barth 2004, 4:1:191.
[209] For all this, Barth 2004, 2:1:370; also, 1:1:139–40.
[210] Barth 2004, 4:2:357.
[211] Wilcoxen 2019, 152; cf. 196–97. Even as Moltmann found much to criticize in Barth's work (cf. Wilcoxen 2019, 150–53).
[212] "[Berkouwer] decries Barth's inclusion of an intra-Trinitarian 'obedience of God' as something that exceeds the boundaries of revelation and leads inevitably to a Theopaschitism that will have to posit the death of God, God's own division against himself. Berkouwer's contention with Barth is that he goes beyond the proper location of mystery and attempts to 'comprehend the incarnation'" (Wilcoxen 2019, 121, citing Berkouwer).
[213] Cf. the "impassible" suffering of the Son (Cyril of Alexandria, *On the Unity of Christ* 133).
[214] Barth 2004, 4:2:59, emphasis added.
[215] For a study which situates God's impassibility with insight and nuance, allowing for the impassible God's compassion, mercy, and redemptive engagement with humanity (his "emotionally colored" virtues), see Gavrilyuk 2004 (e.g. 50–51).

[216] Wilcoxen's worries about Barth are more forcefully expressed than mine. He may be right. See Wilcoxen 2019, 149–50.
[217] Cf. Johnson 2013, 47–51.
[218] Barth 2004, 4:1:187–88.
[219] See Barth 2004, 2:1:608–40.
[220] Cf. Augustine, *Confessions* Book 11, starting at 11:8.
[221] Barth 2004, 4:2:33, emphasis added.
[222] Cf. Barth 2004, 4:2:35; also 4:2:107.
[223] Cf. Wilcoxen 2019, 141–55.
[224] Cf. Barth 2004, 1:1:172–74.
[225] Vidu 2014, 270.
[226] While some "progressive" paradigms deny validity to any forensic interpretation of the cross, Islamic scholars are unlikely to countenance the cross at all. They *are* likely to affirm legal sanction (Islamic law) as integral to both ethics and soteriology.
[227] The relationship of God to time might compare in some respects to the relationship of Newtonian physics to Relativity Theory. Lesslie Newbigin points out that "there is radical discontinuity in the sense that the new theory is not reached by any process of logical reasoning from the old, [but] there is also a continuity in the sense that the old can be rationally understood from the point of view of the new … [This] is not to surrender to irrationality. Seen from one side there is only a chasm; seen from the other there is a bridge" (Newbigin 1986, 52).
[228] Vidu 2014, 270.
[229] Cf. Vidu 2014, 270.
[230] See also Barth 2004, 1:1:162—§5:4 ("The Speech of God as the Mystery of God"); also Hastings 2019, 99–101.
[231] Vidu 2014, 271; cf. 270–71.
[232] Cf. Vidu 2014, 271.

**Chapter Seven Notes**
[1] Cf. Carbine and Koster 2015; Thiel 2015.
[2] "Honor" is not invariably Tanner's term of choice, but we have already made the connection between it and God's goodness and greatness, transcendence, or distinctness from all else. On these Tanner is profuse. See Tanner 2010, 156–57.
[3] Tanner 2010, "Preface".
[4] Hastings 2019, 92–93, quoting Marcus Johnson.
[5] Cf. Tanner 2001, 9.
[6] von Stosch 2021, 64–65; cf. McGuckin 2017.
[7] "'[The Son] became what we are in order to make us what he is' [Irenaeus, *Against Heresies* 5]. This is the patristic theme of the great and saving exchange" (Hunsinger 2015, 101).
[8] Tanner 2010, 254. Tanner marshals the evidence of several church Fathers (Tanner 2010, 254–56). The incarnation is the driving mechanism even for Gregory of Nyssa's controverted bait-and-hook metaphor (cf. Tanner 2010, 255–56).
[9] See Barth 2004, 4:1:131.
[10] Cf. Tanner 2010, 4–5; cf. 23–24. Against the worries of Augustine, Tanner asserts that there need not be any doubt that on this understanding humans then fail to image God as a whole (but "only" the Son). For, after all, the Logos images God perfectly (cf. Tanner 2010, 5).
[11] Tanner 2010, 6–8.
[12] Tanner 2010, 13. For some of the church Fathers, the "image" of Genesis 1:26, after or for which humanity was formed, was in fact the Logos who eternally and perfectly

images the Father (cf. Tanner 2010, 53–57). See Tanner 2001, 15–23, for her creative appropriation and articulation of two-nature Christology.
[13] See Tanner 2010, 136.
[14] Cf. Tanner 2010, 15.
[15] Tanner 2010, 17.
[16] Tanner 2010, 19. "In line with this idea, Athanasius suggests human beings at their creation were not just given their existence and the sort of participation in the Word that comes from being an intelligent creature: they also knew the very Word of God by way of its presence to them. And through that knowledge they enjoyed 'a life in correspondence with God', 'the true life', which, had they maintained it, would have enabled them to abide forever in blessedness" (Tanner 2010, 20–21, referencing Athanasius, *On the Incarnation*, sections 3–5).
[17] Tanner 2010, 23–24.
[18] Tanner 2010, 300. Compare: "Christ's Deity, that is, exhibits all the Divine Perfections. It is Holy Humility; it enters the world as Power that can be rejected, as Presence that can be overlooked. In just this way, the Deity of Christ is not direct Object to us. It does not compel assent as do the sturdy deliverances of our senses, or the firm deductions of our logic. It is the Light by which we see, mingled with the ordinary light of human exchange, human willing and knowing. But because this One is also Almighty God we do not here have an instance of *disguise* or masquerade … Rather, the Deity of Christ is present and manifest as Spirit, Indirect Light … His Omnipotence is sensed, an unmistakable Force that moves in every step of this man of Nazareth. Perhaps we might say that in this Gospel [John], the Transfiguration occupies the whole of Jesus' life" (Sonderegger 2015 *Systematic Theology*, 432).
[19] Tanner 2001, 47; cf. 47–48.
[20] Tanner 2001, 55.
[21] Barth 2004, 4:2:59, 72; cf. 31–36, 59–60.
[22] Barth 2004, 4:1:136; cf. 126–27.
[23] Tanner 2010, 260. Tanner seems to capture Christ's full identification with sinful humanity—without sin—with fitting grit and intensity. One might possibly quibble as to Tanner's intent when she employs phrasing such as, "[Jesus] surpasses failure by suffering it" or "the effects of sin on Jesus' own life" (Tanner 2010, 298). I think we need not. The "perfecting" of Jesus' humanity is a reality in deep solidarity with all humans, but, again, entails no sense of sin attributed to him (cf. Tanner 2001, 52; Heb. 5:8-10). In terms of Jesus' coming in the likeness of sinful human flesh, Gregory of Nazianzus' aphorism on the healing only of that which is assumed comes to mind (Gregory of Nazianzus, *Letter to Cledonius (I)* 440). Hastings describes Calvin's view that incarnation instantly cleanses humanity, while in Barth the process "is more gradual" (Hastings 2019, 136; see also 27–28; 145–48). Barth's existentially tinged verbiage to the effect that Jesus undertook to "be the bearer of human essence in its inward contradiction, to repent as such" is not particularly clarifying (Barth 2004, 4:2:92). Witness too: "[The Son] entered the concrete form of our nature, under which we stand before God as men damned and lost. He did not produce and establish this form differently from all of us; though innocent" (Barth 2004, 1:2:153; cf. 151–59; cf. 2:1:397–98). Jesus as representative in repentance calls to mind John McLeod Campbell (cf. Stevenson 2016); Anatolios 2022 also engages this theme.
[24] Cf. Tanner 2010, 250.
[25] Cf. Tanner 2010, 247–53.
[26] Tanner 2010, 86.
[27] Cf. Tanner 2010, 198–206, and 200 n 97; 2001, 14, 53–56, 62.
[28] Tanner 2010, 198–99.
[29] Tanner 2010, 144; cf. 143–44.

[30] Tanner 2010, 25.
[31] Tanner 2010, 28.
[32] Tanner 2010, 140; cf. 142.
[33] Tanner 2010, 145–46. Tanner portrays the work of God in the economy of salvation as entirely of a piece with the eternal dynamic of Father–Son–Spirit relations *simpliciter*. This "timeless" stability of character and act, potentially speaks to Islamic worries over atonement's implications for God's authority, stature, and unimpeached honor.
[34] Tanner 2010, 147.
[35] Cf. Tanner 2010, 173.
[36] On Trinitarian distinction and unity in salvation, see Tanner 2010, 148–61.
[37] Tanner 2010, 161.
[38] Tanner 2010, 152.
[39] Tanner 2010, 195.
[40] Tanner 2010, 156–57.
[41] "Passages such as 'the Son can do nothing on his own' (John 5:19), 'I do as the Father has commanded me' (John 14:31), 'the Father has given me a commandment about what to say and what to speak' (John 12:49), 'I speak just as the Father has told me' (John 12:50), and 'I have not spoken on my own' (John 12:49), do not, in short, suggest the submission of Jesus' will to an external command. They indicate, instead, simply that the Son's work is the Father's work, that the Father's work is the very work that Jesus does. Jesus is not interpreted in these passages as downplaying his own role by humbly affirming his inferiority to the Father; he is interpreted instead as affirming his exceptional character among men—that what he is doing is by the Father's own charge … Jesus is, indeed, obedient to the Father but in such a perfect way that what we ordinarily mean by obedience no longer holds … 'What the Father knows, the Son does not learn by question and answer; what the Father wills, the Son does not will by command. Since all that the Father has, is his, it is the property of his nature to will and know, exactly as the Father wills and knows'" (Tanner 2010, 184, quoting Hillary of Poitiers).
[42] Tanner 2010, 186.
[43] Tanner 2010, 86, emphasis added; cf. Tanner 2001, 9.
[44] Cf. Anderson 2009, 121–22; cf. 121–27; see too Matthew Baker 2016, 115.
[45] "Looking back, we may well ask with amazement how it was that … Protestantism, as it followed both Luther and Calvin, could overlook this dimension of the Gospel which is so clearly attested in the New Testament—its power as a message of mercifully omnipotent and unconditionally complete liberation from φθορά, death and wrong as the power of evil … In other words, how could it become such a moralistic affair—so dull, so indifferent to the question of man himself, and therefore so lacking in joy? How could it possibly overlook the fact that it was depriving even its specific doctrine of justification and sanctification of so radiant a basis and confirmation by not looking very differently at the character of the self-revelation of God in the Son of Man as it emerges in the miracles of Jesus, in these works of God; by not considering the freedom of the grace which appeared in Him" (Barth 2004, 4:2:233)?
[46] Tanner 2010, 268.
[47] Tanner 2010, 272.
[48] Tanner 2010, 262, emphasis added; cf. 251.
[49] Tanner 2010, 257–58.
[50] Tanner 2010, 256.
[51] Tanner 2010, 260.
[52] Tanner 2010, 257.
[53] Tanner 2010, 101–102.

[54] Tanner 2010, 104.
[55] Tanner 2010, 258. One might find the qualifier "primarily" to be telling here. Something need not be "primary" to be significant and indispensable.
[56] These issues are addressed in Tanner 2004 which is found also in the sixth chapter of Tanner 2010.
[57] Tanner 2010, 261; cf. Tanner 2001, 29–30.
[58] Tanner 2010, 257.
[59] Although, apparently not in any "strong" sense (?).
[60] Tanner 2010, 268. One may wonder how it is that here the cross is all about divine action, hardly with reference to humanity, while in the quote just above, in engaging feminist critics of cross redemption, Tanner seems to situate all the evils of what Jesus suffered in the agency of humanity alone.
[61] Cf. Tanner 2001, 29–30.
[62] We do well to keep in mind that while "ritual" impurity looms large in the cultic system, there is significant conceptual overlap between the "ritual" ways that Israel and the land are polluted and the "moral" pollution that is caused by violence, deceit, idolatry, and so on. So, such behaviors do constitute "impurity" (טמא) and are addressed by God in terms that often entail the extreme, the "violent", and the severe (e.g. Ps. 106:37–39). However one configures the relationship of the sacrificial system to "moral" infractions—and the issue is not simple—it seems implausible to simply divorce the two. (No claim is made here that Tanner does so.) In some way, the sacrificial cult was relevant to ritual and moral impurity.
[63] Tanner 2010, 264.
[64] Tanner 2010, 267.
[65] Tanner 2010, 266; cf. 266–67.
[66] "Despite the fact that it takes place on the cross, this sanctification is not being identified with death but with life. Life is being brought to Jesus on the cross, as his resurrection makes clear. To be sacrificed, so as to be sanctified, is now not to die but to live, in a perfected and purified form" (Tanner 2010, 269). Certainly, through death Jesus overturns death, a victory sealed in the resurrection. But one may question whether this fact warrants Tanner's not-so-subtle attempt to water down the connection between cross and death. See also the appendix on "non-violent" atonement.
[67] Cf. Tanner 2010, 45–50; also, von Stosch above.
[68] Cf. Tanner 2010, 30–32, 44.
[69] Tanner 2010, 41.
[70] "Humans can think of a variety of things that it would be good to do in certain respects and for certain purposes, and what they decide about what is most important to them in the course of such deliberations decides in great part the character of their lives, the identity they come to exhibit in their acts—*that* is just their nature" (Tanner 2010, 48–49; cf. 52–53, 67).
[71] Tanner 2010, 130, quoting de Lubac and Gregory of Nyssa.
[72] Whether one is inclined to follow Tanner in this apparently more optimistic framing of even fallen human anthropology, there should be room for shared acknowledgement of a "hopeful" basic fact: at minimum, humanity was designed with a capacity for fellowship with the good God. "Therefore, if man comes to genesis for these [reasons], for him to become a partaker of divine good things, he is necessarily fashioned like this, so as to suitably have a participation in good things" (Gregory of Nyssa, *Catechetical Discourse,* Part Two: Image of God, 66; cf. Tanner 2010, 37).
[73] Tanner 2010, 65.
[74] Tanner 2010, 135.
[75] Tanner 2010, 59; cf. Florovsky 2016, 145. At this juncture, Tanner's portrayal of the human condition might evince some intriguing affinities with Islamic notions of human

nature and capacity to obey God; salvation in a sort of *gnosis*; and divine "realism" in standards of judgment.
[76] Tanner 2010, 69; cf. 70.
[77] Tanner 2010, 63.
[78] Tanner 2010, 68.
[79] Cf. Tanner 2010, 64–66.
[80] Tanner 2010, 68.
[81] Tanner 2010, 65–66.
[82] J. Behr directs attention to Irenaeus' Christologically framed anthropology: "There is no golden age of primordial perfection when we might not have needed Christ … For Irenaeus, the starting point for all theological reflection (including the Fall) is the given fact of the work of Christ, his life giving and saving death" (Behr 2017, 570, referencing Barr). So, even an "unfallen" Adam "could not have become a partaker in incorruptibility, nor have been united to the Spirit, had God not united himself to the human being in Christ" (Behr 2017, 573; cf. 571–73).
[83] Cf. Tanner 2010, 58–59.
[84] Tanner 2010, 60, emphasis added.
[85] Tanner 2010, 61.
[86] Tanner 2010, 62. One may be reminded here of Rahman's exposition of the Qur'an on humanity's tendency to "gravitate downward".
[87] Tanner 2010, 129.
[88] Tanner 2010, 133; cf. 130.
[89] Tanner 2010, 33, quoting Cyril of Alexandria on John 7, emphasis added.
[90] Tanner 2010, 33.
[91] Tanner 2010, 35; cf. Augustine, *On the Trinity* 2:6:11.
[92] Tanner 2010, 70–71, emphasis added; cf. 58, 254. See too: "So he is called man … that by himself he may sanctify humanity and be as it were a leaven to the whole lump; and by uniting to himself that which was condemned may release it from condemnation" (Gregory of Nazianzus, *Oration* 30:21, 317; Tanner 2010, 255).
[93] Cf. Tanner 2010, 256, citing Cyril of Alexandria, *On the Unity of Christ,* 132–33.
[94] Cf. Tanner 2001, 36–37.
[95] Tanner 2010, 70.
[96] Tanner 2010, 72–73; cf. 75, 88, 104.
[97] Tanner 2010, 14, drawing on Augustine; cf. 53–54; Tanner 2019, 158, 202.
[98] There are alternate translations of this phrase. See Anatolios 2020, 268–69.
[99] Tanner 2010, 297, quoting *Theology in Reconciliation*; cf. Hastings 2019, 38.
[100] Cf. Tanner 2001, 81–83.
[101] Tanner 2010, 236.
[102] Cf. Tanner 2010, 236–37.
[103] Tanner 2010, 241.
[104] Tanner 2001, 71.
[105] For Tanner there are distinctive countercultural implications here for the Christian economic outlook which is not based on an economics of "scarcity" or zero-sum competition (cf. Tanner 2019, 203–204).
[106] Cf. Tanner 2001, 90–95.
[107] Cf. Tanner 2019, 218.
[108] Tanner 2019, 205.
[109] Tanner 2019, 210–11.
[110] Cf. Tanner 2019, 210–14.
[111] Cf. Tanner 2019, 214.
[112] Tanner 2019, 206.
[113] Cf. Tanner 2010, 241.

[114] Tanner 2019, 218, referencing especially Augustine.
[115] Tanner 2010, 98.
[116] Tanner 2010, 98–99.
[117] Tanner 2010, 99.
[118] Tanner 2010, 84; cf. 2001, 69.
[119]Tanner 2010, 272, emphasis added.
[120] Tanner 2010, 243.
[121] Cf. Tanner 2001, 79–81, 122. Tanner (2019) is concerned with praxis to a degree but, again, not in detail.
[122] Some of our Islamic critics might appreciate Tanner's accentuation of the loyalty every Christian owes God, a fidelity that should determine every domain of life, freeing one from market idolatries even as one participates in this world (cf. Tanner 2019, chapter three).
[123] Cf. Tanner 2001, 63.
[124] Cf. Tanner 2019, 201.
[125] Tanner 2019, 164; cf. 163–64.
[126] Tanner 2001, 124.
[127] Tanner 2010, 93.
[128] "Sharply distinguishing justification from sanctification is itself a way of cleanly separating divine from human, in order to give the clear priority to God's own action for our sakes" (Tanner 2010, 96).
[129] Tanner 2001, 86.
[130] Tanner 2010, 87; cf. 2001, 69.
[131] Tanner 2010, 88–89.
[132] Tanner 2010, 89.
[133] Tanner 2010, 89–90.
[134] Tanner 2010, 90.
[135] "A man, then, who remains the same and yet prattles to himself about the change for the better he has undergone in baptism should attend to what Paul says, 'If anyone thinks he is something when he is nothing, he deceives himself'" (Gregory of Nyssa, *Catechetical Oration* 40, quoted in Anatolios 2020, 389).
[136] Tanner 2010, 274.
[137] Tanner 2010, 298.
[138] Tanner 2010, 298–99.
[139] Tanner 2019, 158.
[140] In Tanner's ethics of the atoned, one could well argue for a certain overlap with Islamic notions (e.g. God's "realistic" expectations of us) or not (is she too permissive and pessimistic?). It depends on where one puts the accent. In any case, it must be said that unlike many of our chosen Muslim interlocutors, Tanner does not hew to the "linear" and predictable, nor does she shy away from mystery, paradox, or the sense that appearances can be deceiving.
[141] Tanner 2010, 301.
[142] Tanner 2001, 58.
[143] Tanner 2019, 160; cf. Tanner 2001, 58–59, 71, 75. Tanner's further theorizing of eschatology is provocative and, to my mind, ambiguous. I cannot address it here.
[144] Cragg 1999, 202–203.
[145] Anatolios 2011, 203, quoting Gregory of Nyssa, *Catechetical Oration* 24.
[146] Cf. Tanner 2010, 8–9.
[147] Cf. Tanner 2001, 41–46.
[148] Tanner 2010, 11.
[149] Tanner 2010, 156.
[150] Cf. Soars 2021, 127.

[151] Hastings 2019, 100; cf. 99–101.
[152] Tanner 2010, 12.
[153] Tanner 2010, 235.
[154] Soars 2021, 128. Soars notes Tanner's impact on Burrell's thought.
[155] Tanner 2010, 117.
[156] Tanner 2010, 133, quoting Augustine, *City of God* 11:10.
[157] Tanner 2001, 10, emphasis added. See also, p. 11.
[158] Tanner 2001, 69.
[159] Cf. Tanner 2001, 76–77.
[160] Cf. Tanner 2010, 79.
[161] Tanner 2010, 76–78.
[162] Tanner 2019, 161; cf. 57–59.
[163] Cragg 1999, 198.
[164]Tanner 2001, 68; cf. 68–69.
[165] Cf. Tanner 2001, 2–5.
[166] Cf. Tanner 2001, 11; cf. 11–12; Barth 2004, 4:1:186–87.
[167] Tanner 2010, 114, 116, emphasis added.
[168] Tanner 2010, 260, emphasis added.
[169] "The expiatory rite associated with the cross is not then preparatory to communion sacrifice; a communion sacrifice has already taken place in Jesus' person, in and through the incarnation … It is through direct contact of the human with the divine by way of the incarnation that sacrifice is overturned: Jesus is the sacrifice that ends sacrifice (Heb. 10)" (Tanner 2010, 270–71).
[170] Compare Behr 2017 on Irenaeus' holistic summing up of salvation's apparent sequencing.
[171] Tanner 2010, 259.
[172] Tanner 2019, 128–29; cf. 132–33.
[173] Tanner 2019, 133.
[174] Georges Florovsky in Matthew Baker *et al* (eds.) 2016, 155. See too Hunsinger 2015.
[175] Sonderegger 2020, 308.
[176] Generally, a Muslim is likely to find the life of Jesus as model and prophetic challenge more congenial terrain than, say, his death as sacrifice, payment, or even "victory". But, Jesus still will not be received as the incarnate Son.

**Chapter Eight Notes**

[1] David Moffit's work (2022) at this juncture manifests a more constructive angle of attack in that he is at pains to insist that a victim's death is hardly the whole of atonement, but he does so without creating an unnecessary oppositional polarity between sacrifice as "death" or as "life"; he resists underplaying the obvious and thematic relevance of "death" for atonement.
[2] Madigan 2021, 26–27.
[3] Cf. Macchia 2023, 78.
[4] al-Faruqi directly criticized Barth (e.g. *Christian Ethics* 1999, 195–96).
[5] See too Madigan 2021, 15–16, 28.
[6] Madigan 2021, 28.
[7] "The act of Adam and his wife in the Qur'an, no less than in Genesis, seems to be a choice to treat God as a rival and to seek autonomy from God in an immortality and a lasting sovereignty that are not granted by God but grasped by humans in spite of God's prohibition. Although many commentators will minimize Adam's sin, when the verses that speak of eating the fruit are read together with the verses that give the motivations for that transgression, it can be seen that disobedience of the first humans is anything but trivial" (Madigan 2021, 20; cf. 26, 29).

[8] Webster 1988, 20.
[9] Both Christians and Muslims must grapple with the imponderables of divine sovereignty, time, and human agency (consider *qadar*). Compare: "We rightly recoil from the idea that each newborn begins life with the personal moral status of a sinner, already carrying a debt incurred by her forebears. At the same time, however, it is almost impossible to conceive of a human being whose own freedom is not constrained in some way right from the beginning by the history and culture of sin into which she is born" (Madigan 2021, 20–21).
[10] Crisp 2020, 174.
[11] "In Athanasius the incarnate one is the Word who is the means of God's continuing presence to the world. Therefore, the 'intervention' of God for his world is not isolated from the rest of his action, because it is the mediator of creation who comes to ensure … the original purposes of God" (Gunton 1988, 146; cf. 146–55, 169; Johnson 2015, 42; Rom. 1:3; 8:18-24; Eph. 1:4-10, 20-23; Col. 1:15-20; 1 Pet. 1:18-20; cf. Rev. 13:8).
[12] Cf. Behr 2017.
[13] Cf. al-Faruqi 1999, 138.
[14] Recall Tabatabai's comments on the relative triviality of Adam's sin.
[15] Madigan 2021, 30.
[16] That is, without the provision of further information, a judge's acting on justice, as such, reveals little one way or the other about the judge's disposition in terms of love and mercy. Indeed, it may even be that severe consequences are in fact the most loving response available in a given scenario—whether one has the offender or perhaps the larger community in view.
[17] Vidu 2015, 40. Indeed, here Tanner's participatory metaphysics might well assist our thinking on objective atonement; unfortunately, she is little interested in retrieving anything from constructs such as PSA, settling rather for negation.
[18] Cf. Anatolios 2011.
[19] Ralston 2021, 222.
[20] Cragg 1999, 181.
[21] Hastings 2019, 271.
[22] Madigan 2021, 28.
[23] Or, in Ralston's words: "Jesus dies because of his persistence in and commitment to the kingdom of God, not in order to appease God's wrath or render a ransom back to God" (Ralston 2021, 230).
[24] Madigan 2021, 29.
[25] On Ralston, see the quote just above in note 23.
[26] I focus here on what I take to be infelicitous characterizations at specific points in Madigan's and Ralston's (independent) work. This mild criticism is not meant as a totalizing assessment of their generally broad and sophisticated theology and atonement thought.
[27] Burrell 1993, 85. Indeed, in the OT, God is not passive in, at times, "afflicting" his people. But this is hardly to the side of Israel's agency. And it is ultimately to her restoration. Cf. Hos. 6:1-3; Ps. 90:15-17; cf. Ps. 105:25.
[28] Again, I intend no comprehensive characterization of Madigan (or Ralston) as a proponent of moral exemplar atonement. This would be inaccurate (with respect to Ralston and exemplar approaches, see Ralston 2021, 225–27). But these are the vulnerabilities I discern at this juncture.
[29] Ralston 2021, 229.
[30] Ralston 2021, 230.
[31] Ralston 2021, 232.
[32] Cf. Cragg 1999, 198.

[33] Among many, see, for example, Feinberg 2001, chapter nine; Hasker 2009, 81–84; Mullins 2016.
[34] Ralston 2021, 224.
[35] Sonderegger 2020, 347; cf. 97.
[36] Cragg 1999, 203; Q 17:111.
[37] Cf. Cragg 1999, 203–205.
[38] Burrell 2009, 94–95.
[39] Compare Cragg 1999, 201.
[40] Johnson 2015, 147.
[41] Cragg 1999, 198–99; cf. Q 3:19.
[42] W. Wright 2015, 123.
[43] W. Wright 2015, 124–25.
[44] Johnson 2013, 78.
[45] Sonderegger 2020, 235; cf. 235–37.
[46] Cf. Cragg 1999, 166–69.
[47] Cf. Cragg 1999, 200.
[48] McGuckin 2016, 84; cf. Gregory of Nyssa, *Catechetical Oration* 24.
[49] Cf. Cragg 1999, 180–81, 201.
[50] Gavrilyuk 2004, 175.
[51] Cf. Barth 2004, 4:1:186; 4:1:191.
[52] Perhaps the Pentecostal or charismatic centering of healing as the heritage of redemption can be drawn on at this juncture in ways that the theologians featured here do not.
[53] Cf. al-Faruqi 1999, 161.
[54] Cf. Treier 2023, chapter one.
[55] See Anatolios 2020, 268–69, 307; Irenaeus, *Against Heresies* 4:14:1.
[56] It is, after all, the Lord's *death* proclaimed in his supper, the primal occasion of which Jesus used to invest his looming suffering with existential, covenantal, and expiatory weight (cf. Mt. 26:27-28; 1 Cor. 11:26; Phil. 2:8; also Heb. 2:14-15).
[57] Cf. Vidu 2015, 41; compare Stamps 2015, 135–36.
[58] *On the Incarnation* 19; cf. 25; Hunsinger 2015, 108.
[59] In some respects, *both* categories ii and iii can represent areas of potential engagement, if not agreement, in Muslim–Christian discussion. The only reason for a distinction is that the issues in category ii represent apparent problems to be clarified or rectified (a "defensive" response) and those in iii represent more positive overtures.
[60] See Ralston 2020.
[61] Of course, Ralston has already embarked (cf. Ralston 2020, chapter four).
[62] Cf. Cragg 1995, 400.
[63] M. Baker *et al* 2016, 10.
[64] Anatolios, in effect, works to see cross in resurrection and resurrection in cross (cf. Anatolios 2020, 326).
[65] A phraseology transmitted from Barth through Gunton.
[66] Heb. 2:8; cf. Barth 2004, 4:1:325–26.
[67] See Barth 2004, 4:1:349–50; Sonderegger 1995, 191–92.
[68] Anatolios 2020, 300, following von Balthasar.

**Appendix A Notes**

[1] See, for example, J. Brown and Khalil in Mosher and Marshall 2016; Shabana 2016; also Azumah 2018 and Sarbah 2018—both in Tieszen, ed., 2018.
[2] See, for example, Crowther *et al*, eds. 2017; cf. Haddad and Haddad, eds. 1995; Lazarus-Yafeh 2014; Poorthuis *et al*, eds. 2005; Reeves, ed. 2003.
[3] Ralston also credits Madigan's work; see Ralston 2020, 36–37.

[4] Zahniser 2008, 235–44.
[5] Cf. Tennent 2007, 16–18.
[6] This is true especially of Tennent's chapter two. But even his eighth chapter relies on few, if any, Islamic authors, leaning more on missiological writings.
[7] Clooney 2001, 25–28. Though it is not his own agenda, he does leave space for persons to judge one religious stance superior to another and even for the possibility of "conversion" (cf. Clooney 2001, 11, 28).
[8] Takács 2017, 99 n 3.
[9] Takács 2017, 105; cf. 100.
[10] Cf. Takács 2017, 106–12.
[11] Consider the paradox of the incarnation of the Son—a doctrine which Takács seems to affirm (cf. Takács 2017, 115). On my understanding, the incarnation is not the sort of mysterious reality that can acceptably be true and not-true—true for "my tradition", but not necessarily true for all. That is not where any "paradox" in the incarnation lies (cf. Clooney 2001, 65–68 on von Balthasar; also 124–25). Also see Takács on Ibn 'Arabi's concept of simultaneous "God/not-God" reality (Takács 2017, 102; cf. 104, 114).
[12] Takács 2017, 116, emphasis added.
[13] Cf. M. Bennett 2019, 11, 13, 38–39, 51, 119.
[14] Allow me to add: von Stosch's contribution attempts to leverage Q 5:75 to enhance Christian apprehension of the humanity of Christ and his solidarity "with us in our despair and hopelessness, in our struggles and doubts" (von Stosch 2021, 74). To my mind, von Stosch's modernistic ruminations on death, eschatological hope, Christology, and Prophet Jesus' vulnerability are unlikely to commend themselves to orthodox thinkers—either Christian or Muslim.
[15] Madigan 2021, 14.
[16] Ralston 2021, 227.
[17] See too Ralston 2016.
[18] Ralston 2020, 29. Ralston here invokes J. Fredericks.
[19] Cf. Burrell 1986; 1993; 2011; see Ralston 2020, 32–37.
[20] Ralston 2020, 35.
[21] See Kärkkäinen 2013; 2019; 2020.
[22] Kärkkäinen 2020, 20–21.

**Appendix B Notes**

[1] Cf. Gunton 1988, 116.
[2] Barth 2004, 4:1:81.
[3] Cf. Cone 2011; Weaver 2011, chapters four to six.
[4] "Joanne Carlson Brown and Rebecca Parker … write, 'Christianity is an abusive theology that glorifies suffering [fostering conceptualities] of "divine child abuse" … Christianity … must be liberated from this theology'" (Crisp 2020, 136; cf. Sondergger 2020, 304–306).
[5] Baker and Green 2011, 214 and 215–16.
[6] See Gudmundsdóttir 2017, 343.
[7] Cf. Gudmundsdóttir 2017, 344; cf. 349.
[8] Crisp 2020, 131.
[9] B. Harrison and C. Heyward quoted in Baker and Green 2011, 116; also Weaver 2011.
[10] Vidu 2014, 185.
[11] Cf. Vidu 2014, 188–89, 217–23.
[12] See Placher 2009, 24–26.
[13] Holmes 2017, 303, emphasis added. My overview of Girard relies primarily on Placher; on Girard's "depth hermeneutics" see Vidu 2014, 206.

[14] In later years, Girard was apparently moving towards an integration of the "sacrifice paradigm", though not, of course, as manifesting God's judgment (see Hurlbert 2020; Anatolios 2020, 396–400).
[15] Cf. Placher 2009, 25–26.
[16] Kärkkäinen 2013, 320. Johnson argues that "Girard has uncovered a significant aspect of the work of Christ which belongs in a fuller account" (Johnson 2017 "René Girard", 507; cf. 2013, 158–63).
[17] Davidson 2017, 52–53.
[18] Cf. Baker and Green 2011, 117–20.
[19] Consider Weaver's assertion: "Social practices which prescribe set roles for women and limit their opportunities are examples of violence" (Weaver 2011, 8). I suspect that I actually agree with Weaver in terms of women's access to various roles, status, and leadership. What I object to is the apparently facile manner in which he can relegate *any demurral* on such issues to the invidious category of "violence". My point here in no way undermines the claim that the spectrum of violence extends beyond grossly "physical" acts. The trope of destructive speech ("speech act") is prominent in Scripture. (I was recently reminded of this reality in a recorded discussion of Lynch 2020.)
[20] M. Volf quoted in Hastings 2019, 67; cf. 43.
[21] Sonderegger 2020, 301.
[22] Cf. Kärkkäinen 2013, 321–22.
[23] Gunton 1988, 159; cf. 165; cf. Stott 2012, chapters five to six.

**Appendix C Notes**

[1] The published commentary runs to Q 12.52 (cf. Pink 2016, 3). The influence of 'Abduh is evident in the *tafsir*, but it is Rida's work (cf. Pink 2016, 2–3; Sirry 2014, 14–15).
[2] Cf. Hamzah 2013; Pink 2016; Voll 2004, 609.
[3] Cf. Shepard 2006, 570.
[4] McAuliffe 1991, 85. Our primary source is Rida's *tafsir* (1948). See too Rida 1996 and Wood 2008. In addition to Rida's Qur'an commentary, a few other Arabic-only Qur'an commentators are occasionally consulted; for example: al-Azhar Islamic Research Group (1992); al-Sha'rawi (Egyptian, d. 1998); Ibn al-'Uthamin (Saudi, d. 2001).
[5] Cf. Akhavi 2009, 497; Euben and Zaman, eds., 2009, 129–35; Robinson 2001, 159; Shepard 2013, 489.
[6] Shepard 2006, 568. David Cook suggests that the intellectual fountainhead for Islamic radicalism in our day is comprised of three pivotal thinkers: Qutb, Mawdudi, and Ayatollah Khomayni (Cook 2007, 138).
[7] Lawson 2009, 129, note 37; cf. Robinson 2001, 176; Shepard 2006, 569; 2013, 489.
[8] Or, Husayn.
[9] *The Balance (or Scales) in Interpretation of the Qur'an*. See McAuliffe 1991, 85–89; Elmi and Shah-Kazemi 2005.
[10] Tabatabai offers discourses on "Jesus and Christianity" (Tabatabai 2020 "Discourse on Jesus and Christianity", 134–72/Arabic, Tabatabai 1997, 3:321–53) and on "Jesus and the Gospels" (Tabatabai 2020 "Discourse on Jesus and the Gospels", 175–202/Arabic, Tabatabai 1997, 3:357–78).
[11] See Esposito and Voll 2001, chapter one; al-Faruqi 1998, 1999, 2013.
[12] Moosa 2009, xiii.
[13] Nasr, ed. 2015.
[14] Cf. Ayoub 2007.
[15] Cf. Ayoub 2007, 135–36.
[16] See Siddiqui 2013 *Christians, Muslims, and Jesus.*

**Appendix D Notes**

[1] Ralston 2021, 225 has a heading with wording similar to mine here.

[2] Akhtar 2018, 231.

[3] Cf. Roberts 2013, 318, 326; Siddiqui 2013 *Christians, Muslims, and Jesus*, 231; Talia 2019, 194–95; see also Akhtar 2018, 147. Nancy Roberts' effort to somehow embrace cruciform redemption and atonement *as a Muslim* might be an exception proving the rule (cf. Roberts 2013, especially 318).

[4] Cf. al-Faruqi 2013, 213; 1999, 166; Leirvik 2010, 247.

[5] Aziz-us-Samad quoted in M. Bennett 2019, 132.

[6] Cf. al-Nowaihi 1976, 218. The model of Jesus may call the observer away from rote law observance to a spirit of service and sacrifice; the gospel narratives may rightly evince mystery and the uncanny wisdom and victory of God in the face of looming defeat; but salvation remains a matter of *guidance*, not vicarious atonement (cf. al-'Aqqad 2001, 172-177; 228; chapter eighteen).

[7] Siddiqui 2013 *Christians, Muslims, and Jesus*, 242–43; cf. 225, 231, 238, 245–46.

[8] Ayoub 2007, 158–59; cf. 93-94, 115, 171. "Christ, as were all the messengers of God before and after him, was a savior in that he, by his message, helped to save humanity from error and to guide its steps further on the path to God, to whom we all belong and to whom we all shall return (Q. 2:156)" (Ayoub 2007, 137).

[9] cf. Ayoub 2007, 177. Again, I do not attempt a comparison between Christian atonement theology and Shi'i ideas of the redemptive suffering of Imam Hussein; see, among others, Ayoub's work (Ayoub 2007, 92–96, 136–53; also Ayoub 1978; cf. Roberts 2013, 322–23).

[10] See Ralston on Mustafa Akyol and on the limits of moral exemplar models in Christian–Muslim dialogue (Ralston 2021, 225–26).

**Appendix E Notes**

[1] Hart 1998, 336–37, approximating the précis of *CDH* by Adolph von Harnack.